THE ESSENTIAL
PASTA
COOKBOOK

THE ESSENTIAL
Pasta
COOKBOOK

WHITECAP
BOOKS

This edition first published in the United States and Canada by Whitecap Books.

Published by Murdoch Books® a division of Murdoch Magazines Pty Ltd,
45 Jones Street, Ultimo NSW 2007

CEO & Publisher: Anne Wilson
Publishing Director: Catie Ziller
General Manager: Mark Smith
International Sales Director: Mark Newman

ISBN 1-55110-655-8 (cased edition) 1-55110-656-6 (limp edition)

Printed by Toppan Printing (S) Pte Ltd

Whitecap Books Ltd
Vancouver Office,
351 Lynn Avenue, North Vancouver, BC
Canada V7J 2C4

Whitecap Books
Toronto Office
47 Coldwater Road, North York, ON
Canada M3B IY8

Graphic Arts Center Publishing
P.O. Box 10306, Portland, OR
USA 97296-0306

NUTRITION: The nutritional information given for each recipe does not include any
accompaniments, such as rice or pasta, unless they are included in the ingredients list. The
nutritional values are approximations and can be affected by biological and seasonal variations
in foods, the unknown composition of some manufactured foods and uncertainty in the dietary
database. Nutrient data given are derived primarily from the official NUTTAB95 database.

OUR STAR RATING: When we test recipes, we rate them for ease of preparation.
The following cookery ratings are used in this book:
★ A single star indicates a recipe that is simple and generally quick to make—perfect for beginners.
★★ Two stars indicate the need for just a little more care, or perhaps a little more time.
★★★ Three stars indicate special dishes that need more investment in time,
care and patience—but the results are worth it. Even beginners can make these
dishes as long as the recipe is followed carefully.

PASTA... A FEAST FOR THE GODS

We have finally discovered a cookery secret the Italians have known for centuries... it is difficult to go wrong with pasta. What could be simpler or more appealing than butter and shavings of Parmesan melting over a bowl of fresh tagliatelle? As comfort food, pasta is unbeatable. It is warming, filling and, above all, mouthwateringly delicious.

It was said that Marco Polo brought pasta noodles to Italy from China in 1295, a rumour that does great disservice to the ancient Italians, who had been tucking in since the days of Imperial Rome. Cicero himself, so legend has it, was inordinately fond of laganum, the flat, ribbon pasta we now call tagliatelle. And, from the middle ages, Tasso's story tells how an innkeeper invented tortellini in the image of Venus' navel. So, if you're enjoying your pasta, you're in good company. *Buon appetito.*

CONTENTS

Pasta... a feast for the gods   5

Pasta secrets   8

Dried and fresh pastas   10

Making pasta   16

Classic sauces   20

Soups   34

Pasta with meat   54

Pasta with chicken   78

Pasta with seafood   92

Pasta with vegetables   114

Creamy pasta   144

Pasta salads   170

Gnocchi 196
  Making gnocchi 202

Filled pasta 210
  Filling pasta 218

Baked pasta 228

Pasta pronto 252

Pasta desserts 284

Index 293

SPECIAL FEATURES

ANTIPASTO 50

COLD MEATS 66

OLIVES 134

CHEESE 166

BREAD 184

PASTA SECRETS

There are good reasons why pasta is such a popular food: it's cheap, it's quick and easy to prepare (you'll notice most of our recipes have an 'easy' rating), it's delicious, it's nutritious and, as this book demonstrates, it's amazingly versatile. You can dress up pasta for a dinner party with a creamy smoked salmon sauce, or serve it simply, with Parmesan or bacon and eggs. You can serve it cold in salads, warm in soups or piping hot from the oven, stuffed with spinach and ricotta. You can serve it for dessert and you can even serve it as a hangover cure... according to the Italians, spaghetti with garlic and chilli oil, eaten before going to sleep, will ward off the aftereffects of too much vino. You can eat pasta every day of the week (as indeed many Italians do) and never tire of it. Pasta goes well with anything, including breads, vegetables and salads, which is why we have included ideas for these throughout the book.

And of course, there is the traditional accompaniment to some pasta dishes, Parmesan. Although small amounts of grated Parmesan, or little shavings, do look *so* attractive, resist the temptation to serve it with everything. Avoid it with seafood sauces, in particular, as the flavours do not always mix well. If you can't resist decorating your pasta, garnish with the gremolata suggested on page 113.

DRIED OR FRESH?

Many people think that fresh pasta must be better than dried. This is not always the case—some sauces are better teamed with fresh pasta and some are best with dried. Fresh pasta works well with rich sauces made from cream, butter and cheese, because its soft texture absorbs the sauce. Alfredo is one of the nicest sauces to serve on fresh home-made pasta, as is a simple topping of butter and grated Parmesan. Dried pasta is the one to choose if you're serving a heartier, tomato-based sauce. If your sauce has olives, anchovies, chilli, meat or seafood, you'll almost certainly need dried.

Pasta is a combination of flour, water and sometimes eggs and oil. Pasta made with wholewheat flour is darker. If dried pasta is made with durum wheat flour, it is considered to be of superior quality. Other dried pastas that are available include those made from different flours and cereals such as buckwheat, corn, rice and soya beans. Pastas are sometimes flavoured with a purée of herbs, tomato, spinach or other vegetables. Dried pasta will last up to six months, stored in an airtight container in a cool dark place. However, dried wholewheat pasta will only last for one month before turning rancid. Fresh pasta can be wrapped in plastic and frozen for five days. If double wrapped, it will last up to four months. Don't thaw before cooking.

WHICH PASTA SHAPE?

There are good reasons for matching one pasta shape with a particular sauce. Apart from the traditional regional preference for a local shape, its ability to hold and support the sauce is all important. Tubular shapes such as penne capture thick sauces, while flat or long pastas are traditionally served with thin, smooth sauces. But there are no hard and fast rules and part of the fun of pasta is trying out all those fabulous colours, flavours and shapes. See the following pages for photographs of some of the many fresh and dried pastas now available.

A lot of information about the pasta contained in the packet can be gleaned from its name. A name ending in *-ricce* means the pasta has a wavy edge; *-nidi* indicates that the lengths are formed into nests; *-rigate* means ridged and *-lisce*, smooth surfaced. And, if your Italian is up to scratch, you can pretty much visualise your pasta from its

name... although sometimes you may find this a little offputting. *Orecchiette* are little ears; *eliche*, propellers; *ditali*, thimbles; *conchiglie*, conch shells; *linguine*, little tongues; and *vermicelli*, little worms. If the name of the pasta ends with *-oni*, this indicates a larger size: for example, *conchiglioni* are large *conchiglie*. Likewise, *-ini* and *-ette* means smaller versions, as in *farfallini*. However, before we become too embroiled in the importance of names, let us point out that they do vary from manufacturer to manufacturer and book to book... one man's tortelloni can be another man's agnolotti. Luckily, if a little commonsense is used, this isn't going to pose problems of life-threatening importance.

HOW MUCH PASTA?

Another highly charged subject as far as pasta aficionados are concerned, is how much pasta each person should be served and, even more controversially, how much sauce should be served on that pasta. As a general guide, use 60 g (2 oz) of fresh pasta per person for a starter, and 125 g (4 oz) for a main dish. You should allow a little bit more if you are using dried (it contains less moisture, so is lighter), about 90 g (3 oz) each for a starter and 150 g (5 oz) per person for a main course.

How much sauce is obviously a matter of personal taste, but the biggest mistake non-Italian cooks make is to use too much sauce: the pasta should be lightly coated, not drenched. When the pasta and sauce are tossed, there shouldn't be extra sauce swimming around at the bottom.

COOKING YOUR PASTA

Unsalted water will come to the boil faster than salted water, so add the salt once the water is boiling. Use a large pan of water, enough so that the pasta has plenty of room to move around, and only add the pasta when the water has reached a rapid boil. Some people like to add a tablespoon of olive oil to help prevent the

water boiling over or the pasta sticking together. After the pasta has been added, cover the pan to help bring the water back to the boil as quickly as possible, then remove the lid as soon as the water returns to the boil.

Perfectly cooked pasta should be *al dente*, tender but still firm 'to the tooth'. It is important to drain the pasta and then turn it immediately into a heated dish, into the pan with the sauce, or back into its cooking pan. It should never be overdrained, as it needs to be slippery for the sauce to coat it well. Never leave it sitting in the colander or it will become a sticky mass. A little oil or butter tossed through the drained pasta will stop it sticking together. Alternatively, lightly spray the pasta with some boiling water and toss it gently (it is always a good idea to keep a little of the cooking water for this, in case you overdrain). Timing can make all the difference between a good pasta meal and a great one. Always read the recipe through first and then coordinate your cooking times. Try to have the sauce ready to dress the pasta as soon as it is cooked, especially if the pasta is fresh (it will continue to cook if it is left to sit around). Pasta that is to be used in cold pasta salads should be rinsed under cold water to remove excess starch and tossed with a small amount of oil. Cover and refrigerate until ready to use.

FAR LEFT: Lemon grass and lime scallop pasta (page 165)
ABOVE: Green olive and eggplant toss (page 120)

9

DRIED PASTA

Traditionally, long thin pastas, such as spaghetti, are served with thin oily sauces, while shorter fatter pastas hold chunky sauces better.

SPAGHETTI

LUMACONI or PIPE RIGATE

PAPPARDELLE

RISSONI

MACARONI or MACCHERONI

ANELLI

PENNE or PENNE RIGATE

RIGATONI

FUSILLI or ELICHE

ORECCHIETTE

CANNELLONI

FUSILLI or BUCATI LUNGHI

SARDI or GNOBETTI

FETTUCINE

LASAGNE

COTELLI or CAVATAPPI

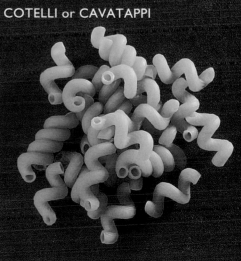

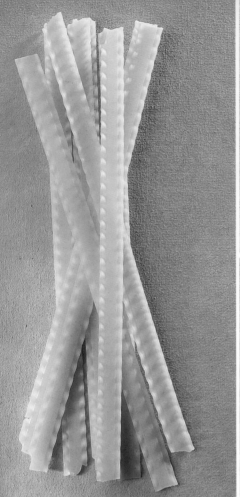

LASAGNETTE or MAFALDINI

PASSATELLI

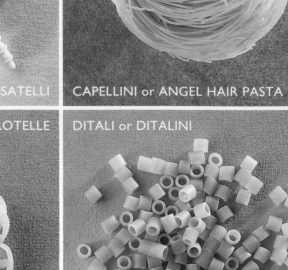

CAPELLINI or ANGEL HAIR PASTA

RUOTE or ROTELLE

DITALI or DITALINI

FARFALLE

GNOCCHI

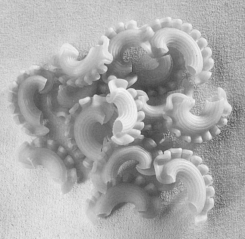

CRESTI DI GALLO

CAVATIELLI

TAGLIATELLE

GARGANELLI

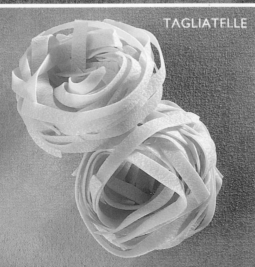

TAGLIARINI

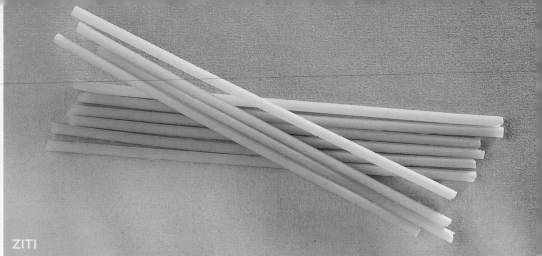

ZITI

FRICELLI

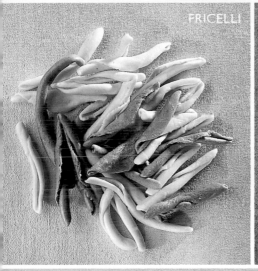

CONCHIGLIE

STELLINI

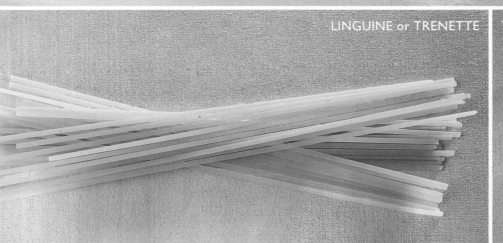

VERMICELLI

LINGUINE or TRENETTE

TORTELLINI

FRESH PASTA

Wonderful with creamy butter- or cream-based sauces, as the soft texture absorbs the flavours. Make your own or buy one of the supermarket or delicatessen varieties.

MALTAGLIATI

GNOCCHI

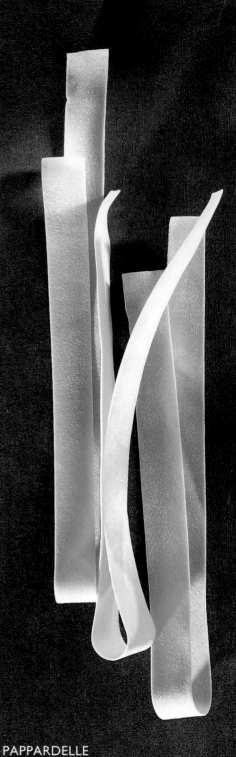

TORTELLINI

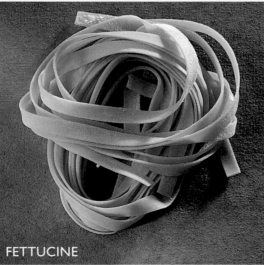

FETTUCINE

PAPPARDELLE

RAVIOLI

MEZZALUNA

AGNOLOTTI

CAPPELLETTI

TONARELLI

LASAGNE

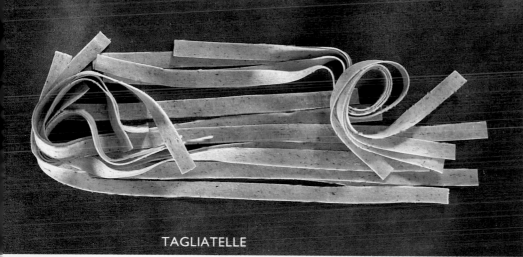

TAGLIATELLE

QUADRUCCI

GARGANELLI

LINGUINE

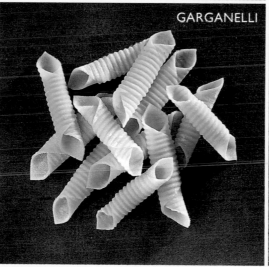

SPAGHETTI

PANSOTTI

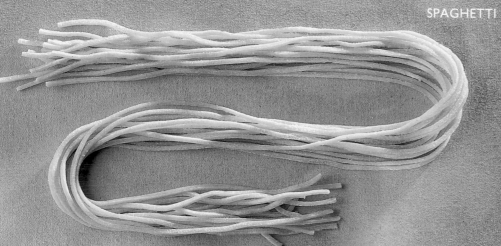

MAKING PASTA What could be more

satisfying and soothing? With a little practice and good-quality ingredients you'll

soon be creating your own pasta in a variety of shapes, tastes and textures.

Making pasta isn't difficult—in fact, it can be extremely relaxing—but there are a few tips that will help. One important element that is often overlooked is a well-ventilated kitchen without breezes or air-conditioning. Also, humidity can cause unruly dough, so don't make pasta on a rainy day.

Kneading is an important part of the process, as it is necessary to work the gluten content of the flour to give a firm but tender dough. Knead the dough until it is pliable, adding small amounts of flour at a time if it is too soft.

Home-made pasta can be refrigerated for up to 48 hours, loosely packed in an airtight container. Turn it over once to check for moisture. Freezing works quite well, but sometimes the pasta becomes brittle. Don't defrost frozen pasta, just put it straight into boiling water. Lasagne sheets store best if blanched first, then stacked between layers of waxed paper before being refrigerated or frozen.

EQUIPMENT
No special equipment is necessary to make pasta but some will save time. Work on a large work area or rolling board with a hard, even surface. Wood or marble is ideal. If making the dough by hand, a long rolling pin gives an evenly-rolled dough and requires less strokes, and a large ceramic bowl makes mixing tidier. A food processor will mix the dough quickly and reduce kneading time. For cutting, you'll need a long,

sharp knife, perhaps a pastry wheel, and a dough scraper is handy. The hand-cranked pasta machines are highly recommended. They knead the dough as it is being rolled, give even sheets of pasta with good texture and are easy to handle. The better brands are sturdy, with a strong holding clamp and rollers that adjust easily as well as crank smoothly.

INGREDIENTS

All the ingredients for pasta dough should be brought to room temperature before you start. The proportion of flour to eggs depends on the weather, the quality of the flour and the age and size of the eggs. Oil makes it easier to work with but you don't have to use it.

Use plain or unbleached flour. It gives a well-textured, light dough with good manageability. A percentage of durum wheat semolina is favoured by some pasta makers as it improves flavour, colour and texture. However, its hard wheat qualities sometimes make it difficult to work, particularly on a hand-cranked machine, and any proportion greater than equal parts durum wheat semolina to plain flour can cause problems.

BASIC PLAIN DOUGH

To make enough pasta dough to serve 6 as a first course or 4 as a main course, you will need 300 g (10 oz) of plain flour, 3 large (60 g/2 oz) eggs, 30 ml (1 fl oz) of olive oil, optional, and a pinch of salt.

1 To mix the dough by hand, mound the plain flour on a work surface or in a large ceramic bowl and then make a well in the centre.

2 Break the eggs into the well and add the oil, if using, and a large pinch of salt. Using a fork, begin to whisk the eggs and oil together, incorporating a little of the flour as you do so.

3 Gradually blend the flour with the eggs, working from the centre out. Use your free hand to hold the mound in place and stop leakage if any of the egg escapes.

4 Knead the dough on a lightly floured surface with smooth, light strokes, turning it as you fold and press. It should be soft and pliable, but dry to the touch. If it is sticky, knead in a little flour.

5 It will take at least 6 minutes kneading to achieve a smooth and elastic texture with a slightly glossy appearance. If durum wheat semolina is used, the kneading will take a little longer, at least 8 minutes. Put the dough in a plastic bag without sealing, or cover with a tea towel or an upturned bowl. Allow to rest for 30 minutes. The dough can be made in a food processor.

MAKING PASTA

ROLLING AND CUTTING BY HAND

1 Divide the dough into three or four manageable portions and cover them.

2 Lightly flour a large work surface. Flatten one portion of dough onto the surface and using a long, floured rolling pin, roll out the dough from the centre to the outer edge.

3 Continue rolling, always from in front of you outward, and rotating the dough often. Keep the work surface dusted with just enough flour to prevent sticking. When you have rolled a well-shaped circle, fold the dough in half and roll it out again. Continue in this way seven or eight times to give a smooth circle of pasta about 5 mm (¼ inch) thick.

4 Roll the sheet quickly and smoothly to a thickness of 2.5 mm (⅛ inch). Patch any tears with a piece of dough from the edge and a little water to help it stick.

5 As each sheet is done, transfer it to a dry tea towel. If the pasta is to be used to make filled pasta keep it covered, but if they are to be cut into lengths or shapes, leave them uncovered while the others are being rolled, so that the surface moisture will dry slightly.

6 For lasagne sheets, simply cut the pasta into the sizes required. The best way to cut lengths such as fettucine is to roll each pasta sheet up like a swiss roll, then cut this into uniform widths with a long, sharp knife. For tagliatelle, cut at 8 mm (⁴⁄10 inch) intervals, 5 mm (¼ inch) for fettucine, or about 3 cm (1¼ inches) for pappardelle. Discard the offcuts. Place the lengths in a single layer on a tea towel to surface dry for no more than 10 minutes. Or hang long pasta strips to surface dry on broom handles or long wooden spoons between two chairs.

Lengths can also be cut from the flat sheet using a long, sharp knife or a pastry wheel. You may find it easier to run the wheel beside a ruler for straight cutting. A zig-zag pastry wheel will give an interesting edge to pasta shapes such as lasagnette and farfalle.

Don't dry pasta in a cold place or in a draught or it may become brittle. It is better if it dries slowly.

ROLLING AND CUTTING WITH A HAND-CRANKED MACHINE

1 Clamp the machine securely onto the edge of your work surface. Divide the

dough into three or four portions and shape each into a rough log. Keeping the unworked portions covered, take one and flatten it by one or two rolls with a rolling pin. Dust lightly with flour.

2 With the machine's rollers at their widest setting, crank the dough through two or three times. Fold it in thirds, turn the dough 90 degrees and feed through again. If the dough feels damp or tends to stick, lightly flour the outside surfaces each time it is rolled until it passes through cleanly. Repeat this folding and rolling process eight to ten times, or until the dough is a smooth and elastic sheet with a velvety appearance. From now on the dough is not folded.

3 Reduce the width of the rollers by one setting and pass the dough through. Repeat, setting the rollers one notch closer each time until you have rolled the desired thickness. Some machines may roll the sheets too thinly on their last setting, tearing them. A way around this is to stop at the second last setting and roll the dough through several times. It will come out a little thinner each time. This step also applies to machines that don't roll the pasta thinly enough on the last setting.

4 As each sheet is completed, place it on a dry tea towel. Leave uncovered to surface dry for 10 minutes if the sheets are to be cut, but cover them if they are to be used for filled pasta.

5 For lasagne sheets, cut the pasta to the desired size. For narrower lengths, select the appropriate cutters on the machine and crank each pasta sheet through it. Spread them on the tea towel until ready to be cooked, only covering them if they appear to be drying too much. Long pasta such as tagliatelle can be hung to surface dry on broom handles or long wooden spoons between two chairs.

MAKING SHAPES

To make **farfalle** you will need sheets of pasta dough freshly rolled to a standard thickness of 2.5 mm (1/8 inch). Using a zig-zag pastry wheel against a ruler, cut rectangles about 2½ x 5½ cm (1 x 2¼ inches). Pinch the centres together to form a bow tie shape and spread them on a dry tea towel to surface dry for 10–12 minutes. After 5 minutes, re-pinch any that look a little wayward.

To make **orecchiette** start with unrolled, but rested dough. Divide into manageable portions and with your hands, roll each into a long, thin log about 1 cm (1/2 inch) in diameter. Working with one log at a time, cut slices about 2.5 mm (1/8 inch) wide. Roll each slice between your thumb and a lightly floured wooden board. Little ear-like shells form, thicker than most pasta shapes and with an obvious hand-made look. Spread on a tea towel to surface dry.

CLASSIC SAUCES

Sometimes it's difficult to determine whether you're eating pasta with your sauce or sauce with your pasta. While the difference is subtle, the Italians intended their pasta to be evenly dressed by its sauce, rather than swimming in it. Prepare these classic sauces using the freshest ingredients and toss them through a bowl of pasta. And remember the Italian philosophy regarding sauce. To eat your pasta any other way is to do it a great injustice.

After cooking, squeeze the beans out of their skins. If they will not come out easily, gently slit or break the ends first.

Use a small knife to trim the stalks from the sugar snap peas. Break the woody ends from the asparagus.

PRIMAVERA

Preparation time: 25 minutes
Total cooking time: 10–15 minutes
Serves 4

☆

500 g (1 lb) pasta
1 cup (155 g/5 oz) frozen broad beans
200 g (6¹/2 oz) sugar snap peas
155 g (5 oz) fresh aparagus spears
30 g (1 oz) butter
1 cup (250 ml/8 fl oz) cream
60 g (2 oz) freshly grated Parmesan

1 Cook the pasta in a large pan of rapidly boiling salted water until *al dente*. Drain and return to the pan to keep warm.
2 Cook the beans in a pan of boiling water for 2 minutes. Plunge them into iced water and then drain. Remove and discard the skins from the broad beans—you can usually just squeeze them out, otherwise carefully slit the skins first.
3 Trim the stalks from the peas and break the woody ends from the asparagus spears. Cut the asparagus into short lengths.
4 Melt the butter in a heavy-based frying pan. Add the vegetables, cream and Parmesan. Simmer gently over medium heat for 3–4 minutes, or until the peas and asparagus are bright green and just tender. Season with some salt and pepper. Pour the sauce over the warm pasta and toss to combine. Serve immediately.
NOTE: Traditionally, primavera sauce is served with spaghetti. We have shown it with spaghettini, a thin spaghetti.

NUTRITION PER SERVE: *Protein 30 g; Fat 35 g; Carbohydrate 95 g; Dietary Fibre 12 g; Cholesterol 105 mg; 3420 kJ (815 cal)*

POMODORO

Preparation time: 15 minutes
Total cooking time: 10–15 minutes
Serves 4

★

500 g (1 lb) pasta
1 1/2 tablespoons olive oil
1 onion, very finely chopped
2 x 400 g (13 oz) cans Italian tomatoes, chopped
1/4 cup (7 g / 1/4 oz) fresh basil leaves

1 Cook the pasta in a large pan of rapidly boiling salted water until *al dente*. Drain, return to the pan and keep warm.
2 Heat the oil in a large frying pan. Add the onion and cook over medium heat until softened. Stir in the chopped tomato and simmer for 5–6 minutes, or until the sauce has reduced slightly and thickened. Season with salt and freshly ground pepper. Stir in the basil leaves and cook for another minute. Pour the sauce over the warm pasta and gently toss through. Serve immediately. This is a sauce suitable for serving with freshly grated Parmesan.
NOTE: Traditionally, pomodoro is served with tagliatelle. We have shown it with fettucine.

NUTRITION PER SERVE: *Protein 20 g; Fat 10 g; Carbohydrate 95 g; Dietary Fibre 10 g; Cholesterol 5 mg; 2295 kJ (545 cal)*

STEP-BY-STEP

To finely chop the onion, use a sharp knife to cut it in half, then thinly slice it horizontally, without cutting all the way through.

Next, make cuts close together across one way, and then in the opposite direction, making fine cubes.

23

Finely chop the thick bacon rashers or speck, after removing any rind.

Grate a little of the whole nutmeg, using the finest cutting side of the grater.

CLASSIC BOLOGNESE

Preparation time: 25 minutes
Total cooking time: at least 3 hours
Serves 4

☆

50 g (1 3/4 oz) butter
180 g (6 oz) thick bacon rashers or speck, with rind removed, finely chopped
1 large onion, finely chopped
1 carrot, finely chopped
1 celery stick, finely chopped
400 g (13 oz) lean beef mince
150 g (5 oz) chicken livers, finely chopped
2 cups (500 ml/16 fl oz) beef stock
1 cup (250 ml/8 fl oz) tomato purée (passata)
1/2 cup (125 ml/4 fl oz) red wine
1/4 teaspoon freshly grated nutmeg
500 g (1 lb) pasta
freshly grated Parmesan, for serving

1 Heat half the butter in a heavy-based frying pan. Add the speck and cook until golden. Add the onion, carrot and celery and cook over low heat for 8 minutes, stirring occasionally.
2 Increase the heat, add the remaining butter and, when the pan is hot, add the mince. Break up any lumps with a fork and stir until brown. Add the chicken livers and stir until they change colour. Add the beef stock, tomato purée, wine, nutmeg, and salt and pepper, to taste.
3 Bring to the boil and simmer, covered, over very low heat for 2–5 hours, adding a little more stock if the sauce becomes too dry. The longer the sauce is cooked, the more flavour it will have.
4 Cook the pasta in a large pan of rapidly boiling salted water until *al dente*. Drain and divide among warmed serving bowls. Serve the sauce over the top and sprinkle with freshly grated Parmesan.
NOTE: Traditionally, bolognese was served with tagliatelle, but now we serve it with spaghetti.

NUTRITION PER SERVE: *Protein 45 g; Fat 35 g; Carbohydrate 95 g; Dietary Fibre 9 g; Cholesterol 145 mg; 3860 kJ (920 cal)*

ALFREDO

Preparation time: 10 minutes
Total cooking time: 15 minutes
Serves 4–6

★

500 g (1 lb) pasta
90 g (3 oz) butter
1½ cups (150 g/5 oz) freshly grated
   Parmesan
1¼ cups (315 ml/10 fl oz) cream
3 tablespoons chopped fresh parsley

1 Cook the pasta in a large pan of rapidly boiling salted water until *al dente*. Drain and return to the pan.
2 While the pasta is cooking, melt the butter in a pan over low heat. Add the Parmesan and cream and bring to the boil, stirring constantly. Reduce the heat and simmer, stirring, until the sauce has thickened slightly. Add the chopped fresh parsley, salt and pepper, to taste, and stir until well combined.
3 Add the sauce to the pasta and toss well so the sauce coats the pasta. This dish can be garnished with chopped herbs or sprigs of fresh herbs such as thyme.
NOTE: Traditionally, plain fettucine, as shown in the picture, is used with this sauce, but you can use any style of pasta. It is a very simple sauce to make and should be prepared just before the pasta is cooked.

NUTRITION PER SERVE (6): *Protein 20 g; Fat 40 g; Carbohydrate 60 g; Dietary Fibre 4 g; Cholesterol 125 mg; 2875 kJ (685 cal)*

STEP-BY-STEP

Ideally, Parmesan is grated from a piece just before using. This prevents loss of flavour and drying out.

Use a large, sharp knife to chop the fresh parsley. A swivel action is easiest, holding the point of the knife in one place.

For this sauce, the vegetables should be chopped into quite small pieces before adding to the hot oil.

The tomatoes should also be cut into small pieces, before adding with the parsley, sugar and water.

NAPOLITANA

Preparation time: 20 minutes
Total cooking time: 1 hour
Serves 4–6

★

2 tablespoons olive oil
1 onion, finely chopped
1 carrot, finely chopped
1 celery stick, finely chopped
500 g (1 lb) very ripe tomatoes, chopped
2 tablespoons chopped fresh parsley
2 teaspoons sugar
500 g (1 lb) pasta

1 Heat the oil in a heavy-based pan. Add the onion, carrot and celery. Cover and cook for 10 minutes over low heat, stirring occasionally.
2 Add the tomato to the vegetables with the parsley, sugar and ½ cup (125 ml/4 fl oz) of water. Bring to the boil, reduce the heat to low, cover and simmer for 45 minutes, stirring occasionally. Season with salt and freshly ground black pepper, to taste. If necessary, add up to ¾ cup (185 ml/6 fl oz) more water until the required consistency is reached.
3 About 15 minutes before serving, add the pasta to a large pan of rapidly boiling salted water and cook until *al dente*. Drain and return to the pan. Pour the sauce over the pasta and gently toss until combined. Serve in individual bowls or on plates.
NOTE: Traditionally, spaghetti is used with this sauce, but you can use any pasta. We have shown penne rigate. The sauce can be reduced to a concentrated version by cooking it for a longer period. Store it in the refrigerator and add water or stock to thin it, if necessary, when reheating.

NUTRITION PER SERVE (6): *Protein 10 g; Fat 7 g; Carbohydrate 65 g; Dietary Fibre 6 g; Cholesterol 0 mg; 1540 kJ (365 cal)*

PASTA WITH SEAFOOD

It is hardly a mystery why pasta and seafood go together so well. Italy is surrounded on almost all sides by the tranquil blueness of the Mediterranean sea and the Italians have been reaping its fruits since the dawn of their civilization. It's only natural that they should cook up their catch of fresh prawns, clams and succulent fish and toss them together with their beloved pasta to come up with some spectacular dishes.

CALAMARI

Calamari, Italian for squid, is a member of the *cephalopod* family, along with octopus and cuttlefish. Like the octopus, the squid has eight limbs, but also two longer tentacles with suckers on the end. The body sac is elongated and does not contain a true skeleton, and both this body and the tentacles can be eaten. The flesh is firm, mildy sweet and doesn't have a 'fishy' flavour. Calamari is eaten whole, stuffed and stewed, or cut into strips or rings and fried. It can be rubbery and tasteless if cooked without care.

ABOVE: Spaghetti marinara

SPAGHETTI MARINARA

Preparation time: 40 minutes
Total cooking time: 50 minutes
Serves 6

★

12 fresh mussels

Tomato Sauce

2 tablespoons olive oil
1 onion, finely diced
1 carrot, sliced
1 red chilli, seeded and chopped
2 cloves garlic, crushed
425 g (14 oz) can crushed tomatoes

1/2 cup (125 ml/4 fl oz) white wine
1 teaspoon sugar
pinch of cayenne pepper

1/4 cup (60 ml/2 fl oz) white wine
1/4 cup (60 ml/2 fl oz) fish stock
1 clove garlic, crushed
375 g (12 oz) spaghetti
30 g (1 oz) butter
125 g (4 oz) small calamari tubes, sliced
125 g (4 oz) boneless white fish fillets, cut into cubes
200 g (6 1/2 oz) raw prawns, shelled and deveined
1/2 cup (30 g/1 oz) fresh parsley, chopped
200 g (6 1/2 oz) can clams, drained

CARBONARA
(CREAMY EGG AND BACON SAUCE)

Preparation time: 15 minutes
Total cooking time: 25 minutes
Serves 4–6

★

8 bacon rashers
500 g (1 lb) pasta
4 eggs
1/2 cup (50 g/13/4 oz) freshly grated Parmesan
11/4 cups (315 ml/10 fl oz) cream

1 Remove and discard the bacon rind and cut the bacon into thin strips. Cook in a heavy-based pan over medium heat until crisp. Drain on paper towels.
2 Add the pasta to a large pan of rapidly boiling salted water and cook until *al dente*. Drain and return to the pan.
3 While the pasta is cooking, beat the eggs, Parmesan and cream in a bowl until well combined. Stir the bacon through the mixture. Pour the sauce over the hot pasta and toss gently until the sauce coats the pasta.
4 Return the pan to very low heat and cook for 1/2–1 minute, or until the sauce has slightly thickened. Freshly ground black pepper can be added, to taste.
NOTE: Traditionally, fettucine is used with this dish, but you can use any pasta of your choice. It has been pictured with tagliatelle.

NUTRITION PER SERVE (6): *Protein 30 g; Fat 35 g; Carbohydrate 60 g; Dietary Fibre 4 g; Cholesterol 225 mg; 2895 kJ (690 cal)*

STEP-BY-STEP

Cook the bacon strips in a heavy-based pan, stirring until crisp, being careful not to let them burn.

Drain the bacon on paper towels. After beating the eggs, Parmesan and cream together, mix in the bacon.

STEP-BY-STEP

Process the pine nuts, basil leaves, garlic, salt and cheeses until finely chopped, about 20 seconds.

With the motor running, add the olive oil in a thin steady stream, until a paste is formed.

PESTO

Preparation time: 10–15 minutes
Total cooking time: Nil
Serves 4–6

★

500 g (1 lb) pasta

3 tablespoons pine nuts

2 cups (100 g/3½ oz) fresh basil leaves

2 cloves garlic, peeled

½ teaspoon salt

3 tablespoons freshly grated Parmesan

2 tablespoons freshly grated Pecorino
   cheese, optional

½ cup (125 ml/4 fl oz) olive oil

1 Cook the pasta in a large pan of rapidly boiling salted water until *al dente*. Drain, return to the pan and keep warm.

2 About 5 minutes before the pasta is cooked, add the pine nuts to a heavy-based pan and stir over low heat for 2–3 minutes, or until golden. Allow to cool. Process the pine nuts, basil leaves, garlic, salt and cheeses in a food processor for 20 seconds, until finely chopped. Scrape down the sides of the bowl.

3 With the motor running, gradually add the oil in a thin steady stream until a paste is formed. Add freshly ground black pepper, to taste. Toss the sauce with the warm pasta until the pasta is well coated.

NOTE: Traditionally, linguine, as shown, is used with pesto but you can serve it with any pasta of your choice. Pesto sauce can be made up to one week in advance and refrigerated in an airtight container. Ensure the pesto is tightly packed and seal the surface with some plastic wrap or pour some extra oil over the top, to prevent the pesto going black.

NUTRITION PER SERVE (6): *Protein 15 g; Fat 30 g; Carbohydrate 60 g; Dietary Fibre 5 g; Cholesterol 8 mg; 2280 kJ (540 cal)*

AMATRICIANA
(SPICY BACON AND TOMATO SAUCE)

Preparation time: 45 minutes
Total cooking time: 20 minutes
Serves 4–6

⭐

6 thin slices pancetta or 3 bacon rashers

1 kg (2 lb) very ripe tomatoes

500 g (1 lb) pasta

1 tablespoon olive oil

1 small onion, very finely chopped

2 teaspoons very finely chopped fresh chilli

Parmesan shavings, for serving

1 Finely chop the pancetta or bacon. Score a cross in the base of each tomato. Soak in boiling water for 1–2 minutes, drain and plunge into cold water briefly. Peel back the skin from the cross. Halve, remove the seeds and chop the flesh.

2 Add the pasta to a large pan of rapidly boiling water and cook until *al dente*. Drain and return to the pan.

3 About 5 minutes before the pasta is cooked, heat the oil in a heavy-based frying pan. Add the pancetta or bacon, onion and chilli and stir over medium heat for 3 minutes. Add the tomato and salt and pepper, to taste. Reduce the heat and simmer for another 3 minutes. Add the sauce to the pasta and toss until well combined. Serve garnished with shavings of Parmesan. Freshly ground black pepper can be added, to taste.

NOTE: It is believed this dish originated in the town of Amatrice, where bacon is a prized local product. For a change from regular tomatoes, you can try Roma (egg) tomatoes in this recipe. They are firm-fleshed, with few seeds and have a rich flavour when cooked. Traditionally, bucatini, as shown, is used with this sauce, but you can use any pasta you prefer.

NUTRITION PER SERVE (6): *Protein 15 g; Fat 9 g; Carbohydrate 60 g; Dietary Fibre 6 g; Cholesterol 15 mg; 1640 kJ (390 cal)*

STEP-BY-STEP

Remove the tomatoes from the cold water and peel the skin down from the cross.

Halve the tomatoes and use a teaspoon to scrape out the seeds before chopping the flesh.

Add a little of the cream and scrape the bottom of the pan with a wooden spoon to dislodge any bacon that has stuck.

Cook the sauce over high heat until it is thick enough to coat the back of a wooden spoon.

CREAMY BOSCAIOLA

Preparation time: 15 minutes
Total cooking time: 20–25 minutes
Serves 4

★

500 g (1 lb) pasta
6 bacon rashers, trimmed of rind
  and chopped
200 g (6½ oz) button mushrooms, sliced
2½ cups (600 ml/20 fl oz) cream
2 spring onions, sliced
1 tablespoon chopped fresh parsley

1 Cook the pasta in a large pan of rapidly boiling salted water until *al dente*. Drain, return to the pan and keep warm.
2 While the pasta is cooking, heat about 1 tablespoon of oil in a large frying pan, add the bacon and mushroom and cook, stirring, for 5 minutes, or until golden brown.

3 Stir in a little of the cream and scrape the wooden spoon on the bottom of the pan to dislodge any bacon that has stuck.
4 Add the remaining cream, bring to the boil and cook over high heat for 15 minutes, or until the sauce is thick enough to coat the back of a spoon. Stir the spring onion through the mixture. Pour the sauce over the pasta and toss to combine. Serve sprinkled with the chopped fresh parsley.
NOTE: This sauce is normally served with spaghetti, but you can use any pasta. We have shown it with casereccie. If you are short on time and don't have 15 minutes to reduce the sauce, it can be thickened with 2 teaspoons of cornflour mixed in 1 tablespoon of water. Stir until the mixture boils and thickens. 'Boscaiola' means woodcutter—collecting mushrooms is part of the heritage of the woodcutters.

NUTRITION PER SERVE: *Protein 30 g; Fat 60 g; Carbohydrate 95 g; Dietary Fibre 8 g; Cholesterol 200 mg; 4310 kJ (1025 cal)*

PUTTANESCA
(SAUCE WITH CAPERS, OLIVES AND ANCHOVIES)

Preparation time: 20 minutes
Total cooking time: 20 minutes
Serves 4

☆

500 g (1 lb) pasta
2 tablespoons olive oil
3 cloves garlic, crushed
2 tablespoons chopped fresh parsley
1/4 – 1/2 teaspoon chilli flakes
   or powder
2 x 425 g (14 oz) cans chopped
   tomatoes
1 tablespoon capers
3 anchovy fillets, thinly sliced
1/4 cup (45 g / 1 1/2 oz) black olives
freshly grated Parmesan, for serving

1 Cook the pasta in a large pan of rapidly boiling salted water until *al dente*. Drain, return to the pan and keep warm.
2 While the pasta is cooking, heat the oil in a large heavy-based frying pan. Add the garlic, parsley and chilli flakes and stir constantly, for about 1 minute, over medium heat.
3 Add the tomato to the pan and bring to the boil. Reduce the heat and simmer, covered, for 5 minutes.
4 Add the capers, anchovies and olives and stir for another 5 minutes. Season, to taste, with black pepper. Add the sauce to the pasta and toss gently until the sauce is evenly distributed. Serve immediately, with freshly grated Parmesan.
NOTE: Traditionally, spaghetti is used with the sauce, but you can use other pasta if you prefer. The lasagnette we have shown here creates an unusual look.

NUTRITION PER SERVE: *Protein 20 g; Fat 15 g; Carbohydrate 95 g; Dietary Fibre 9 g; Cholesterol 8 mg; 2510 kJ (595 cal)*

STEP-BY-STEP

To make peeling easier, squash each clove of garlic with the flat side of a knife, pressing with the palm of your hand.

Roughly chop the garlic, with a little salt, then scrape the knife at an angle to finely crush the garlic.

Remove the stalks and slice the chillies in half. Wear rubber gloves to protect your skin.

Finely chop the chillies. The seeds and membrane are left in as this is a fiery sauce, but remove them if you prefer a milder taste.

ARRABBIATA
(FIERY TOMATO SAUCE)

Preparation time: 30 minutes
Total cooking time: 50 minutes
Serves 4

☆

1/2 cup (75 g/2 1/2 oz) bacon fat
2–3 fresh red chillies
2 tablespoons olive oil
1 large onion, finely chopped
1 clove garlic, finely chopped
500 g (1 lb) very ripe tomatoes,
    finely chopped
500 g (1 lb) pasta
2 tablespoons chopped
    fresh parsley
freshly grated Parmesan or Pecorino
    cheese, for serving

1 Use a large knife to finely chop the bacon fat. Chop the chillies, taking care to avoid skin irritation—wearing rubber gloves will help. Heat the oil in a heavy-based pan and add the bacon fat, chilli, onion and garlic. Cook for 8 minutes over medium heat, stirring occasionally.

2 Add the chopped tomato along with 1/2 cup (125 ml/4 fl oz) of water and season with salt and freshly ground black pepper, to taste. Cover and simmer for about 40 minutes, or until the sauce is thick and rich.

3 When the sauce is almost cooked, cook the pasta in a large pan of rapidly boiling salted water until *al dente*. Drain and return to the pan.

4 Add the parsley to the sauce. Taste and season again, if necessary. Pour the sauce over the pasta in the pan and toss gently. Serve with the freshly grated Parmesan or Pecorino cheese sprinkled over the top.

NOTE: Penne rigate, as shown, is traditionally used with this sauce, but you can use other pasta.

NUTRITION PER SERVE: *Protein 20 g; Fat 25 g; Carbohydrate 95 g; Dietary Fibre 9 g; Cholesterol 20 mg; 2880 kJ (685 cal)*

MARINARA

Preparation time: 50 minutes
Total cooking time: 30 minutes
Serves 4

★

1 onion, chopped
2 cloves garlic, crushed
1/2 cup (125 ml/4 fl oz) red wine
2 tablespoons tomato paste
425 g (14 oz) can chopped tomatoes
1 cup (250 ml/8 fl oz) bottled tomato pasta sauce
1 tablespoon each of chopped fresh
   basil and oregano
12 mussels, beards removed, and scrubbed
   (discard any which are already open)
30 g (1 oz) butter
125 g (4 oz) small calamari tubes, sliced
125 g (4 oz) boneless white fish fillets, cubed
200 g (61/2 oz) raw prawns, shelled and
   deveined, leaving tails intact
500 g (1 lb) pasta

1 Heat a little olive oil in a large pan. Add the onion and garlic and cook over low heat for 2–3 minutes. Increase the heat to medium and add the wine, tomato paste, tomato and pasta sauce. Simmer, stirring occasionally, for 5–10 minutes or until the sauce reduces and thickens slightly. Stir in the herbs and season, to taste. Keep warm.

2 While the sauce is simmering, heat 1/2 cup (125 ml/4 fl oz) water in a pan. Add the mussels, cover and steam for 3–5 minutes, or until the mussels have changed colour and opened. Discard any unopened mussels. Remove and set aside. Stir the remaining liquid into the tomato sauce.

3 Heat the butter in a pan and sauté the calamari, fish and prawns, in batches, for 1–2 minutes, or until cooked. Add the seafood to the warm tomato sauce and stir gently.

4 Cook the pasta in a large pan of rapidly boiling salted water until al dente; drain. Combine the seafood sauce with the hot pasta and serve.
NOTE: Traditionally served with spaghetti.

NUTRITION PER SERVE: *Protein 40 g; Fat 10 g; Carbohydrate 100 g; Dietary Fibre 10 g; Cholesterol 205 mg; 2840 kJ (675 cal)*

STEP-BY-STEP

Pull the beards away from the mussels and discard any open mussels. Scrub the shells to remove any dirt or grit.

Remove the quills from inside the calamari tubes and slice the tubes into thin rings.

SOUPS

Soup is food for the soul—spreading warmth and comfort and memories of winter suppers. The best kind of soup is made by simmering all your favourite ingredients in a tasty stock, and what better way to beef it up than by throwing in a handful of pasta? Conchiglie and fusilli make a soup almost a stew, while tortellini or ravioli make a meal of any elegant clear consommé. There are even special tiny pastas for floating in your soup. In fact, pasta and soup go together like, well, like macaroni and minestrone.

low heat. Remove the lemon rind from the pan and bring the mixture to the boil.

3 Add the tortellini and parsley to the pan and season with black pepper. Cook for 6–7 minutes, or until the pasta is *al dente*. Garnish with the fine strips of lemon rind.

NOTE: You can use chopped fresh basil instead of parsley. Serve with a sprinkling of freshly grated Parmesan if you wish.

NUTRITION PER SERVE (6): *Protein 10 g; Fat 2 g; Carbohydrate 45 g; Dietary Fibre 4 g; Cholesterol 10 mg; 1060 kJ (250 cal)*

CHICKEN, LEEK AND CHICKPEA SOUP

Preparation time: 15 minutes
Total cooking time: 20 minutes
Serves 4

✴

4 cups (1 litre) chicken stock
125 g (4 oz) miniature pasta shapes
20 g (³/₄ oz) butter
1 leek, sliced
1 clove garlic, crushed
¹/₂ cup (110 g/3¹/₂ oz) roasted chickpeas
1 tablespoon plain flour
2 tablespoons finely chopped fresh
    flat-leaf parsley
pinch of cayenne pepper
200 g (6¹/₂ oz) chopped cooked chicken meat

1 Bring the chicken stock to the boil in a large saucepan. Add the pasta to the stock and cook until just tender. Remove the pasta with a slotted spoon, keeping the stock on the heat and just boiling.

2 Meanwhile, melt the butter in a large saucepan, add the leek and garlic and stir until golden, but not brown. Add the chickpeas, toss for a minute and then sprinkle with the flour. Fry for about 10 seconds, then gradually blend in the boiling stock.

3 Add the parsley, cayenne, and salt and black pepper, to taste. Add the pasta and the chicken meat to the saucepan and bring back to the boil before serving.

NUTRITION PER SERVE: *Protein 15 g; Fat 8 g; Carbohydrate 30 g; Dietary Fibre 4 g; Cholesterol 50 mg; 1075 kJ (255 cal)*

LEMON-SCENTED BROTH WITH TORTELLINI

Preparation time: 10 minutes
Total cooking time: 20 minutes
Serves 4–6

✴

1 lemon
¹/₂ cup (125 ml/4 fl oz) good-quality white wine
440 g (14 oz) can chicken consommé
375 g (12 oz) fresh or dried veal- or
    chicken-filled tortellini
4 tablespoons chopped fresh parsley

1 Using a vegetable peeler, peel wide strips from the lemon. Remove the white pith with a small sharp knife and cut three of the wide pieces into fine strips. Set aside for garnishing.

2 Combine the wide lemon strips, white wine, consommé and 3 cups (750 ml/24 fl oz) of water in a large deep pan. Cook for 10 minutes over

ABOVE: Lemon-scented broth with tortellini

MINESTRONE

Preparation time: 30 minutes + overnight
soaking
Total cooking time: 3 hours
Serves 6–8

★

250 g (8 oz) dried borlotti beans, soaked
in water overnight
2 onions, chopped
2 cloves garlic, crushed
3 bacon rashers, chopped
4 egg (Roma) tomatoes, peeled and chopped
3 tablespoons chopped fresh parsley
9 cups (2.25 litres) beef or vegetable stock
1/4 cup (60 ml/2 fl oz) red wine
1 carrot, chopped
1 swede, diced
2 potatoes, diced
3 tablespoons tomato paste (tomato purée,
double concentrate)

2 zucchini (courgettes), sliced
1/2 cup (80 g/2³/4 oz) peas
1/2 cup (80 g/2³/4 oz) small macaroni
freshly grated Parmesan and pesto, for serving

1 Drain and rinse the borlotti beans, cover with
cold water in a pan. Bring to the boil, stir, lower
the heat and simmer for 15 minutes. Drain.
2 Heat 2 tablespoons of oil in a large heavy-
based pan and cook the onion, garlic and
bacon, stirring, until the onion is soft and the
bacon golden.
3 Add the tomato, parsley, borlotti beans, stock
and red wine. Simmer, covered, over low heat
for 2 hours. Add the carrot, swede, potato and
tomato paste, cover and simmer for 20 minutes.
4 Add the zucchini, peas and macaroni. Cover
and simmer for 10–15 minutes, or until the
vegetables and macaroni are tender. Season, to
taste, and serve topped with Parmesan and a
little pesto. Fresh herbs can be used to garnish.

NUTRITION PER SERVE (8): *Protein 15 g; Fat 7 g;
Carbohydrate 35 g; Dietary Fibre 8 g; Cholesterol 8 mg;
1135 kJ (270 cal)*

BORLOTTI BEANS
Borlotti beans, also known
as cranberry or red
haricot, are the large,
beautifully marked kidney
beans so loved in northern
and central Italy. They
have a nutty flavour and
creamy flesh that is
especially fine in soups
and stews, but they are
also suited to salads and
puréeing. They can be
found fresh in spring and
summer. Otherwise, dried
are used, or pre-cooked
from cans for convenience.

ABOVE: Minestrone

SNOW PEA (MANGETOUT), PRAWN AND PASTA SOUP

Preparation time: 30 minutes
Total cooking time: 15 minutes
Serves 4

★

12 raw king prawns

100 g (3¹/₂ oz) snow peas (mangetout)

1 tablespoon oil

2 onions, chopped

6 cups (1.5 litres) chicken stock

¹/₂ teaspoon grated fresh ginger

200 g (6¹/₂ oz) angel hair pasta or spaghettini

fresh basil leaves, to garnish

BELOW: Snow pea, prawn and pasta soup

1 Peel and devein the prawns, leaving the tails intact. Trim the snow peas and if they are big ones, slice them into smaller pieces.
2 Heat the oil in a pan, add the onion and cook over low heat until soft. Add the chicken stock to the pan and bring to the boil.
3 Add the fresh ginger, snow peas, prawns and pasta. Cook over medium heat for 4 minutes. Season with salt and pepper and serve immediately, garnished with fresh basil leaves.

NUTRITION PER SERVE: *Protein 20 g; Fat 6 g; Carbohydrate 40 g; Dietary Fibre 4 g; Cholesterol 85 mg; 1255 kJ (300 cal)*

RISSONI AND MUSHROOM BROTH

Preparation time: 15 minutes
Total cooking time: 20–25 minutes
Serves 4

★

90 g (3 oz) butter

2 cloves garlic, sliced

2 large onions, sliced

375 g (12 oz) mushrooms, thinly sliced

5 cups (1.25 litres) chicken stock

125 g (4 oz) rissoni

1¹/₄ cups (315 ml/10 fl oz) cream

1 Melt the butter in a large pan over low heat. Add the garlic and onion and cook for 1 minute. Add the sliced mushrooms and cook gently, without colouring, for 5 minutes. Set aside a few mushroom slices to use as a garnish. Add the chicken stock and cook for 10 minutes.
2 Meanwhile, add the rissoni to a large pan of rapidly boiling salted water and cook until *al dente*. Drain and set aside.
3 Allow the mushroom mixture to cool a little before mixing in a blender or food processor until smooth.
4 Return the mixture to the pan and stir in the rissoni and cream. Heat through and season with salt and pepper, to taste. Serve from a soup terrine or in individual bowls. Garnish with the reserved mushrooms.

NUTRITION PER SERVE: *Protein 10 g; Fat 55 g; Carbohydrate 30 g; Dietary Fibre 5 g; Cholesterol 165 mg; 2660 kJ (635 cal)*

BEAN SOUP
WITH SAUSAGE

Preparation time: 25 minutes
Total cooking time: 40 minutes
Serves 4–6

☆

4 Italian sausages

2 teaspoons olive oil

2 leeks, sliced

1 clove garlic, crushed

1 large carrot, chopped into
   small cubes

2 celery sticks, sliced

2 tablespoons plain flour

2 beef stock cubes, crumbled

8 cups (2 litres) hot water

1/2 cup (125 ml/4 fl oz) white wine

125 g (4 oz) conchiglie
   (shell pasta)

440 g (14 oz) can three-bean
   mix, drained

1 Cut the sausages into small pieces. Heat the oil in a large heavy-based pan and add the sausage pieces. Cook over medium heat for 5 minutes or until golden, stirring regularly. Remove from the pan and drain on paper towels.

2 Add the leek, garlic, carrot and celery to the pan and cook for 2–3 minutes or until soft, stirring occasionally.

3 Add the flour and stir for 1 minute. Gradually stir in the combined stock cubes and water and the wine. Bring to the boil, reduce the heat and simmer for 10 minutes.

4 Add the pasta and beans to the pan. Increase the heat and cook for 8–10 minutes, or until the pasta is tender. Return the sausage to the pan and season with salt and pepper, to taste. Serve with chopped fresh parsley, if desired.

NOTE: Use dried beans, if preferred. Put them in a bowl, cover with water and soak overnight. Drain and add to a large pan with enough water to cover the beans well. Bring to the boil, reduce the heat and simmer for 1 hour. Drain well before adding to the soup.

NUTRITION PER SERVE (6): *Protein 15 g; Fat 10 g; Carbohydrate 30 g; Dietary Fibre 9 g; Cholesterol 20 mg; 1145 kJ (270 cal)*

LEEKS
Like onions, leeks are a member of the *allium* family. They are favoured for their delicate, mildly sweet flavour and are used both raw and cooked. Leeks have cylindrical, not rounded bulbs and the leaves are flattened and solid. These leaves are tightly compacted and grit tends to stick between the layers, so careful rinsing is necessary after the green tops have been discarded. Only the tender white part is used.

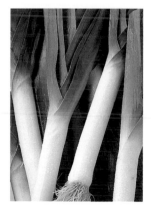

*ABOVE: Bean
soup with sausage*

39

1 Put the chicken pieces, carrot, celery and leek in a large heavy-based pan. Push the chicken to one side and add the egg whites to the vegetables. Using a wire whisk, beat for a minute or so, until frothy (take care not to use a pan that can be scratched by the whisk).

2 Warm the stock in another pan, then add gradually to the first pan, whisking continuously to froth the egg whites. Continue whisking while slowly bringing to the boil. Make a hole in the froth on top with a spoon and leave to simmer for 30 minutes, without stirring.

3 Line a large strainer with a damp tea towel or double thickness of muslin and strain the broth into a clean bowl (discard the chicken and vegetables). Season with salt, pepper and Tabasco sauce, to taste. Set aside until you are ready to serve.

4 To make the coriander pasta, sift the flour into a bowl and make a well in the centre. Whisk the egg and oil together and pour into the well. Mix together to make a soft pasta dough and knead on a lightly floured surface for 2 minutes, until smooth.

5 Divide the pasta dough into four even portions. Roll one portion out very thinly and cover with a layer of evenly spaced coriander leaves. Roll out another portion of pasta and lay this on top of the leaves, then gently roll the layers together. Repeat with the remaining pasta and coriander.

6 Cut out squares of pasta around the leaves. The pasta may then be left to sit and dry out if it is not needed immediately. When you are ready to serve, heat the chicken broth gently in a pan. As the broth simmers, add the pasta and cook for 1 minute. Serve immediately.

NOTE: The egg whites added to the vegetable and chicken stock make the broth very clear, rather than leaving it with the normal cloudy appearance of chicken stock. This is called clarifying the stock. When you strain the broth through muslin or a tea towel, don't press the solids to extract the extra liquid or the broth will become cloudy. It is necessary to make a hole in the froth on top to prevent the stock boiling over.

NUTRITION PER SERVE: *Protein 25 g; Fat 5 g; Carbohydrate 20 g; Dietary Fibre 5 g; Cholesterol 95 mg; 920 kJ (220 cal)*

FRESH CORIANDER

Coriander, also known as cilantro or Chinese parsley, is widely used throughout the world. All parts of the plant are eaten, in one country or another. In Asia and the Middle East, the dried seeds are used for their fragrance, and they form the basis for curry powders when ground. In Mexican cooking, fresh leaves are used extensively, while in Thailand the stems and roots are eaten as well as the leaves.

ABOVE: Spicy chicken broth with coriander pasta

SPICY CHICKEN BROTH WITH CORIANDER PASTA

Preparation time: 1 hour
Total cooking time: 50 minutes
Serves 4

★★★

350 g (11 oz) chicken thighs or wings, skin removed

2 carrots, finely chopped

2 celery sticks, finely chopped

2 small leeks, finely chopped

3 egg whites

6 cups (1.5 litres) chicken stock

Tabasco sauce

Coriander pasta

1/2 cup (60 g/2 oz) plain flour

1 egg

1/2 teaspoon sesame oil

90 g (3 oz) coriander leaves

TOMATO SOUP WITH PASTA AND BASIL

Preparation time: 25 minutes
Total cooking time: 35–40 minutes
Serves 4

★

3 large very ripe tomatoes (about 750 g/1 1/2 lb)

2 tablespoons olive oil

1 onion, finely chopped

1 clove garlic, crushed

1 small red pepper (capsicum), finely chopped

4 cups (1 litre) chicken or vegetable stock

1/4 cup (60 g/2 oz) tomato paste (tomato purée, double concentrate)

1 teaspoon sugar

1/4 cup (15 g/1/2 oz) fresh basil leaves

1 cup (155 g/5 oz) conchiglie (shell pasta) or macaroni

1 Score a small cross in the top of each tomato. Plunge the tomatoes into boiling water for 1–2 minutes, then into cold water. Peel the skin down from the cross and discard. Remove the seeds and roughly chop the tomatoes. Heat the oil in a large heavy-based pan and cook the onion, garlic and red pepper, stirring, for 10 minutes, or until soft. Add the tomato and cook for another 10 minutes.

2 Add the stock, tomato paste, sugar and salt and pepper, to taste. Cover and simmer for 15 minutes. Remove from the heat and add the basil leaves. Allow to cool slightly before processing the mixture, in batches, in a food processor or blender until smooth. Return the mixture to the pan and reheat gently.

3 While the soup is cooking, add the pasta to a large pan of rapidly boiling salted water and cook until *al dente*. Drain, add to the soup and heat through. Garnish with basil leaves if you wish.

NOTE: Basil is added at the end of cooking so that its flavour is not impaired.

NUTRITION PER SERVE: *Protein 10 g; Fat 10 g; Carbohydrate 40 g, Dietary Fibre 5 g; Cholesterol 0 mg; 1200 kJ (285 cal)*

BASIL

There are many varieties of this spicy, aromatic herb, but sweet basil is the most commonly used. Basil plays an important role in Italian and Asian, especially Indonesian, cuisine. It is most often used fresh and added at the last minute, the dried form only being successful in dishes of complex flavours needing long cooking. Basil leaves have a high moisture content and bruise easily. They are best if shredded, not chopped, and the less they are cut, the less blackening will occur.

LEFT: Tomato soup with pasta and basil

1 In a large pan, heat the oil and butter. Add the peeled whole garlic cloves and the onion and cook over low heat for 2–3 minutes.
2 Add the celery and carrot and fry until the vegetables are golden but do not allow them to brown. Add the parsley, basil and cayenne. Stir briefly, add the prawns and toss through. Remove the garlic cloves.
3 Pour in the sherry, increase the heat and cook for 2–3 minutes. Add the chicken stock, bring back to the boil, reduce the heat and simmer for 5 minutes.
4 Add the conchiglie and simmer until the pasta is *al dente*. Stir in the cream and add salt and freshly ground black pepper, to taste.

NUTRITION PER SERVE: *Protein 25 g; Fat 20 g; Carbohydrate 20 g; Dietary Fibre 5 g; Cholesterol 270 mg; 1710 kJ (410 cal)*

BROCCOLI SOUP

Preparation time: 15 minutes
Total cooking time: 20 minutes
Serves 4

★

2 tablespoons olive oil
1 large onion, thinly sliced
50 g (1 3/4 oz) diced prosciutto or
   unsmoked ham
1 clove garlic, crushed
5 cups (1.25 litres) chicken stock
50 g (1 3/4 oz) stellini or other miniature
   pasta shapes
250 g (8 oz) broccoli, tops cut into small
   florets and the tender stems julienned
freshly grated Parmesan, for serving

1 Heat the oil in a large pan over low heat, add the onion, prosciutto and garlic and cook for 4–5 minutes.
2 Pour in the chicken stock, bring to the boil, reduce the heat slightly and simmer for 10 minutes with the lid three-quarters on.
3 Add the stellini and broccoli and cook until the pasta is *al dente* and the broccoli is crisp but tender. Season, to taste, with salt and freshly ground black pepper. Serve in warm bowls with the grated Parmesan.

NUTRITION PER SERVE: *Protein 10 g; Fat 15 g; Carbohydrate 10 g; Dietary Fibre 5 g; Cholesterol 10 mg; 850 kJ (250 cal)*

BROCCOLI
Broccoli belongs to the cabbage family. It is so closely related to the cauliflower that they both have the same varietal name, *botrytis*, from the Greek meaning "formed in a cluster" like a bunch of grapes. Broccoli adds not only colour and flavour to a meal, but nutritive value, as it has high levels of vitamins and essential minerals. It boils or steams well and, if trimmed and cut into separate florets, will cook fast and evenly. Broccoli is also suitable for puréeing and the bulk of the florets gives volume to salads and stir-fries.

ABOVE: Prawn and basil soup (top); Broccoli soup

PRAWN AND BASIL SOUP

Preparation time: 45 minutes
Total cooking time: 15–20 minutes
Serves 4

★

2 tablespoons olive oil
20 g (3/4 oz) butter
2 cloves garlic
1 small red onion, thinly sliced
2 celery sticks, cut into julienne strips
3 small carrots, cut into julienne strips
1 tablespoon finely chopped fresh parsley
1 1/2 tablespoons finely chopped
   fresh basil
pinch of cayenne pepper
500 g (1 lb) raw prawns, peeled
   and deveined
1/2 cup (125 ml/4 fl oz) medium-dry sherry
4 cups (1 litre) chicken stock
70 g (2 1/4 oz) conchiglie (shell pasta)
3 tablespoons cream

BACON AND PEA SOUP

Preparation time: 20 minutes
Total cooking time: 15 minutes
Serves 4–6

★

4 bacon rashers
50 g (1 3/4 oz) butter
1 large onion, finely chopped
1 celery stick, thinly sliced
8 cups (2 litres) chicken stock
1 cup (155 g/5 oz) frozen peas
250 g (8 oz) rissoni
2 tablespoons chopped fresh parsley

1 Trim the rind and excess fat from the bacon and chop into small pieces.
2 Melt the butter in a large heavy-based pan and cook the bacon, onion and celery over low heat for 5 minutes, stirring occasionally. Add the stock and peas and simmer, covered, for 5 minutes. Increase the heat, add the rissoni and cook, uncovered, stirring occasionally, for 5 minutes, or until the rissoni is tender.

3 Add the chopped fresh parsley and season with salt and pepper, to taste, just before serving.

NUTRITION PER SERVE (6): *Protein 10 g; Fat 10 g; Carbohydrate 35 g; Dietary Fibre 5 g; Cholesterol 35 mg; 1130 kJ (270 cal)*

ON THE SIDE

HERB BREAD To make herb bread, combine 125 g (4 oz) of softened butter with 1/2 cup (30 g/1 oz) of chopped mixed herbs and a finely chopped garlic clove. Slice a breadstick diagonally, almost all the way through, and spread each piece with the herb butter. Reshape into a loaf, wrap in aluminium foil and bake in a moderate 180°C (350°F/Gas 4) oven for 30 minutes, or until the loaf is crisp and hot. If you don't want the garlic flavour, you can leave it out.

CELERY
An important flavouring vegetable for many dishes, celery is also delicious in its own right, whether it be braised, baked or served fresh in a salad. All the sticks are stringy, and the darker, outer ones might need to be stripped before use. These are more likely to be chopped for use in stews, while the pale, milder inner stalks can be eaten raw. Celery hearts do not need stringing and are ideal for braising. The dried seeds of the plant, aromatic and slightly bitter, are used as a seasoning.

ABOVE: Bacon and pea soup

EGGPLANT (AUBERGINE)
One of the most attractive of vegetables, the eggplant or aubergine comes in an amazing range of shapes and colours. It can be large and bulbous, thin and finger-like, or small and round like a cherry tomato. The colours range from deep purple to green or white and sometimes they are striped. Look for a glossy wrinkle-free skin, and firm, not hard, flesh.

ABOVE: Ratatouille and pasta soup

RATATOUILLE AND PASTA SOUP

Preparation time: 25 minutes + standing
Total cooking time: 40 minutes
Serves 6

☆

1 medium eggplant (aubergine)
2 tablespoons olive oil
1 large onion, chopped
1 large red pepper (capsicum), chopped
1 large green pepper (capsicum), chopped
2 cloves garlic, crushed
3 zucchini (courgettes), sliced
2 x 400 g (13 oz) cans crushed tomatoes
1 teaspoon dried oregano leaves
1/2 teaspoon dried thyme leaves
4 cups (1 litre) vegetable stock
1/2 cup (45 g/1 1/2 oz) fusilli
Parmesan shavings, for serving

1 Chop the eggplant. To remove any bitterness, spread the eggplant pieces out in a colander and sprinkle generously with salt. Set aside for 20 minutes and then rinse thoroughly and pat dry with paper towels.
2 Heat the oil in a large heavy-based pan and cook the onion over medium heat for 10 minutes, or until soft and lightly golden. Add the peppers, garlic, zucchini and eggplant and stir-fry for 5 minutes.
3 Add the tomato, herbs and vegetable stock to the pan. Bring to the boil, reduce the heat and simmer for 10 minutes, or until the vegetables are tender. Add the fusilli and cook for another 15 minutes, or until the fusilli is tender. Serve with shavings of Parmesan.
NOTE: This delicious soup can be served with Italian bread.

NUTRITION PER SERVE: *Protein 5 g; Fat 5 g; Carbohydrate 20 g; Dietary Fibre 5 g; Cholesterol 0 mg; 640 kJ (150 cal)*

SOUPE AU PISTOU
(VEGETABLE SOUP WITH BASIL SAUCE)

Preparation time: 1 hour
Total cooking time: 35–40 minutes
Serves 8

★

3 stalks fresh parsley
1 large sprig fresh rosemary
1 large sprig fresh thyme
1 large sprig fresh marjoram
1 bay leaf
1/4 cup (60 ml/2 fl oz) olive oil
2 onions, thinly sliced
1 leek, thinly sliced
375 g (12 oz) pumpkin, cut into
   small pieces
250 g (8 oz) potato, cut into small pieces
1 carrot, cut in half lengthways and
   thinly sliced
2 small zucchini (courgettes),
   thinly sliced
1 teaspoon salt
8 cups (2 litres) water or vegetable stock
1/2 cup (80 g/2³/4 oz) fresh or frozen
   broad beans
1/2 cup (80 g/2³/4 oz) fresh or frozen peas
2 very ripe tomatoes, peeled and chopped
1/2 cup (80 g/2³/4 oz) short macaroni
   or conchiglie (shell pasta)

Pistou

1/2 cup (25 g/³/4 oz) fresh basil leaves
2 large cloves garlic, crushed
1/2 teaspoon black pepper
1/3 cup (35 g/1¹/4 oz) freshly grated Parmesan
1/3 cup (80 ml/2³/4 fl oz) olive oil

1 Tie the fresh parsley, rosemary, thyme, marjoram and the bay leaf together with string. Heat the oil in a heavy-based pan, add the sliced onion and leek and cook over low heat for 10 minutes, or until soft.
2 Add the herb bunch, pumpkin, potato, carrot, zucchini, salt, and water or stock to the pan. Cover and simmer for 10 minutes, or until the vegetables are almost tender.
3 Add the broad beans, peas, tomato and pasta. Cover and cook for another 15 minutes, or until the vegetables are very tender and the pasta is cooked (add more water if necessary). Remove the herbs. While the soup is cooking, prepare the pistou.
4 To make the pistou, process the fresh basil leaves with the garlic, pepper and Parmesan in a food processor for 20 seconds, or until finely chopped. With the motor running, pour in the oil gradually, processing until smooth. Serve small amounts of the pistou spooned over the top.
NOTE: This hearty soup is suitable for a main course. It can be made with any seasonal vegetable of your choice. Serve the soup with slices of fresh bread, bread rolls or pieces of Lebanese bread.

NUTRITION PER SERVE: *Protein 5 g; Fat 20 g, Carbohydrate 20 g; Dietary Fibre 5 g; Cholesterol 5 mg; 1150 kJ (275 cal)*

BROAD BEANS
Broad beans, also known as fava, Windsor and horse beans, are the most widely used bean in Europe. Only the bean itself is eaten. Very young broad beans can be eaten raw. When older, the skin toughens and should be removed unless going into a stew or soup, where they will be cooked until tender. Skinning can be done easily once the bean has been steamed or boiled. Dried broad beans have a unique flavour, mealy flesh and dull colour.

ABOVE: Soupe au pistou

PASTA AND BEANS

Combining pasta and beans may seem strange, but they have an affinity recognised in a number of cuisines. In Italy, each region seems to have its own version of *pasta e fagioli*, with the local pasta and favourite beans matched with vegetables, sausage, or perhaps just Parmesan. Pasta combined with beans creates a complete protein, making it a good vegetarian meal.

BELOW: Pasta and bean soup

PASTA AND BEAN SOUP

Preparation time: 20 minutes
   + overnight soaking
Total cooking time: 1 hour 25 minutes
Serves 4–6

☆

250 g (8 oz) borlotti beans, soaked
   in water overnight
1 ham hock
1 onion, chopped
pinch of ground cinnamon
pinch of cayenne pepper
2 teaspoons olive oil
2 cups (500 ml/16 fl oz) chicken stock
125 g (4 oz) tagliatelle (plain or spinach),
   broken into short lengths

1 Drain and rinse the borlotti beans, cover with cold water in a pan and bring to the boil. Stir, lower the heat and simmer for 15 minutes.
2 Drain the beans and transfer to a large pan, with a tight-fitting lid. Add the ham hock, onion, cinnamon, cayenne, olive oil and stock, and cold water to cover. Cover the pan and simmer over low heat for 1 hour, or until the beans are cooked and have begun to thicken the stock. Remove the hock and cut off any meat. Chop the meat and return to the pan, discarding the bone.
3 Taste for seasonings and add salt, if necessary. Bring the soup back to the boil, toss in the tagliatelle and cook until *al dente*. Remove the pan from the heat and set aside for 1–2 minutes before serving. Can be garnished with fresh herbs.

NUTRITION PER SERVE (6): *Protein 15 g; Fat 3 g; Carbohydrate 40 g; Dietary Fibre 6 g; Cholesterol 4 mg; 1025 kJ (245 cal)*

CHICKEN AND PASTA SOUP

Preparation time: 20 minutes
Total cooking time: 20 minutes
Serves 4

★

2 chicken breast fillets
90 g (3 oz) mushrooms
2 tablespoons olive oil
1 onion, finely diced
180 g (6 oz) spaghetti, broken into
    short lengths
6 cups (1.5 litres) chicken stock
1 cup (35 g/1¼ oz) torn fresh basil leaves

1 Finely dice the chicken breast fillets and roughly chop the mushrooms. Heat the olive oil in a pan and cook the onion until soft and golden. Add the chicken, mushrooms, spaghetti pieces and chicken stock. Bring to the boil.
2 Reduce the heat and simmer for 10 minutes. Stir in the fresh basil leaves. Season with salt and freshly ground black pepper, to taste.
NOTE: This is quite a chunky soup. If you prefer a thinner style of soup, you can add more stock. The soup is best enjoyed immediately.

NUTRITION PER SERVE: *Protein 20 g; Fat 10 g; Carbohydrate 35 g; Dietary Fibre 4 g; Cholesterol 30 mg; 1380 kJ (330 cal)*

GARLIC, PASTA AND FISH SOUP

Preparation time: 30 minutes
Total cooking time: 40 minutes
Serves 4–6

★

4 tablespoons olive oil
1 leek, sliced
20–30 cloves garlic, thinly sliced
2 potatoes, chopped
2 litres fish stock
½ cup (75 g/2½ oz) miniature pasta shapes
10 baby yellow squash, halved
2 zucchini, cut into thick slices
300 g (10 oz) ling fillets, cut into
    large pieces
1–2 tablespoons lemon juice
2 tablespoons shredded fresh basil

1 Heat the oil in a large pan, add the leek, garlic and potato and cook over medium heat for 10 minutes. Add 500 ml (16 fl oz) of the stock and cook for 10 minutes.
2 Allow to cool slightly before puréeing, in batches, in a food processor or blender.
3 Pour the remaining stock into the pan and bring to the boil. Add the pasta, squash and zucchini, along with the purée, and simmer for 15 minutes.
4 When the pasta is soft, add the fish and cook for 5 minutes, or until tender. Add the lemon juice and basil, and season with salt and pepper, to taste.

NUTRITION PER SERVE (6): *Protein 15 g; Fat 15 g; Carbohydrate 20 g; Dietary Fibre 4 g; Cholesterol 35 mg; 1165 kJ (275 cal)*

ABOVE: Chicken and pasta soup

PUMPKIN

Pumpkins are related to marrows and squash. Because of their relatively high moisture content, they cook more quickly than vegetables such as potatoes. When cooking pumpkin for a puréed soup, try baking the pumpkin instead of boiling it. The resulting texture is firmer and the flavour is richer and has a slightly nutty edge.

ABOVE: Country pumpkin and pasta soup

COUNTRY PUMPKIN AND PASTA SOUP

Preparation time: 25 minutes
Total cooking time: 20 minutes
Serves 4–6

✫

700 g (1 lb 6½ oz) pumpkin

2 potatoes

1 tablespoon olive oil

30 g (1 oz) butter

1 large onion, finely chopped

2 cloves garlic, crushed

12 cups (3 litres) ready-made liquid chicken stock

125 g (4 oz) stellini or rissoni

chopped fresh parsley, for serving

1 Chop the peeled pumpkin and potatoes into small cubes. Heat the oil and butter in a large pan. Add the onion and garlic and stir over low heat for 5 minutes.

2 Add the chopped pumpkin, potato and chicken stock. Increase the heat, cover the pan and cook for 10 minutes, or until the vegetables are tender.

3 Add the pasta and cook, stirring occasionally, for 5 minutes or until the pasta is just tender. Sprinkle with the chopped fresh parsley. Serve immediately.

NOTE: Butternut or jap pumpkin will give the sweetest flavour. Use a good-quality chicken stock to give the best flavour and to ensure that the soup does not finish up too salty.

NUTRITION PER SERVE (6): *Protein 5 g; Fat 10 g; Carbohydrate 35 g; Dietary Fibre 5 g; Cholesterol 15 mg; 1000 kJ (240 cal)*

LAMB AND FUSILLI SOUP

Preparation time: 25 minutes
Total cooking time: 40 minutes
Serves 6–8

☆

500 g (1 lb) lean lamb meat, cut
   into cubes
2 onions, finely chopped
2 carrots, diced
4 celery sticks, diced
425 g (14 oz) can crushed
   tomatoes
8 cups (2 litres) beef stock
500 g (1 lb) fusilli
chopped fresh parsley,
   for serving

1 Heat a little oil in a large pan and cook the cubed lamb, in batches, until golden brown. Remove each batch as it is done and drain on paper towels. Add the onion to the pan and cook for 2 minutes or until softened. Return the meat to the pan.
2 Add the carrot, celery, tomato, and beef stock. Stir to combine and bring to the boil. Reduce the heat to low and simmer, covered, for 15 minutes.
3 Add the fusilli to the pan. Stir briefly to prevent the pasta from sticking to the pan. Simmer, uncovered, for another 10 minutes or until the lamb and pasta are tender. Sprinkle with chopped fresh parsley before serving.

NUTRITION PER SERVE (8): *Protein 25 g; Fat 5 g; Carbohydrate 50 g; Dietary Fibre 5 g; Cholesterol 40 mg; 1400 kJ (330 cal)*

BEEF STOCK
Beef stock is the base of many soups and adds flavour to casseroles and stews. A good stock can be drunk as a light broth. When reduced to a concentrated form, it becomes a flavouring agent for sauces. Beef or chicken stock is used in recipes containing lamb and pork, as lamb gives a strong, muttony stock and pork, a thin, sweet flavour.

*ABOVE: Lamb
and fusilli soup*

ANTIPASTO
What better way to whet the appetite? Literally translated as 'before the pasta', the antipasto platter is a colourful reminder of the days of the Roman banquet. Excellent for serving at parties.

SALAMI AND POTATO FRITTATA WEDGES

Fry 2 finely diced potatoes in about 2 tablespoons of oil in a 20 cm (8 inch) diameter non-stick frying pan. Add 50 g (1¾ oz) of roughly chopped spicy Italian salami and fry, stirring occasionally, for 10 minutes, or until the potato softens. Add 8 lightly beaten eggs and cook over medium heat for 10 minutes. Transfer the pan to a preheated grill and cook for 3 minutes or until the frittata is set. Remove from the pan and allow to cool slightly before cutting into wedges. Serves 6–8.

NUTRITION PER SERVE (8): *Protein 8 g; Fat 10 g; Carbohydrate 4 g; Dietary Fibre 1 g; Cholesterol 185 mg; 660 kJ (155 cal)*

STUFFED MUSSELS

Scrub 500 g (1 lb) of mussels and remove the beards. Discard any open mussels. Cook in boiling water for 3 minutes, or until the mussels open (discard any that don't open). Drain and cool. Remove the top shells and put the mussels in the shell in a baking dish. Preheat the oven to moderately hot 200°C (400°F/Gas 6).

Fry 1 finely chopped onion in 1 tablespoon of olive oil until golden. Add 2 chopped ripe tomatoes and 2 crushed cloves of garlic. Remove from the heat and season, to taste. Spoon a little sauce into each shell. Combine 1 cup (80 g/2¾ oz) of fresh breadcrumbs and 20 g (¾ oz) of finely grated Parmesan and sprinkle on top. Bake for 10 minutes, or until the crumbs are crisp. Serves 6–8.

NUTRITION PER SERVE (8): *Protein 15 g; Fat 5 g; Carbohydrate 8 g; Dietary Fibre 1 g; Cholesterol 65 mg; 545 kJ (130 cal)*

POLENTA SHAPES WITH CHORIZO AND SALSA

Bring 3 cups (750 ml/24 fl oz) of water to the boil in a saucepan. Gradually add ¾ cup (110 g/3½ oz) of polenta (cornmeal) and stir constantly over medium heat until the mixture comes away from the side of the pan. Stir in 100 g (3½ oz) of grated Cheddar cheese, 50 g (1¾ oz) of grated Mozzarella cheese and 1 tablespoon of chopped fresh oregano. Spread the mixture into a greased tin, about 28 x 18 cm (11 x 7 inches). Chill for 2 hours, or until set. Cut out shapes using biscuit cutters about 5 cm (2 inches) in diameter. Brush lightly with oil and cook under a preheated grill until golden. Thinly slice 4 chorizo sausages and brown on both sides in a non-stick frying pan. Top the polenta shapes with bottled tomato salsa and a piece of chorizo. Garnish with fresh oregano leaves. Serves 6–8.

NUTRITION PER SERVE (8): *Protein 9 g; Fat 15 g; Carbohydrate 10 g; Dietary Fibre 1 g; Cholesterol 30 mg; 945 kJ (225 cal)*

BARBECUED SARDINES

Combine 3 tablespoons of lemon juice, 2 tablespoons of olive oil and 1 or 2 peeled and halved garlic cloves. Lightly oil a preheated barbecue or chargrill pan and brown 20 butterflied sardine fillets over high heat. Brush the sardines with the lemon mixture during cooking. Arrange the sardines on a platter. Makes 20.

NUTRITION PER SARDINE: *Protein 3 g; Fat 4 g; Carbohydrate 0 g; Dietary Fibre 0 g; Cholesterol 15 mg; 220 kJ (50 cal)*

ABOVE, FROM LEFT: Salami and potato frittata wedges; Stuffed mussels; Polenta shapes with chorizo and salsa; Barbecued sardines

ANTIPASTO

GRILLED EGGPLANT (AUBERGINE) AND PEPPERS (CAPSICUMS)

Cut 1 large eggplant into 1 cm (½ inch) thick slices. Cut 2 large red peppers (capsicums) in half and remove the seeds and membrane. Put the red pepper, skin-side-up, under a hot grill and cook for 8 minutes, or until the skins blister and blacken. Remove from the heat and cover with a damp tea towel. When cool enough to handle, peel away the skin and cut the pepper flesh into thick strips. Brush the eggplant slices liberally with olive oil and cook under a medium grill until deep golden brown. Carefully turn the slices over, brush the other sides with oil and grill again until golden. Do not rush this process by having the grill too hot, as slow cooking allows the sugar in the eggplant to caramelize. Combine the eggplant and peppers in a bowl with 2 crushed cloves of garlic, 2 tablespoons of extra virgin olive oil, a pinch of sugar and about 2 tablespoons of chopped fresh parsley. Cover and marinate in the refrigerator overnight. Bring to room temperature for serving. Serves 4–6.

NUTRITION PER SERVE (6): *Protein 1 g; Fat 15 g; Carbohydrate 3 g; Dietary Fibre 2 g; Cholesterol 0 mg; 670 kJ (160 cal)*

PESTO BOCCONCINI BALLS

Blend 1 cup (50 g/1¾ oz) of fresh basil leaves, 3 tablespoons each of pine nuts and freshly grated Parmesan with 2 cloves of garlic, in a food processor until finely chopped. With the motor running, gradually add 1/3 cup (80 ml/2¾ fl oz) of olive oil and process until a paste is formed. Transfer the pesto to a bowl and add 300 g (10 oz) of baby bocconcini. Mix very gently, cover and marinate in the refrigerator for 2 hours. Serves 4–6.

NUTRITION PER SERVE (6): *Protein 15 g; Fat 30 g; Carbohydrate 1 g; Dietary Fibre 1 g; Cholesterol 35 mg; 1400 kJ (335 cal)*

SLOW-ROASTED BALSAMIC TOMATOES

Preheat the oven to warm 160°C (315°F/Gas 2). Cut 500 g (1 lb) of egg (Roma) tomatoes in half. Put them on a non-stick baking tray and brush lightly with extra virgin olive oil. Sprinkle with salt and drizzle with 2 tablespoons of balsamic vinegar. Roast for 1 hour, basting every 15 minutes with another 2 tablespoons of balsamic vinegar. Serves 6–8.

NUTRITION PER SERVE (8): *Protein 1 g; Fat 2 g; Carbohydrate 1 g; Dietary Fibre 1 g; Cholesterol 0 mg; 135 kJ (30 cal)*

BRUSCHETTA

Cut 1 loaf of Italian bread into thick slices. Chop 500 g (1 lb) of ripe tomatoes into very small cubes. Finely dice 1 red (Spanish) onion. Combine the tomato and onion in a bowl with 2 tablespoons of olive oil. Season, to taste, with salt and freshly ground pepper. Lightly toast the bread and, while still hot, rub both sides with a whole garlic clove. Top each piece with some of the tomato mixture and serve warm, topped with strips of finely shredded fresh basil leaves. Serves 6–8.

NUTRITION PER SERVE (8): *Protein 6 g; Fat 6 g; Carbohydrate 30 g; Dietary Fibre 3 g; Cholesterol 0 mg; 875 kJ (210 cal)*

CAULIFLOWER FRITTERS

Cut 300 g (10 oz) of cauliflower into large florets. Cook the florets in a large pan of salted boiling water until just tender. Be careful that you do not overcook them or they will fall apart. Drain thoroughly and set aside to cool slightly. Cut 200 g (6½ oz) of fontina cheese into small cubes and carefully tuck the cheese inside the florets. Beat 3 eggs together in a bowl and dip each floret in the egg. Next, roll the florets in ½ cup (40 g/1¼ oz) of fresh breadcrumbs. When they are all crumbed, deep-fry them in hot oil, in batches, until they are crisp and golden. Serve hot. Serves 4–6.

NUTRITION PER SERVE (6): *Protein 15 g; Fat 30 g; Carbohydrate 5 g; Dietary Fibre 1 g; Cholesterol 120 mg; 1440 kJ (340 cal)*

ABOVE, FROM LEFT: Grilled eggplant and peppers; Pesto bocconcini balls; Slow-roasted balsamic tomatoes; Bruschetta; Cauliflower fritters

PASTA WITH MEAT

Undoubtedly the most famous pasta dish of all, and the most popular standby meal for many families, is spaghetti bolognese, the superb combination of minced meat sauce with pasta. Although most commonly made with beef, in Bologna pork is often added and sometimes lamb is used. All these meats, and many others, when flavoured with herbs, and married with tomatoes, vegetables and wine, turn a straightforward bowl of pasta into a hearty, nutritious and truly delicious meal.

SPAGHETTI BOLOGNESE
This is one of the most popular pasta dishes ever created and almost every family has their own favourite unique version. Within this book you will find three different recipes for this well-loved classic: the traditional (page 24), flavoured with chicken livers and requiring several hours of loving attention; a quick bolognese (page 60); and this recipe (right), ideal for family dinners.

ABOVE: Spaghetti bolognese

SPAGHETTI BOLOGNESE

Preparation time: 20 minutes
Total cooking time: 1 hour 40 minutes
Serves 4–6

⭐

2 tablespoons olive oil
2 cloves garlic, crushed
1 large onion, chopped
1 carrot, chopped
1 celery stick, chopped
500 g (1 lb) beef mince
2 cups (500 ml/16 fl oz) beef stock
1½ cups (375 ml/12 fl oz) red wine
2 x 425 g (14 oz) cans crushed tomatoes
1 teaspoon sugar
¼ cup (7 g/¼ oz) fresh parsley, chopped
500 g (1 lb) spaghetti
freshly grated Parmesan, for serving

1 Heat the olive oil in a large deep pan. Add the garlic, onion, carrot and celery and stir for 5 minutes over low heat until the vegetables are golden.
2 Increase the heat, add the mince and brown well, stirring and breaking up any lumps with a fork as it cooks. Add the stock, wine, tomato, sugar and parsley.
3 Bring the mixture to the boil, reduce the heat and simmer for 1½ hours, stirring occasionally. Season, to taste.
4 While the sauce is cooking and shortly before serving, cook the pasta in a large pan of rapidly boiling salted water until *al dente*. Drain and then divide among serving bowls. Serve the sauce over the top of the pasta and sprinkle with the freshly grated Parmesan.

NUTRITION PER SERVE (6): *Protein 30 g; Fat 20 g; Carbohydrate 65 g; Dietary Fibre 5 g; Cholesterol 55 mg; 2470 kJ (590 cal)*

TAGLIATELLE WITH VEAL, WINE AND CREAM

Preparation time: 15 minutes
Total cooking time: 20 minutes
Serves 4

★

500 g (1 lb) veal scaloppine or escalopes,
    cut into thin strips
plain flour, seasoned with salt and pepper
60 g (2 oz) butter
1 onion, sliced
1/2 cup (125 ml/4 fl oz) dry white wine
3–4 tablespoons beef stock or chicken stock
2/3 cup (170 ml/5 1/2 fl oz) cream
600 g (1 1/4 lb) fresh plain or spinach tagliatelle
    (or a mixture of both)
freshly grated Parmesan

1 Coat the veal strips with the seasoned flour. Melt the butter in a pan. Add the veal strips and fry quickly until browned. Remove with a slotted spoon and set aside.

2 Add the onion slices to the pan and stir until soft and golden, about 8–10 minutes. Pour in the wine and cook rapidly to reduce the liquid. Add the stock and cream and season with salt and pepper, to taste. Reduce the sauce again, and add the veal towards the end.

3 Meanwhile, cook the tagliatelle in a large pan of rapidly boiling salted water until *al dente*. Drain and transfer to a warm serving dish.

4 Stir 1 tablespoon of Parmesan through the sauce. Pour the sauce over the pasta. Serve with a sprinkle of Parmesan. Some chopped herbs can be used as an extra garnish and will add flavour.

NOTE: This dish is lovely served with a mixed salad. If you prefer a lighter sauce, you can omit the cream. The flavour is just as delicious.

NUTRITION PER SERVE: *Protein 45 g; Fat 35 g; Carbohydrate 75 g; Dietary Fibre 5 g; Cholesterol 205 mg; 3355 kJ (800 cal)*

ON THE SIDE

ROAST PUMPKIN WITH SAGE

Preheat the oven to 220°C (425°C/Gas 7). Cut a pumpkin into small cubes and toss well in olive oil. Transfer to a baking dish and scatter with 2 tablespoons of chopped fresh sage and salt and pepper, to taste. Bake for 20 minutes, or a little longer, to brown the cubes a little more. Serve scattered with a little more fresh sage.

CUCUMBER WITH TOASTED SESAME SEEDS
Thinly slice a long cucumber, season and add 2 tablespoons of sesame oil and 1 tablespoon of toasted sesame seeds. Toss and leave to stand for about 20 minutes before serving.

WHITE WINE
White wine contributes a delicate body to dishes. The taste should never be discernible and only a small amount should be used, which must then be completely cooked off to dispel the alcohol. The wine should be the same quality as a good drinking wine. Non-fruity dry white wines are used in savoury cooking, particularly with seafood, and for sweet dishes fortified wines or liqueurs are chosen, but not sweet white wine.

ABOVE: Tagliatelle with veal, wine and cream

PASTA WITH BRAISED OXTAIL AND CELERY

Preparation time: 20 minutes
Total cooking time: 3 hours 45 minutes
Serves 4

☆

1.5 kg (3 lb) oxtail, jointed

1/4 cup (30 g/1 oz) plain flour, seasoned

1/4 cup (60 ml/2 fl oz) olive oil

1 onion, finely chopped

2 cloves garlic, crushed

2 cups (500 ml/16 fl oz) beef stock

425 g (14 oz) can crushed tomatoes

1 cup (250 ml/8 fl oz) dry white wine

6 whole cloves

2 bay leaves

3 celery sticks, finely chopped

500 g (1 lb) penne

30 g (1 oz) butter

3 tablespoons freshly grated Parmesan

ABOVE: Pasta with braised oxtail and celery

1 Preheat the oven to warm 160°C (315°F/ Gas 2−3).

2 Dust the oxtail in seasoned flour and shake off any excess. Heat half the oil in a large pan and brown the oxtail over high heat, a few pieces at a time. Transfer to a large casserole dish.

3 Wipe the pan clean with paper towels. Heat the remaining oil in the pan and add the onion and garlic. Cook over low heat until the onion is tender. Stir in the stock, tomato, wine, cloves, bay leaves and salt and pepper, to taste. Bring to the boil. Pour over the oxtail.

4 Bake, covered, for 2½−3 hours. Add the celery to the dish. Bake, uncovered, for another 30 minutes. Towards the end of cooking time, cook the pasta in a large pan of rapidly boiling salted water until *al dente*. Drain and toss with the butter and Parmesan. Serve the oxtail and sauce with the pasta.

NOTE: Seasoned flour is plain flour to which seasonings of your choice have been added, for example, herbs, salt, pepper, dried mustard.

NUTRITION PER SERVE: *Protein 50 g; Fat 70 g; Carbohydrate 100 g; Dietary Fibre 10 g; Cholesterol 110 mg; 5200 kJ (1240 cal)*

SPAGHETTI WITH SALAMI AND PEPPERS (CAPSICUMS)

Preparation time: 15 minutes
Total cooking time: 55 minutes
Serves 4–6

★

2 tablespoons olive oil
1 large onion, finely chopped
2 cloves garlic, crushed
150 g (5 oz) sliced spicy salami,
  cut into strips
2 large red peppers (capsicums), chopped
825 g (1 lb 11 oz) can crushed tomatoes
1/2 cup (125 ml/4 fl oz) dry white wine
500 g (1 lb) spaghetti

1 Heat the oil in a heavy-based frying pan. Add the onion, garlic and salami and cook for 5 minutes, stirring, over medium heat. Add the pepper, cover and cook for 5 minutes.
2 Add the tomato and the dry white wine and bring to the boil. Reduce the heat and simmer, covered, for 15 minutes. Remove the lid and cook for another 15 minutes, or until the liquid is reduced and the sauce is the desired consistency. Add salt and pepper, to taste.
3 About 15 minutes before the sauce is ready, cook the spaghetti in a large pan of rapidly boiling salted water until *al dente*. Drain and return to the pan. Toss half the sauce with the pasta and divide among serving dishes. Top with the remaining sauce and serve.

NUTRITION PER SERVE (6): *Protein 20 g; Fat 15 g; Carbohydrate 70 g; Dietary Fibre 5 g; Cholesterol 25 mg; 2150 kJ (510 cal)*

ON THE SIDE

POTATO SALAD Cook 1 kg (2 lb) of baby potatoes, with the skins left on, in boiling salted water. Drain and set aside to cool. In a large bowl, thoroughly mix 2 tablespoons of mayonnaise, 2 tablespoons of sour cream and 4 finely chopped spring onions. Add the potatoes and toss until covered in the mixture. Sprinkle with a little cayenne pepper.

SALAMI

Salami, uncooked cured sausage, comes in numerous shapes, flavours and blends of meats. They can be mild or strong, fresh or mature, hard or soft, fine or coarse grained. The meats that are favoured are beef, pork and pork fat in varying proportions, and game meat is sometimes used. Most salamis are cured in salt, but there are some types that originated in mountainous regions which are air-cured. Salami should not be cooked too long as this draws out the fat content.

BELOW: Spaghetti with salami and peppers

EXTRA VIRGIN OLIVE OIL

Extra virgin olive oil is traditionally made from the first pressing of slightly under-ripe olives, where no heating of the fruit takes place (cold pressed) and no chemicals are used. It has almost no acidity and is thick and rich in colour, and often unfiltered. However, by the terms set down by the European Union, the only distinction an olive oil must have to qualify as extra virgin is to have less then 1% acidity. So it is more economical for large olive oil companies in Spain, Italy and France to chemically rectify lower grade oils. This reduces the acid level to the required percentage. Ironically, farmers and small co-ops find this refining too expensive and stick to their traditional methods. It is almost impossible for the consumer to tell the difference, so the only ways to judge quality are by tasting and testing.

ABOVE: Quick spaghetti bolognese

QUICK SPAGHETTI BOLOGNESE

Preparation time: 15 minutes
Total cooking time: 30 minutes
Serves 4

★

2 teaspoons extra virgin olive oil
75 g (2¹/₂ oz) bacon or pancetta, finely chopped
400 g (13 oz) lean beef mince
2 cups (500 g/1 lb) ready-made tomato pasta sauce
2 teaspoons red wine vinegar
2 teaspoons sugar
1 teaspoon dried oregano
500 g (1 lb) spaghetti
freshly grated Parmesan, for serving

1 Heat the oil in a large frying pan and fry the bacon or pancetta until lightly browned. Add the beef mince and brown well over high heat, breaking up any lumps with a fork.
2 Add the pasta sauce, wine vinegar, sugar and dried oregano to the pan and bring to the boil. Lower the heat and simmer for 15 minutes, stirring often to prevent the sauce from catching on the bottom of the pan.
3 About 10 minutes before the sauce is ready, cook the spaghetti in a large pan of rapidly boiling salted water and cook until *al dente*. Drain and divide among four serving bowls. Top with a generous portion of Bolognese sauce and serve sprinkled with the freshly grated Parmesan.

NUTRITION PER SERVE: *Protein 40 g; Fat 30 g; Carbohydrate 100 g; Dietary Fibre 10g; Cholesterol 150 mg; 3505 kJ (835 cal)*

BAKED PASTA AND MINCE

Preparation time: 20 minutes
Total cooking time: 2 hours
Serves 8

★

2 tablespoons olive oil
1 large onion, chopped
1 kg (2 lb) beef mince
¼ cup (60 ml/2 fl oz) red wine
700 ml (23 fl oz) chunky tomato pasta sauce
2 chicken stock cubes, crumbled
2 tablespoons finely chopped
   fresh parsley
500 g (1 lb) bucatini
2 egg whites, lightly beaten
2 tablespoons dry breadcrumbs

Cheese sauce

50 g (1¾ oz) butter
2 tablespoons plain flour
2½ cups (600 ml/20 fl oz) milk
2 egg yolks, lightly beaten
1 cup (125 g/4 oz) grated
   Cheddar cheese

1 Heat the oil in a heavy-based pan. Add the onion and cook over medium heat for 2 minutes, or until soft. Add the mince and stir over high heat until well browned and almost all the liquid has evaporated.
2 Add the wine, sauce and stock cubes and bring to the boil. Reduce to a simmer and cook, covered, for 1 hour, stirring occasionally. Remove from the heat. Add the parsley and allow to cool.
3 To make the cheese sauce, heat the butter in a medium pan over low heat, add the flour and stir for 1 minute, or until golden and smooth. Remove from the heat and gradually stir in the milk. Return to the heat and stir constantly over medium heat for 5 minutes, or until the sauce boils and begins to thicken. Simmer for another minute. Remove from the heat, allow to cool slightly and stir in the egg yolks and cheese.
4 Preheat the oven to moderate 180°C (350°F/Gas 4). Cook the bucatini in a large pan of rapidly boiling salted water until *al dente*. Drain, rinse under cold water and drain thoroughly, then mix with the egg whites. Place half the bucatini over the base of a lightly oiled, deep ovenproof dish. Cover with the mince mixture.
5 Combine the remaining bucatini with the cheese sauce and spread over the mince.

Sprinkle with the dry breadcrumbs. Bake in the oven for 45 minutes, or until the top is lightly golden.

NUTRITION PER SERVE: *Protein 40 g; Fat 30 g; Carbohydrate 80 g; Dietary Fibre 5 g; Cholesterol 160 mg; 3210 kJ (765 cal)*

ON THE SIDE

BEAN SALAD WITH VINAIGRETTE
Toss cooked cannellini or haricot beans in a vinaigrette dressing made by thoroughly whisking together some walnut oil and balsamic vinegar with a crushed clove of garlic. Add 2 tablespoons of finely chopped fresh parsley, 4 finely chopped spring onions and a handful of torn basil. Season well with salt and pepper. Before serving, allow to stand for about 10 minutes so the beans soak up the flavour.

ABOVE: Baked pasta and mince

CHORIZO SAUSAGE

Chorizo is a hard, deep red sausage from Spain. It is well spiced and coarsely grained and is made primarily from pork and pork fat with garlic and paprika. Some types are intended for eating raw, while others with less fat are suited to cooking in stews and soups. If unobtainable, substitute Italian pepperoni or any other firm, spicy garlic sausage.

ABOVE: Rigatoni with chorizo and tomato

RIGATONI WITH CHORIZO AND TOMATO

Preparation time: 15 minutes
Total cooking time: 20–25 minutes
Serves 4

★

2 tablespoons olive oil
1 onion, sliced
250 g (8 oz) chorizo sausage, sliced
425 g (14 oz) can crushed tomatoes
1/2 cup (125 ml/4 fl oz) dry white wine
1/2–1 teaspoon chopped chilli, optional
375 g (12 oz) rigatoni
2 tablespoons chopped fresh parsley
2 tablespoons freshly grated Parmesan

1 Heat the oil in a frying pan. Add the onion and stir over low heat until tender.
2 Add the sausage to the pan and cook, turning frequently, for 2–3 minutes. Add the tomato, wine, chilli and salt and pepper, to taste, and stir. Bring to the boil, reduce the heat and simmer for 15–20 minutes.
3 While the sauce is cooking, cook the rigatoni in a large pan of rapidly boiling salted water until *al dente*. Drain and return to the pan. Add the sauce to the hot pasta. Toss well to combine. Serve sprinkled with the combined fresh parsley and grated Parmesan.

NUTRITION PER SERVE: *Protein 25 g; Fat 30 g; Carbohydrate 70 g; Dietary Fibre 5 g; Cholesterol 50 mg; 2990 kJ (715 cal)*

ZITI WITH VEGETABLES AND SAUSAGE

Preparation time: 30 minutes
Total cooking time: 40 minutes
Serves 4

☆

1 red pepper (capsicum)
1 green pepper (capsicum)
1 small eggplant (aubergine), sliced
1/4 cup (60 ml/2 fl oz) olive oil
1 onion, sliced
1 clove garlic, crushed
250 g (8 oz) chipolatas, sliced
425 g (14 oz) can crushed tomatoes
1/2 cup (125 ml/4 fl oz) red wine
1/4 cup (35 g/1 1/4 oz) halved pitted
   black olives
1 tablespoon chopped fresh basil
1 tablespoon chopped fresh parsley
500 g (1 lb) ziti
freshly grated Parmesan, for serving

1 Cut the peppers into large flat pieces and discard the seeds and membrane. Put, skin-side-up, under a hot grill and cook for 8 minutes, or until the skin is black and blistered. Remove from the heat and cover with a damp tea towel. When cool, peel away the skin, chop the flesh and set aside.
2 Brush the eggplant with a little of the oil. Grill until golden on each side, brushing with more oil as required. Set aside.
3 Heat the remaining oil in a frying pan. Add the onion and garlic and stir over low heat until the onion is tender. Add the chipolatas and cook until well browned.
4 Stir in the tomato, wine, olives, basil, parsley and salt and pepper, to taste. Bring to the boil, reduce the heat and simmer for 15 minutes. Add the vegetables and then heat through.
5 While the sauce is cooking, cook the ziti in a large pan of rapidly boiling salted water until *al dente*. Drain and return to the pan. Toss the vegetables and sauce through the hot pasta. Sprinkle with Parmesan before serving.
NOTE: Ziti is a wide tubular pasta that is excellent with this dish but you can substitute fettucine or spaghetti if you prefer.

NUTRITION PER SERVE: *Protein 30 g; Fat 35 g; Carbohydrate 105 g; Dietary Fibre 10 g; Cholesterol 35 mg; 3760 kJ (900 cal)*

ON THE SIDE

ASPARAGUS WITH LEMON HAZELNUT BUTTER Lightly steam or microwave fresh asparagus spears until just tender. Heat a little butter in a small pan until it starts to turn a nutty brown. Stir in some toasted and roughly chopped hazelnuts and finely grated lemon rind. Spoon over the asparagus and serve at once.

CHIVE AND GARLIC CORN COBS Boil, steam or microwave corn cobs in the husk until tender. Remove the husks and silks. Cut the cobs into three and toss in a little extra virgin olive oil, butter, crushed garlic and chopped fresh chives. Sprinkle generously with cracked black pepper and sea salt.

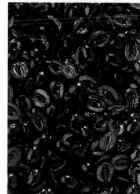

ABOVE: Ziti with vegetables and sausage

RED WINE

Where a richer, more mellow taste is called for in a dish, red wine is used. Its earthy, robust flavours make it a good companion to red meats and game and the colour makes it better suited to tomato-based sauces and gravies. Very rarely is it used with dairy produce, such as in a cream sauce. The red wine best suited for cooking is young, full-bodied and well balanced, one that would be enjoyed as a table wine.

BELOW: Rigatoni with Italian-style oxtail sauce

RIGATONI WITH ITALIAN-STYLE OXTAIL SAUCE

Preparation time: 25 minutes
Total cooking time: 2 hours
Serves 4

★

2 tablespoons olive oil
1.5 kg (3 lb) oxtail, jointed
2 large onions, sliced
4 cloves garlic, chopped
2 celery sticks, sliced
2 carrots, thinly sliced
2 large sprigs rosemary
1/4 cup (60 ml/2 fl oz) red wine
1/4 cup (60 g/2 oz) tomato paste (tomato purée, double concentrate)
4 tomatoes, peeled and chopped
6 cups (1.5 litres) beef stock
500 g (1 lb) rigatoni or ditaloni

1 Heat the oil in a large heavy-based pan. Brown the oxtail, remove from the pan and set aside. Add the onion, garlic, celery and carrot to the pan and stir for 3–4 minutes, or until the onion is lightly browned.

2 Return the oxtail to the pan and add the rosemary and red wine. Cover and cook for 10 minutes, shaking the pan occasionally to prevent the meat from sticking to the bottom. Add the tomato paste and chopped tomato to the pan with 2 cups (500 ml/16 fl oz) of the beef stock and simmer, uncovered, for 30 minutes, stirring the mixture occasionally.

3 Add another 2 cups of beef stock to the pan and cook for 30 minutes. Add 1 cup of stock and cook for 30 minutes. Finally, add the remaining stock and cook until the oxtail is tender and the meat is falling from the bone. The liquid should have reduced to produce a thick sauce.

4 Just before the meat is cooked, cook the pasta in a large pan of rapidly boiling salted water until *al dente*. Serve the meat and sauce over the hot pasta.

NOTE: For a different flavour, you can add 250 g (8 oz) of bacon to the cooked onion, garlic and vegetables. Proceed as above.

NUTRITION PER SERVE: *Protein 50 g; Fat 55 g; Carbohydrate 100 g; Dietary Fibre 10 g; Cholesterol 90 mg; 4600 kJ (1100 cal)*

ON THE SIDE

SPICY CUCUMBER SALAD Peel and slice a long cucumber and arrange the slices on a platter. Mix 1 finely chopped spring onion with 2 tablespoons of rice vinegar or white wine vinegar, 1 teaspoon of honey, 1 tablespoon of sesame oil and a finely chopped red chilli. Drizzle the dressing over the cucumber slices and sprinkle with about 3 tablespoons of chopped roasted peanuts.

GARLIC DILL MUSHROOMS Fry sliced button mushrooms in a mixture of olive oil and butter. Add some finely chopped garlic and some sliced spring onions and cook until the mushrooms are browned and tender. Drain off any excess liquid, fold through a little chopped fresh dill and season, to taste, with salt and cracked black pepper.

RIGATONI WITH KIDNEY BEANS AND ITALIAN SAUSAGE

Preparation time: 25 minutes
Total cooking time: 30 minutes
Serves 4–6

★

1 tablespoon olive oil

1 large onion, chopped

2 cloves garlic, crushed

4 Italian sausages, chopped

825 g (1 lb 11 oz) can crushed tomatoes

425 g (14 oz) can kidney or borlotti beans, drained

2 tablespoons chopped fresh basil

1 tablespoon chopped fresh sage

1 tablespoon chopped fresh parsley

500 g (1 lb) rigatoni

freshly grated Parmesan, for serving

1 Heat the oil in a heavy-based pan. Add the onion, garlic and sausage to the pan and cook, stirring occasionally, over medium heat for 5 minutes.

2 Add the tomato, beans, basil, sage, parsley and salt and pepper, to taste. Reduce the heat and simmer for 20 minutes.

3 While the sauce is cooking, add the pasta to a large pan of rapidly boiling salted water and cook until *al dente*. Drain. Divide the pasta among serving bowls and top with the sauce. Sprinkle with Parmesan and serve immediately.

NOTE: Dried beans can be used. Soak them overnight in water, drain and transfer to a pan. Cover well with water, bring to the boil and cook for 20 minutes, or until tender. Giant conchiglie (shell pasta) can be used instead of rigatoni as they hold the sauce well.

NUTRITION PER SERVE (6): *Protein 25 g; Fat 30 g; Carbohydrate 75 g; Dietary Fibre 10 g; Cholesterol 60 mg; 2810 kJ (670 cal)*

FRESH ITALIAN SAUSAGES

Italian sausages are distinguished by a coarse grain and well-balanced spicing. They are made with various combinations of pork, pork fat and beef, and rely on the quality of these for good flavour and texture. For use in a stew or sauce, choose one that is compact, with good meat to fat ratio and an even grain. The skins can be removed before cooking without the sausage losing shape. Italian sausages are available at delicatessens.

ABOVE: Rigatoni with kidney beans and Italian sausage

COLD MEATS
While Italy is famous for its pasta, cold meats and salamis are also close to the Italian cook's heart. Each region is passionately adamant about the superiority of its own speciality.

PANCETTA is the Italian version of bacon. The rind is removed and the meat is seasoned with salt and pepper and spices which include nutmeg, juniper, cloves, cinnamon, depending on the person who is packing it. It is cured for two weeks, then tightly rolled and packed in a case similar to that used for salami. The flavour is less salty than prosciutto, though it can be eaten raw as you would

prosciutto. It is prized for the flavour it imparts to cooked dishes where it has no real substitute for its savoury sweet taste.

PROSCIUTTO is the salt- and air-dried hind leg of a pig. The salt removes the moisture from the meat and the slow process of air-curing produces a soft delicate flavour. Prosciutto can be cured for up 18 months and the most prized

are judged against genuine Italian Parma ham. Sliced prosciutto should be consumed as soon as possible after cutting as it gradually loses its flavour. Remove it from the refrigerator 1 hour before you plan to serve it. Parma ham gets its unique flavour from the pigs being fed the whey left over from cheese-making. Traditionally served with melon or figs on an antipasto platter.

MORTADELLA from Bologna takes its name from the mortar used to grind the pork. Flavoured with peppercorns, stuffed olives, pistachios and garlic and flecked with strips of fat, it can measure up to 40 cm (16 inches) in diameter. Mortadella is chopped and used on pizzas, in sandwiches or in tortellini.

SALAMI

A cured dry sausage made from minced pork and seasoned with garlic, herbs and spices. Thought to have originated in Salamis in Cyprus, most Italian salamis take their names from the towns in which they are produced. Distinctive types of salami are also made in Denmark, Spain, Hungary, Austria and Germany.

CACCIATORE is made from pork and beef, garlic and spices, and can be mild or hot.

MILANO SALAMI is a mildly-flavoured Italian salami made with lean pork, beef and pork fat. It has a fine texture and is seasoned with garlic, pepper and wine.

FINOCCHIONA TOSCANA is a salami made from pork and seasoned with fennel seeds that are distributed throughout the salami. Mild or hot.

PEPPERONI is a dried Italian sausage made from ground pork and beef, highly seasoned with pepper. It is used as a topping for pizzas and in pasta sauces.

COPPA is made from the pork shoulder that has been cured. It is fattier than prosciutto and is sold rolled and cased like salami. Coppa is frequently served as a part of an antipasto platter.

SPECK is the fatty top part of a leg of bacon, usually smoked and salted. It is available in small pieces. Austrian in origin, it can be sliced for a cold snack or chopped into small cubes to use to add flavour to cooked dishes.

CHORIZO is a coarsely-textured Spanish sausage that comes in many varieties, although it is always made from pork and seasoned with pimiento. It is sliced, fried and used in pasta sauces or, as it is best known, in paella.

CLOCKWISE, FROM TOP LEFT: Prosciutto on the bone, pancetta, prosciutto slices off the bone, Milano, Finocchiona Toscana, Coppa, Cacciatore, Speck, Chorizo, Pepperoni, Mortadella

PORK, PAPRIKA AND POPPY SEEDS WITH PASTA

Preparation time: 15 minutes
Total cooking time: 15–20 minutes
Serves 4

✭

500 g (1 lb) pappardelle

20 g (3/4 oz) butter

1 1/2 tablespoons vegetable oil

1 onion, thinly sliced

1 clove garlic, crushed

2 teaspoons sweet paprika

pinch of cayenne pepper

500 g (1 lb) lean pork (fillet or leg steaks),
    thinly sliced

1 tablespoon finely chopped fresh parsley

1 tablespoon port or other dry
    fortified wine

1 tablespoon tomato paste (tomato purée,
    double concentrate)

300 g (10 oz) sour cream

150 g (5 oz) button mushrooms, sliced

2 teaspoons poppy seeds

2 tablespoons chopped fresh parsley

ABOVE: Pork, paprika and poppy seeds with pasta

1 Cook the pappardelle in a large pan of rapidly boiling salted water until *al dente*. Drain and return to the pan.

2 Heat the butter and 1/2 tablespoon of oil in a frying pan and gently fry the sliced onion for 6–8 minutes, or until soft. Add the garlic, paprika, cayenne pepper, pork and parsley and season, to taste, with freshly ground pepper. Sauté quickly over high heat until the pork is cooked. Add the port, bring to the boil and stir briefly, for about 10 seconds. Add the tomato paste and sour cream and stir until combined. Stir in the mushrooms and adjust the seasoning. Reduce the heat to low.

3 Stir the remaining oil and the poppy seeds through the warm pasta. Serve the pork spooned over the pasta. Garnish with fresh parsley just before serving.

NUTRITION PER SERVE: *Protein 40 g; Fat 45 g; Carbohydrate 65 g; Dietary Fibre 6 g; Cholesterol 170 mg; 3525 kJ (840 cal)*

TURKISH RAVIOLI

Preparation time: 1 hour
Total cooking time: 30 minutes
Serves 4–6

★ ★

Filling

1 tablespoon oil
1 small onion, finely grated
1 red chilli, finely chopped
1 teaspoon ground cinnamon
1 teaspoon ground cloves
500 g (1 lb) finely minced lamb
2 teaspoons grated lemon rind
2 teaspoons chopped fresh dill
3 tablespoons chopped fresh flat-leaf parsley

Sauce

1 cup (250 ml/8 fl oz) chicken stock
2 cups (500 ml/16 fl oz) natural yoghurt
4 cloves garlic, crushed

1¾ cups (215 g/7 oz) plain flour
⅓ cup (50 g/1¾ oz) plain wholemeal flour
½ cup (125 ml/4 fl oz) water
1 egg
1 egg yolk
½ cup fresh mint leaves, finely chopped

1 To make the filling, heat the oil in a large frying pan, add the onion, chilli and spices and cook over medium heat for 5 minutes, or until the onion is golden. Add the mince and cook over high heat until the meat is browned, stirring constantly to break up any lumps. Remove from the heat, stir in the lemon rind and chopped herbs. Set aside to cool.

2 To make the sauce, bring the chicken stock to the boil in a pan and cook until the stock is reduced by half. Remove from the heat, and whisk the stock with the yoghurt and garlic. Season, to taste, with salt and pepper.

3 Combine the flours, water, egg and yolk in a food processor until the mixture comes together to form a smooth dough. Turn the dough out onto a lightly floured surface. If the dough is too sticky you may need to add a little extra flour. (It is much easier to add more flour to a wet dough than add more egg to a dry dough.)

4 Divide the dough into quarters, open the rollers on your pasta machine to the widest setting, sprinkle the rollers generously with flour and roll the dough through the machine.

Fold the dough into three, so that the width of the pasta remains the same and the length should now be one-third of what it was.

5 Pass the dough through the rollers again, and repeat the folding and rolling process, turning the dough right on a 90 degree angle each time. Repeat this at least ten times, dusting the machine and dough lightly with flour if you need to. When the pasta is smooth, set the rollers in a groove closer, pass the pasta through and keep setting the rollers closer until the pasta is 1 mm (¹⁄₁₆ inch) thick. Cover and set aside. Repeat with the remaining dough.

6 Cut the dough into 12 cm (5 inch) squares and place 1 tablespoon of the filling on the centre of each square, brush the edges lightly with water and fold each square into a triangle. Press the edges together to seal and place the ravioli in a single layer on a lightly floured baking tray. Keep them covered while making the rest of the ravioli.

7 Cook the ravioli, in batches, in a large pan of rapidly boiling salted water for 3 minutes, or until *al dente*. Drain and toss through the sauce. Garnish with chopped mint.

NUTRITION PER SERVE (6): *Protein 25 g; Fat 20 g; Carbohydrate 30 g; Dietary Fibre 3 g; Cholesterol 120 mg; 1595 kJ (380 cal)*

NATURAL YOGHURT

Made by fermenting cow's or ewe's milk, yoghurt originated in the Balkans. It was used then as a pharmaceutical remedy but is now enjoyed for the fresh, slightly sour flavour and used in cooking for the complexity of tastes that its acidity creates. Yoghurt is produced when selected milk is treated with an active lactic culture. Under controlled temperatures, this action brings about a natural fermentation. The resulting curd is semi-set, smooth and a clean white colour. Fresh yoghurt keeps for 4–5 days, refrigerated, before deteriorating.

BELOW: Turkish ravioli

GINGER
Ginger is a rhizome, the root of a tropical plant which originated in Bengal and the Malabar Coast of southern India. It is used as a condiment for savoury foods and as a flavouring ingredient for savoury and sweet dishes. Ginger has a fresh but hot taste and a very firm flesh. The fragrance, which is clean and aromatic, is intensified when heated. The longer ginger is in the ground, the stronger the flavour becomes, but unfortunately this is accompanied by an increase in the fibrousness of the root, which makes it harder to chop or grate. When buying fresh ginger choose a plump, firm root that isn't limp or spongey, and store it in the refrigerator, wrapped first in a paper towel and then a plastic bag.

OPPOSITE PAGE:
Stir-fried chilli beef with spaghettini (top);
Moroccan lamb and roasted pepper with fusilli

STIR-FRIED CHILLI BEEF WITH SPAGHETTINI

Preparation time: 40 minutes
Total cooking time: 20 minutes
Serves 4

★

500 g (1 lb) spaghettini
3 tablespoons peanut oil
1 onion, sliced
1 clove garlic, crushed
1/2 teaspoon finely chopped fresh ginger
1/4 teaspoon chilli flakes
400 g (13 oz) lean beef (rump or scotch fillet), cut into thin strips
1 1/2 teaspoons soy sauce
few drops sesame oil
155 g (5 oz) bean sprouts, trimmed
1 heaped tablespoon chopped fresh coriander

1 Cook the spaghettini in a large pan of rapidly boiling salted water until *al dente*. Drain, return to the pan and cover with cold water. Drain again and return to the pan. Stir 1 tablespoon of peanut oil through the pasta and set aside.
2 Heat 1 tablespoon of peanut oil in a large frying pan or wok and cook the onion, without browning, until softened. Stir in the garlic, ginger and chilli flakes. Add the beef and stir-fry over high heat until browned.
3 Stir in the soy sauce, sesame oil, bean sprouts and coriander. Taste for salt, pepper and chilli, adjust if necessary, and continue stirring until all the ingredients have heated through. Remove from the pan or wok. Add some peanut oil to the wok or pan and add the pasta, tossing it briefly over high heat to heat it through. Serve the spaghettini topped with the beef.
NOTE: As with all stir-fries, this dish requires quick, attentive cooking over high heat. Although it's tempting to take short cuts, rinsing the spaghettini in cold water is necessary to stop the cooking process and give the correct texture and flavour to the pasta.

NUTRITION PER SERVE: *Protein 35 g; Fat 20 g; Carbohydrate 70 g; Dietary Fibre 7 g; Cholesterol 65 mg; 2455 kJ (585 cal)*

MOROCCAN LAMB AND ROASTED PEPPER (CAPSICUM) WITH FUSILLI

Preparation time: 25 minutes
+ overnight marinating
Total cooking time: 25 minutes
Serves 4–6

★

500 g (1 lb) lamb fillets
3 teaspoons ground cumin
1 tablespoon ground coriander
2 teaspoons ground allspice
1 teaspoon ground cinnamon
1/2 teaspoon ground cayenne pepper
4 cloves garlic, crushed
1/3 cup 80 ml (2 3/4 fl oz) olive oil
1/2 cup (125 ml/4 fl oz) lemon juice
2 red peppers (capsicums)
400 g (13 oz) fusilli
1/4 cup (60 ml/2 fl oz) extra virgin olive oil
2 teaspoons harissa
150 g (5 oz) rocket

1 Cut the fillets in half if they are very long. Mix the cumin, coriander, allspice, cinnamon, cayenne, garlic, olive oil and half the lemon juice in a bowl. Add the lamb, stir to coat and marinate, covered, in the refrigerator overnight.
2 Cut the peppers into large pieces and discard the seeds and membrane. Put skin-side-up, under a hot grill and cook for 8 minutes, or until the skin is black and blistered. Remove from the heat and cover with a damp tea towel. When cool, peel away the skin and slice thinly.
3 Cook the fusilli in a large pan of rapidly boiling salted water until *al dente*. Drain; keep warm.
4 Drain the lamb, heat 1 tablespoon of the extra virgin olive oil in a large frying pan and cook the lamb over high heat until done to your liking. Remove from the pan; cover with foil.
5 Heat 1 teaspoon of the oil in the frying pan and cook the harissa over medium heat for a few seconds. Be careful as the mixture may spit. Remove and place in a small screw top jar with the remaining oil and lemon juice and shake the jar until well combined. Season, to taste.
6 Thinly slice the lamb fillets and toss with the warm pasta, sliced pepper and rocket. Toss the harissa dressing through the pasta. Serve warm.

NUTRITION PER SERVE (6): *Protein 25 g; Fat 30 g; Carbohydrate 50 g; Dietary Fibre 5 g; Cholesterol 55 mg; 2365 kJ (565 cal)*

MARJORAM

Also known as sweet or knotted marjoram, common marjoram (*majorana hortensis*) is very closely related to oregano. Sweet marjoram is milder and more subtle in flavour, and has a fresh, fragrant aroma. It is used in soups and with fish, and goes well with most vegetables. It is easy to grow and it dries easily. For best results when drying, cut sprigs just before the flowers come into bloom as this is when the herb is in full fragrance.

ABOVE: Rigatoni with salami and fresh herbs

RIGATONI WITH SALAMI AND FRESH HERBS

Preparation time: 35 minutes
Total cooking time: 40 minutes
Serves 4

★

20 g (3/4 oz) butter
1 tablespoon olive oil
1 onion, thinly sliced
1 carrot, cut into julienne strips
1 bay leaf
75 g (2 1/2 oz) bacon rashers, chopped
200 g (6 1/2 oz) spicy Italian salami, skinned and sliced
400 g (13 oz) can peeled egg (Roma) tomatoes
1/2 cup (125 ml/4 fl oz) beef or chicken stock
400 g (13 oz) rigatoni
1 tablespoon fresh oregano or marjoram leaves

1 Heat the butter and oil in a frying pan and cook the onion and carrot with the bay leaf until the onion is transparent and softened. Add the chopped bacon and sliced salami and cook, stirring often, until brown.

2 Squeeze half the tomatoes dry over the sink, pulp the flesh with your hand and add to the pan. Add the rest whole and break up loosely with the spoon while stirring. Season well with salt and pepper, to taste, and simmer for 30 minutes over low heat, gradually adding the stock as the sauce reduces.

3 Cook the rigatoni in a large pan of rapidly boiling salted water until *al dente*. Drain and transfer to a warm serving dish. Add the oregano or marjoram and sauce, and toss together lightly before serving.

NOTE: Use good-quality salami to ensure the success of this sauce. The use of fresh herbs is also important to produce the best flavour.

NUTRITION PER SERVE: *Protein 25 g; Fat 25 g; Carbohydrate 75 g; Dietary Fibre 10 g; Cholesterol 65 mg; 2755 kJ (660 cal)*

MEATBALLS WITH FUSILLI

Preparation time: 35 minutes
Total cooking time: 35 minutes
Serves 4

☆

750 g (1 1/2 lb) pork and veal or beef mince
1 cup (80 g/2¾ oz) fresh breadcrumbs
3 tablespoons freshly grated Parmesan
1 onion, finely chopped
2 tablespoons chopped fresh parsley
1 egg, beaten
1 clove garlic, crushed
rind and juice of 1/2 lemon
1/4 cup (30 g/1 oz) plain flour, seasoned
2 tablespoons olive oil
500 g (1 lb) fusilli

Sauce

425 g (14 oz) can tomato purée (passata)
1/2 cup (125 ml/4 fl oz) beef stock
1/2 cup (125 ml/4 fl oz) red wine
2 tablespoons chopped fresh basil
1 clove garlic, crushed

1 In a large bowl, combine the mince, breadcrumbs, Parmesan, onion, parsley, egg, garlic, lemon rind and juice and salt and pepper, to taste. Roll tablespoons of the mixture into balls and roll the balls in the seasoned flour.
2 Heat the oil in a large frying pan and fry the meatballs until golden. Remove from the pan and drain on paper towels. Remove the excess fat and meat juices from the pan.
3 To make the sauce, in the same pan, combine the tomato purée, stock, wine, basil, garlic, salt and pepper. Bring to the boil.
4 Reduce the heat and return the meatballs to the pan. Allow to simmer for 10–15 minutes.
5 While the meatballs and sauce are cooking, add the fusilli to a large pan of rapidly boiling salted water and cook until *al dente*. Drain and serve with meatballs and sauce over the top.

NUTRITION PER SERVE: *Protein 60 g; Fat 35 g; Carbohydrate 115 g; Dietary Fibre 10 g; Cholesterol 170 mg; 4110 kJ (980 cal)*

ON THE SIDE

BEETROOT, GOATS CHEESE AND PISTACHIO NUT SALAD

Boil, steam or microwave about 1 kg (2 lb) of trimmed baby beetroot until quite tender. Allow to cool slightly before cutting into quarters. Line a serving plate with rocket leaves, top with the beetroot quarters, along with 1 thinly sliced red (Spanish) onion, 100 g (3½ oz) of crumbled goats cheese and 100 g (3½ oz) of toasted and roughly chopped pistachio nuts. Make a dressing by whisking together 3 tablespoons of raspberry vinegar, 1 teaspoon of Dijon mustard, 1 teaspoon of honey and 1/3 cup (80 ml/2¾ fl oz) of oil. Drizzle over the salad ingredients and serve immediately.

SEASONED FLOUR

When plain flour has salt added to it, it is called seasoned flour. Pepper, and sometimes other spices or herbs, may be included. It is used to dredge meats and vegetables before searing them for braising. The flour gives an even coating that colours well and helps to thicken sauce. It also enhances the flavour of the dish.

ABOVE: Meatballs with fusilli

MACARONI

Macaroni, or *maccheroni*, is short tubular lengths of pasta. It can be quite short and thin, or fat and as long as 4 cm (1¹/₂ inches), but it is always hollow. Various sizes are known by specific names, and different regions in Italy may have different names for the same shape and size. Along with many of the improbable stories regarding the origins of macaroni, one fact is known, that it has been called *maccherone* since at least 1041 when it was a word used to describe a man who was a bit of a dunce.

*ABOVE: Penne
with prosciutto*

PENNE WITH PROSCIUTTO

Preparation time: 15 minutes
Total cooking time: 25 minutes
Serves 4

★

1 tablespoon olive oil
6 thin slices prosciutto, chopped
1 onion, finely chopped
1 tablespoon chopped fresh rosemary
825 g (1 lb 11 oz) can crushed tomatoes
500 g (1 lb) penne or macaroni
¹/₂ cup (50 g/1³/₄ oz) freshly grated Parmesan

1 Heat the oil in a heavy-based frying pan. Add the prosciutto and onion and cook, stirring occasionally, over low heat for 5 minutes, or until golden.

2 Add the rosemary, tomato and salt and pepper, to taste. Simmer for 10 minutes.
3 While the sauce is cooking, add the pasta to a large pan of rapidly boiling salted water and cook until *al dente*. Drain. Divide the pasta among serving bowls and top with the sauce. Sprinkle with grated Parmesan.
NOTE: Rosemary, commonly used in Mediterranean cookery, adds a distinctive flavour to this dish.

NUTRITION PER SERVE: *Protein 20 g; Fat 9 g; Carbohydrate 65 g; Dietary Fibre 6 g; Cholesterol 20 mg; 1725 kJ (410 cal)*

PARSEE LAMB WITH CUMIN, EGGS AND TAGLIATELLE

Preparation time: 40 minutes
Total cooking time: 1 hour 15 minutes
Serves 4

★

20 g (³/4 oz) butter
1 large onion, finely chopped
2 cloves garlic, crushed
1 teaspoon finely chopped fresh ginger
³/4 teaspoon each of chilli flakes, turmeric,
    garam masala and ground cumin
600 g (1¹/4 lb) minced lamb
2 large very ripe tomatoes, chopped
¹/2 teaspoon sugar
1 tablespoon lemon juice
3 tablespoons finely chopped fresh
    coriander
1 small red chilli, finely chopped, optional
350 g (11 oz) tagliatelle
1 tablespoon vegetable oil
3 hard-boiled eggs, chopped

1 Heat the butter in a frying pan and add the onion, garlic and ginger. Fry over low heat until the onion is soft but not browned. Stir in the chilli flakes, turmeric, garam masala and cumin.
2 Add the mince, increase the heat and cook until the meat is well browned, stirring occasionally. Stir in the tomato, sugar, a good pinch of salt and 1 cup (250 ml/8 fl oz) of water. Reduce the heat and simmer, covered, for 50–60 minutes, or until the sauce thickens and darkens. Increase the heat and add the lemon juice, 2 tablespoons of the chopped coriander and the red chilli. Check the seasoning, add salt if required and cook, uncovered, for 2–3 minutes.
3 Cook the tagliatelle in a large pan of rapidly boiling salted water until *al dente*. Drain, return to the pan and stir in the oil. Transfer to warmed serving dishes and spoon the lamb mixture on top. Sprinkle with hard-boiled eggs and the remaining fresh coriander before serving.

NUTRITION PER SERVE: *Protein 45 g; Fat 35 g; Carbohydrate 65 g; Dietary Fibre 7 g; Cholesterol 275 mg; 3270 kJ (780 cal)*

GARAM MASALA
Garam masala is a blend of ground spices used in Indian cooking. If stored in an airtight container and kept in a cool, dark spot it will keep for 3 months. There are many versions of garam masala, probably as many as there are cooks in India, but they will always include cardamom, cloves, nutmeg and cinnamon. Other possible components are cumin, coriander or black peppercorns. In Kashmir, black cumin is popular.

ABOVE: Parsee lamb with cumin, eggs and tagliatelle

75

MEATBALLS STROGANOFF

Preparation time: 40 minutes
Total cooking time: 20–25 minutes
Serves 4

☆

500 g (1 lb) macaroni
750 g (1 1/2 lb) lean beef mince
2 cloves garlic, crushed
2–3 tablespoons plain flour
1 teaspoon sweet paprika
2 tablespoons oil
50 g (1 3/4 oz) butter
1 large onion, thinly sliced
250 g (8 oz) small button mushrooms, halved
2 tablespoons tomato paste (tomato purée, double concentrate)
2–3 teaspoons Dijon mustard
1/4 cup (60 ml/2 fl oz) white wine
1/2 cup (125 ml/4 fl oz) beef stock
3/4 cup (185 g/6 oz) sour cream
3 tablespoons finely chopped fresh parsley

1 Cook the macaroni in a large pan of rapidly boiling water until *al dente*. Drain; keep warm.
2 Combine the beef mince, garlic and some salt and cracked pepper in a bowl. Use your hands to mix well. Roll 2 heaped teaspoons of the mince into balls. Combine the flour, paprika and some freshly ground black pepper on a clean surface or sheet of greaseproof paper. Dust the meatballs in the seasoned flour.
3 Heat the oil and half the butter in a frying pan. When foaming, cook the meatballs over medium heat, in batches, until brown. Remove from the pan and drain on paper towels.
4 Melt the remaining butter in the pan, add the onion and cook until soft. Stir in the mushrooms and cook until the mushrooms are tender. Pour in the combined tomato paste, mustard, wine and stock. Return the meatballs to the pan and gently reheat. Bring the mixture to the boil, reduce the heat and simmer for 5 minutes, stirring occasionally. Season to taste. Stir the sour cream through until smooth. Sprinkle with a little parsley and serve with the pasta.

NUTRITION PER SERVE: *Protein 60 g; Fat 50 g; Carbohydrate 100 g; Dietary Fibre 10 g; Cholesterol 205 mg; 4615 kJ (1095 cal)*

ABOVE: Meatballs stroganoff

GARLIC

Garlic is a bulbous liliaceous plant and the most pungent member of the *allium* family, which includes onions and leeks. Straight from the ground it has a crisp, sharp taste which mellows and becomes less intense as the bulb dries. Garlic has a high oil content and this is what determines pungency; the fresher the bulb, the more oil it contains and the stronger the flavour. Used with discretion, garlic gives a kick to otherwise flat flavours, and when subjected to slow cooking it gives body to a dish. As well, it has medicinal properties and stimulates the gastric juices, thus acting as a digestive and as a flavouring.

PASTA WITH LAMB AND VEGETABLES

Preparation time: 20 minutes
Total cooking time: 20 minutes
Serves 4

★

2 tablespoons oil

1 large onion, chopped

2 cloves garlic, crushed

500 g (1 lb) minced lamb

125 g (4 oz) small mushroom caps, halved

1 red pepper (capsicum), seeded and chopped

150 g (5 oz) shelled broad beans

440 g (14 oz) can crushed tomatoes

2 tablespoons tomato paste (tomato purée, double concentrate)

500 g (1 lb) penne

125 g (4 oz) feta cheese

2 tablespoons shredded fresh basil

1 Heat the oil in a heavy-based pan over medium heat. Add the onion and garlic and stir-fry for 2 minutes or until lightly browned. Add the mince and stir-fry over high heat for 4 minutes or until the meat is well browned and all the liquid has evaporated. Use a fork to break up any lumps as the mince cooks.

2 Add the mushrooms, red pepper, broad beans, undrained tomato and tomato paste to the pan. Bring to the boil, reduce the heat and simmer, covered, for 10 minutes or until the vegetables are tender. Stir occasionally.

3 While the sauce is cooking, cook the pasta in a large pan of rapidly boiling salted water until *al dente*. Drain. Spoon into serving bowls, top with the lamb and vegetable sauce, crumble cheese over the top and sprinkle with basil.

NOTE: The sauce can be made up to two days ahead. Refrigerate, covered with plastic wrap. Reheat the sauce and cook the pasta just before serving. Unsuitable for freezing.

NUTRITION PER SERVE: *Protein 50 g; Fat 30 g; Carbohydrate 100 g; Dietary Fibre 15 g; Cholesterol 100 mg; 3730 kJ (890 cal)*

ABOVE: Pasta with lamb and vegetables

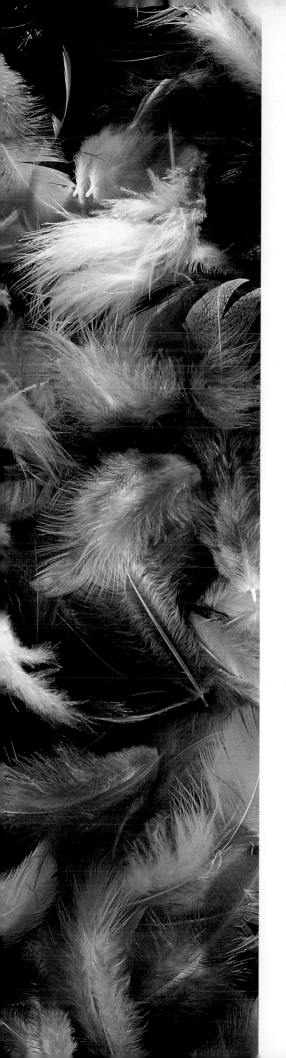

PASTA WITH CHICKEN

As tradition has it chicken would not, in days gone by, have been served with pasta, but we can now look back and wonder 'whyever not?' With the added flavour of fresh herbs, spices, tomatoes or mushrooms, chicken combines perfectly with pasta, especially as a filling for tiny parcels such as tortellini or ravioli. The versatility of chicken is shown in dishes such as meatballs, lasagne and even bolognese: a new twist on recipes in which you would normally expect to find meat.

BAY LEAVES

Bay or bay laurel is a symbol of fame and victory. Wreaths of laurel have been presented to honour achievement ever since the Ancient Greeks wove it into crowns for victorious athletes, poets and statesmen. The leaves have been used in the kitchen for just as long, although at first they were favoured as a flavouring for sweet dishes. Nowadays they are used mainly in marinades and in pickling, and to enhance the taste of white sauces, soups and stews.

ABOVE: Spaghetti with chicken meatballs

SPAGHETTI WITH CHICKEN MEATBALLS

Preparation time: 45 minutes + chilling
Total cooking time: 1 hour 30 minutes
Serves 4–6

☆

500 g (1 lb) chicken mince
60 g (2 oz) freshly grated Parmesan
2 cups (160 g/5½ oz) fresh white breadcrumbs
2 cloves garlic, crushed
1 egg
1 tablespoon chopped fresh flat-leaf parsley
1 tablespoon chopped fresh sage
3 tablespoons vegetable oil
500 g (1 lb) spaghetti
2 tablespoons chopped fresh oregano, to serve

Tomato sauce

1 tablespoon olive oil
1 onion, finely chopped
2 kg (4 lb) very ripe tomatoes, chopped
2 bay leaves
1 cup (30 g/1 oz) fresh basil leaves, loosely packed
1 teaspoon coarsely ground black pepper

1 In a large bowl, mix the chicken mince, Parmesan, breadcrumbs, garlic, egg and herbs. Season, to taste, with salt and freshly ground black pepper. Shape tablespoonsful of the mixture into small balls and chill for about 30 minutes, to firm.

2 Heat the oil in a shallow pan and fry the balls, in batches, until golden brown. Turn them often by gently shaking the pan. Drain on paper towels.

3 To make the tomato sauce, heat the oil in a large pan, add the onion and fry for about 1–2 minutes, until softened. Add the tomato and bay leaves, cover and bring to the boil, stirring occasionally. Reduce the heat to low, partially cover and cook for 50–60 minutes.

4 Add the meatballs to the sauce, along with the basil leaves and freshly ground black pepper and simmer, uncovered, for 10–15 minutes.

5 While the sauce is simmering, cook the spaghetti in a large pan of rapidly boiling salted water until *al dente*. Drain and return to the pan. Add some sauce to the pasta and toss to distribute. Serve the pasta in individual bowls with sauce and meatballs, sprinkled with chopped fresh oregano and perhaps some extra Parmesan.

NUTRITION PER SERVE (6): *Protein 40 g; Fat 20 g; Carbohydrate 85 g; Dietary Fibre 10 g; Cholesterol 95 mg; 2915 kJ (670 cal)*

CHICKEN TORTELLINI WITH TOMATO SAUCE

Preparation time: 1 hour
  + resting of dough
Total cooking time: 30 minutes
Serves 4

★★

Pasta

2 cups (250 g/8 oz) plain flour
3 eggs
1 tablespoon olive oil

Filling

20 g (3/4 oz) butter
90 g (3 oz) chicken breast fillet, cubed
2 slices pancetta, chopped
1/2 cup (50 g/13/4 oz) freshly grated Parmesan
1/2 teaspoon nutmeg
1 egg, lightly beaten

Tomato sauce

1/3 cup (80 ml/23/4 fl oz) olive oil
11/2 kg (3 lb) very ripe tomatoes, peeled
  and chopped
1/4 cup (7 g/1/4 oz) chopped fresh oregano
1/2 cup (50 g/13/4 oz) freshly grated Parmesan

100 g (31/2 oz) bocconcini, thinly sliced,
  for serving

1 To make the pasta, sift the flour and a pinch of salt into a bowl and make a well in the centre. In a jug, whisk together the eggs, oil and 1 tablespoon of water. Add the egg mixture gradually to the flour, mixing to a firm dough. Gather together into a ball, adding a little extra water if necessary.
2 Knead on a lightly floured surface for 5 minutes, or until the dough is smooth and elastic. Put in a lightly oiled bowl, cover with plastic wrap and set aside for 30 minutes.
3 To make the filling, heat the butter in a frying pan, add the chicken cubes and cook, stirring, until golden brown. Drain and allow to cool slightly. Process the chicken and pancetta in a food processor or mincer until finely chopped. Transfer to a bowl and add the Parmesan, nutmeg, egg and salt and pepper, to taste. Set aside.
4 Roll out the dough very thinly on a lightly floured surface. Using a floured cutter, cut into 5 cm (2 inch) rounds and spoon 1/2 teaspoon of filling into the centre of each. Brush the edges with a little water. Fold in half to form semi-circles, pressing the edges together. Wrap each around your finger to form a ring and then press the ends of the dough together firmly.
5 To make the tomato sauce, put the oil, tomato and oregano in a frying pan and cook over high heat for 10 minutes. Stir the Parmesan through and set aside.
6 Cook the tortellini in two batches in a large pan of rapidly boiling water for about 6 minutes each batch, or until *al dente*. Drain and return to the pan. Reheat the tomato sauce, add to the tortellini and toss to combine. Divide the tortellini among individual bowls, top with bocconcini and allow the cheese to melt a little before serving.

NUTRITION PER SERVE: *Protein 40 g; Fat 55 g; Carbohydrate 55 g; Dietary Fibre 5 g; Cholesterol 300 mg; 3660 kJ (875 cal)*

TORTELLINI AND CAPPELLETTI

Manufacturers invariably sell cappelletti as tortellini. The difference is minimal. Tortellini are small rolls of filled pasta that were originally twisted around a finger so that the two ends folded over each other. Cappelletti are like little hats and their ends are pinched together. The two are interchangeable.

ABOVE: Chicken tortellini with tomato sauce

CHICKEN AND SPINACH LASAGNE

Preparation time: 30 minutes
Total cooking time: 1 hour 10 minutes
Serves 8

★

500 g (1 lb) English spinach
1 kg (2 lb) chicken mince
1 clove garlic, crushed
3 bacon rashers, chopped
425 g (14 oz) can crushed tomatoes
1/2 cup (125 g/4 oz) tomato paste (tomato purée, double concentrate)
1/2 cup (125 ml/4 fl oz) tomato sauce
1/2 cup (125 ml/4 fl oz) chicken stock
12 instant lasagne sheets
1 cup (125 g/4 oz) grated Cheddar cheese

Cheese sauce

60 g (2 oz) butter
1/3 cup (40 g/1 1/4 oz) plain flour
2 1/2 cups (600 ml/20 fl oz) milk
1 cup (125 g/4 oz) grated Cheddar cheese

ABOVE: Chicken and spinach lasagne

1 Preheat the oven to moderate 180°C (350°F/Gas 4). Remove and discard the stalks from the spinach leaves. Plunge the leaves in a pan of boiling water for 2 minutes, or until tender. Remove, plunge immediately into a bowl of iced water and then drain.

2 Heat a little oil in a heavy-based frying pan. Add the mince, garlic and bacon. Cook over medium heat for 5 minutes, or until browned. Stir in the tomato, tomato paste, sauce and stock and bring to the boil. Reduce the heat and simmer, partially covered, for 10 minutes, or until the sauce is slightly thickened. Season with salt and pepper, to taste.

3 To make the cheese sauce, melt the butter in a medium pan, add the flour and stir over low heat for 1 minute, or until the mixture is lightly golden and smooth. Remove from the heat and gradually stir in the milk. Return to the heat and stir constantly over medium heat for 4 minutes, or until the sauce boils and thickens. Remove from the heat and stir in the cheese.

4 To assemble the lasagne, brush a deep, 3-litre, ovenproof dish with melted butter or oil. Spread one-quarter of the chicken mixture over the base. Top with 4 sheets of lasagne. Spread with one-third of the cheese sauce, then another layer of the chicken filling. Top with all of the spinach, a layer of lasagne, a layer of cheese sauce and the remaining chicken filling. Spread evenly with the remaining cheese sauce and sprinkle with the grated cheese. Bake for 50 minutes, or until cooked through and golden brown.

NUTRITION PER SERVE: *Protein 50 g; Fat 45 g; Carbohydrate 35 g; Dietary Fibre 5 g; Cholesterol 230 mg; 3145 kJ (750 cal)*

LEMONS
The rind, flesh and juice of lemons are all put to good use in savoury foods as well as desserts, cakes and sweets. The lemon is perhaps the most acid of citrus fruits and is highly scented. Bush lemons, with their thick and crinkly skins, are valued for their clean acid taste, which stays pure when blended with other flavours. The many types of smooth-skinned lemons tend to be sweeter and the fresh fruit is more attractive for use as a decoration or garnish.

CHICKEN WITH LEMON, PARSLEY AND ORECCHIETTE

Preparation time: 10 minutes
Total cooking time: 20 minutes
Serves 4

★

375 g (12 oz) orecchiette
1 tablespoon oil
60 g (2 oz) butter
4 small chicken breast fillets
1/3 cup (80 ml/2¾ fl oz) lemon juice
1/3 cup (20 g/¾ oz) finely chopped fresh parsley plus some extra, to garnish
lemon slices, to garnish

1 Cook the pasta in a large pan of rapidly boiling salted water until *al dente*. Drain.
2 While the pasta is cooking, heat the oil and half the butter in a large, heavy-based pan. Add the chicken fillets and cook for 2 minutes each side; set aside. Add the lemon juice, parsley and the remaining butter to the pan. Stir to combine and return the fillets to the pan. Cook over low heat for 3–4 minutes, turning once, or until cooked through. Season, to taste, with salt and freshly ground black pepper.
3 Serve the pasta topped with a chicken fillet and sauce. Garnish with lemon slices and sprinkle with some chopped fresh parsley.

NUTRITION PER SERVE: *Protein 40 g; Fat 20 g; Carbohydrate 25 g; Dietary Fibre 0 g; Cholesterol 120 mg; 1880 kJ (450 cal)*

ON THE SIDE

BACON, LETTUCE AND TOMATO SALAD Grill or fry 4 rashers of bacon until they are crisp. Allow to cool on paper towels before roughly chopping. Combine in a bowl with the leaves of a cos lettuce, 200 g (6½ oz) of halved cherry tomatoes, and 1 chopped avocado. Toss gently to combine. Top with a dressing made by mixing together ½ cup (125 g/4 oz) of natural yoghurt with 1 tablespoon of wholegrain mustard, 1 tablespoon of lemon juice and 1 teaspoon of honey.

ABOVE: Chicken with lemon, parsley and orecchiette

ORIENTAL CHICKEN PASTA

Preparation time: 25 minutes
Total cooking time: 10 minutes
Serves 4

☆

1 barbecued chicken
1 onion
1 carrot
150 g (5 oz) tagliatelle
1 tablespoon oil
1 clove garlic, crushed
2 teaspoons curry powder
2 teaspoons bottled crushed chilli
1 large red pepper (capsicum), thinly sliced
150 g (5 oz) snow peas (mangetout), halved

3 spring onions, sliced
2 teaspoons sesame oil
1/4 cup (60 ml/2 fl oz) soy sauce

1 Remove the chicken meat from the bones and discard the bones. Slice the chicken into thin strips. Cut the onion into thin wedges and the carrot into long strips.
2 Cook the tagliatelle in a large pan of rapidly boiling salted water until *al dente*. Drain well.
3 Heat the oil in a wok or heavy-based pan, swirling gently to coat the base and sides. Add the onion, carrot, garlic, curry powder and chilli. Stir until aromatic and the garlic is soft. Add the pasta and the remaining ingredients. Stir-fry over medium heat for 4 minutes, or until heated through. Add salt, to taste.

NUTRITION PER SERVE: *Protein 40 g; Fat 25 g; Carbohydrate 40 g; Dietary Fibre 5 g; Cholesterol 105 mg; 2355 kJ (560 cal)*

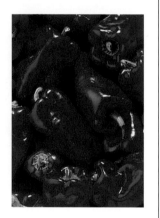

RIGHT: Oriental chicken pasta

ROSEMARY
Rosemary is an important herb in European cookery where it is used in particular for outdoor cooking and to flavour meats. It should be added to food towards the end of cooking, as the essential oils that contain the flavour evaporate with lengthy cooking. The perennial plant is not difficult to grow as it tolerates most conditions, and the leaves, when dried, carry a true rosemary taste, rich and piney.

SPAGHETTI WITH CHICKEN BOLOGNESE

Preparation time: 20 minutes
Total cooking time: 15 minutes
Serves 4

★

2 tablespoons olive oil

2 leeks, thinly sliced

1 red pepper (capsicum), diced

2 cloves garlic, crushed

500 g (1 lb) chicken mince

2 cups (500 g/1 lb) tomato pasta sauce

1 tablespoon chopped fresh thyme

1 tablespoon chopped fresh rosemary

2 tablespoons seeded and chopped black olives

400 g (13 oz) spaghetti

125 g (4 oz) feta cheese, crumbled

1 Heat the oil in a large, heavy-based pan. Add the leek, pepper and garlic and cook over medium high heat for 2 minutes, or until lightly browned.

2 Add the chicken mince and cook over high heat for 3 minutes, or until browned and any liquid has evaporated. Stir occasionally and break up any lumps as the mince cooks.

3 Add the tomato pasta sauce, thyme and rosemary and bring to the boil. Reduce the heat and simmer for 5 minutes, or until the sauce has reduced and thickened. Add the olives and stir to combine. Season, to taste.

4 Cook the spaghetti in a large pan of rapidly boiling salted water until *al dente*. Drain. Place the spaghetti on individual serving plates or pile into a large deep serving dish and pour the Chicken Bolognese over the top. (The sauce can be mixed through the pasta.) Sprinkle with feta and serve immediately.

NOTE: Chicken Bolognese can be cooked up to 2 days ahead. Refrigerate, covered, or freeze for up to four weeks. Reheat the sauce and cook the spaghetti just before serving. Any type of pasta, dried or fresh, is suitable to use. Freshly grated Parmesan or pecorino can be used instead of feta cheese.

NUTRITION PER SERVE: *Protein 45 g; Fat 35 g; Carbohydrate 85 g; Dietary Fibre 10 g; Cholesterol 120 mg; 3540 kJ (845 cal)*

ABOVE: Spaghetti with chicken bolognese

*ABOVE: Fettucine
with chicken and
mushroom sauce*

FETTUCINE WITH CHICKEN AND MUSHROOM SAUCE

Preparation time: 20 minutes
Total cooking time: 20 minutes
Serves 4

★

400 g (13 oz) fettucine
2 large chicken breast fillets
1 tablespoon olive oil
30 g (1 oz) butter
2 bacon rashers, chopped
2 cloves garlic, crushed
250 g (8 oz) button mushrooms, sliced
1/3 cup (80 ml/2³/4 fl oz) white wine
2/3 cup (170 ml/5¹/2 fl oz) cream
4 spring onions, chopped
1 tablespoon plain flour
2 tablespoons water
1/3 cup (35 g/1¹/4 oz) freshly grated
   Parmesan, for serving

1 Cook the fettucine in a large pan of rapidly
boiling salted water until *al dente*. Drain and
return to the pan.
2 Trim the chicken of excess fat and cut into
thin strips. Heat the oil and butter in a heavy-
based frying pan, add the chicken and cook over
medium heat for 3 minutes, or until browned.
Add the bacon, garlic and mushrooms and cook
for 2 minutes, stirring occasionally.
3 Add the wine and cook until the liquid has
reduced by half. Add the cream and spring
onion and bring to the boil. Blend the flour
with the water until smooth, add to the pan and
stir until the mixture boils and thickens. Reduce
the heat and simmer for 2 minutes. Season with
salt and pepper, to taste.
4 Add the sauce to the pasta and stir over low
heat until combined. Sprinkle with Parmesan.
Serve immediately with a green salad and
perhaps some hot herb bread.

NUTRITION PER SERVE: *Protein 40 g; Fat 35 g;
Carbohydrate 75 g; Dietary Fibre 5 g; Cholesterol 135 mg;
3355 kJ (800 cal)*

PESTO CHICKEN PASTA

Preparation time: 20 minutes
Total cooking time: 20 minutes
Serves 4

★

250 g (8 oz) fusilli or penne
1 small barbecued chicken
1 cup (125 g/4 oz) walnuts
4 bacon rashers
250 g (8 oz) cherry tomatoes, halved
60 g (2 oz) pitted and sliced olives
1/2 cup (125 g/4 oz) bottled pesto sauce
1/2 cup (30 g/1 oz) finely shredded fresh basil
shavings of Parmesan, for serving

1 Cook the pasta in a large pan of rapidly boiling salted water until *al dente*. Drain.
2 While the pasta is cooking, discard the skin of the chicken. Remove the meat from the chicken, cut or shred it into bite-sized pieces and put in a large bowl.
3 Toast the walnuts for 2–3 minutes under a hot grill, allow to cool and then chop roughly.

4 Remove the rind from the bacon rashers and grill the bacon for 3–4 minutes, or until crisp. Allow to cool and then chop into small pieces. Add the nuts, bacon, cherry tomatoes and olives to the chicken.
5 Add the pasta to the chicken mixture, along with the pesto sauce and the fresh basil. Toss until thoroughly mixed. Serve at room temperature, with Parmesan shavings.

NUTRITION PER SERVE: *Protein 55 g; Fat 45 g; Carbohydrate 25 g; Dietary Fibre 5 g; Cholesterol 190 mg; 2960 kJ (705 cal)*

ON THE SIDE

ROASTED TOMATOES TOPPED WITH HERBED GOATS CHEESE

Brush halved egg (Roma) tomatoes with a little olive oil, sprinkle with salt, sugar and pepper and bake in a moderate 180°C (350°F/Gas 4) oven for 30 minutes, or until tender and slightly dried. Make a mixture of goats cheese and fresh herbs and press a little onto the top of each piece of cooked tomato. Cook under a grill until the goats cheese begins to soften and colour.

BELOW: Pesto chicken pasta

based pan. Cook the chicken quickly over high heat until browned but not cooked through; drain on paper towels. Add the onion, carrot and bacon to the pan. Stir over medium heat for 10 minutes. Add the zucchini and soup, bring to the boil and simmer for 5 minutes. Remove from the heat.

3 Combine the pasta, chicken, tomato mixture and sour cream. Season with salt and pepper, to taste. Spread into a shallow ovenproof dish and top with cheese. Bake for 20 minutes, or until golden and cooked through.

NUTRITION PER SERVE: *Protein 45 g; Fat 30 g; Carbohydrate 45 g; Dietary Fibre 5 g; Cholesterol 115 mg; 2665 kJ (635 cal)*

LASAGNETTE WITH MUSHROOMS AND CHICKEN

Preparation time: 15 minutes
Total cooking time: 20 minutes
Serves 4

✫

1/4 cup (60 ml/2 fl oz) milk
1/2 teaspoon dried tarragon or
  2 teaspoons chopped fresh
400 g (13 oz) lasagnette
25 g (3/4 oz) butter
2 cloves garlic
200 g (61/2 oz) chicken breast fillet, sliced
100 g (31/2 oz) button mushrooms,
  thinly sliced
ground nutmeg
2 cups (500 ml/16 fl oz) cream
few sprigs fresh tarragon, to garnish

CHICKEN AND MACARONI BAKE

Preparation time: 20 minutes
Total cooking time: 55 minutes
Serves 6

✫

4 chicken breast fillets
2 cups (310 g/10 oz) macaroni elbows
1/4 cup (60 ml/2 fl oz) olive oil
1 onion, chopped
1 carrot, chopped
3 bacon rashers, chopped
2 zucchini, chopped
440 g (14 oz) can tomato soup
1/3 cup (90 g/3 oz) sour cream
11/2 cups (185 g/6 oz) grated Cheddar cheese

1 Trim the chicken of excess fat and sinew. Preheat the oven to moderate 180°C (350°F/ Gas 4). Cook the macaroni in a large pan of rapidly boiling salted water until *al dente*; drain.
2 Slice the chicken breasts into long strips and then cut into cubes. Heat the oil in a heavy-

ABOVE: Chicken and macaroni bake
RIGHT: Lasagnette with mushrooms and chicken

1 Bring the milk and tarragon to the boil in a small pan. Remove from the heat, strain and reserve the milk. Set aside.

2 Cook the lasagnette in a large pan of rapidly boiling salted water until *al dente*. Drain and return to the pan.

3 While the pasta is cooking, melt the butter in a frying pan and gently sauté the whole garlic cloves, sliced chicken and button mushrooms until the chicken is golden and cooked through. Discard the garlic cloves and add the nutmeg and salt and pepper, to taste. Stir for 10 seconds before stirring in the cream and tarragon milk. Bring to the boil, reduce the heat and simmer until the sauce thickens. Spoon the sauce over the pasta and decorate with fresh tarragon.

NUTRITION PER SERVE: *Protein 25 g; Fat 60 g; Carbohydrate 75 g; Dietary Fibre 5 g; Cholesterol 215 mg; 4005 kJ (955 cal)*

CHICKEN LIVERS WITH PENNE

Preparation time: 15 minutes
Total cooking time: 15 minutes
Serves 4

★★

350 g (11 oz) chicken livers

500 g (1 lb) penne

50 g (1³/₄ oz) butter

1 onion, diced

2 cloves garlic, crushed

2 teaspoons finely grated orange rind

2 bay leaves

¹/₂ cup (125 ml/4 fl oz) red wine

2 tablespoons tomato paste (tomato purée, double concentrate)

2 tablespoons cream

1 Wash the chicken livers and trim off any membrane. Cut each liver into six pieces.

2 Cook the penne in a large pan of rapidly boiling salted water until *al dente*. Drain and keep warm.

3 While the pasta is cooking, melt the butter in a frying pan and cook the onion until softened. Add the crushed garlic, chicken livers, orange rind and bay leaves, and stir for 3 minutes. Remove the chicken livers with a slotted spoon. Stir in the red wine, tomato paste and cream. Simmer until the sauce reduces and thickens.

4 Return the chicken livers to the pan and warm through. Season with salt and freshly ground pepper, to taste. Spoon the chicken liver sauce over the pasta.

NUTRITION PER SERVE: *Protein 35 g; Fat 20 g; Carbohydrate 90 g; Dietary Fibre 10 g; Cholesterol 460 mg; 3010 kJ (720 cal)*

ON THE SIDE

ROAST BROCCOLI WITH CUMIN SEEDS Gently boil or steam some evenly sized broccoli florets for a couple of minutes. Drain thoroughly and then toss them in a mixture of olive oil, crushed garlic and lightly toasted crushed cumin seeds. Put on an oven tray and bake in a very hot oven until the broccoli is browned at the edges.

CHERRY TOMATOES WITH BUTTER AND DILL Pan-fry some cherry tomatoes in a little butter until the skins are beginning to split, season well with salt and cracked black pepper and sprinkle with some chopped dill. Gently toss and serve immediately.

ABOVE: Chicken livers with penne

CHICKEN RAVIOLI WITH FRESH TOMATO SAUCE

Preparation time: 40 minutes
Total cooking time: 40 minutes
Serves 4

★ ★

1 tablespoon oil
1 large onion, chopped
2 cloves garlic, crushed
1/3 cup (90 g/3 oz) tomato paste (tomato purée, double concentrate)
1/4 cup (60 ml/2 fl oz) red wine
2/3 cup (170 ml/5 1/2 fl oz) chicken stock
2 very ripe tomatoes, chopped
1 tablespoon chopped fresh basil

Ravioli

200 g (6 1/2 oz) chicken mince
1 tablespoon chopped fresh basil
1/4 cup (25 g/3/4 oz) grated Parmesan

BELOW: Chicken ravioli with fresh tomato sauce

3 spring onions, finely chopped
50 g (1 3/4 oz) fresh ricotta cheese
250 g (8 oz) packet (48) gow gee wrappers

1 Heat the oil in a medium pan and add the onion and garlic. Cook for 2–3 minutes and stir in the tomato paste, red wine, chicken stock and chopped tomato and simmer for 20 minutes. Stir in the basil and season, to taste.
2 To make the ravioli, combine the chicken mince, basil, Parmesan, spring onion, ricotta and some salt and pepper. Lay 24 of the wrappers on a flat surface and brush with a little water. Place slightly heaped teaspoons of mixture in the centre of each wrapper. Place another wrapper on top and press the edges firmly together.
3 Bring a large pan of water to the boil and cook the ravioli a few at a time for 2–3 minutes, or until tender. Drain well. Serve with sauce.

NUTRITION PER SERVE: *Protein 20 g; Fat 25 g; Carbohydrate 50 g; Dietary Fibre 5 g; Cholesterol 75 mg; 2210 kJ (530 cal)*

BRANDY CHICKEN FETTUCINE

Preparation time: 40 minutes
Total cooking time: 40 minutes
Serves 4–6

★

10 g (¼ oz) porcini mushrooms
2 tablespoons olive oil
2 cloves garlic, crushed
200 g (6½ oz) button mushrooms, sliced
125 g (4 oz) prosciutto, chopped
375 g (12 oz) fettucine
¼ cup (60 ml/2 fl oz) brandy
1 cup (250 ml/8 fl oz) cream
1 barbecued chicken, shredded
1 cup (155 g/5 oz) frozen peas
⅓ cup (20 g/¾ oz) finely chopped
  fresh parsley

1 Put the porcini mushrooms in a bowl and cover with boiling water. Set aside for 10 minutes, then drain, squeeze dry and chop.
2 Heat the oil in a large, heavy-based pan. Add the crushed garlic and cook, stirring, for 1 minute over low heat. Add the button and porcini mushrooms, along with the prosciutto, and cook over low heat, stirring often, for 5 minutes.
3 Meanwhile, cook the pasta in a large pan of rapidly boiling salted water until *al dente*. Drain and return to the pan.
4 Add the brandy and cream to the mushroom mixture. Cook, stirring, over low heat for 2 minutes. Add the chicken, peas and parsley. Cook, stirring, for 4–5 minutes, until heated through. Add the chicken mixture to the hot pasta and mix through.
NOTE: Cut the slices of prosciutto separately, otherwise they stick together. Use bacon slices instead, if preferred. If porcini mushrooms are not available, use 30 g (1 oz) of dried Chinese mushrooms.

NUTRITION PER SERVE (6): *Protein 40 g; Fat 35 g; Carbohydrate 45 g; Dietary Fibre 5 g; Cholesterol 130 mg, 2900 kJ (690 cal)*

ON THE SIDE

PANZANELLA Tear 2 slices of day-old country-style bread into pieces and sprinkle with crushed garlic and oil. Toss it in a bowl with chopped cucumber, tomatoes, red (Spanish) onion and some fresh basil leaves. Drizzle with olive oil and red wine vinegar and season well. The bread should be slightly moist but not too soggy. You can also add anchovies or hard-boiled eggs.

BEANS WITH PARSLEY BUTTER Cook some green beans in salted boiling water until they are tender but still bright green. Drain and place in a bowl with some pieces of herb butter and some salt and black pepper. Toss well so that the beans are all coated in the buttery mixture.

ABOVE: Brandy chicken fettucine

1 Remove the beards from the mussels and scrub away any grit. Discard any opened or damaged mussels.

2 To make the tomato sauce, heat the oil in a medium pan, add the onion and carrot and stir over medium heat for about 10 minutes, or until the vegetables are lightly browned. Add the chilli, garlic, tomato, white wine, sugar and cayenne pepper and simmer for 30 minutes, stirring occasionally.

3 Meanwhile, heat the ¼ cup wine with the stock and garlic in a large pan and add the unopened mussels. Cover the pan and shake it over high heat for 3–5 minutes. After 3 minutes, start removing any opened mussels and set them aside. After 5 minutes discard any unopened mussels and reserve the wine mixture.

4 Cook the pasta in a large pan of rapidly boiling salted water until *al dente*. Drain and keep warm. Meanwhile, melt the butter in a frying pan, add the calamari rings, fish and prawns and stir-fry for 2 minutes. Set aside. Add the reserved wine mixture, mussels, calamari, fish, prawns, parsley and clams to the tomato sauce and reheat gently. Gently combine the sauce with the pasta and serve at once.

NUTRITION PER SERVE: *Protein 30 g; Fat 15 g; Carbohydrate 50 g; Dietary Fibre 5 g; Cholesterol 225 mg; 2000 kJ (480 cal)*

FARFALLE WITH TUNA, MUSHROOMS AND CREAM

Preparation time: 15 minutes
Total cooking time: 15 minutes
Serves 4

☆

500 g (1 lb) farfalle
60 g (2 oz) butter
1 tablespoon olive oil
1 onion, chopped
1 clove garlic, crushed
125 g (4 oz) button mushrooms, sliced
1 cup (250 ml/4 fl oz) cream
450 g (14 oz) can tuna, drained and flaked
1 tablespoon lemon juice
1 tablespoon chopped fresh parsley

1 Cook the farfalle in a large pan of rapidly boiling salted water until *al dente*. Drain and return to the pan.

2 While the pasta is cooking, heat the butter and oil in a large frying pan. Add the chopped onion and crushed garlic and stir over low heat until the onion is tender. Add the sliced mushroom and cook for 2 minutes. Pour in the cream and bring to the boil. Reduce the heat and simmer until the sauce begins to thicken.

3 Add the flaked tuna, lemon juice, parsley and salt and pepper, to taste, to the cream mixture and stir to combine. Heat gently, stirring constantly. Add the sauce to the farfalle and toss gently to combine.

NOTE: You can use a can of salmon, drained and flaked, instead of tuna.

NUTRITION PER SERVE: *Protein 45 g; Fat 50 g; Carbohydrate 90 g; Dietary Fibre 10 g; Cholesterol 145 mg; 4100 kJ (980 cal)*

TUNA
Tuna are surface fish and strong swimmers so they have tight, muscular and close-grained flesh. This makes tuna well suited to stewing and long cooking, but it is also eaten lightly sautéed or uncooked, as in Japanese sashimi. The raw flesh is an attractive dark rose colour and can be cut into firm slices without breaking up.

ABOVE: Farfalle with tuna, mushrooms and cream

CREAMY PRAWNS WITH FETTUCINE

Preparation time: 30 minutes
Total cooking time: 15 minutes
Serves 4

★

500 g (1 lb) fettucine

500 g (1 lb) raw prawns

30 g (1 oz) butter

1 tablespoon olive oil

6 spring onions, chopped

1 clove garlic, crushed

1 cup (250 ml/8 fl oz) cream

2 tablespoons chopped fresh parsley,
    for serving

*BELOW: Creamy
prawns with fettucine*

1 Cook the fettucine in a large pan of rapidly boiling water until *al dente*. Drain and return to the pan.

2 While the fettucine is cooking, peel and devein the prawns. Heat the butter and oil in a frying pan, add the spring onion and garlic and stir over low heat for 1 minute. Add the prawns and cook for 2–3 minutes, or until the flesh changes colour. Remove the prawns from the pan and set aside. Add the cream to the pan and bring to the boil. Reduce the heat and simmer until the sauce begins to thicken. Return the prawns to the pan, add salt and pepper, to taste, and simmer for 1 minute.

3 Add the prawns and sauce to the warm fettucine and toss gently. Serve sprinkled with chopped parsley.

NOTE: For variations, in step 1, add 1 sliced red pepper (capsicum) and 1 very finely sliced leek. Use scallops instead of prawns or a mixture of both.

NUTRITION PER SERVE: *Protein 35 g; Fat 40 g; Carbohydrate 90 g; Dietary Fibre 7 g; Cholesterol 320 mg; 3660 kJ (875 cal)*

ON THE SIDE

WATERCRESS, SALMON AND CAMEMBERT SALAD Remove the sprigs of watercress (about 500 g/1 lb) from the tough stems and arrange the sprigs over the base of a large platter. Top with ten slices of smoked salmon, 200 g (6½ oz) of thinly sliced camembert cheese, 2 tablespoons of capers and 1 thinly sliced red (Spanish) onion. Make a dressing by thoroughly combining 2 tablespoons of freshly squeezed lime juice, 1 teaspoon of honey and ⅓ cup (90 ml/3 fl oz) of olive oil. Drizzle over the salad and garnish generously with cracked black pepper and snipped fresh chives.

MARINATED MUSHROOM SALAD Trim and halve 500 g (1 lb) of button mushrooms. Put them in a large bowl, add 4 thinly sliced spring onions, 1 finely diced red pepper (capsicum) and 2 tablespoons of chopped fresh flat-leaf parsley. Make a dressing by combining 3 crushed cloves of garlic, 3 tablespoons of white wine vinegar, 2 teaspoons of Dijon mustard and ⅓ cup (80 ml/2¾ fl oz) of olive oil. Pour the dressing over the mushrooms and toss to coat. Cover and refrigerate for 3 hours before serving.

CRAB CAKES WITH HOT SALSA

Preparation time: 40 minutes
  + 30 minutes refrigeration
Total cooking time: 35 minutes
Serves 6

★

Hot salsa

2 large very ripe tomatoes
1 onion, finely chopped
2 cloves garlic, crushed
1 teaspoon dried oregano leaves
2 tablespoons sweet chilli sauce

100 g (3½ oz) angel hair pasta, broken into
  short lengths
600 g (1¼ lb) crab meat
2 tablespoons finely chopped fresh parsley
1 small red pepper (capsicum), finely chopped
3 tablespoons freshly grated Parmesan
¼ cup (30 g/1 oz) plain flour
2 spring onions, finely chopped
2 eggs, lightly beaten
2–3 tablespoons oil, for frying

1 To make the hot salsa, combine all the ingredients in a small bowl and allow to stand at room temperature for 1 hour.
2 Cook the pasta in a large pan of rapidly boiling salted water until *al dente*. Drain.
3 Squeeze the excess moisture from the crab meat and combine in a large bowl with the pasta, parsley, red pepper, grated Parmesan, flour, onions and pepper, to taste. Add the beaten egg and mix well.
4 Shape the mixture into twelve flat patties, cover and refrigerate for 30 minutes.
5 Heat the oil in a large heavy-based pan and cook the crab cakes, in batches, over medium high heat until golden brown. Serve immediately with hot salsa.

NUTRITION PER SERVE: *Protein 20 g; Fat 10 g; Carbohydrate 25 g; Dietary Fibre 3 g; Cholesterol 150 mg; 1200 kJ (290 cal)*

ON THE SIDE

BLACK BEANS WITH TOMATO, LIME AND CORIANDER Peel 3 large very ripe tomatoes, remove the seeds and finely chop the flesh. Combine in a bowl with the juice of 1 lime, some finely chopped cucumber and a large handful of fresh coriander leaves. Mix with 2 cups of cooked black beans (turtle beans) and 1 tablespoon of olive oil and season well.

ZUCCHINI WITH TOMATO AND GARLIC Fry little cubes of zucchini in olive oil with a crushed clove of garlic until they are crisp and browned on all sides. Add some fresh chopped tomato and season well with salt and pepper. Serve while the zucchini is still crisp.

CRAB
Crab, a crustacean, does not have a high flesh to bulk ratio. Small swimmer and shore crabs have a low meat yield and are used for flavouring stocks and stews. But if caught while their new shells are still soft, they can be eaten whole, shells, claws and all. Some, such as the Alaskan crab, have huge claws and the amount of flesh is significant. Crab meat is mild and sweet.

ABOVE: Crab cakes with hot salsa

SALMON

Salmon is prized for its delicate taste, warm pink colour and the fine, succulent grain of the flesh. It conserves well and can be dried, smoked or canned. Salmon are a migratory fish that live in the sea but spawn in fresh water. They do not feed when in fresh water so their meat is at its worst by the time they head back to the sea. There are exceptions to this rule, however, and salmon in some places are known to live in fresh water lakes, travelling up their tributaries to spawn. The flesh of these fish is considered by some to be inferior in both flavour and texture, but in these days of farming and controlled production the quality of salmon in the marketplace is consistently high.

ABOVE: Salmon and pasta mornay

SALMON AND PASTA MORNAY

Preparation time: 15 minutes
Total cooking time: 10–15 minutes
Serves 4

★

400 g (13 oz) conchiglie (shell pasta)

30 g (1 oz) butter

6 spring onions, chopped

2 cloves garlic, crushed

1 tablespoon plain flour

1 cup (250 ml/8 fl oz) milk

1 cup (250 g/8 oz) sour cream

1 tablespoon lemon juice

425 g (14 oz) can salmon,
   drained and flaked

1/2 cup (30 g/1 oz) chopped fresh parsley

1 Cook the pasta in a large pan of rapidly boiling salted water until *al dente*. Drain and return to the pan.

2 While the pasta is cooking, melt the butter in a medium pan, add the onion and garlic and stir over low heat for 3 minutes, or until tender. Add the flour and stir for 1 minute. Combine the milk, sour cream and lemon juice in a jug. Add gradually to the onion mixture, stirring constantly. Stir over medium heat for 3 minutes, or until the mixture boils and thickens.

3 Add the salmon and parsley to the pan and stir for 1 minute, or until heated through. Add to the drained pasta and toss until well combined. Season with salt and pepper, to taste, before serving.

NOTE: As a variation, use a can of drained and flaked tuna instead of salmon, or add 1 teaspoon of mustard to the sauce.

NUTRITION PER SERVE: *Protein 40 g; Fat 40 g; Carbohydrate 80 g; Dietary Fibre 5 g; Cholesterol 190 mg; 3550 kJ (850 cal)*

SPAGHETTI WITH CHILLI CALAMARI

Preparation time: 20 minutes
Total cooking time: 20 minutes
Serves 4

★★

500 g (1 lb) calamari, cleaned

500 g (1 lb) spaghetti

2 tablespoons olive oil

1 leek, chopped

2 cloves garlic, crushed

1–2 teaspoons chopped chilli

1/2 teaspoon cayenne pepper

425 g (14 oz) can crushed tomatoes

1/2 cup (125 ml/4 fl oz) fish stock (see margin note)

1 tablespoon chopped fresh basil

2 teaspoons chopped fresh sage

1 teaspoon chopped fresh marjoram

1 Pull the tentacles from the body of the calamari. Using your fingers, pull the quill from the pouch of the calamari. Pull the skin away from the flesh and discard. Use a sharp knife to slit the tubes up one side. Lay out flat and score one side in a diamond pattern. Cut each tube into four.

2 Cook the spaghetti in a large pan of rapidly boiling salted water until *al dente*. Drain and keep warm.

3 While the pasta is cooking, heat the oil in a large frying pan. Add the leek and cook for 2 minutes. Add the garlic and stir over low heat for 1 minute. Stir in the chilli and cayenne. Add the tomato, stock and herbs and bring to the boil. Reduce the heat and simmer for 5 minutes.

4 Add the calamari to the pan. Simmer for another 5–10 minutes, or until tender. Serve the chilli calamari over the spaghetti.

NUTRITION PER SERVE: *Protein 35 g; Fat 15 g; Carbohydrate 90 g; Dietary Fibre 10 g; Cholesterol 250 mg; 2670 kJ (640 cal)*

FISH STOCK

Fish stock is not widely available ready-made, so you may want to make your own and freeze it. Melt 1 tablespoon butter in a large pan and cook 2 finely chopped onions over low heat for 10 minutes, or until soft but not browned. Add 2 litres of water, 1.5 kg (3 lb) of fish bones, heads and tails and a bouquet garni. Simmer for about 20 minutes, skimming off any froth. Strain the stock through a fine sieve before refrigerating. Use white-fleshed fish for stock as darker, oily fish tends to make it greasy.

ABOVE: Spaghetti with chilli calamari

3 Add the prawns and cook for 5 minutes, or until the prawns are browned. Stir in the salsa and cream and bring to the boil. Reduce the heat and simmer for 3–5 minutes, or until the sauce thickens slightly. Divide the pasta among four plates, top with sauce and garnish with parsley.

NUTRITION PER SERVE: *Protein 55 g; Fat 40 g; Carbohydrate 95 g; Dietary Fibre 8 g; Cholesterol 385 mg; 4105 kJ (975 cal)*

FRAGRANT HERB TAGLIATELLE WITH KAFFIR LIME AND PRAWNS

Preparation time: 1 ½ hours + 1 hour drying
Total cooking time: 12–15 minutes
Serves 4

★★★

Tagliatelle

2 cups (250 g/8 oz) plain flour, sifted, plus
   extra flour
¼ cup (15 g/½ oz) parsley, minced or very
   finely chopped
3 teaspoons herb-flavoured oil
3 teaspoons pure lime oil
1 teaspoon salt
3 eggs, beaten

Sauce

20 g (¾ oz) butter
1 onion, chopped
1 teaspoon grated fresh ginger
½ cup (125 ml/3½ fl oz) fish sauce
⅓ cup (90 ml/3 fl oz) sweet chilli sauce
juice and rind of 1 lime
6 kaffir lime leaves, roughly chopped
1¾ cups (440 ml/14 fl oz) coconut milk
1 kg (2 lb) raw king prawns, peeled
   and deveined, leaving tails intact
½ cup (125 ml/4 fl oz) cream

1 To make the tagliatelle, mix the flour, parsley, oils, salt and eggs in a food processor for 2–3 minutes, or until the mixture forms a soft dough. It will not form a ball, but will come together. Transfer to a lightly floured cutting board and cut into three or four equal pieces, using a floured knife. Cover with a damp cloth.
2 Adjust the rollers of the pasta machine to fully open. Lightly flour one piece of dough and pass it through the rollers to a lightly floured surface.

ABOVE: Spicy prawn mexicana

SPICY PRAWN MEXICANA

Preparation time: 20 minutes
Total cooking time: 15 minutes
Serves 4

★

500 g (1 lb) rigatoni
1 tablespoon oil
2 cloves garlic, crushed
2 red chillies, finely chopped
3 spring onions, sliced
750 g (1 ½ lb) raw prawns, peeled
   and deveined
300 g (10 oz) hot bottled salsa
1 ½ cups (375 ml/12 fl oz) cream
2 tablespoons chopped fresh parsley

1 Cook the rigatoni in a large pan of rapidly boiling salted water until *al dente*. Drain.
2 Heat the oil, add the garlic, chilli and spring onion and cook over medium heat for 2 minutes, or until the garlic is soft and golden.

Fold the dough into thirds, turn the dough by 90 degrees and feed through again. Lightly dust with flour so that the dough does not stick to the rollers. This process kneads the dough and must be repeated about ten times. Gradually decrease the width of the dough by adjusting the notches. This is a thinning process and the dough should not be folded. Each time you pass the dough through, tighten a notch until it has reached the third narrowest setting (the narrowest is too thin). You may want to cut the thinned pasta strip in half as you reach notch 3 or 4. If the pasta strip gets too long, it is hard to handle.

3 Trim rough edges of the pasta sheets and cut the sheets into tagliatelle with cutters. Hang the pasta up to dry, over a clean stick, supported by the backs of two chairs, for 10–15 minutes. (Be careful not to leave it too long or in a draught, or it will dry out and crack.) Place in loosely coiled piles and dust well with flour. Leave on a floured tea towel to dry for at least 1 hour.

4 Add 1 teaspoon each of lime oil, olive oil and salt to a large pan of water. Bring to the boil, add the tagliatelle and cook until *al dente*. Drain and keep warm.

5 To make the sauce, melt the butter in heavy-based pan, add the onion and cook over medium heat until tender. Add the ginger, fish sauce, sweet chilli sauce, lime juice and rind, and kaffir lime leaves. Cook for 1–2 minutes. Stir in the coconut milk and simmer over low heat for 10 minutes.

6 Add the prawns and cream. Simmer for another 3–4 minutes, being careful not to overcook the prawns or they will become tough.

7 To serve, divide the tagliatelle among warmed plates and spoon the sauce over the top.

NOTE: Fragrant herb oil can be made by mincing ½ cup (30 g/1 oz) basil leaves and ½ cup (15 g/½ oz) parsley leaves in a food processor. Add to ½ cup (125 ml/4 fl oz) of extra virgin olive oil and simmer very gently for 2 minutes. Cool and strain. As an alternative to lime oil, use 3 teaspoons of olive oil with 2 teaspoons of finely grated lime rind.

NUTRITION PER SERVE: *Protein 70 g; Fat 50 g; Carbohydrate 70 g; Dietary Fibre 4 g; Cholesterol 555 mg; 4245 kJ (1010 cal)*

ABOVE: Fragrant herb tagliatelle with kaffir lime and prawns

RED CAVIAR

The roe of various members of the sturgeon family is known as caviar. There are different qualities, depending on the fish from which the roe is extracted, and the colour can be black, dark brown, grey, golden or salmon. What is known as red caviar is actually a pale orange. The eggs should be glossy and firm, and taste neither too salty nor too fishy.

BELOW: Fettucine with caviar

FETTUCINE WITH CAVIAR

Preparation time: 15 minutes
Total cooking time: 15 minutes
Serves 4

☆

2 hard-boiled eggs
4 spring onions
1 cup (150 g/5 oz) light sour cream
50 g (1¾ oz) red caviar
2 tablespoons chopped fresh dill
1 tablespoon lemon juice
500 g (1 lb) fettucine

1 Peel the eggs and chop into small pieces. Trim the spring onions, discarding the dark green tops, and chop finely.
2 In a small bowl, mix the sour cream, egg, spring onion, caviar, dill, lemon juice and pepper, to taste. Set aside.

3 Cook the fettucine in a large pan of rapidly boiling salted water until *al dente*. Drain and return to the pan.
4 Toss the caviar mixture through the hot pasta. Serve garnished with a sprig of fresh dill, if desired.
NOTE: Use large red roe, not the small supermarket variety.

NUTRITION PER SERVE: *Protein 20 g; Fat 15 g; Carbohydrate 90 g; Dietary Fibre 5 g; Cholesterol 165 mg; 2950 kJ (700 cal)*

FRAGRANT SEAFOOD PASTA

Preparation time: 30 minutes
Total cooking time: 20 minutes
Serves 4

☆

500 g (1 lb) conchiglie (shell pasta)
2–3 tablespoons light olive oil
4 spring onions, finely sliced
1 small chilli, finely chopped
500 g (1 lb) raw prawns, peeled and deveined, tails intact
250 g (8 oz) scallops, halved
¼ cup (15 g/½ oz) chopped fresh coriander
¼ cup (60 ml/2 fl oz) lime juice
2 tablespoons sweet chilli sauce
1 tablespoon fish sauce
1 tablespoon sesame oil
shredded lime rind, to garnish

1 Cook the conchiglie in a large pan of rapidly boiling salted water until *al dente*.
2 While the pasta is cooking, heat the oil in a pan and add the spring onion, chilli, prawns and scallops. Stir constantly over medium heat until the prawns turn pink and the scallops are lightly cooked. Remove from the heat immediately. Stir in the coriander, lime juice, chilli sauce and fish sauce.
3 Drain the pasta and return to the pan. Toss the sesame oil through, add the prawn mixture and mix gently to combine. Serve the pasta garnished with lime rind, if desired.

NUTRITION PER SERVE: *Protein 45 g; Fat 40 g; Carbohydrate 90 g; Dietary Fibre 5 g; Cholesterol 260 mg; 3885 kJ (925 cal)*

CHILLI SEAFOOD IN TOMATO SAUCE

Preparation time: 25 minutes
Total cooking time: 30 minutes
Serves 4

★

8 fresh mussels
1 teaspoon olive oil
1 large onion, chopped
3 cloves garlic, finely chopped
2 small red chillies, seeded and finely chopped
820 g (1 lb 13 oz) can tomatoes
2 tablespoons tomato paste (tomato purée, double concentrate)
1/2 teaspoon cracked black pepper
1/2 cup (125 ml/4 fl oz) vegetable stock
2 tablespoons Pernod
650 g (1 lb 5 oz) marinara mix
2 tablespoons chopped fresh flat-leaf parsley
1 tablespoon chopped fresh dill
350 g (11 oz) bucatini

1 Remove the beards from the mussels and scrub away any grit.
2 Heat the oil in a large pan. Add the onion, garlic and chilli and cook for 1–2 minutes. Stir in the tomato, tomato paste, pepper, stock and Pernod. Reduce the heat and simmer for 8–10 minutes. Remove the sauce from the heat and cool slightly. Transfer to a food processor and process until smooth.

3 Return the tomato mixture to the pan, add the marinara mix and simmer for 4 minutes. Add the mussels and herbs to the pan and simmer for another 1–2 minutes, or until the mussels have opened. Discard any mussels that do not open.
4 Meanwhile, cook the pasta in a large pan of rapidly boiling water until *al dente*; drain thoroughly. Divide the pasta among 4 serving bowls and spoon the sauce over the top.
NOTE: Marinara mix is a combination of uncooked seafood available from fish shops. It usually contains scallops, prawns, mussels and calamari rings. You can use just one favourite type of seafood, such as prawns or calamari.

NUTRITION PER SERVE: *Protein 45 g; Fat 5 g; Carbohydrate 80 g; Dietary Fibre 10 g; Cholesterol 265 mg; 2380 kJ (570 cal)*

ABOVE: Fragrant seafood pasta
BELOW: Chilli seafood in tomato sauce

2 While the pasta is cooking, heat 2 tablespoons of olive oil in a heavy-based pan and cook the garlic and chilli for 1 minute over low heat. Add the chopped tomato with any juices, and the sugar. Stir gently over low heat for 5 minutes, or until the tomato is just warmed through.

3 Add the salmon and basil and season with salt and pepper, to taste. Toss the sauce through the pasta before serving.

NUTRITION PER SERVE: *Protein 25 g; Fat 10 g; Carbohydrate 60 g; Dietary Fibre 5 g; Cholesterol 55 mg; 1930 kJ (460 cal)*

SPAGHETTINI WITH ROASTED SALMON AND GARLIC

Preparation time: 10 minutes
Total cooking time: 20 minutes
Serves 4–6

★

4 small fillets fresh baby salmon, about
  100 g (3 1/2 oz) each
4–5 tablespoons extra virgin olive oil
8–10 cloves garlic, peeled
300 g (10 oz) dry spaghettini
50 g (1 3/4 oz) thinly sliced fennel
1 1/2 teaspoons finely grated lime rind
2 tablespoons lime juice
4 sprigs fennel fronds, to garnish

1 Preheat the oven to hot 220°C (425°F/Gas 7) and oil a ceramic baking dish. Brush the salmon fillets with 2 tablespoons of the olive oil, salt lightly and position in a single layer in the dish.

2 Slice the garlic cloves lengthways and spread them all over the salmon fillets. Brush lightly with olive oil. Bake for 10–15 minutes, or until the salmon is cooked through.

3 Meanwhile, cook the spaghettini in a large pan of rapidly boiling salted water until *al dente*. Drain and stir through enough extra virgin olive oil to make it glisten. Toss the fennel and lime rind through the pasta and arrange on warmed serving plates.

4 Top each serving with a salmon fillet then spoon the pan juices over them, with any stray slices of garlic. Drizzle with lime juice. Garnish with fennel fronds and serve accompanied by a plain tomato salad.

NUTRITION PER SERVE (6): *Protein 30 g; Fat 30 g; Carbohydrate 55 g; Dietary Fibre 5 g; Cholesterol 70 mg; 2640 kJ (630 cal)*

PAPPARDELLE

Pappardelle are long flat noodles, similar to fettucine but a lot wider at around 30 mm (1 1/4 inches). They are excellent for sauces that are strong, rich or heavy and ideal with game and offal. Sometimes one or both sides are crimped, causing confusion with lasagnette, which is only half the width. One can be substituted for the other in most recipes.

ABOVE: Pappardelle with salmon

PAPPARDELLE WITH SALMON

Preparation time: 15 minutes
Total cooking time: 25 minutes
Serves 6

★

500 g (1 lb) pappardelle
2 cloves garlic, finely chopped
1 teaspoon chopped fresh chilli
500 g (1 lb) very ripe tomatoes, chopped
1 teaspoon soft brown sugar
425 g (14 oz) can pink salmon, drained
  and flaked
1/2 cup (30 g/1 oz) fresh basil leaves, chopped

1 Cook the pappardelle in a large pan of rapidly boiling salted water until *al dente*. Drain and return to the pan.

TAGLIATELLE WITH OCTOPUS

Preparation time: 30 minutes
Total cooking time: 25 minutes
Serves 4

☆

500 g (1 lb) mixed tagliatelle

1 kg (2 lb) baby octopus

2 tablespoons olive oil

1 onion, sliced

1 clove garlic, crushed

425 g (14 oz) can tomato purée
   (passata)

1/2 cup (125 ml/4 fl oz) dry white wine

1 tablespoon bottled chilli sauce

1 tablespoon chopped fresh basil

1 Cook the tagliatelle in a large pan of rapidly boiling salted water until *al dente*. Drain and return to the pan.

2 Clean the octopus by using a small sharp knife to remove the gut—either cut off the head entirely or slice open the head and remove the gut. Pick up the body and use your index finger to push the beak up. Remove the beak and discard. Clean the octopus thoroughly, pat dry and, if you prefer, cut in half. Set aside.

3 While the pasta is cooking, heat the oil in a large frying pan. Add the onion and garlic and stir over low heat until the onion is tender. Add the tomato purée, wine, chilli sauce, basil, and salt and pepper, to taste, to the pan. Bring to the boil, reduce the heat and simmer for 10 minutes.

4 Add the octopus to the pan and simmer for 5–10 minutes, or until tender. Serve over the pasta.

NUTRITION PER SERVE: *Protein 50 g; Fat 15 g; Carbohydrate 95 g; Dietary Fibre 10 g; Cholesterol 00 mg; 3130 kJ (750 cal)*

ABOVE: Tagliatelle with octopus

TOMATO PASTA WITH SMOKED COD AND SESAME

Preparation time: 25 minutes
Total cooking time: 10 minutes
Serves 4

☆

320 g (11 oz) smoked cod or other fresh
smoked large fish, e.g. haddock
1/2 cup (125 ml/4 fl oz) milk
400 g (13 oz) tomato casereccie
1 carrot
4 tablespoons peanut oil
1 small onion, sliced
150 g (5 oz) bean sprouts
1 1/2 teaspoons soy sauce
1 teaspoon sesame oil
1 tablespoon sesame seeds, toasted

1 Put the fish in a pan with the milk, add
enough water to cover, and poach for 5 minutes,
or until tender. Rinse under cold water to cool
and to remove milk scum. Break the fish into
large flakes, discarding the skin and bones.
Set aside.
2 Cook the pasta in a large pan of rapidly
boiling salted water until *al dente*. Drain.
3 Thinly slice the carrot diagonally. Heat
3 tablespoons of the peanut oil in a large frying
pan or wok and toss the carrot and onion until
cooked but still crisp. Stir in the bean sprouts,
soy sauce and sesame oil. Season, to taste, with
salt and freshly ground black pepper.
4 Add the pasta to the pan with the sesame
seeds, prepared fish and the remaining
1 tablespoon peanut oil. Lightly toss and
serve immediately.

NUTRITION PER SERVE: *Protein 30 g; Fat 25 g;
Carbohydrate 75 g; Dietary Fibre 8 g; Cholesterol 45 mg;
2725 kJ (650 cal)*

TROUT, FETTUCINE AND FENNEL FRITTATA

Preparation time: 20 minutes
Total cooking time: 1 hour
Serves 4

☆

250 g (8 oz) whole smoked trout
200 g (6 1/2 oz) dried fettucine
1 cup (250 ml/8 fl oz) milk
1/2 cup (125 ml/4 fl oz) cream
4 eggs
pinch of nutmeg
40 g (1 1/4 oz) finely sliced fennel, plus fennel
greens for garnish
4 spring onions, sliced
2/3 cup (85 g/3 oz) grated Cheddar cheese

1 Preheat the oven to moderate 180°C
(350°F/Gas 4). Lightly brush a 23 cm (9 inch)
ovenproof frying pan or flan dish with oil.
Remove and discard the skin and bones from
the trout.
2 Cook the fettucine in a large pan of rapidly
boiling salted water until *al dente*. Drain.
3 Combine the milk, cream, eggs and nutmeg in
a large bowl and whisk until smooth. Season
with salt and pepper, to taste. Add the trout,
fettucine, fennel and spring onion and toss to
distribute evenly. Pour into the prepared dish,
sprinkle with the cheese and bake until set,
about 1 hour. Garnish with 2–3 sprigs of fennel
greens and serve.

NUTRITION PER SERVE: *Protein 25 g; Fat 20 g;
Carbohydrate 25 g; Dietary Fibre 2 g; Cholesterol 195 mg;
1615 kJ (385 cal)*

ON THE SIDE

TABOULI Soak 3/4 cup (130 g/4 1/4 oz) of
burghul in 3/4 cup (185 ml/6 fl oz) of water
for about 15 minutes, or until the water has
been absorbed. Finely chop the leaves from
2 bunches (300 g/10 oz) of flat-leaf parsley
and combine with 1/2 cup (25 g/3/4 oz) of
chopped fresh mint, 3 chopped vine-
ripened tomatoes and 4 finely chopped
spring onions. Make a dressing by
thoroughly combining 3 crushed cloves of
garlic, 1/3 cup (80 ml/2 3/4 fl oz) of lemon
juice and 1/4 cup (60 ml/2 fl oz) of olive oil.
Pour the dressing over the salad and toss
well to combine.

FENNEL
Bulb fennel has an
unmistakable aniseed
flavour and a crunchy
texture. Uncooked and
sliced, it is used in salads
and as antipasto. Cooked,
it braises well and is a
good companion to
seafood and pork. Look
for crisp bulbs that are
fully formed with many
stalks. The white inner
stalks are used as well as
the leaves, which are very
good chopped and
sprinkled on salads and
fish, or as a flavouring in
seafood sauces. Dried
fennel seeds are important
in spice mixtures and are
used to flavour a diverse
range of foods, from bread
to salami.

*OPPOSITE PAGE: Tomato
pasta with smoked cod
and sesame (top);
Trout, fettucine and
fennel frittata*

SCALLOPS

Scallops are one of the molluscs that are cooked for eating. Out of the shell they may be poached, sautéed or baked; in the half shell they are lightly grilled, and often with a minimum of flavourings. Scallops are complemented well by milk, butter and cream, and are often put with white wine. The cooking time should be brief to avoid the flesh becoming rubbery.

ABOVE: Creamy seafood ravioli

CREAMY SEAFOOD RAVIOLI

Preparation time: 1 hour
+ 30 minutes standing
Total cooking time: 30 minutes
Serves 4

☆

Pasta

2 cups (250 g/8 oz) plain flour
3 eggs
1 tablespoon olive oil
1 egg yolk, extra

Filling

50 g (1³/4 oz) butter, softened
3 cloves garlic, finely chopped
2 tablespoons finely chopped flat-leaf parsley
100 g (3¹/2 oz) scallops, cleaned and
    finely chopped
100 g (3¹/2 oz) raw prawn meat, finely chopped

Sauce

75 g (2¹/2 oz) butter
3 tablespoons plain flour
1¹/2 cups (375 ml/12 fl oz) milk
300 ml (10 fl oz) cream
¹/2 cup (125 ml/4 fl oz) white wine
¹/2 cup (50 g/1³/4 oz) grated Parmesan
2 tablespoons chopped flat-leaf parsley

1 To make the pasta, sift the flour and a pinch of salt into a bowl and make a well in the centre. Whisk the eggs, oil and 1 tablespoon water in a jug, then add gradually to the flour and mix to a firm dough. Gather into a ball.
2 Knead on a lightly floured surface for 5 minutes, or until smooth and elastic. Transfer to a lightly oiled bowl, cover with plastic wrap and set aside for 30 minutes.
3 To make the filling, mix together the softened butter, chopped garlic, parsley, scallops and prawn meat. Set aside.

4 Roll out a quarter of the pasta dough at a time until very thin (each portion of dough should be roughly 10 cm/4 inches wide when rolled). Place 1 teaspoonful of filling at 5 cm (2 inch) intervals down one side of each strip. Whisk the extra egg yolk with 3 tablespoons water. Brush along one side of the dough and between the filling. Fold the dough over the filling to meet the other side. Repeat with the remaining filling and dough. Press the edges of the dough together firmly to seal.

5 Cut between the mounds with a knife or a fluted pastry cutter. Cook, in batches, in a large pan of rapidly boiling salted water for 6 minutes each batch (while the pasta is cooking make the sauce). Drain well and return to the pan to keep warm.

6 To make the sauce, melt the butter in a pan, add the flour and cook over low heat for 2 minutes. Remove from the heat and gradually stir in the combined milk, cream and wine. Cook over low heat until the sauce begins to thicken, stirring constantly to prevent lumps forming. Bring to the boil and simmer gently for 5 minutes. Add the Parmesan and parsley and stir until combined. Remove from the heat, add to the ravioli and toss well.

NOTE: The pasta dough is set aside for 30 minutes to let the gluten in the flour relax. If you don't do this, you run the risk of making tough pasta.

NUTRITION PER SERVE: *Protein 30 g; Fat 70 g, Carbohydrate 60 g; Dietary Fibre 5 g; Cholesterol 430 mg; 4255 kJ (1020 cal)*

MUSSELS WITH TOMATO SAUCE

Preparation time: 20 minutes
Total cooking time: 20 minutes
Serves 4

★

500 g (1 lb) penne or rigatoni

1 tablespoon olive oil

1 small onion, finely chopped

1 clove garlic, chopped

1 large carrot, diced

1 stick celery, diced

3 tablespoons chopped fresh parsley

800 ml (24 fl oz) tomato pasta sauce

1/2 cup (125 ml/4 fl oz) white wine

375 g (12 oz) tub marinated green mussels

1/4 cup (60 ml/2 fl oz) cream, optional

1 Cook the pasta in a large pan of rapidly boiling salted water until *al dente*. Drain and return to the pan.

2 Heat the oil in a pan and add the onion, garlic, carrot and celery. Cook until the vegetables are tender and add the parsley, tomato pasta sauce and wine. Simmer, stirring occasionally, for 15 minutes.

3 Drain the mussels, add to the sauce with the cream, if using, and stir to combine. Add to the pasta and stir to combine.

NOTE: If you can't buy bottled tomato pasta sauce, use canned crushed tomatoes.

NUTRITION PER SERVE: *Protein 35 g; Fat 25 g; Carbohydrate 100 g; Dietary Fibre 10 g; Cholesterol 105 mg; 3280 kJ (780 cal)*

ABOVE: Mussels with tomato sauce

SPAGHETTI

Spaghetti arrived in Italy via Sicily, where it was introduced by the Arabs after they invaded in 827 A.D. Being great wanderers and traders, they needed their pasta in a form that could be stored and easily transported and so their preference for dried spaghetti was passed on. Known then as *itriyah* (Persian for string), it developed into *tria* and then *trii*, a form of spaghetti still popular in Sicily and parts of southern Italy.

BELOW: Spaghetti with creamy garlic mussels

SPAGHETTI WITH CREAMY GARLIC MUSSELS

Preparation time: 20 minutes
Total cooking time: 10–15 minutes
Serves 4

★

500 g (1 lb) spaghetti
1.5 kg (3 lb) fresh mussels
2 tablespoons olive oil
2 cloves garlic, crushed
½ cup (125 ml/4 fl oz) white wine
1 cup (250 ml/8 fl oz) cream
2 tablespoons chopped fresh basil

1 Cook the spaghetti in a large pan of rapidly boiling salted water until *al dente*. Drain.
2 While the spaghetti is cooking, remove the beards from the mussels and scrub away any grit. Discard any open mussels. Set aside. Heat the oil in a large pan. Add the garlic and stir over low heat for 30 seconds.

3 Add the wine and mussels. Simmer, covered, for 5 minutes. Remove the mussels, discarding any that don't open, and set aside.
4 Add the cream, basil and salt and pepper, to taste, to the pan. Simmer for 2 minutes, stirring occasionally. Serve the sauce and mussels over the spaghetti.

NUTRITION PER SERVE: *Protein 80 g; Fat 40 g; Carbohydrate 90 g; Dietary Fibre 7 g; Cholesterol 445 mg; 4510 kJ (1075 cal)*

ON THE SIDE

ROASTED VEGETABLE AND BRIE SALAD Roast 300 g (10 oz) each of peeled and halved potatoes, parsnips, sweet potato and baby carrots and onions in oil until crisp and tender. While still hot, drizzle with a dressing made by whisking together 2 tablespoons of orange juice, 1 teaspoon of horseradish cream and 2 tablespoons of oil. Serve warm, topped with 200 g (6 ½ oz) of sliced Brie cheese and plenty of cracked black pepper.

FETTUCINE WITH SMOKED SALMON

Preparation time: 10 minutes
Total cooking time: 10–15 minutes
Serves 4

★

100 g (3½ oz) smoked salmon

¼ cup (35 g/1¼ oz) sun-dried tomatoes

1 tablespoon olive oil

1 clove garlic, crushed

1 cup (250 ml/8 fl oz) cream

¼ cup (15 g/½ oz) snipped fresh chives, plus extra, to garnish

¼ teaspoon mustard powder

2 teaspoons lemon juice

375 g (12 oz) fettucine

2 tablespoons freshly grated Parmesan, for serving

1 Cut the smoked salmon into bite-sized pieces and the sun-dried tomatoes into small pieces.
2 Heat the olive oil in a frying pan, add the garlic and stir over low heat for 30 seconds. Add the cream, chives, mustard powder, and salt and pepper, to taste. Bring to the boil, reduce the heat and simmer, stirring, until the sauce begins to thicken.
3 Add the salmon and lemon juice to the pan and stir to combine. Heat gently.
4 While the sauce is cooking, cook the fettucine in a large pan of rapidly boiling salted water until *al dente*. Drain well and return to the pan. Toss the sauce through the hot pasta. Serve immediately topped with the sun-dried tomato, Parmesan and chives.

NUTRITION PER SERVE: *Protein 20 g; Fat 30 g; Carbohydrate 70 g; Dietary Fibre 5 g; Cholesterol 90 mg; 2685 kJ (640 cal)*

SUN-DRIED TOMATOES
These preserved tomatoes are available dry, loosely packed, or in jars. They are useful in pasta dishes and salads or on top of pizzas. The flavour is intense and sweet. Some come packed in olive or canola oil and need to be drained. Others are available dry and must be soaked in boiling water for 5 minutes before use. Sun-dried tomatoes combine well with cheese, salad greens, olives, seafood, chicken and meat.

ABOVE: Fettucine with smoked salmon

CLAMS

Long thought of as the poor relative in the mollusc family, clams are used for their succulent flesh and mild flavour. When bought live in the shells, they are eaten raw or lightly cooked. Shelled, they are preserved in cans or bottles and in this form the flesh is used in sauces and stews. Jars of cooked clams still in their shell are also available, and are an excellent alternative to preparing clams from scratch. The juice in which clams are preserved makes a lightly flavoured seafood stock, good for use in soups and sauces.

ABOVE: Spaghetti vongole

SPAGHETTI VONGOLE
(SPAGHETTI WITH CLAM SAUCE)

Preparation time: 25 minutes + soaking
Total cooking time: 20–35 minutes
Serves 4

☆

1 kg (2 lb) fresh small clams in shells or
   750 g (1 1/2 lb) can clams in brine
1 tablespoon lemon juice
1/3 cup (80 ml/2 3/4 fl oz) olive oil
3 cloves garlic, crushed
2 x 425 g (14 oz) cans crushed tomatoes
250 g (8 oz) spaghetti
4 tablespoons chopped fresh parsley

1 If using fresh clams, clean thoroughly (see Note). Place in a large pan with the lemon juice. Cover the pan and shake over medium heat for 7–8 minutes until the shells open, discarding any that don't open. Remove the clam flesh from the shell of the opened clams and set aside; discard the empty shells. If using canned clams, drain, rinse well and set aside.

2 Heat the oil in a large pan. Add the garlic and cook over low heat for 5 minutes. Add the tomato and stir to combine. Bring to the boil and simmer, covered, for 20 minutes. Add freshly ground black pepper, to taste, and the clams, and stir until heated through.

3 While the sauce is cooking, cook the spaghetti in a large pan of rapidly boiling salted water until *al dente*. Drain and return to the pan. Gently stir in the sauce and the chopped parsley until combined. Serve immediately in a warm dish. Caperberries and a slice of lemon peel make an attractive garnish for special occasions.
NOTE: To clean the clams, any sand and grit needs to be drawn out of the shells. Combine 2 tablespoons each of salt and plain flour with enough water to make a paste. Add to a large bucket or bowl of cold water and soak the clams in this mixture overnight. Drain and scrub the shells well, then rinse thoroughly and drain again.

NUTRITION PER SERVE: *Protein 35 g; Fat 25 g; Carbohydrate 55 g; Dietary Fibre 7 g; Cholesterol 355 mg; 2420 kJ (580 cal)*

SPAGHETTI AND MUSSELS IN TOMATO AND HERB SAUCE

Preparation time: 15 minutes
Total cooking time: 30 minutes
Serves 4

★

1.5 kg (3 lb) fresh mussels
2 tablespoons olive oil
1 onion, finely sliced
2 cloves garlic, crushed
425 g (14 oz) can crushed tomatoes
1 cup (250 ml/8 fl oz) white wine
1 tablespoon chopped fresh basil
2 tablespoons chopped fresh parsley
500 g (1 lb) spaghetti

1 Remove the beards from the mussels and scrub away any grit. Discard any open mussels.
2 Heat the olive oil in a large pan. Add the onion and garlic and stir over low heat until the onion is tender. Add the tomato, white wine, fresh basil and parsley, and salt and pepper, to taste. Bring the sauce to the boil, reduce the heat and simmer for 15–20 minutes, or until the sauce begins to thicken.
3 Add the prepared mussels to the pan and cook, covered, for 5 minutes, shaking the pan occasionally. Be sure to discard any mussels that don't open.
4 While the sauce is cooking, add the spaghetti to a large pan of rapidly boiling salted water and cook until *al dente*. Drain. Serve the mussels and sauce over the pasta.

NUTRITION PER SERVE: *Protein 50 g; Fat 15 g; Carbohydrate 95 g; Dietary Fibre 10 g; Cholesterol 190 mg; 3050 kJ (730 cal)*

ON THE SIDE

POTATO, EGG AND BACON

SALAD Boil, steam or microwave 1 kg (2 lb) of whole baby potatoes. Fry 4 sliced rashers of bacon until crisp; drain on paper towels. Peel and quarter 6 hard-boiled eggs and combine with the warm potatoes, 4 sliced spring onions and 2 tablespoons each of chopped fresh mint and chives. Fold through 1 cup (250 g/8 oz) of natural yoghurt and top with the crisp bacon.

GREMOLATA

It is not usual to serve grated cheese with seafood pasta sauces, but for those who can't resist sprinkling a little something on top, there is an alternative! Mix the grated rind of half a lemon, with a finely chopped clove of garlic and about a cup of loosely packed chopped fresh parsley. Adjust the proportions to suit your tastes. Called gremolata or gremolada, this mix was traditionally used to accompany osso buco.

ABOVE: Spaghetti and mussels in tomato and herb sauce

PASTA WITH VEGETABLES

The key to great food is freshness. While the Italian cook makes good use of pantry staples such as canned tomatoes and olive oil, it is the fresh vegetables and herbs which lift the dishes into the sublime. Herbs are generally used fresh, often gathered from the surrounding area in great basketfuls. Tomatoes, peppers and artichokes ripen under the Mediterranean sun and, tossed together with a bowl of pasta, are as colourful and delicious as they are good for you.

ZUCCHINI

Zucchini or courgettes are Italian summer squash. Green or yellow in colour, they should be harvested within 4–6 days of flowering to give a tender rind and crisp flesh. If they are too old or too big, the flesh tends to be bitter. Zucchini require little preparation and short cooking time. They can be steamed, boiled, sautéed, baked or deep-fried, and larger ones can be stuffed and baked.

ABOVE: Fettucine with zucchini and crisp-fried basil

FETTUCINE WITH ZUCCHINI (COURGETTES) AND CRISP-FRIED BASIL

Preparation time: 15 minutes
Total cooking time: 15 minutes
Serves 6

★

1 cup (250 ml/8 fl oz) olive oil
a handful of fresh basil leaves
500 g (1 lb) fettucine or tagliatelle
60 g (2 oz) butter
2 cloves garlic, crushed
500 g (1 lb) zucchini (courgettes), grated
3/4 cup (75 g/2 1/2 oz) freshly grated Parmesan

1 To crisp-fry the basil leaves, heat the oil in a small pan, add 2 leaves at a time and cook for 1 minute, or until crisp. Remove with a slotted spoon and drain on paper towels. Repeat with the remaining basil leaves.
2 Cook the pasta in a large pan of rapidly boiling salted water until *al dente*. Drain and return to the pan.
3 While the pasta is cooking, heat the butter in a deep heavy-based pan over low heat until the butter is foaming. Add the garlic and cook for 1 minute. Add the zucchini and cook, stirring occasionally, for 1–2 minutes or until softened. Add to the hot pasta. Add the Parmesan and toss well. Serve the pasta garnished with the crisp basil leaves.
NOTE: The basil leaves can be fried up to 2 hours in advance. Store in an airtight container after cooling.

NUTRITION PER SERVE: *Protein 15 g; Fat 55 g; Carbohydrate 60 g; Dietary Fibre 5 g; Cholesterol 35 mg; 3245 kJ (775 cal)*

OLIVE AND MOZZARELLA SPAGHETTI

Preparation time: 20 minutes
Total cooking time: 15 minutes
Serves 4

★

500 g (1 lb) spaghetti
50 g (1 3/4 oz) butter
2 cloves garlic, crushed
1/2 cup (70 g/2 1/4 oz) pitted black olives, halved
3 tablespoons olive oil
1/3 cup (20 g/3/4 oz) chopped fresh parsley
150 g (5 oz) mozzarella cheese, cut into small cubes

1 Cook the spaghetti in a large pan of rapidly boiling salted water until *al dente*. Drain and return to the pan.
2 While the spaghetti is cooking, heat the butter in a small pan until it begins to turn nutty brown. Add the crushed garlic and cook over low heat for 1 minute.
3 Add to the pasta with the black olives, olive oil, fresh parsley and mozzarella cheese. Toss until well combined.

NUTRITION PER SERVE: *Protein 25 g; Fat 35 g; Carbohydrate 90 g; Dietary Fibre 5 g; Cholesterol 55 mg; 3320 kJ (770cal)*

FARFALLE WITH ARTICHOKE HEARTS AND OLIVES

Preparation time: 20 minutes
Total cooking time: 20 minutes
Serves 4

★

500 g (1 lb) farfalle
400 g (13 oz) marinated
   artichoke hearts
3 tablespoons olive oil
3 cloves garlic, crushed

1/2 cup (95 g/3 oz) pitted black
   olives, chopped
2 tablespoons chopped fresh chives
200 g (6 1/2 oz) fresh ricotta cheese

1 Cook the farfalle in a large pan of rapidly boiling salted water until *al dente*. Drain and return to the pan.
2 While the pasta is cooking, drain and thinly slice the artichoke hearts. Heat the olive oil in a large frying pan. Add the garlic and cook over low heat until softened, but don't let the garlic burn or brown or it will become bitter.
3 Add the artichoke hearts and olives to the pan and stir until heated through. Add the chives and ricotta, breaking up the ricotta with a spoon. Cook until the ricotta is heated through.
4 Combine the sauce with the pasta. Season with salt and freshly ground black pepper and serve immediately.
NOTE: This dish is wonderful made with fresh cooked artichoke hearts. Use 5 artichoke hearts and follow the recipe as above.

NUTRITION PER SERVE: *Protein 15 g; Fat 15 g; Carbohydrate 60 g; Dietary Fibre 5 g; Cholesterol 15 mg; 1840 kJ (440 cal)*

ABOVE: Olive and mozzarella spaghetti (left); Farfalle with artichoke hearts and olives

SUN-DRIED TOMATO SAUCE ON TAGLIATELLE

Preparation time: 20 minutes
Total cooking time: 20 minutes
Serves 4

☆

500 g (1 lb) tagliatelle
2 tablespoons olive oil
1 onion, chopped
1/2 cup (80 g/2 3/4 oz) thinly sliced
    sun-dried tomatoes
2 cloves garlic, crushed
425 g (14 oz) can chopped tomatoes
1 cup (125 g/4 oz) pitted black olives
1/3 cup (20 g/3/4 oz) chopped fresh basil
freshly grated Parmesan, for serving

1 Cook the tagliatelle in a large pan of rapidly
boiling salted water until *al dente*. Drain and
return to the pan.
2 Meanwhile, heat the oil in a large frying pan.
Add the onion and cook for 3 minutes, stirring
occasionally, until soft. Add the sliced sun-dried
tomato along with the crushed garlic and cook
for another minute.
3 Add the chopped tomato, olives and basil to
the pan and season with freshly ground black
pepper. Bring to the boil, reduce the heat, and
simmer for 10 minutes.
4 Add the sauce to the hot pasta and gently
toss through. Serve immediately, topped with
some Parmesan.
NOTE: Sun-dried tomatoes are available either
dry or loosely packed, or in jars with olive or
canola oil. The tomatoes in oil need only to be
drained, but the dry tomatoes must be soaked
in boiling water for 5 minutes to rehydrate and
soften before using.

NUTRITION PER SERVE: *Protein 20 g; Fat 15 g;
Carbohydrate 95 g; Dietary Fibre 10 g; Cholesterol 5 mg;
2415 kJ (575 cal)*

CREAMY ASPARAGUS LINGUINE

Preparation time: 15 minutes
Total cooking time: 15 minutes
Serves 4

☆

200 g (6 1/2 oz) fresh full-fat ricotta cheese
1 cup (250 ml/8 fl oz) cream
3/4 cup (75 g/2 1/2 oz) freshly grated Parmesan
freshly ground nutmeg, to taste
500 g (1 lb) linguine
500 g (1 lb) fresh asparagus spears, cut into
    short lengths
1/2 cup (45 g/1 1/2 oz) toasted flaked almonds,
    for serving

1 Put the ricotta in a bowl and stir until smooth.
Stir in the cream, Parmesan and nutmeg and
season with salt and freshly ground black pepper,
to taste.
2 Cook the linguine in a large pan of rapidly
boiling salted water until not quite tender. Add
the asparagus to the pan and cook for another
3 minutes.
3 Drain the pasta and asparagus, reserving
2 tablespoons of the cooking water. Return
the pasta and asparagus to the pan.
4 Add the reserved cooking water to the ricotta
mixture, stirring well to combine. Spoon the
mixture over the pasta and toss gently. Serve
sprinkled with the toasted almonds.
NOTE: To toast flaked almonds, you can heat
them under a moderately hot grill for about
2 minutes. Stir them occasionally and be careful
to avoid burning them.

NUTRITION PER SERVE: *Protein 35 g; Fat 45 g;
Carbohydrate 90 g; Dietary Fibre 10 g; Cholesterol 125 mg;
3850kJ (920 cal)*

BLACK OLIVES

Olives when picked young
are green and hard. They
ripen and darken on the
tree. Olives are preserved
in oil, sometimes with
herbs, or in brine.
Featured in a great many
Mediterranean dishes,
olives are suitable for
salads and stuffings, are
baked into breads and are
an attractive addition to
pasta and rice dishes.
Olives should be used as
soon after purchase as
possible, and it is wisest to
buy the best you can
afford. Greek and Italian
olives are thought to be
the finest.

*OPPOSITE PAGE: Sun-
dried tomato sauce on
tagliatelle (top); Creamy
asparagus linguine*

GREEN OLIVE AND EGGPLANT (AUBERGINE) TOSS

Preparation time: 20 minutes
Total cooking time: 20 minutes
Serves 4

☆

500 g (1 lb) fettucine or tagliatelle
1 cup (175 g/6 oz) green olives
1 large eggplant (aubergine)
2 tablespoons olive oil
2 cloves garlic, crushed
1/2 cup (125 ml/4 fl oz) lemon juice
2 tablespoons chopped fresh parsley
1/2 cup (50 g/1¾ oz) freshly grated Parmesan

1 Cook the pasta in a large pan of rapidly boiling salted water until *al dente*. Drain and return to the pan.
2 While the pasta is cooking, slice the olives and cut the eggplant into small cubes.
3 Heat the oil in a heavy-based frying pan. Add the garlic and stir for 30 seconds. Add the eggplant and cook over medium heat, stirring frequently, for 6 minutes, or until tender. Add the olives, lemon juice and salt and pepper, to taste. Add the sauce to the pasta and toss. Sprinkle with parsley and grated Parmesan.
NOTE: To draw out bitter juices, eggplant can be chopped and salted, left to stand for 30 minutes, then rinsed well before using.

NUTRITION PER SERVE: *Protein 20 g; Fat 15 g; Carbohydrate 95 g; Dietary Fibre 10 g; Cholesterol 10 mg; 2585 kJ (615 cal)*

ON THE SIDE

WARM VEGETABLE SALAD Boil or steam 200 g (6½ oz) each of baby carrots, sugar snap peas, yellow squash, zucchini and new potatoes until just tender. Do not overcook or the vegetables will lose their bright colours. To make the dressing, combine 2 crushed cloves of garlic, 2 tablespoons each of chopped fresh dill and chives, 1 tablespoon lime juice, 1 tablespoon Dijon mustard and ⅓ cup (80 ml/2¾ fl oz) of olive oil.

BELOW: Green olive and eggplant toss

SPAGHETTI WITH FRESH TOMATO SAUCE

Preparation time: 15 minutes
  + 2 hours refrigeration
Total cooking time: 10–15 minutes
Serves 4

☆

4 firm ripe tomatoes
8 stuffed green olives
2 tablespoons capers
4 spring onions, finely chopped
2 cloves garlic, crushed
1/2 teaspoon dried oregano
1/3 cup (20 g/3/4 oz) fresh parsley, chopped
1/3 cup (80 ml/2 3/4 fl oz) olive oil
375 g (12 oz) spaghetti or spaghettini

1 Chop the tomatoes into small pieces. Chop the olives and capers. Combine all the ingredients, except the pasta, in a bowl and mix well. Cover and refrigerate for at least 2 hours.
2 Cook the pasta in a large pan of rapidly boiling salted water until *al dente*. Drain and return to the pan. Add the cold sauce to the hot pasta and mix well.
NOTE: For a different taste, add 1/2 cup (30 g/1 oz) of shredded fresh basil leaves to the sauce.

NUTRITION PER SERVE: *Protein 15 g; Fat 20 g; Carbohydrate 70 g; Dietary Fibre 10 g; Cholesterol 0 mg; 2190 kJ (525cal)*

LINGUINE WITH ROASTED VEGETABLE SAUCE

Preparation time: 30 minutes
Total cooking time: 50 minutes
Serves 4

☆

4 large red peppers (capsicums)
500 g (1 lb) firm ripe tomatoes
3 large red (Spanish) onions, peeled
1 bulb garlic
1/2 cup (125 ml/4 fl oz) balsamic vinegar
1/4 cup (60 ml/2 fl oz) olive oil
2 teaspoons coarse salt
2 teaspoons freshly ground black pepper
500 g (1 lb) linguine
100 g (3 1/2 oz) fresh Parmesan, shaved
100 g (3 1/2 oz) black olives

1 Preheat the oven to moderate 180°C (350°F/Gas 4). Cut the peppers in half and remove the seeds and membrane. Cut the tomatoes and onions in half and separate and peel the garlic cloves.
2 Arrange the vegetables in a large baking dish in a single layer. Pour the vinegar and oil over them and sprinkle with the salt and pepper.
3 Bake for 50 minutes. Allow to cool for 5 minutes before puréeing in a food processor for 3 minutes, or until the mixture is smooth. Season with more salt and pepper, if necessary.
4 When the vegetables are almost cooked, cook the linguine in a large pan of rapidly boiling salted water until *al dente*. Drain.
5 Serve the roasted vegetable sauce over the linguine with the Parmesan, olives and some extra black pepper.

NUTRITION PER SERVE: *Protein 30 g; Fat 30 g; Carbohydrate 100 g; Dietary Fibre 10 g; Cholesterol 25 mg; 3320 kJ (790 cal)*

ABOVE: *Spaghetti with fresh tomato sauce*

EGG TOMATOES
Favoured for their high flesh-to-seed ratio, egg tomatoes are ideal for cooking. Also known as Roma or plum tomatoes, their colour is a bright, even red and their walls are thick and firm, thus making peeling easy. They are perfect for preserving and are used for canned peeled tomatoes and sun-dried tomatoes.

ABOVE: Grilled vegetables on pasta

GRILLED VEGETABLES ON PASTA

Preparation time: 30 minutes
Total cooking time: 20 minutes
Serves 4

✹

500 g (1 lb) tomato- or chilli-flavoured
    fettucine or tagliatelle
1 red pepper (capsicum)
1 yellow pepper (capsicum)
250 g (8 oz) egg (Roma) tomatoes,
    thickly sliced
2 large zucchini (courgettes), sliced
1/3 cup (80 ml/2¾ fl oz) olive oil
3 cloves garlic, crushed
10 fresh basil leaves, roughly chopped
4 bocconcini, sliced

1 Cook the pasta in a large pan of rapidly boiling salted water until *al dente*. Drain and return to the pan. Cut the peppers into large flat pieces and discard the seeds and membrane. Cook skin-side-up under a hot grill for 8 minutes, or until the skin is black and blistered. Remove from the heat and cover with a damp tea towel. When cool, peel the skin away and finely chop the pepper flesh.
2 Sprinkle the cut sides of the tomatoes lightly with salt. Brush the zucchini with 1 tablespoon of the oil. Cook the vegetables under a hot grill for 10 minutes, or until tender, turning once.
3 Toss the pasta with the vegetables, garlic, basil, the remaining oil and the sliced bocconcini. Season with salt and freshly ground black pepper, to taste. Serve immediately.
NOTE: Use plain pasta if flavoured is not available. Add a little chopped chilli to the dish, if you like the spicy taste.

NUTRITION PER SERVE: *Protein 25 g; Fat 30 g; Carbohydrate 95 g; Dietary Fibre 10 g; Cholesterol 20 mg; 3060 kJ (730 cal)*

VEGETABLE LASAGNE

Preparation time: 40 minutes
Total cooking time: 1 hour 15 minutes
Serves 6

★

3 large red peppers (capsicums)
2 large eggplants (aubergines)
2 tablespoons oil
1 large onion, chopped
3 cloves garlic, crushed
1 teaspoon dried mixed herbs
1 teaspoon dried oregano
500 g (1 lb) mushrooms, sliced
440 g (14 oz) can crushed tomatoes
440 g (14 oz) can red kidney beans, drained
1 tablespoon sweet chilli sauce
250 g (8 oz) packet instant lasagne
500 g (1 lb) English spinach, chopped
1 cup (30 g/1 oz) fresh basil leaves
90 g (3 oz) sun-dried tomatoes, sliced
3 tablespoons grated Parmesan
3 tablespoons grated Cheddar cheese

Cheese sauce

60 g (2 oz) butter
3 tablespoons plain flour
2 cups (500 ml/16 fl oz) milk
600 g (1 1/4 lb) ricotta cheese

1 Preheat the oven to moderate 180°C (350°F/Gas 4). Brush a 35 x 28 cm (14 x 11 inch) ovenproof baking dish with oil.
2 Cut the red peppers into large flat pieces and remove the seeds and membrane. Cook, skin-side-up, under a hot grill for 8 minutes, or until the skin is black and blistered. Cover with a damp tea towel and when cool, peel away the skin and cut the flesh into long thin strips. Set aside.
3 Slice the eggplant into 1 cm (1/2 inch) rounds and place in a large pan of boiling water. Cook for 1 minute, or until just tender. Drain, pat dry with paper towels and set aside.
4 Heat the oil in a large heavy-based frying pan and add the onion, garlic and herbs. Cook over medium heat for 5 minutes, or until the onion is soft. Add the sliced mushrooms and cook for 1 minute.
5 Add the tomato, red kidney beans, chilli sauce and salt and pepper, to taste. Bring to the boil, reduce the heat and simmer for 15 minutes, or until the sauce thickens. Remove from the heat and set aside.
6 To make the cheese sauce, heat the butter in a pan and stir in the flour over medium heat for 1 minute, or until smooth. Remove from the heat and gradually stir in the milk. Return to the heat and stir constantly until the sauce boils and begins to thicken. Simmer for another minute. Add the ricotta and stir until smooth.
7 Dip the lasagne sheets, if necessary, in hot water to soften slightly and arrange 4 sheets on the base of the prepared dish. Build up layers on top of the pasta, using half of the eggplant, the spinach, the basil, the grilled pepper strips, the mushroom sauce and then the sun-dried tomatoes. Top with a layer of pasta and press gently. Repeat the layers, finishing with a layer of lasagne. Top with the cheese sauce and sprinkle with the combined cheeses. Bake for 45 minutes, or until the pasta is soft.

NUTRITION PER SERVE: *Protein 35 g; Fat 35 g; Carbohydrate 65 g; Dietary Fibre 15 g; Cholesterol 95 mg; 2965 kJ (710 cal)*

ABOVE: Vegetable lasagne

FLAT-LEAF PARSLEY
Also known as Italian or continental parsley, the flat-leafed variety is stronger tasting than curly-leafed and more widely used as a flavouring agent. However, it is mild enough to use in quantity and so can be added to thicken dishes and also to temper other ingredients. The taste of the stems is more delicate and they can be used instead of the leaves for a milder flavour.

ABOVE: Chunky spaghetti napolitana

CHUNKY SPAGHETTI NAPOLITANA

Preparation time: 20 minutes
Total cooking time: 1 hour
Serves 6

★

2 tablespoons olive oil
1 onion, finely chopped
1 carrot, diced
1 celery stick, diced
500 g (1 lb) very ripe tomatoes
1/2 cup (125 ml/4 fl oz) white wine
2 teaspoons sugar
500 g (1 lb) spaghetti
1 tablespoon chopped fresh parsley
1 tablespoon chopped fresh oregano

1 Heat the oil in a heavy-based pan. Add the onion, carrot and celery, cover and cook for 10 minutes over low heat, stirring occasionally, taking care not to let the vegetables colour.
2 Chop the tomatoes and add to the vegetables with the wine and sugar. Bring the sauce to the boil, reduce the heat to low, cover and simmer for 45 minutes, stirring occasionally. Season with salt and freshly ground black pepper. If the sauce becomes too thick, add up to 3/4 cup (185 ml/6 fl oz) of water to thin it out.
3 About 15 minutes before serving time, cook the spaghetti in a large pan of rapidly boiling salted water until *al dente*. Drain and return to the pan. Pour two-thirds of the sauce over the pasta, add the parsley and oregano and gently toss. Serve in bowls or on a platter with the remaining sauce in a jug at the table.

NUTRITION PER SERVE: *Protein 10 g; Fat 7 g; Carbohydrate 65 g; Dietary Fibre 7 g; Cholesterol 0 mg; 1595 kJ (380 cal)*

SPAGHETTI WITH OLIVES AND CAPERS

Preparation time: 20 minutes
Total cooking time: 20 minutes
Serves 4

★

2/3 cup (170 ml/5 1/2 fl oz) extra virgin olive oil
1 1/2 cups (125 g/4 oz) fresh white breadcrumbs
3 cloves garlic, finely chopped
45 g (1 1/2 oz) can anchovies, drained and
   finely chopped, optional
300 g (10 oz) black olives, finely chopped
6 Roma (egg) tomatoes, peeled
   and chopped
2 tablespoons tiny capers
500 g (1 lb) spaghetti or spaghettini

1 Heat 2 tablespoons of the olive oil in a medium frying pan. Add the breadcrumbs and cook, stirring continuously, until golden brown and crispy. Remove from the pan and set aside to cool completely.
2 Add the remaining oil to the pan and heat for 1 minute. Add the garlic, anchovies and black olives and cook over medium heat for 30 seconds. Add the tomato and capers and cook for 3 minutes.
3 Cook the pasta in a large pan of rapidly boiling salted water until *al dente*. Drain and return to the pan. Add the tomato mixture and breadcrumbs and toss to combine. Serve immediately, with herbs as a garnish if you like.

NUTRITION PER SERVE: *Protein 25 g; Fat 45 g; Carbohydrate 11.5 g; Dietary Fibre 15 g; Cholesterol 10 mg; 4065 kJ (970 cal)*

CAPERS

Capers are the small, unripe bud of the caper bush. They are preserved in vinegar or salt and their piquant flavour makes them an ideal companion for fish and meat dishes. Salted ones have a more subtle flavour without vinegar overtones, but they need to have the salt rinsed off before use. Tiny capers have a finer flavour and a crunchier texture, but are more expensive because of the extra labour required for picking.

ABOVE: Spaghetti with olives and capers

125

4 While the pasta is cooking, heat the oil in a heavy-based frying pan. Cook the bacon and spring onion over medium heat, stirring occasionally, for 5 minutes. Add the basil, cream and salt and pepper, to taste, and simmer for 5 minutes. Add the tomato and cook for 2–3 minutes, or until heated through. Serve the sauce over the pasta.

NUTRITION PER SERVE: *Protein 15 g; Fat 25 g; Carbohydrate 65 g; Dietary Fibre 6 g; Cholesterol 80 mg; 2325 kJ (555 cal)*

FARFALLE WITH MUSHROOMS

Preparation time: 20 minutes
Total cooking time: 15 minutes
Serves 4

★

500 g (1 lb) farfalle
50 g (1 3/4 oz) butter
2 cloves garlic, thinly sliced
500 g (1 lb) button mushrooms, thinly sliced
2 tablespoons dry sherry
1/4 cup (60 ml/2 fl oz) chicken stock
1/3 cup (90 g/3 oz) sour cream
2 tablespoons fresh thyme leaves
2 tablespoons chopped fresh chives
2 tablespoons chopped fresh parsley
freshly grated Parmesan, for serving

1 Cook the farfalle in a large pan of rapidly boiling salted water until *al dente*. Drain and return to the pan.
2 While the pasta is cooking, melt the butter in a large frying pan, add the garlic and cook for 1 minute over medium heat.
3 Add the mushrooms and, when all the butter is absorbed, add the sherry, stock and sour cream. Stir to combine and bring to the boil. Reduce the heat and simmer for 4 minutes.
4 Add the mushroom sauce and herbs to the pasta and toss to combine. Serve sprinkled with grated Parmesan and maybe some cracked black pepper or seasoned pepper.

NUTRITION PER SERVE: *Protein 20 g; Fat 25 g; Carbohydrate 90 g; Dietary Fibre 10 g; Cholesterol 65 mg; 2790 kJ (665 cal)*

PENNE WITH CREAMY TOMATO SAUCE

Preparation time: 25 minutes
Total cooking time: 20 minutes
Serves 6

★

2 bacon rashers, optional
4 large ripe tomatoes
500 g (1 lb) penne
1 tablespoon olive oil
2 spring onions, chopped
2 tablespoons chopped fresh basil
1 1/4 cups (315 ml/10 fl oz) cream

1 Discard the bacon rind and cut the bacon into small pieces. Cut a small cross on the base of each tomato. Put in boiling water for 1–2 minutes and then plunge into cold water. Peel the skin down from the cross.
2 Cut the tomatoes in half and scoop out the seeds with a teaspoon. Finely chop the tomatoes.
3 Cook the pasta in a large pan of rapidly boiling salted water until *al dente*. Drain and keep warm.

ABOVE: Penne with creamy tomato sauce

RIGATONI WITH PUMPKIN SAUCE

Preparation time: 15 minutes
Total cooking time: 25 minutes
Serves 6

★

500 g (1 lb) rigatoni or large penne
1 kg (2 lb) pumpkin
2 leeks
30 g (1 oz) butter
1/2 teaspoon ground nutmeg
1 1/4 cups (315 ml/10 fl oz) cream
3 tablespoons pine nuts, toasted

1 Cook the pasta in a large pan of rapidly boiling salted water until *al dente*. Drain and return to the pan.
2 Peel the pumpkin, remove and discard the seeds and cut the pumpkin into small cubes. Wash the leeks thoroughly to remove all traces of grit and then slice very finely. Heat the butter in a large pan over low heat. Add the sliced leek, cover the pan and cook, stirring occasionally, for 5 minutes.
3 Add the pumpkin and nutmeg, cover and cook for 8 minutes. Add the cream and 3 tablespoons of water to the pumpkin and bring the sauce to the boil. Cook, stirring occasionally, for 8 minutes, or until the pumpkin is tender.
4 Divide the pasta among serving bowls and top with sauce. Sprinkle with pine nuts and serve immediately.

NOTE: Butternut or jap pumpkin will give the sweetest flavour to this sauce. To toast pine nuts, stir over low heat in a non-stick frying pan until lightly golden. Alternatively, spread on a baking tray and grill. Be sure to check frequently as they brown quickly.

NUTRITION PER SERVE: *Protein 15 g; Fat 35 g; Carbohydrate 70 g; Dietary Fibre 7 g; Cholesterol 85 mg; 2710 kJ (645 cal)*

BELOW: *Rigatoni with pumpkin sauce*

LINGUINE WITH RED PEPPER (CAPSICUM) SAUCE

Preparation time: 20 minutes
Total cooking time: 30 minutes
Serves 6

★

3 red peppers (capsicums)
3 tablespoons olive oil
1 large onion, sliced
2 cloves garlic, crushed
1/4–1/2 teaspoon chilli powder or flakes
1/2 cup (125 ml/4 oz) cream
2 tablespoons chopped fresh oregano
500 g (1 lb) linguine or spaghetti (plain or spinach)

1 Cut the red peppers into large flat pieces and discard the seeds and membrane. Place skin-side up, under a hot grill and cook for 8 minutes, or until black and blistered. Remove from the heat, cover with a damp tea towel and, when cool, peel away the skin and cut the flesh into thin strips.
2 Heat the oil in a large heavy-based pan. Add the onion and stir over low heat for 8 minutes, or until soft. Add the pepper strips, garlic, chilli and cream and cook for 2 minutes, stirring occasionally. Add the oregano and salt and pepper, to taste.
3 About 15 minutes before the sauce is cooked, cook the pasta in a large pan of rapidly boiling salted water until *al dente*. Drain and return to the pan. Add the sauce to the hot pasta and toss until well combined.
NOTE: If necessary, you can substitute dried oregano. Use about one-third of the quantity as dried herbs have a much stronger flavour. For a stronger red pepper flavour, just omit the cream.

NUTRITION PER SERVE: *Protein 10 g; Fat 20 g; Carbohydrate 65 g; Dietary Fibre 5 g; Cholesterol 30 mg; 2050 kJ (490 cal)*

FUSILLI WITH GREEN SAUCE

Preparation time: 10 minutes
Total cooking time: 15 minutes
Serves 6

★

500 g (1 lb) fusilli or spiral pasta
1 onion
2 zucchini (courgettes)
5–6 large silverbeet leaves
2 anchovies, optional
2 tablespoons olive oil
1 tablespoon capers
50 g (1 3/4 oz) butter
1/4 cup (60 ml/2 fl oz) white wine

1 Cook the pasta in a large pan of rapidly boiling salted water until *al dente*. Drain and return to the pan.
2 While the pasta is cooking, chop the onion very finely and grate the zucchini into fine pieces. Remove and discard the stalks from the silverbeet and chop or shred the leaves into small pieces. Roughly chop the anchovies, if using. Heat the olive oil and butter in a large heavy-based pan. Add the onion and zucchini and stir with a wooden spoon for 3 minutes over medium heat.
3 Add the anchovies, capers, wine and salt and pepper, to taste, to the pan and cook, stirring, for 2 minutes. Add the prepared silverbeet to the pan and cook for 1–2 minutes, or until the silverbeet has softened. Add the green sauce to the warm pasta and toss until well distributed through the sauce.
NOTE: If you prefer, you can use 500 g (1 lb) of English spinach instead of silverbeet. Cut the ends off and shred the leaves into small pieces.

NUTRITION PER SERVE: *Protein 10 g; Fat 15 g; Carbohydrate 60 g; Dietary Fibre 10 g; Cholesterol 20 mg; 1815 kJ (430 cal)*

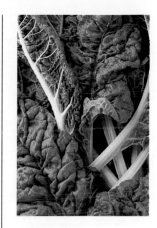

SILVERBEET
Silverbeet, also known as Swiss chard or seakale spinach, is unusual in that the stalks and leaves are used as separate vegetables. The white stalks or ribs have a sweet and nutty flavour. They are cut from the leaves, then rinsed and trimmed of the stringy outer membrane before being boiled or par-boiled for braising. Silverbeet leaves are tougher and less sweet than those of English spinach, but they can be used in fillings and stuffings and they are strong enough to roll up into parcels for baking or braising.

OPPOSITE PAGE:
Linguine with red pepper sauce (top); Fusilli with green sauce

MAKING FRESH BREADCRUMBS

Fresh breadcrumbs are easily made in a food processor. Discard the crusts, cut the bread into chunks and process until crumbed. For smaller, more even crumbs, simply grate frozen bread and use straight away. Don't use bread that is more than two days old as the flavour of some breads deteriorates with age and their crumbs will carry the stale taste into your dish.

ABOVE: Spaghetti with herbs and tomato

SPAGHETTI WITH HERBS AND TOMATO

Preparation time: 20 minutes
Total cooking time: 15 minutes
Serves 4

★

1/4 cup (20 g/3/4 oz) fresh breadcrumbs

500 g (1 lb) spaghetti

3 tablespoons olive oil

2 cloves garlic, diced

1 cup (30 g/1 oz) chopped fresh herbs
   (basil, coriander, parsley)

4 tomatoes, chopped

1/4 cup (30 g/1 oz) chopped walnuts

1/4 cup (25 g/3/4 oz) grated Parmesan, plus
   extra for serving

1 Heat the grill to medium and put the fresh breadcrumbs under for a few seconds, or until slightly golden.
2 Cook the spaghetti in boiling salted water until *al dente*, then drain.

3 Heat 2 tablespoons of the olive oil in a large frying pan and cook the garlic until soft.
4 Add the remaining oil and the herbs, tomato, walnuts and Parmesan. Add the pasta to the pan and toss for 1–2 minutes. Top with the breadcrumbs and extra Parmesan.

NUTRITION PER SERVE: *Protein 20 g; Fat 25 g; Carbohydrate 95 g; Dietary Fibre 9 g; Cholesterol 6 mg; 2825 kJ (620 cal)*

ON THE SIDE

WALDORF SALAD Combine in a bowl 3 cored and chopped red apples, 100 g (3½ oz) of toasted walnuts, 2 sliced sticks of celery, and 200 g (6½ oz) of black grapes. Remove the skin and bones from a barbecued chicken, finely shred the chicken flesh and add it to the salad. To make the dressing, combine 1 cup (250 g/8 oz) whole egg mayonnaise, ¼ cup (60 g/2 oz) of natural yoghurt and 1 teaspoon of mild curry powder. Fold through the salad just before serving.

FETTUCINE PRIMAVERA

Preparation time: 35 minutes
Total cooking time: 15 minutes
Serves 6

☆

500 g (1 lb) fettucine
155 g (5 oz) fresh asparagus spears
1 cup (155 g/5 oz) frozen (or fresh)
   broad beans
30 g (1 oz) butter
1 celery stick, sliced
1 cup (155 g/5 oz) peas
1 1/4 cups (315 ml/10 fl oz) cream
1/2 cup (50 g/1 3/4 oz) freshly grated Parmesan

1 Cook the pasta in a large pan of rapidly boiling salted water until *al dente*. Drain and return to the pan.
2 While the pasta is cooking, cut the asparagus into small pieces. Bring a pan of water to the boil, add the asparagus and cook for 2 minutes. Using a slotted spoon, remove the asparagus from the pan and plunge the pieces into a bowl of ice cold water.
3 Add the broad beans to the pan of boiling water. Remove immediately and cool in cold water. Drain, then peel and discard any rough outside skin. If fresh broad beans are used, cook them for 2–5 minutes or until tender. If the beans are young, the skin can be left on, but old beans should be peeled.
4 Heat the butter in a heavy-based frying pan. Add the celery and stir for 2 minutes. Add the peas and the cream and cook gently for 3 minutes. Add the asparagus, broad beans, Parmesan, and salt and pepper, to taste. Bring the sauce to the boil and cook for 1 minute. Add the sauce to the cooked fettucine and toss well to combine.
NOTE: In this classic dish, any vegetables, usually spring vegetables, may be used. Choose your favourite such as leeks, zucchini, beans, sugar snap peas or snowpeas.

NUTRITION PER SERVE: *Protein 20 g; Fat 10 g; Carbohydrate 95 g; Dietary Fibre 10 g; Cholesterol 5 mg; 2295 kJ (545 cal)*

ON THE SIDE

BEETROOT AND NECTARINE SALAD Boil, steam or microwave 2 bunches of trimmed baby beetroot until tender. Drain and allow to cool before cutting into quarters. Cut 4 fresh nectarines into thick wedges. Combine the beetroot, nectarines, 2 tablespoons of toasted sunflower seeds and 2 tablespoons of fresh chervil leaves. Make up a dressing by mixing together 1 tablespoon of wholegrain mustard, 2 tablespoons of raspberry vinegar, 2 tablespoons of honey, 3 tablespoons of natural yoghurt and 3 tablespoons of oil. Drizzle the dressing over the salad just before serving.

WARM BROCCOLI FLORETS WITH ALMONDS Cook broccoli florets until tender, then refresh in iced water, sprinkle with toasted flaked almonds and drizzle with a dressing made by mixing together melted butter, crushed garlic and lemon juice.

ABOVE: Fettucine primavera

CHICKPEAS
Chickpeas, garbanzos or ceci originated in the Mediterranean regions and are particularly popular today in Spain, southern Italy and North Africa. Their nut-like taste makes them highly suitable for blending with other flavours and their crunchy texture works well in salads. Chickpea flour (besan) is used in both sweet and savoury pastry making. Dried chickpeas must be soaked overnight before use. Canned, pre-cooked chickpeas are a time-saving alternative.

PENNE WITH PUMPKIN AND CINNAMON SAUCE

Preparation time: 25 minutes
Total cooking time: 30 minutes
Serves 4

★

340 g (11 oz) pumpkin
500 g (1 lb) penne
25 g (³/₄ oz) butter
1 onion, finely chopped
2 cloves garlic, crushed
1 teaspoon ground cinnamon
1 cup (250 ml/8 fl oz) cream
1 tablespoon honey
¹/₃ cup (35 g/1¹/₄ oz) freshly grated Parmesan
chopped fresh chives, to garnish

1 Peel the pumpkin, remove the seeds and cut the flesh into small cubes. Boil, steam or microwave the pumpkin until just tender. Drain well.
2 Cook the penne in a large pan of rapidly boiling salted water until *al dente*. Drain and return to the pan.
3 While the pasta is cooking, melt the butter in a frying pan and cook the onion over medium heat until soft and golden. Add the garlic and cinnamon and cook for another minute.
4 Pour the cream into the pan, add the pumpkin and the honey and simmer for 5 minutes, until the sauce reduces and thickens slightly and is heated through.
5 Add the Parmesan and stir until it has melted. Season, to taste, with salt and freshly ground black pepper. Pour the sauce over the penne and toss until well combined. Serve sprinkled with chopped fresh chives.

NUTRITION PER SERVE: *Protein 20 g; Fat 35 g; Carbohydrate 105 g; Dietary Fibre 10 g; Cholesterol 110 mg; 3465 kJ (830 cal)*

CONCHIGLIE WITH CHICKPEAS

Preparation time: 15 minutes
Total cooking time: 20 minutes
Serves 4

★

500 g (1 lb) conchiglie (pasta shells)
2 tablespoons extra virgin olive oil
1 red (Spanish) onion, finely sliced
2–3 cloves garlic, crushed
425 g (14 oz) can chickpeas
¹/₂ cup (75 g/2¹/₂ oz) sun-dried tomatoes, drained and thinly sliced
1 teaspoon finely grated lemon rind
1 teaspoon chopped fresh red chilli
2 tablespoons lemon juice
1 tablespoon chopped fresh oregano leaves
1 tablespoon finely chopped fresh parsley
fresh Parmesan shavings, for serving

1 Cook the conchiglie in a large pan of rapidly boiling salted water until *al dente*. Drain and return to the pan.
2 While the pasta is cooking, heat the oil in a frying pan, add the onion and cook until soft and lightly golden.
3 Add the garlic to the pan and cook for another minute. Add the rinsed and drained chickpeas, sun-dried tomato, lemon rind and chopped chilli and cook over high heat until heated through. Stir in the lemon juice along with the chopped fresh herbs.
4 Toss the chickpea mixture through the pasta. Season with salt and pepper, to taste, and serve immediately, scattered with Parmesan shavings.

NUTRITION PER SERVE: *Protein 40 g; Fat 20 g; Carbohydrate 145 g; Dietary Fibre 25 g; Cholesterol 2 mg; 3725 kJ (890 cal)*

OPPOSITE PAGE:
Penne with pumpkin and cinnamon sauce (top);
Conchiglie with chickpeas

OLIVES
The sour, pungent taste of these shiny black, green or brown fruits makes a vital contribution to the flavour, not only of the myriad Mediterranean dishes with which we associate them, but many others as well.

OLIVES

The olive tree is the oldest cultivated tree. It originated in Africa and Asia Minor and has been grown in the Mediterranean for over 6,000 years. An olive tree takes five years to bear fruit, but its life span is usually over 100 years. Known as a symbol of longevity, it is able to withstand harsh climates. The olive branch has long been used as a symbol of peace. Black and green olives come from the same tree, green is merely the unripe fruit. To preserve your own fresh olives, soak 1 kg (2 lb) of fresh black olives in a bucket of cold water for 6 weeks, draining and replacing the water every second day. After 6 weeks, drain the olives in a large colander and cover completely with rock salt. Set aside for 2 days. Rinse and set aside to dry thoroughly. Layer the olives in sterilised jars with slivers of preserved lemon skin, slivers of garlic, coriander seeds and sprigs of lemon thyme. Cover with a mixture of half oil and half white wine vinegar. Seal; set aside for 2 weeks. Store in a cool dark place for up to 6 months.

SAUTÉED BLACK OLIVES

Soak 500 g (1 lb) wrinkled cured black olives in warm water overnight. Rinse and drain. Heat 3 tablespoons of oil in a large frying pan, add 1 sliced onion and cook over medium heat for 2 minutes. Add the olives and cook for 10 minutes, or until soft. Remove the olives and onion with a slotted spoon and drain in a colander. Add several sprigs of oregano, toss and cool completely. Transfer to a sterilised jar. Refrigerate up to 3 weeks.

NUTRITION PER 100 G: *Protein 0 g; Fat 25 g; Carbohydrate 1 g; Dietary Fibre 0 g; Cholesterol 0 mg; 770 kJ (185 cal)*

CHILLI GARLIC OLIVES

Rinse and drain 500 g (1 lb) of brined Kalamata olives. Make a small incision in the side of each olive. Layer the olives in a sterilised jar with fine strips of orange rind, 1 teaspoon of chilli flakes, 4 halved small red chillies, 2 finely sliced cloves of garlic and 4 sprigs of rosemary. Combine 2 tablespoons of lemon juice with 1 cup (250 ml/8 fl oz) of olive oil and pour it over the olives. Add extra olive oil to cover, if necessary. Cover and marinate in a cool dark place for 2 weeks.

NUTRITION PER 100 G: *Protein 0 g; Fat 40 g; Carbohydrate 1 g; Dietary Fibre 0 g; Cholesterol 0 mg; 1380 kJ (330 cal)*

OLIVE AND TOMATO TAPENADE

Soak 3 anchovy fillets in milk for 10 minutes. Rinse and drain. Roughly chop the anchovies, 1 cup (155 g/5 oz) of pitted black Niçoise olives, 2 garlic cloves, 2 tablespoons chopped capers and the rind of 1 lemon in a food processor for a few seconds. Transfer to a bowl, add ½ cup (80 g/2¾ oz) chopped sun-dried tomato, 2 tablespoons lemon juice, 1 tablespoon of chopped parsley and 2 tablespoons of extra virgin olive oil. Serve on sliced woodfired Italian bread.

NUTRITION PER 100 G: *Protein 2 g; Fat 15 g; Carbohydrate 2 g; Dietary Fibre 1 g; Cholesterol 3 mg; 620 kJ (145 cal)*

ABOVE, FROM TOP LEFT: Preserved fresh olives; Sautéed black olives; Chilli garlic olives; Olive and tomato tapenade

SPAGHETTI SIRACUSANI

Preparation time: 15 minutes
Total cooking time: 1 hour
Serves 6

★

1 large green pepper (capsicum)

2 tablespoons olive oil

2 cloves garlic, crushed

2 x 425 g (14 oz) cans crushed tomatoes

2 zucchini (courgettes), chopped

2 anchovy fillets, chopped, optional

1 tablespoon capers, chopped

1/4 cup (35 g/1 1/4 oz) black olives, pitted
   and halved

2 tablespoons chopped fresh basil leaves

500 g (1 lb) spaghetti or linguine

1/2 cup (50 g/1 3/4 oz) freshly grated Parmesan,
   for serving

*BELOW: Spaghetti
siracusani*

1 Remove the membrane and seeds from the green pepper. Slice the flesh into thin strips. Heat the oil in a large deep pan. Add the garlic and stir for 30 seconds over low heat. Add 1/2 cup (125 ml/4 fl oz) of water along with the green pepper, tomato, zucchini, anchovies, if using, capers and olives. Cook for 20 minutes, stirring occasionally. Stir in the basil and salt and pepper, to taste.

3 While the sauce is cooking, cook the pasta in a large pan of rapidly boiling salted water until *al dente*. Drain. Serve the sauce over the pasta. Sprinkle with Parmesan.

NUTRITION PER SERVE: *Protein 15 g; Fat 10 g; Carbohydrate 65 g; Dietary Fibre 10 g; Cholesterol 10 mg; 1790 kJ (430 cal)*

ON THE SIDE

WARM GINGER AND SESAME CARROT SALAD Scrub or peel 500 g (1 lb) of baby carrots and steam or microwave until just tender. Transfer to a bowl, add 1 tablespoon honey, 1/4 teaspoon of ground ginger, 50 g (1 3/4 oz) of melted butter, 1 teaspoon of lemon thyme leaves and 1 tablespoon of toasted sesame seeds. Toss lightly to coat and serve immediately.

FETTUCINE BOSCAIOLA
(FETTUCINE WITH MUSHROOM AND TOMATO SAUCE)

Preparation time: *20 minutes*
Total cooking time: *25 minutes*
Serves 6

☆

500 g (1 lb) button mushrooms

1 large onion

2 tablespoons olive oil

2 cloves garlic, finely chopped

2 x 425 g (14 oz) cans tomatoes,
   roughly chopped

500 g (1 lb) fettucine

2 tablespoons chopped fresh parsley

1 Carefully wipe the mushrooms with a damp paper towel and then slice finely, including the stems.
2 Chop the onion roughly. Heat the oil in a heavy-based frying pan and cook the onion and garlic over medium heat, stirring occasionally, for about 6 minutes, or until the vegetables are light golden. Add the tomato including the juice, along with the mushrooms, to the pan and bring the mixture to the boil. Reduce the heat, cover the pan and simmer for 15 minutes.
3 While the sauce is cooking, cook the fettucine in a large pan of rapidly boiling salted water until *al dente*. Drain and return to the pan.
4 Stir the parsley into the sauce and season well with salt and pepper, to taste. Toss the sauce through the pasta.
NOTE: If you would like a creamy sauce, add ½ cup (125 ml/4 fl oz) of cream when adding the parsley (do not reboil or it may curdle).

NUTRITION PER SERVE: *Protein 15 g; Fat 10 g; Carbohydrate 65 g; Dietary Fibre 10 g; Cholesterol 0 mg; 1640 kJ (390 cal)*

BUTTON MUSHROOMS
Cultivated button mushrooms would have to be the most widely used mushroom today. Because of their mild flavour, clean colour and appearance, and compact size, they are suited to most cooking styles. As well as being good for flavouring sauces and fillings, they can be eaten raw. As they mature, their caps partially open and become known as cup or cap mushrooms. These taste stronger and have more visible and browner gills. Cap mushrooms complement foods of a robust nature and make rich sauces when sautéed in butter or cooked with red wine.

ABOVE: Fettucine boscaiola

BLUE CHEESE AND BROCCOLI WITH RIGATONI

Preparation time: 15 minutes
Total cooking time: 15 minutes
Serves 4

☆

500 g (1 lb) rigatoni
500 g (1 lb) broccoli
1 tablespoon vegetable oil
1 onion, sliced
1/2 cup (125 ml/4 fl oz) dry white wine
1 cup (250 ml/8 fl oz) cream
1/2 teaspoon spicy paprika
150 g (5 oz) blue Brie, chopped
  into small pieces
2 tablespoons flaked almonds, toasted

1 Cook the rigatoni in a large pan of rapidly boiling salted water until *al dente*. Drain and return to the pan.
2 Cut the broccoli into florets, steam or microwave them for 2–3 minutes, until tender, and drain well.
3 Heat the oil in a large pan and fry the onion until soft. Add the wine and cream and simmer for 4–5 minutes, until reduced and thickened slightly. Stir in the paprika and cheese, and season with salt and pepper, to taste.
4 Add the broccoli and sauce to the pasta and gently toss over low heat until well mixed and heated through. Serve sprinkled with the toasted, flaked almonds.
NOTE: You can use a stronger blue cheese, such as gorgonzola, if you like.

NUTRITION PER SERVE: *Protein 30 g; Fat 50 g; Carbohydrate 95 g; Dietary Fibre 15 g; Cholesterol 120 mg; 4005 kJ (955 cal)*

ON THE SIDE

CRISPY ZUCCHINI RIBBONS

Using a sharp vegetable peeler, cut large zucchinis into ribbons by running the peeler along them horizontally. Lightly coat the ribbons firstly in beaten egg, then in a mixture of dried breadcrumbs, finely grated Parmesan and some chopped fresh herbs. Deep-fry the ribbons, in batches, in hot oil until crisp and golden brown. Serve with a tangy tomato salsa.

PUMPKIN AND PINE NUT TAGLIATELLE

Preparation time: 25 minutes
Total cooking time: 25 minutes
Serves 4

☆

30 g (1 oz) butter
1 large onion, chopped
2 cloves garlic, crushed
1 1/2 cups (375 ml/12 fl oz) vegetable stock
750 g (1 1/2 lb) butternut pumpkin, peeled
  and chopped into small pieces
1/4 teaspoon ground nutmeg
1/2 teaspoon freshly ground black pepper
1 cup (250 ml/8 fl oz) cream
500 g (1 lb) fresh tagliatelle
1/2 cup (80 g/2 3/4 oz) pine nuts, toasted
2 tablespoons chopped fresh chives
freshly grated Parmesan, for serving

1 Melt the butter in a large pan. Add the onion and cook for 3 minutes, or until soft and golden. Add the garlic and cook for another minute. Stir in the vegetable stock and add the pumpkin. Bring to the boil, reduce the heat slightly and cook until the pumpkin is tender.
2 Reduce the heat to very low and season with the nutmeg and pepper. Stir in the cream until just warmed through; do not boil. Transfer to a food processor and process for about 30 seconds, until the mixture forms a smooth sauce.
3 Meanwhile, cook the tagliatelle in a large pan of rapidly boiling salted water until *al dente*. Drain and return to the pan.
4 Return the sauce to the pan and gently reheat. Add to the pasta with the pine nuts and toss well. Serve sprinkled with chives and offer Parmesan in a separate bowl. Pictured garnished with bay leaves.
NOTE: To toast pine nuts, stir over low heat in a non-stick frying pan until lightly golden.

NUTRITION PER SERVE: *Protein 25 g; Fat 50 g; Carbohydrate 105 g; Dietary Fibre 10 g; Cholesterol 110 mg; 4115 kJ (980 cal)*

PINE NUTS
These are small, elongated, creamy white kernels taken from the nuts of pine trees, in particular the Pinon and Stone pines. Sometimes these trees are called parasol pines because of their umbrella shape, and they typify the Mediterranean landscape, where they are native. The nuts are always sold shelled and blanched, and their flavour can be enhanced by toasting or roasting them before use. Pine nuts are used in dessert and sweet making as well as in savoury dishes.

OPPOSITE PAGE: Blue cheese and broccoli with rigatoni (top); Pumpkin and pine nut tagliatelle

CHERRY TOMATOES

Cherry tomatoes come in a number of varieties including Red Currant, Green Grape, Sweet 100 and Yellow Pear. All are perfect for use in salads and some, such as the Sweet 100, can withstand quick cooking. They are all low in acid and can be extremely sweet. At approximately 5 mm (1/4 inch) diameter, Red Currant is the smallest and is often displayed for sale in loose clusters.

SPICY PENNE WITH PEPPERS (CAPSICUMS)

Preparation time: 30 minutes
Total cooking time: 12 minutes
Serves 4

★

1 large red pepper (capsicum)
1 large green pepper (capsicum)
1 large yellow pepper (capsicum)
500 g (1 lb) penne
1/3 cup (80 ml/2¾ fl oz) olive oil
2 tablespoons sweet chilli sauce
1 tablespoon red wine vinegar
1/3 cup (20 g/¾ oz) chopped fresh coriander
250 g (8 oz) cherry tomatoes, halved
freshly grated Parmesan, for serving

1 Cut the peppers into large flat pieces, and discard the seeds and membrane. Cook skin-side-up under a hot grill for 8 minutes, or until the skin is black and blistered. Remove from the heat and cover with a damp tea towel. When cool, peel away the skin and cut the pepper flesh into thin strips.
2 Meanwhile, cook the penne in a large pan of rapidly boiling salted water until *al dente*. Drain and return to the pan.
3 While the penne is cooking, whisk together the oil, chilli sauce and red wine vinegar, and season with salt and pepper, to taste.
4 Add the oil mixture, fresh coriander, peppers and cherry tomatoes to the pasta. Serve sprinkled with Parmesan.
NOTE: This dish can be served warm as a main meal, or at room temperature as a salad. It makes an excellent accompaniment to chicken or barbecued meat.

NUTRITION PER SERVE: *Protein 20 g; Fat 25 g; Carbohydrate 95 g; Dietary Fibre 10 g; Cholesterol 5 mg; 2795 kJ (665 cal)*

FETTUCINE WITH SNOW PEAS (MANGETOUT) AND WALNUTS

Preparation time: 30 minutes
Total cooking time: 15 minutes
Serves 4

★

500 g (1 lb) fettucine or linguine
1/2 cup (60 g/2 oz) chopped walnuts
30 g (1 oz) butter
1 large onion, chopped
4 bacon rashers, chopped, optional
1 clove garlic, crushed
3/4 cup (185 ml/6 fl oz) dry white wine
1 cup (250 ml/8 fl oz) cream
250 g (8 oz) snow peas (mangetout), cut into pieces

1 Cook the fettucine in a large pan of rapidly boiling salted water until *al dente*. Drain and return to the pan.
2 While the pasta is cooking, scatter the walnuts on a foil-lined grill tray. Cook under a moderately hot grill for 2 minutes, or until lightly toasted. Stir after 1 minute, and be careful they don't burn. Set aside to cool.
3 Melt the butter in a large pan. Add the onion and bacon and cook until the onion is soft and the bacon lightly browned. Add the garlic and cook for another minute.
4 Pour in the white wine and cream, bring to the boil and reduce the heat. Simmer for 4 minutes, add the snow peas and simmer for another minute. Toss the sauce and walnuts through the pasta. Season with salt and pepper, to taste.
NOTE: Don't be tempted to save time by not toasting the nuts. Raw nuts may be bitter and stale in flavour, particularly if they are old, or have been kept in the refrigerator.

NUTRITION PER SERVE: *Protein 30 g; Fat 45 g; Carbohydrate 95 g; Dietary Fibre 10 g; Cholesterol 125 mg; 3930 kJ (940 cal)*

OPPOSITE PAGE: Spicy penne with peppers (top); Fettucine with snow peas and walnuts

WALNUTS

Walnuts are encased in a hard, round shell, with two distinct halves. The nut inside consists of two deeply ridged, creamy-white lobes of mild-flavoured flesh. Chopped walnuts are used in pasta sauces as well as fruit cakes, salads and biscuits. Walnuts in their shells can be refrigerated for up to 6 months. Shelled nuts should be bought in airtight containers or cans and stored, after opening, in a glass, airtight jar in the refrigerator.

ABOVE: Tagliatelle with tomato and walnuts

TAGLIATELLE WITH TOMATO AND WALNUTS

Preparation time: 20 minutes
Total cooking time: 45 minutes
Serves 6

★

4 very ripe tomatoes

1 carrot

2 tablespoons oil

1 onion, finely chopped

1 celery stick, finely chopped

2 tablespoons chopped fresh parsley

1 teaspoon red wine vinegar

1/4 cup (60 ml/2 fl oz) white wine

500 g (1 lb) tagliatelle or fettucine

3/4 cup (90 g/3 oz) walnuts, roughly chopped

1/3 cup (35 g/1 1/4 oz) freshly grated Parmesan, for serving

1 Score a small cross on the base of each tomato. Place in a bowl of boiling water for 1–2 minutes and then plunge into cold water. Peel the skin down from the cross and roughly chop the flesh. Peel and grate the carrot.
2 Heat 1 tablespoon of the oil in a large heavy-based pan and cook the onion and celery for 5 minutes over low heat, stirring regularly. Add the tomato, carrot, parsley and combined vinegar and wine. Reduce the heat and simmer for 25 minutes. Season with salt and pepper.
3 About 15 minutes before the sauce is ready, cook the pasta in a large pan of rapidly boiling water until *al dente*. Drain and return to the pan. Add the sauce to the pasta and toss.
4 Before the sauce is cooked, heat the remaining oil in a frying pan, add the chopped walnuts and stir over low heat for 5 minutes. Serve the pasta and sauce topped with walnuts and sprinkled with Parmesan.

NUTRITION PER SERVE: *Protein 15 g; Fat 20 g; Carbohydrate 65 g; Dietary Fibre 10 g; Cholesterol 5 mg; 2105 kJ (500 cal)*

TORTELLINI WITH EGGPLANT (AUBERGINE)

Preparation time: 10 minutes
Total cooking time: 20 minutes
Serves 4

☆

500 g (1 lb) fresh cheese and
    spinach tortellini
1/4 cup (60 ml/2 fl oz) oil
2 cloves garlic, crushed
1 red pepper (capsicum), cut into
    small squares
500 g (1 lb) eggplant (aubergine), cut into
    small cubes
425 g (14 oz) can crushed tomatoes
1 cup (250 ml/8 fl oz) vegetable stock
1/2 cup (125 ml/4 fl oz) chopped fresh basil

1 Cook the tortellini in a large pan of rapidly boiling salted water until *al dente*. Drain and return to the pan.
2 While the pasta is cooking, heat the oil in a large pan, add the garlic and red pepper and stir over medium heat for 1 minute.
3 Add the cubed eggplant to the pan and stir gently over medium heat for 5 minutes, or until lightly browned.
4 Add the undrained tomato and vegetable stock to the pan. Stir and bring to the boil. Reduce the heat to low, cover the pan and cook for 10 minutes, or until the vegetables are tender. Add the basil and pasta and stir until mixed through.
NOTE: Cut the eggplant just before using. It turns brown when exposed to the air.

NUTRITION PER SERVE: *Protein 20 g; Fat 15 g; Carbohydrate 100 g; Dietary Fibre 10 g; Cholesterol 0 mg; 2555 kJ (610 cal)*

TORTELLINI

Once, an innkeeper, a local gastronome, had the good fortune of being host to the goddess Venus. Overtaken with curiosity, he couldn't help taking a peek at her through the keyhole of her door. One look at her bellybutton, surrounded by the outline of the keyhole, was enough to inspire him to rush to his kitchen and create something in its image —the tortellini. This tale reflects the love the citizens of Bologna have for one of their most famous pastas.

ABOVE: Tortellini with eggplant

CREAMY PASTA

Pasta and cream, a culinary marriage made in heaven. There are times when only the best will do... when only a bowl of fresh tagliatelle, tossed in a rich creamy sauce and topped with Parmesan shavings and cracked black pepper will satisfy your hunger for a taste of decadence. Traditionally, the long thin pastas are served with cream sauces, but these days, the possibilities are limitless.

FUSILLI WITH BROAD BEAN SAUCE

Preparation time: 30 minutes
Total cooking time: 25 minutes
Serves 6

⭐

2 cups (310 g/10 oz) frozen broad beans
4 bacon rashers
2 leeks
2 tablespoons olive oil
1¼ cups (315 ml/10 fl oz) cream
2 teaspoons grated lemon rind
500 g (1 lb) fusilli or penne

1 Plunge the broad beans into a pan of boiling water. Remove, drain and plunge immediately in cold water. Drain again and allow to cool before peeling (see note) and discard any rough outside skin.
2 Remove and discard the bacon rind. Chop the bacon into small pieces. Wash the leeks thoroughly to remove any dirt and grit and slice finely.
3 Heat the oil in a heavy-based frying pan. Add the leek and bacon and cook over medium heat, stirring occasionally, for 8 minutes, or until the leek is golden. Add the cream and lemon rind, bring to the boil, reduce the heat and simmer until the sauce thickens and coats the back of a spoon. Add the broad beans and season with salt and pepper, to taste.
4 While the sauce is simmering, cook the pasta in a large pan of rapidly boiling salted water until *al dente*. Drain and return to the pan.
5 Add the sauce to the pasta and toss well to combine. Serve at once in warmed pasta bowls.
NOTE: Broad beans can be cooked and peeled in advance and refrigerated in a covered container until needed. To peel them, slit or break off the top and squeeze the beans out. Leaving the hard outside skin on the broad bean will change the delicate texture and flavour of this dish so it is worth the extra effort of peeling them.
Fresh broad beans can also be used. If very young, leave the skin on. Old beans should be peeled before cooking. Cook for 15 minutes and then add to the dish.

NUTRITION PER SERVE: *Protein 20 g; Fat 30 g; Carbohydrate 60 g; Dietary Fibre 10 g; Cholesterol 85 mg; 2575 kJ (615 cal)*

ON THE SIDE

WARM SPRING VEGETABLE SALAD Lightly blanch some baby carrots, broccoli, snow peas (mangetout), beans, squash and baby corn in boiling water until just tender. Drain and toss through some chopped fresh herbs and some melted butter and honey mustard.

GREEK SALAD Mix together 1 red (Spanish) onion, cut into thin wedges, 1 red, yellow and green pepper (capsicum), all chopped, 200 g (6½ oz) of halved cherry tomatoes, 50 g (1¾ oz) of marinated black olives, 2 thickly sliced Lebanese cucumbers and 200 g (6½ oz) of feta broken into large pieces. Top with a dressing of 2 crushed cloves of garlic, 1 tablespoon of red wine vinegar and 3 tablespoons of olive oil.

ABOVE: Fusilli with broad bean sauce

TAGLIATELLE WITH CHICKEN LIVERS AND CREAM

Preparation time: 20 minutes
Total cooking time: 15 minutes
Serves 4

⭐

375 g (12 oz) tagliatelle
300 g (10 oz) chicken livers
2 tablespoons olive oil
1 onion, finely chopped
1 clove garlic, crushed
1 cup (250 ml/8 fl oz) cream
1 tablespoon snipped fresh chives
1 teaspoon seeded mustard
2 eggs, beaten
freshly grated Parmesan and some snipped
    chives, for serving

1 Cook the tagliatelle in a large pan of rapidly boiling salted water until *al dente*. Drain and return to the pan.
2 While the pasta is cooking, trim the chicken livers and slice. Heat the oil in a large frying pan. Add the onion and garlic and stir over low heat until the onion is tender.
3 Add the chicken livers to the pan and cook gently for 2–3 minutes. Remove from the heat and stir in the cream, chives, mustard, and salt and pepper, to taste. Return to the heat and bring to the boil. Add the beaten eggs and stir quickly to combine. Remove from the heat.
4 Add the sauce to the hot pasta and toss well to combine. Serve sprinkled with Parmesan and snipped chives.

NUTRITION PER SERVE: *Protein 35 g; Fat 50 g; Carbohydrate 70 g; Dietary Fibre 5 g; Cholesterol 575 mg; 3675 kJ (880 cal)*

MUSTARD
The condiment mustard is made by blending mustard seeds, sometimes ground, with vinegar or wine, food acid, salt and aromatic herbs and spices. The seeds come from various species of the mustard plant and have differing strengths, colours and sizes. Mustard powder is a mix of ground mustard seeds and wheat flour, often flavoured with turmeric and other spices.

ABOVE: Tagliatelle with chicken livers and cream

PENNE WITH CHICKEN AND MUSHROOMS

Preparation time: 30 minutes
Total cooking time: 25 minutes
Serves 4

⭐

30 g (1 oz) butter
1 tablespoon olive oil
1 onion, sliced
1 clove garlic, crushed
60 g (2 oz) prosciutto, chopped
250 g (8 oz) chicken thigh fillets, trimmed
   and sliced
125 g (4 oz) mushrooms, sliced
1 tomato, peeled, halved and sliced
1 tablespoon tomato paste (tomato purée,
   double concentrate)
1/2 cup (125 ml/4 fl oz) white wine
1 cup (250 ml/8 fl oz) cream
500 g (1 lb) penne
freshly grated Parmesan, for serving

1 Heat the butter and oil in a large frying pan. Add the onion and garlic and stir over low heat until the onion is tender. Add the prosciutto to the pan and fry until crisp.
2 Add the chicken and cook over medium heat for 3 minutes. Add the mushrooms and cook for another 2 minutes. Add the tomato and tomato paste and stir until combined. Stir in the wine and bring to the boil. Reduce the heat and simmer until the liquid is reduced by half.
3 Stir in the cream and salt and pepper, to taste, and bring to the boil. Reduce the heat and simmer until the sauce begins to thicken.
4 While the sauce is cooking, cook the penne in a large pan of rapidly boiling salted water until *al dente*. Drain well and return to the pan. Add the sauce to the pasta and toss to combine. Serve immediately, sprinkled with Parmesan.
NOTE: If you prefer, you can use chicken mince in this recipe instead of the sliced chicken thigh fillets.

NUTRITION PER SERVE: *Protein 35 g; Fat 45 g; Carbohydrate 95 g; Dietary Fibre 10 g; Cholesterol 145 mg; 3980 kJ (950 cal)*

RIGATONI WITH SAUSAGE AND PARMESAN

Preparation time: 15 minutes
Total cooking time: 15 minutes
Serves 4

⭐

2 tablespoons olive oil
1 onion, sliced
1 clove garlic, crushed
500 g (1 lb) Italian pork sausage, cut
   into chunks
60 g (2 oz) mushrooms, sliced
1/2 cup (125 ml/4 fl oz) dry white wine
500 g (1 lb) rigatoni
1 cup (250 ml/8 fl oz) cream
2 eggs
1/2 cup (50 g/1 3/4 oz) freshly grated Parmesan
2 tablespoons chopped fresh parsley

1 Heat the oil in a large frying pan. Add the onion and garlic and stir over low heat until the onion is tender. Add the sausage and mushroom and cook until the sausage is cooked through. Stir in the wine and bring to the boil. Reduce the heat and simmer until the liquid is reduced by half.
2 While the sauce is cooking, cook the rigatoni in a large pan of rapidly boiling salted water until *al dente*. Drain and return to the pan.
3 In a large jug, whisk together the cream, eggs, half the Parmesan, the parsley and salt and pepper, to taste. Add to the rigatoni with the sausage mixture and toss. Serve sprinkled with the remaining Parmesan.
NOTE: You can freeze leftover wine for use in recipes such as this one. You can use salami instead of Italian pork sausage.

NUTRITION PER SERVE: *Protein 40 g; Fat 85 g; Carbohydrate 90 g; Dietary Fibre 5 g; Cholesterol 295 mg; 5585 kJ (1335 cal)*

BLACK PEPPER
Peppercorns are the berry of the tropical vine *Piper nigrum*. They are green and soft when immature, and red or yellow when ripe. Black peppercorns are picked when ripe then sun-dried, which gives them their hard, black, wrinkled appearance. These have the strongest flavour and aroma. Peppercorns lose their sharpness once ground, and it is recommended to keep them whole and grind just before use.

OPPOSITE PAGE: Penne with chicken and mushrooms (top); Rigatoni with sausage and parmesan

BUCATINI WITH GORGONZOLA SAUCE

Preparation time: 10 minutes
Total cooking time: 20 minutes
Serves 6

★

375 g (12 oz) bucatini or spaghetti
200 g (6½ oz) gorgonzola cheese
20 g (¾ oz) butter
1 celery stick, chopped
1¼ cups (315 ml/10 fl oz) cream
250 g (8 oz) fresh ricotta cheese, beaten until smooth

1 Cook the pasta in a large pan of rapidly boiling salted water until *al dente*. Drain and return to the pan.
2 While the pasta is cooking, chop the gorgonzola cheese into small cubes.
3 Heat the butter in a medium pan, add the celery and stir for 2 minutes. Add the cream, ricotta and gorgonzola and season, to taste, with freshly ground black pepper.

4 Bring to the boil over low heat, stirring constantly, and then simmer for 1 minute. Add the sauce to the warm pasta and toss well.

NUTRITION PER SERVE: *Protein 20 g; Fat 40 g; Carbohydrate 45 g; Dietary Fibre 5 g; Cholesterol 135 mg; 2690 kJ (640 cal)*

ON THE SIDE

KUMERA, YOGHURT AND DILL SALAD Boil, steam or microwave 1 kg (2 lb) of peeled and thickly sliced sweet potato until just tender. Transfer to a bowl and cool slightly before adding 1 red (Spanish) onion, cut into thin wedges, 200 g (6½ oz) of natural yoghurt and plenty of chopped fresh dill, to your taste.

TOMATO AND FETA SALAD Slice egg (Roma) tomatoes in half lengthways and roast in a slow 150°C (300°F/Gas 2) oven until sweet and tender. Arrange on a platter, top with crumbled feta cheese, sliced anchovies and some fresh oregano leaves. Drizzle with olive oil.

GORGONZOLA CHEESE Gorgonzola is an Italian blue-veined cheese. It is creamy and sweet when young, and sharp, strong and slightly crumbly when mature. As well as being a delicious table cheese which goes well with apples and pears, it is a good companion for cooked vegetables and meats. It melts well when heated and makes a rich, mellow flavouring for cream-based sauces. It can be replaced by a creamy mild blue-vein such as Blue Castello, or half Blue Castello and half Danish Blue for a stronger taste.

RIGHT: Bucatini with gorgonzola sauce

FETTUCINE WITH CREAMY MUSHROOM AND BEAN SAUCE

Preparation time: 20 minutes
Total cooking time: 20 minutes
Serves 4

☆

280 g (9 oz) fettucine

250 g (8 oz) green beans

2 tablespoons oil

1 onion, chopped

2 cloves garlic, crushed

250 g (8 oz) mushrooms, thinly sliced

1/2 cup (125 ml/4 fl oz) white wine

1 1/4 cups (315 ml/10 fl oz) cream

1/2 cup (125 ml/4 fl oz) vegetable stock

1 egg

3 tablespoons chopped fresh basil

2/3 cup (100 g/3 1/2 oz) pine nuts, toasted

1/4 cup (35 g/1 1/4 oz) sun-dried tomatoes, cut into thin strips

50 g (1 3/4 oz) shaved Parmesan

1 Cook the fettucine in a large pan of rapidly boiling salted water until *al dente*. Drain, return to the pan and keep warm.

2 Trim the tops and tails of the beans and cut into long thin strips. Heat the oil in a large heavy-based frying pan. Add the onion and garlic and cook over medium heat for 3 minutes or until softened. Add the sliced mushrooms and cook, stirring, for 1 minute. Add the wine, cream and stock. Bring to the boil, reduce the heat and simmer for 10 minutes.

3 Lightly beat the egg in a small bowl. Stirring constantly, add a little cooking liquid. Pour the mixture slowly into the pan, stirring constantly for 30 seconds. Keep the heat low because if the mixture boils, it will curdle. Add the beans, basil, pine nuts and tomato and stir until heated through. Season, to taste, with salt and pepper. Serve the sauce over the pasta. Garnish with shavings of Parmesan, as well as sprigs of fresh herbs if you like.

NUTRITION PER SERVE: *Protein 25 g; Fat 70 g; Carbohydrate 55 g; Dietary Fibre 10 g; Cholesterol 165 mg; 3955 kJ (945 cal)*

VEGETABLE STOCK
A good vegetable stock has a delicate balance of flavours suitable for meat and seafood dishes as well as vegetable sauces, soups and braises. Any combination of aromatic, non-starchy vegetables such as carrots, onions, leeks, celery or turnips are simmered for 30 minutes with a bouquet garni, a clove of garlic and a little salt. The result will be a pale and clear stock with a mild flavour. A simple alternative is to use the water in which vegetables such as carrots or green beans have been boiled.

ABOVE: Fettucine with creamy mushroom and bean sauce

CONCHIGLIE WITH BROCCOLI AND ANCHOVY

Preparation time: 15 minutes
Total cooking time: 20 minutes
Serves 6

★

500 g (1 lb) conchiglie (shell pasta)
450 g (14 oz) broccoli
1 tablespoon oil
1 onion, chopped
1 clove garlic, crushed
3 anchovy fillets, chopped
1 1/4 cups (315 ml/10 fl oz) cream
1/2 cup (50 g/1 3/4 oz) freshly grated Parmesan, for serving

1 Cook the conchiglie in a large pan of rapidly boiling salted water until *al dente*. Drain and return to the pan.
2 While the conchiglie is cooking, cut the broccoli into small florets and cook in a pan of boiling water for 1 minute. Drain, plunge in cold water and drain again. Set aside.
3 Heat the oil in a heavy-based frying pan. Add the onion, garlic and anchovies and cook over low heat, stirring, for 3 minutes.
4 Add the cream to the pan and, stirring constantly, bring to the boil. Reduce the heat and simmer for 2 minutes. Add the broccoli florets and cook for 1 minute. Add salt and freshly ground black pepper, to taste. Add the sauce to the pasta and toss well to combine. Sprinkle with Parmesan and serve immediately.
NOTE: When tossing the sauce with the pasta, make sure all pieces of conchiglie are thoroughly coated with sauce. You can substitute different pastas such as macaroni or farfalle if you prefer.

NUTRITION PER SERVE: *Protein 20 g; Fat 30 g; Carbohydrate 60 g; Dietary Fibre 8 g; Cholesterol 85 mg; 2490 kJ (590 cal)*

SPINACH FETTUCINE WITH MUSHROOM SAUCE

Preparation time: 15 minutes
Total cooking time: 25 minutes
Serves 6

★

500 g (1 lb) spinach or plain fettucine
300 g (10 oz) baby mushrooms
3 spring onions
6 slices smoked ham or pancetta (50 g/1 3/4 oz)
40 g (1 1/4 oz) butter
1 1/4 cups (315 ml/10 fl oz) cream
4 tablespoons chopped fresh parsley

1 Cook the fettucine in a large pan of rapidly boiling salted water until *al dente*. Drain and return to the pan.
2 While the fettucine is cooking, slice the mushrooms finely. Trim the spring onions, removing the dark green section, and chop finely. Slice the smoked ham or pancetta into thin strips.
3 Heat the butter in a medium pan and cook the spring onion and ham over medium heat for 3 minutes. Add the mushrooms, cover, reduce the heat and cook, stirring occasionally, for 5 minutes.
4 Add the cream, half the parsley and salt and pepper, to taste. Simmer for 2 minutes, add the sauce to the fettucine and toss well to combine. Serve immediately, sprinkled with the remaining parsley.
NOTE: Don't add all the pasta to the boiling water at once—add it gradually, making sure that the water continues to boil. If spinach fettucine is unavailable, you can use other varieties of pasta.

NUTRITION PER SERVE: *Protein 15 g; Fat 30 g; Carbohydrate 60 g; Dietary Fibre 6 g; Cholesterol 100 mg; 2430 kJ (580 cal)*

ANCHOVY FILLETS

The most convenient way to buy anchovy fillets is in little tins or jars, preserved in oil. They should be pink, not grey, and have good definable fillets. If they are a little too strong for your taste, drain the amount needed and cover with milk. Leave for 30 minutes before discarding the milk, then pat the fillets dry with a paper towel. For a very mild flavour, use only the oil. Also available are anchovy fillets preserved in salt. These have a more delicate flavour, but must be soaked for 30 minutes before use.

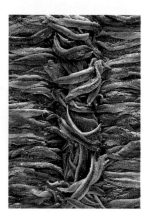

OPPPOSITE PAGE:
Conchiglie with broccoli and anchovy (top); Spinach fettucine with mushroom sauce

ASPARAGUS

Preparing asparagus for cooking takes just a minute. The woody base of the stalk should be removed by simply snapping it off. Starting at the base and moving up towards the tip, gently bend the stalk. The tough end will snap off when you reach crisp flesh. Only thick stalks with coarse skins need to be peeled. This is done with a vegetable peeler or a small sharp knife, and the paring should taper off as you near the tip. When these steps are followed, the stalks will cook evenly from top to bottom and it shouldn't be necessary to tie the bunches together for boiling. The cooking time is critical; too short, and the asparagus will be hard and have a metallic taste; too long, and the flesh becomes stringy and water-logged. Asparagus of average thickness take only 3 minutes to cook. For thick stalks an extra 30–50 seconds is needed.

ABOVE: Tagliatelle with asparagus and fresh herbs

TAGLIATELLE WITH ASPARAGUS AND FRESH HERBS

Preparation time: 15 minutes
Total cooking time: 15 minutes
Serves 6

★

500 g (1 lb) tagliatelle
155 g (5 oz) asparagus spears
40 g (1 1/4 oz) butter
1 tablespoon chopped fresh parsley
1 tablespoon chopped fresh basil
1 1/4 cups (315 ml/10 fl oz) cream
1/2 cup (50 g/1 3/4 oz) freshly grated Parmesan

1 Cook the pasta in a large pan of rapidly boiling salted water until *al dente*. Drain and return to the pan.
2 While the pasta is cooking, cut the asparagus spears into short pieces. Heat the butter in a medium pan, add the asparagus and stir over medium heat for 2 minutes or until just tender. Add the parsley and basil, cream, and salt and pepper, to taste. Cook for 2 minutes.
3 Add the grated Parmesan to the pan and stir well. When thoroughly mixed, add to the warm pasta in the pan and toss gently to distribute ingredients evenly. If serving as a first course, this dish will be sufficient for eight.

NUTRITION PER SERVE: *Protein 15 g; Fat 30 g; Carbohydrate 60 g; Dietary Fibre 5 g; Cholesterol 100 mg; 2470 kJ (590 cal)*

SPAGHETTI CARBONARA
(SPAGHETTI WITH CREAMY EGG AND BACON SAUCE)

Preparation time: 10 minutes
Total cooking time: 20 minutes
Serves 6

✭

500 g (1 lb) spaghetti
8 bacon rashers
4 eggs
1/2 cup (50 g/1³/4 oz) freshly grated
    Parmesan
1 1/4 cups (315 ml/10 fl oz) cream

1 Cook the spaghetti in a large pan of rapidly boiling salted water until *al dente*. Drain and return to the pan.
2 While the pasta is cooking, discard the bacon rind and cut the bacon into thin strips. Cook in a heavy-based pan over medium heat until crisp. Remove and drain on paper towels.
3 Beat the eggs, Parmesan and cream in a bowl until well combined. Add the bacon and pour the sauce over the warm pasta. Toss gently until pasta is well coated.
4 Return the pan to the heat and cook over very low heat for 1/2–1 minute, or until slightly thickened. Serve seasoned with freshly ground pepper. Garnish with herb sprigs if you wish.

NUTRITION PER SERVE: *Protein 25 g; Fat 30 g; Carbohydrate 60 g; Dietary Fibre 5 g; Cholesterol 225 mg; 2665 kJ (635 cal)*

CARBONARA
There is some mystery surrounding the invention and naming of this simple sauce. Some say that Carbonara is relatively new, having appeared in Rome during the Second World War, when American GIs combined their rations of bacon and eggs with the local spaghetti. It is likely that the dish has been around a lot longer than that. Was it simply that it was a quick and easy meal whipped up by the coal vendors, *carbonari*, over street charcoal burners, or was it so named because the flecks of black pepper spotting the creamy sauce looked like coal dust? However it came about, the concept of using egg to thicken and flavour a simple bacon and cream sauce was truly inventive.

ABOVE: Spaghetti carbonara

RAVIOLI WITH MASCARPONE AND PANCETTA

Preparation time: 10 minutes
Total cooking time: 20 minutes
Serves 4

⭐

500 g (1 lb) fresh spinach ravioli
2 teaspoons vegetable oil
90 g (3 oz) pancetta, finely chopped
1/2 cup (125 ml/4 fl oz) chicken stock
185 g (6 oz) mascarpone
1/2 cup (80 g/2 3/4 oz) finely sliced sun-dried
   tomatoes
2 tablespoons finely shredded fresh basil
1/2 teaspoon cracked black pepper

1 Cook the ravioli in a large pan of rapidly boiling salted water until *al dente*.
2 While the pasta is cooking, heat the oil in a frying pan and cook the pancetta for 2–3 minutes. Stir in the stock, mascarpone and sun-dried tomatoes.
3 Bring to the boil, reduce the heat and simmer for 5 minutes, until the sauce reduces and thickens. Stir in the basil and pepper.
4 Drain the ravioli and add to the pan with the sauce. Toss together gently to combine. Serve immediately.

NUTRITION PER SERVE: *Protein 20 g; Fat 35 g; Carbohydrate 90 g; Dietary Fibre 5 g; Cholesterol 145 mg; 3220 kJ (770 cal)*

ON THE SIDE

TOMATO AND BOCCONCINI SALAD Thickly slice 4 large vine-ripened tomatoes and 8 baby bocconcini. Arrange the tomato slices, bocconcini and basil leaves on a serving plate. Drizzle with a little extra virgin olive oil and balsamic vinegar. Sprinkle with pepper and sea salt.

ANTIPASTO SALAD Combine about 200 g (6 1/2 oz) each of sun-dried tomatoes, marinated black olives, chopped marinated eggplant (aubergine), artichoke and sun-dried pepper (capsicum). Toss through 3 tablespoons of chopped basil. Drizzle with a little balsamic vinegar.

FETTUCINE WITH SMOKED CHEESE AND SALAMI

Preparation time: 20 minutes
Total cooking time: 15 minutes
Serves 4

⭐

375 g (12 oz) tomato fettucine
200 g (6 1/2 oz) sun-dried tomatoes in oil
3 bacon rashers
1 large red onion, sliced
2 large cloves garlic, finely chopped
150 g (5 oz) hot or mild salami, sliced
   into strips
2 teaspoons plain flour
1 tablespoon tomato paste (tomato purée,
   double concentrate)
1 1/2 cups (375 ml/12 fl oz) evaporated milk
1/2 cup (60 g/2 oz) grated smoked cheese
1/4 teaspoon cayenne pepper
2 tablespoons chopped fresh flat-leaf parsley
shavings of fresh Parmesan, for serving

1 Cook the fettucine in a large pan of rapidly boiling salted water until *al dente*. Drain and return to the pan.
2 While the pasta is cooking, drain the sun-dried tomatoes, reserving the oil, and cut into strips; set aside. Finely chop the bacon and set aside.
3 Heat the reserved oil in a pan and cook the onion for 3 minutes, or until soft and golden. Add the garlic and cook for another minute. Add the sun-dried tomato, bacon and salami and cook for another 2–3 minutes.
4 Stir in the flour, then the tomato paste and cook for 1 minute. Gradually add the evaporated milk, stirring continuously. Bring to the boil and reduce the heat. Add the smoked cheese, cayenne pepper, parsley and black pepper, to taste, and simmer until the cheese melts.
5 Toss the sauce through the hot pasta. Serve immediately, with shavings of Parmesan.

NUTRITION PER SERVE: *Protein 40 g; Fat 35 g; Carbohydrate 85 g; Dietary Fibre 5 g; Cholesterol 110 mg; 3495 kJ (835 cal)*

CAYENNE PEPPER
Sometimes called Nepal pepper, cayenne pepper is an attractive bright reddish-orange colour and has a pungency somewhere between that of ground chilli and black pepper. It is named after Cayenne, the main port of French Guiana. Cayenne pepper is made by grinding the dried fruit, minus the seeds, of different members of the capsicum family, namely *capsicum frutescens* and *capsicum minimum*, and it is favoured because it has a slight sweetness underlying the hot pepper taste. Cayenne pepper can be used as a flavouring in dishes which require long cooking, but it has an intensity that is equally strong when used at the last minute as a condiment.

OPPOSITE PAGE: Ravioli with mascarpone and pancetta (top); Fettucine with smoked cheese and salami

HONEY

The flavour, consistency, aroma, colour and degree of sweetness in honey is determined by the flowers from which the bees gather their nectar. Most prized for cooking uses is honey from herbs such as thyme and rosemary that have a subtle flavouring and a savoury fragrance. Flowers such as apple blossom give a highly floral perfume and flavour, while others make almost bitter honey.

ABOVE: Linguine in honey basil cream

LINGUINE IN HONEY BASIL CREAM

Preparation time: 15 minutes
Total cooking time: 20 minutes
Serves 6

★

500 g (1 lb) linguine
240 g (7½ oz) fresh basil
1 small red chilli, chopped
3 cloves garlic, crushed
3 tablespoons pine nuts, toasted
3 tablespoons freshly grated Parmesan
juice of 1 lemon
½ cup (125 ml/4 fl oz) olive oil
3 tablespoons honey
1½ cups (375 ml/12 fl oz) cream
½ cup (125 ml/4 fl oz) chicken stock
shavings of fresh Parmesan, for serving

1 Cook the linguine in a large pan of rapidly boiling salted water until *al dente*. Drain and keep warm.
2 While the pasta is cooking, discard the stems of basil and mix the basil leaves, chilli, garlic, pine nuts, Parmesan, lemon juice, oil and honey in a food processor or blender until smooth.
3 Combine the basil mixture, cream and chicken stock in a large pan, bring to the boil and simmer for 15–20 minutes, or until the sauce has thickened. Season, to taste, with cracked pepper.
4 Add the pasta to the pan and toss well. Sprinkle with shavings of Parmesan.

NUTRITION PER SERVE: *Protein 15 g; Fat 70 g; Carbohydrate 75 g; Dietary Fibre 7 g; Cholesterol 100 mg; 4005 kJ (955 cal)*

CARAMELIZED ONION AND BLUE CHEESE RISSONI

Preparation time: 20 minutes
Total cooking time: 35 minutes
Serves 4

★★

500 g (1 lb) rissoni
30 g (1 oz) butter
3 tablespoons olive oil
4 onions, sliced
185 g (6 oz) blue cheese
100 g (3¹/₂ oz) mascarpone
2 cups (130 g/4¹/₂ oz) shredded English
  spinach leaves

1 Cook the rissoni in rapidly boiling salted water until *al dente*. Drain well and return to the pan.
2 While the pasta is cooking, heat the butter and the olive oil in a large heavy-based frying pan.

Add the sliced onion and cook over low heat for about 20–30 minutes, until golden brown and caramelized. Remove from the pan with a slotted spoon and drain on paper towels.
3 Mix the blue cheese, mascarpone and onion in a bowl.
4 Add the cheese and onion mixture, as well as the spinach, to the rissoni and toss through. Season, to taste, with salt and freshly ground black pepper before serving.

NUTRITION PER SERVE: *Protein 30 g; Fat 45 g; Carbohydrate 95 g; Dietary Fibre 9 g; Cholesterol 90 mg; 3755 kJ (895 cal)*

ABOVE: Caramelized onion and blue cheese rissoni

159

GRILLED CARBONARA

Preparation time: 10 minutes
Total cooking time: 15 minutes
Serves 4

★

250 g (8 oz) linguine
4 eggs
3/4 cup (185 ml/6 fl oz) cream
6 slices prosciutto, chopped
3/4 cup (75 g/2 1/2 oz) freshly grated Parmesan
2 tablespoons chopped fresh chives
30 g (1 oz) butter

1 Brush a 23 cm (9 inch) shallow heatproof dish with some melted butter or oil. Preheat the grill to moderately hot.
2 Cook the linguine in a large pan of rapidly boiling salted water until *al dente*. Drain and return to the pan.
3 While the pasta is cooking, whisk the eggs and cream together in a bowl, stir in the prosciutto, the Parmesan (reserving 3 tablespoons) and chives and season with freshly ground black pepper, to taste.
4 Add the egg mixture and the butter to the hot pasta and stir continuously over low heat for 1 minute, or until the egg mixture begins to thicken slightly. Take care not to overcook the mixture, or you will end up with scrambled eggs. The mixture should be quite creamy and moist.
5 Pour the pasta into the prepared dish and sprinkle the top with the reserved Parmesan. Place under the grill for a few minutes, until just set and lightly browned on top. Serve with crusty Italian bread.

NUTRITION PER SERVE: *Protein 25 g; Fat 40 g; Carbohydrate 45 g; Dietary Fibre 5 g; Cholesterol 300 mg; 2710 kJ (645 cal)*

ORECCHIETTE WITH TUNA, LEMON AND CAPER SAUCE

Preparation time: 10 minutes
Total cooking time: 20 minutes
Serves 4

★

500 g (1 lb) orecchiette
30 g (1 oz) butter
1 clove garlic, crushed
1 onion, finely chopped
425 g (14 oz) can tuna in brine, drained
2 tablespoons lemon juice
1 cup (250 ml/8 fl oz) cream
2 tablespoons chopped fresh flat-leaf parsley
1 tablespoon capers, drained
1/4 teaspoon cayenne pepper, optional

1 Cook the orecchiette in a large pan of rapidly boiling salted water until *al dente*. Drain and return to the pan.
2 While the pasta is cooking, heat the butter in a pan and cook the garlic and onion for 1–2 minutes. Add the tuna, lemon juice, cream, half the parsley and the capers. Season with black pepper and cayenne, if using. Simmer over low heat for 5 minutes.
3 Add the tuna sauce to the pasta and toss until thoroughly combined. Serve the pasta sprinkled with the remaining chopped fresh parsley. Pictured here garnished with caperberries.
NOTE: Use two wooden spoons to toss the mixture together.

NUTRITION PER SERVE: *Protein 40 g; Fat 35 g; Carbohydrate 90 g; Dietary Fibre 5 g; Cholesterol 155 mg; 3570 kJ (850 cal)*

ON THE SIDE

SESAME COLESLAW Finely shred one-quarter each of a red cabbage and a green cabbage. Cut 100 g (3 1/2 oz) of snow peas (mangetout), 2 celery sticks, 2 carrots and 1 red pepper (capsicum) into julienne strips. Combine the cabbage and other vegetables in a large bowl and toss through enough whole egg mayonnaise to lightly dress the salad. Top with finely shredded fresh mint leaves and toasted sesame seeds.

PROSCIUTTO
In Italy, prosciutto simply means ham, and it can be bought cooked, *cotto*, which is similar to boiled hams elsewhere, or raw, *crudo*, which is cured on the bone by salting and air-drying. This is the one referred to in recipes and known for its versatility and mellow flavour. It is used in salads, on bread and tossed through pasta sauces, or used to add flavour to cooked sauces, stews and soups. It can be mature, with dark ruby flesh, creamy fat and a concentrated flavour and aroma, or younger and more succulent, with pale pink flesh and white fat.

OPPOSITE PAGE: Grilled carbonara (top); Orecchiette with tuna, lemon and caper sauce

ALFREDO SAUCE

Immortalised by Alfredo in his Rome restaurant, this sauce is a rich blend of butter, cream and Parmesan. Traditionally, it is served with fettucine and eaten as soon as the sauce is tossed through the pasta, to prevent the dish becoming clammy. For this reason it is one of the few pasta dishes that is compiled at the table in restaurants.

ABOVE: Fettucine alfredo

FETTUCINE ALFREDO

Preparation time: 10 minutes
Total cooking time: 15 minutes
Serves 6

★

500 g (1 lb) fettucine or tagliatelle
90 g (3 oz) butter
1 1/2 cups (150 g/5 oz) freshly shredded
   Parmesan
1 1/4 cups (315 ml/10 fl oz) cream
3 tablespoons chopped fresh parsley

1 Cook the pasta in a large pan of rapidly boiling salted water until *al dente*. Drain and return to the pan.
2 While the pasta is cooking, heat the butter in a medium pan over low heat. Add the Parmesan and cream and bring to the boil, stirring constantly. Reduce the heat and simmer for 10 minutes, or until the sauce has thickened

slightly. Add the parsley, and salt and pepper, to taste, and stir well to combine. Add the sauce to the warm pasta and toss well to combine. Serve garnished with a fresh herb sprig, if desired.

NUTRITION PER SERVE: *Protein 20 g; Fat 45 g; Carbohydrate 60 g; Dietary Fibre 5 g; Cholesterol 135 mg; 2985 kJ (710 cal)*

ON THE SIDE

GREEN HERB PILAF Fry a finely sliced onion in a little butter in a large deep frying pan. Add 1 tablespoon each of chopped fresh coriander and parsley. Stir in 1 cup (200 g/6 1/2 oz) of washed basmati rice and 1 1/2 cups (375 ml/12 fl oz) of chicken or vegetable stock. Season, to taste. Bring to the boil and simmer for about 20 minutes, or until the rice is cooked. Drain off any excess liquid and add another tablespoon of each herb. Top with tiny knobs of butter and cracked black pepper.

LINGUINE WITH CREAMY LEMON SAUCE

Preparation time: 10 minutes
Total cooking time: 20 minutes
Serves 4

★

400 g (13 oz) fresh linguine or spaghetti
1/4 teaspoon saffron threads or
  powder, optional
1 1/4 cups (315 ml/10 fl oz) cream
1 cup (250 ml/8 fl oz) chicken stock
1 tablespoon grated lemon rind

1 Cook the pasta in a large pan of rapidly boiling salted water until *al dente*. Drain and keep warm.
2 If using saffron threads, soak them in a little hot water for 5 minutes. While the pasta is cooking, combine the cream, chicken stock and grated lemon rind in a large frying pan. Bring to the boil, stirring occasionally.
3 Reduce the heat and simmer for 10 minutes. Season, to taste, with salt and pepper. Add the cooked pasta and cook for another 2–3 minutes.
4 Add the saffron threads and liquid and stir. Serve garnished with fine strips of lemon rind, if desired.
NOTE: Saffron is available from delicatessens and speciality food shops. If unavailable, use 1/4 teaspoon of turmeric.

NUTRITION PER SERVE: *Protein 15 g; Fat 35 g; Carbohydrate 75 g; Dietary Fibre 5 g; Cholesterol 105 mg; 2755 kJ (660 cal)*

SAFFRON
Saffron is the dried stamens of the saffron or autumn crocus. Available in threads or as a powdered form, it has a dark orange colour that carries into the food, and a sharp taste that mellows when cooked. Steep the threads in tepid water to extract the flavour, or to intensify the flavour, toast until darkened, cool, then crumble to a coarse powder. Saffron is costly because of the labour required to pluck the stamens from each flower.

ABOVE: Linguine with creamy lemon sauce

1 To make the dough, combine the flour, beaten eggs and oil with ⅓ cup (80 ml/2¾ fl oz) of water in a food processor, for 5 seconds, or until the mixture comes together in a ball. Cover with plastic wrap and refrigerate for 15 minutes. If you don't have a food processor, combine the ingredients in a large bowl, using your fingertips.

2 To make the filling, heat the oil in a heavy-based pan, add the spring onion and garlic and stir-fry over medium heat for 2 minutes. Add the mince and stir-fry over high heat for 4 minutes, or until well browned and all the liquid has evaporated. Use a fork to break up any lumps as the mince cooks. Allow to cool and stir in the egg.

3 Roll half the dough out very thinly on a lightly floured surface. Use a large sharp knife to cut the dough into 6 cm (2½ inch) squares. Brush half the squares very lightly with water and place a teaspoon of filling on each. Place another square over each and press down firmly to seal the filling inside. Place in a single layer on well-floured oven trays. Repeat with the remaining dough and filling.

4 To make the sauce, melt the butter in a medium pan, add the mascarpone cheese and stir over medium heat until melted. Add the Parmesan and sage and gently heat while stirring, for 1 minute.

5 Cook the ravioli in a large pan of rapidly boiling water for 5 minutes, or until tender. Drain and serve with the sauce.

NUTRITION PER SERVE: *Protein 35 g; Fat 65 g; Carbohydrate 50 g; Dietary Fibre 4 g; Cholesterol 270 mg; 3855 kJ (915 cal)*

GRATED PARMESAN

For an interesting variation on serving freshly grated Parmesan or Pecorino with pasta dishes, combine grated lemon rind with one of these cheeses. It gives a delicious piquancy that enhances many sauces, especially cream-based ones, and works well with meat-filled ravioli. Mix in proportions that will best complement your sauce. A ratio of 1 tablespoon of cheese to 1 teaspoon of lemon rind is a good starting point.

ABOVE: Pork and veal ravioli with cheesy sauce

PORK AND VEAL RAVIOLI WITH CHEESY SAUCE

Preparation time: 1 hour
Total cooking time: 15 minutes
Serves 4

★

Dough

2 cups (250 g/8 oz) plain flour
2 eggs, lightly beaten
2 tablespoons oil

Filling

1 tablespoon oil
4 spring onions, finely chopped
3 cloves garlic, crushed
250 g (8 oz) pork and veal mince
1 egg, lightly beaten

Sauce

60 g (2 oz) butter
1 cup (220 g/7 oz) mascarpone cheese
⅓ cup (35 g/1¼ oz) freshly grated Parmesan
2 tablespoons chopped fresh sage

ON THE SIDE

DILLED ORANGE CARROTS
Boil, steam or microwave baby carrots until tender. Heat a little orange juice, a cinnamon stick and orange liqueur and honey in a pan, bring to the boil and simmer for 3 minutes. Remove the cinnamon stick. Drizzle the sauce over the carrots and sprinkle with chopped fresh dill.

BRAISED LEEKS WITH PINE NUTS
Fry sliced leeks in a little oil and butter until golden brown. Add enough vegetable stock and white wine to just cover the leeks. Cook until the leeks are tender and fold through lots of chopped fresh herbs. Sprinkle with toasted pine nuts and grated Parmesan.

LEMON GRASS AND LIME SCALLOP PASTA

Preparation time: 20 minutes
Total cooking time: 15 minutes
Serves 4

☆

500 g (1 lb) spaghetti or chilli fettucine
1 tablespoon oil
1 onion, sliced
2 tablespoons finely chopped lemon grass
500 g (1 lb) scallops
1 cup (250 ml/8 fl oz) coconut milk
2 kaffir lime leaves, finely shredded
1/2 cup (15 g/1/2 oz) coriander leaves

1 Cook the pasta in rapidly boiling salted water until *al dente*. Drain.
2 Meanwhile, heat the oil in a large heavy-based frying pan, add the onion and lemon grass and cook over medium heat for 5 minutes, or until the onion is soft. Add the scallops in batches and cook until tender and lightly browned. Remove and keep warm.
3 Add the coconut milk and kaffir lime leaves to the pan and simmer for 5 minutes, or until the sauce thickens slightly.
4 Return the scallops to the pan and cook until heated through. Toss the pasta through the sauce with the coriander leaves. Season, to taste, with salt and pepper.

NUTRITION PER SERVE: *Protein 30 g; Fat 20 g; Carbohydrate 90 g; Dietary Fibre 7 g; Cholesterol 40 mg; 2775 kJ (660 cal)*

LEMON GRASS

Lemon grass is an aromatic plant with a bulbous base and grass-like leaves, used all over Asia for its balmy lemon flavour. The base is trimmed of coarse outer layers and the crisp white heart is chopped or pounded to go into broths, curry pastes and stir-fries. The fresh whole stem or the dried leaves can be added to soups or curries. Dried leaves need to be soaked in water for about 30 minutes before use and the flavour is adequate as a substitute for fresh. Fresh lemon grass can be bought from some greengrocers while Asian food stores stock fresh and dried.

LEFT: Lemon grass and lime scallop pasta

CHEESE
Pasta and Parmesan are a famous combination, but the Italians produce many other cheeses, from soft creamy-white table cheeses to strong blue-veined varieties, of which they are rightfully proud.

MOZZARELLA
A smooth, matured mild-flavoured cheese, originally made from buffalo milk, but now sometimes made from cow's milk or a mixture of the two. Manufactured in large quantities around the world. it is available in a variety of shapes, from pear to block, and has a stringy texture when melted. It is famous for its use in pizzas but can be diced and added to sauces or sliced and melted over veal steaks.

BOCCONCINI AND OVOLINI
Small mozzarella balls are called bocconcini, although sometimes referred to as baby mozzarella. They are fresh, unripened cheeses still made following the traditional method and. unlike matured mozzarella. are enjoyed as a table cheese. Smaller ones are called ovolini. Stored in the refrigerator fully covered in the whey in which they are sold, they will last for up to three weeks. If they show any signs of

yellowing, they should be discarded. Serve drained and cut into thin slices. Used in salads, as a topping for pizzas or bruschetta or in baked pasta dishes.

RICOTTA
A fresh curd cheese made from whey, usually the whey drained off when making mozzarella. It can be made from sheep (ricotta pecora) or cow milk (ricotta vaccina) and is usually sold in the

basket it is produced in, as it is very delicate. Ricotta has a short shelf life and should be bought as required. Avoid any that is discoloured or dry. Drain off the excess whey before using. The flavour is mild, so ricotta can be used in savoury or sweet dishes. Often used in fillings for cannelloni, with pancakes or as a spread. Dried ricotta balls are suitable for grating.

GORGONZOLA

Originally produced in a small village in Milan, gorgonzola is now made throughout the world. It is prized for its rich creamy texture and soft blue flavour. It is less salty than most blue cheeses. Only buy what you need as, like most blues, it has a strong aroma that will permeate other foods in the refrigerator. Gorgonzola is delicious as a cream sauce for pasta, in salads, melted over pears or served with figs. Return to room temperature before serving.

PROVOLONE

Usually sold encased in wax and hanging by a striped red and white string. The younger the cheese, the milder the flavour (it sharpens on ageing). Provolone is often lightly smoked and works well as part of a cheese platter. It is delicious grated in pasta sauces, in fondues or melted over meats. Refrigerate in plastic wrap for up to two weeks.

PECORINO

The name given to a range of hard, cooked sheep milk curd cheeses. These have a grainy texture, similar to that of Parmesan, and are generally grated for cooking, in the same way as Parmesan. *Pecorino romano* is aged for the longest time and is therefore harder and more suitable for grating. *Pecorino pepato* has had black peppercorns added to the curd, and has a subtle peppery flavour.

Pecorino fresco is the name given to the young fresh cheese. Pecorino will keep in the refrigerator for months. Fully enclose it in plastic wrap as it has a strong aroma that can permeate other foods.

MASCARPONE

A fresh curd triple cream cheese that looks more like cream than cheese. It is very high in fat and has a mild yet slightly acidic taste. It can be used in a four-cheese sauce or in a baked béchamel sauce topping. Commonly served with fresh or poached fruit for dessert. Refrigerate for up to five days.

CLOCKWISE, FROM TOP LEFT:
Mozzarella, ricotta, gorgonzola, provolone, mascarpone, pecorino, fresh pecorino, pecorino pepato, baby ricotta, ovolini, bocconcini

CHEESE

FONTINA

A sweet, nutty-flavoured cheese with a soft velvety texture and a few tiny air holes. Fontina is sold in wheels, with a golden brown rind. It is a semi-hard cheese, prized for its melting quality and is the vital ingredient in the Italian-style fondue dish, *fonduta*. Italian law restricts the use of the name *fontina* to cheese produced in the Aosta Valley, near Mount Fontin. There are many copies in other regions of Italy and elsewhere. These are known as *fontal* and are generally softer than fontina. Fontina is delicious melted over polenta or gnocchi as well as in sauces. Will keep in the refrigerator, sealed in plastic wrap, for up to one week.

PARMIGIANO REGGIANO

Parmesan derives its name from the Parma region in northern Italy where it is made. It is a hard cheese with a crumbly texture. Parmesan is aged for 2–3 years in large wooden wheels and can only be stamped *Parmigiano reggiano* if it is produced within the provinces of Parma and Reggio, where it is still made using the original method. It is best to buy Parmesan in a wedge and grate it yourself as pre-grated cheese is often dry and lacking flavour. Select Parmesan with the rind still attached, with no evidence of whitening at the rim. Parmesan can be served on its own or grated or shaved on top of pasta sauces, in salads or soups. Wrap it in

greaseproof paper and foil and store on the bottom shelf of your refrigerator.

GRANA

Like Parmesan, this is a hard grating cheese and, as the name implies, it has a grainy texture. It is easily identified by the imprint on the rind of the cheese that guarantees its authenticity. Grana can be served as a table cheese as it has a more delicate flavour than Parmesan. Refrigerate, wrapped in plastic.

BEL PAESE

Easily identified by the silver and green foil wrapper with a map of Italy on the top, this is a mild, creamy, slightly sweet cheese that can be used on sandwiches, as

a table cheese or melted over casseroles or pizzas. The creamy cheese ripens quickly, in about 4–6 weeks, and should be kept wrapped in the foil until ready to use. It is sold in large wheels or tiny individual serves.

TALEGGIO

This cheese takes its name from the town where it is produced and can be classified into two varieties. One is the cooked curd, with a thin greyish rind and straw-coloured interior with a mild flavour. The uncooked curd is a surface-ripened cheese with a thin, reddish moulded skin with a pale yellow buttery interior. It has a delicate sweet flavour with a slightly acidic tang in towards the centre. Taleggio should be purchased only as required. Return to room temperature before serving as a table cheese. Taleggio is also known as *stracchino*.

ASIAGO

This can either be a table cheese or a grating cheese, depending on how it has been aged and pressed. The younger cheese, *Asiago d'Allevo*, has a thin golden rind that darkens to a rusty brown colour as the cheese ripens. The interior is pale yellow with a slightly grainy texture that is scattered with small holes. The flavour sharpens with age. The aged and pressed cheese, *Asiago Pressato* has a deep golden rind and a very pale straw-coloured interior. It has a pleasant mild flavour and is often used as a dessert cheese. Asiago stores well in the refrigerator, wrapped in plastic.

GOATS CHEESE

Goats cheese has a distinctive, sharp taste. It varies in texture from a soft, crumbly cheese to a firm chalky cheese, depending on the age and method of production. When young and crumbly it can easily be spread on bread, as a table cheese or crumbled over salad and pasta dishes. The firmer cheese can be cut into pieces and marinated in oil and herbs. The cheese should be a clean white with no evidence of drying around the edges. Purchase as required. It should keep for up to two weeks in the refrigerator. Depending on the variety, the rind may vary from black (ash-covered goats cheese) to off-white. Ash goats cheese is made by rolling goats cheese in fresh herbs that have been cooked in a pan until blackened. The cheese is rolled until it has an even coating.

CLOCKWISE, FROM TOP LEFT: Fontina, Parmigiano-Reggiano, Bel Paese, Goats cheese, Ash goats cheese, Asiago, Grana

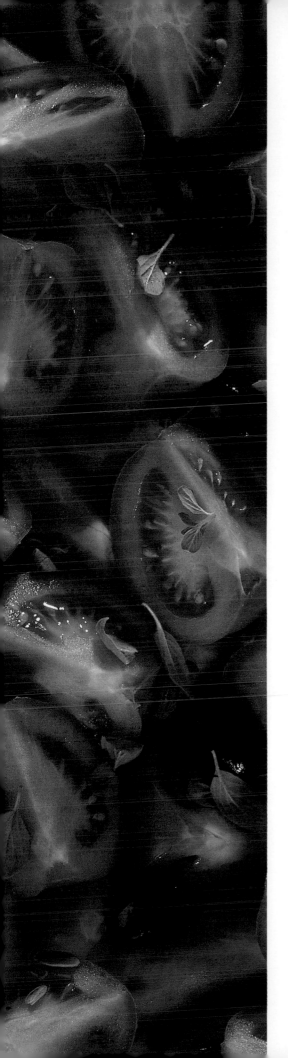

PASTA SALADS

Pasta salads have come about as part of the evolution of pasta. While they are not an authentic Italian creation, the combination of fresh vegetables, finest-quality olive oil and cold *al dente* pasta certainly has a Mediterranean flavour. Few foods are so adaptable that they are delicious when served either hot or cold. Pasta is one exception and these salads are guaranteed to leave Italian cooks with just one thought: 'why didn't we think of that?'

OREGANO

Italian oregano (also known as wild marjoram) is closely related to rigani, which is used in Greek kitchens, and to sweet marjoram, common to French and Northern Italian cooking. It is milder than rigani but more pungent than sweet marjoram. Oregano is very compatible with tomatoes, garlic and onion and is the herb most often found on pizzas. The plants are hardy and the leaves dry well, ensuring a constant supply.

ABOVE: Farfalle salad with sun-dried tomatoes and spinach

FARFALLE SALAD WITH SUN-DRIED TOMATOES AND SPINACH

Preparation time: 20 minutes
Total cooking time: 12 minutes
Serves 6

★

500 g (1 lb) farfalle or spiral pasta
3 spring onions
50 g (1³/₄ oz) sun-dried tomatoes, cut into strips
1 kg (2 lb) English spinach, stalks trimmed and leaves shredded
¹/₃ cup (50 g/1³/₄ oz) toasted pine nuts
1 tablespoon chopped fresh oregano
¹/₄ cup (60 ml/2 fl oz) olive oil
1 teaspoon fresh chopped chilli
1 clove garlic, crushed

1 Cook the pasta in a large pan of rapidly boiling salted water until *al dente*. Drain, rinse under cold water and drain again. Allow to cool and transfer to a large salad bowl.
2 Trim the spring onions and finely slice diagonally. Add to the pasta with the tomato, spinach, pine nuts and oregano.
3 To make the dressing, combine the oil, chilli, garlic and salt and pepper, to taste, in a small screw top jar and shake well.
4 Pour the dressing over the top of the salad. Toss well and serve.

NUTRITION PER SERVE: *Protein 15 g; Fat 15 g; Carbohydrate 60 g; Dietary Fibre 10 g; Cholesterol 0 mg; 1930 kJ (460 cal)*

SPAGHETTI TOMATO SALAD

Preparation time: 25 minutes
Total cooking time: 15 minutes
Serves 6

★

500 g (1 lb) spaghetti or bucatini
1 cup (50 g/1¾ oz) fresh basil leaves, shredded
250 g (8 oz) cherry tomatoes, halved
1 clove garlic, crushed
½ cup (75 g/2½ oz) chopped black olives
¼ cup (60 ml/2 fl oz) olive oil
1 tablespoon balsamic vinegar
½ cup (50 g/1¾ oz) freshly grated Parmesan

1 Cook the pasta in a large pan of rapidly boiling salted water until *al dente*. Drain, rinse under cold water and drain again.
2 Combine the basil, tomato, garlic, olives, oil and vinegar in a salad bowl. Set aside for about 15 minutes. Mix in the drained pasta.

3 Add the Parmesan and salt and pepper, to taste. Toss well and serve immediately.

NUTRITION PER SERVE: *Protein 15 g; Fat 15 g; Carbohydrate 60 g; Dietary Fibre 5 g; Cholesterol 10 mg; 1780 kJ (425 cal)*

ON THE SIDE

PUMPKIN AND SAGE SCONES

Sift 2 cups (250 g/8 oz) of self-raising flour into a bowl with a pinch of salt. Rub 250 g of cooked and puréed pumpkin and 20 g (¾ oz) of butter into the flour and then add 1 tablespoon of chopped fresh sage. Bring the mixture together with a little milk and turn it out onto a baking tray. Shape the mixture into a round and roll it out to about 3 cm (1¼ inches) thick. Gently mark or cut the scone into segments and bake in a moderate 180°C (350°F/Gas 4) oven for 15–20 minutes, until lightly browned and cooked through.

ABOVE: Spaghetti tomato salad

2 While the pasta is cooking, mix the olive oil, garlic, lemon rind and juice, basil, tomato, olives and oregano in a large bowl. Season with salt and pepper, to taste.

3 Cut the chicken into thin strips. Heat the oil in a medium heavy-based frying pan. Add the chicken strips and cook over medium heat, stirring occasionally, for 4 minutes, or until cooked through.

4 Add the drained chicken and warm pasta to the tomato mixture and toss to combine. Serve with the rocket leaves.

NUTRITION PER SERVE: *Protein 20 g; Fat 15 g; Carbohydrate 25 g; Dietary Fibre 5 g; Cholesterol 45 mg; 1330 kJ (320 cal)*

TOMATO AND BASIL PASTA SALAD

Preparation time: 15 minutes
Total cooking time: 10 minutes
Serves 6

★

500 g (1 lb) cooked penne rigate
1/4 cup (15 g/1/2 oz) finely shredded fresh basil
1–2 cloves garlic, crushed
2 tablespoons olive oil
1 tablespoon balsamic vinegar
1 teaspoon soft brown sugar
4 egg (Roma) tomatoes
60 g (2 oz) prosciutto

WARM SALADS

A salad where all or some of the ingredients are warm makes a very appetising first course or light meal. The cooked components, straight from the heat, are still bright and succulent and full of flavour, while the more traditional salad vegetables contribute a contrasting crisp freshness.

ABOVE: Warm chicken and pasta salad
RIGHT: Tomato and basil pasta salad

WARM CHICKEN AND PASTA SALAD

Preparation time: 20 minutes
Total cooking time: 15 minutes
Serves 6

★

180 g (6 oz) penne rigate
1/4 cup (60 ml/2 fl oz) virgin olive oil
2 cloves garlic, crushed
rind of 1 lemon, cut into fine strips
1 tablespoon lemon juice
3 tablespoons shredded fresh basil
4 medium tomatoes, seeded and chopped
18 black olives, pitted and sliced
1/2 teaspoon chopped fresh oregano leaves
400 g (13 oz) chicken breast tenderloins
1 tablespoon oil
1/2 cup (20 g/3/4 oz) rocket leaves

1 Cook the pasta in a large pan of rapidly boiling salted water until *al dente*; drain.

1 Combine the penne, basil, garlic, oil, vinegar, brown sugar and salt and pepper, to taste.
2 Cut the egg tomatoes into wedges and toss with the other ingredients until well distributed.
3 Grill the prosciutto until crisp, crumble into small pieces and sprinkle on top of the salad before serving.

NUTRITION PER SERVE: *Protein 5 g; Fat 5 g; Carbohydrate 30 g; Dietary Fibre 5 g; Cholesterol 5 mg; 910 kJ (215 cal)*

TUNA AND PASTA SALAD

Preparation time: 20 minutes
Total cooking time: 15 minutes
Serves 6

★

500 g (1 lb) conchiglie (shell pasta) or fusilli
200 g (6½ oz) beans, cut into short lengths
2 red peppers (capsicums), thinly sliced
2 spring onions, chopped
425 g (14 oz) can tuna, in oil
2 tablespoons oil
¼ cup (60 ml/2 fl oz) white wine vinegar
1 tablespoon lemon juice
1 clove garlic, crushed
1 teaspoon sugar
1 large cucumber, thinly sliced
6 eggs, hard-boiled and quartered
4 tomatoes, cut into eighths
½ cup (80 g/2¾ oz) black olives
2 tablespoons chopped fresh basil

1 Cook the pasta in a large pan of rapidly boiling salted water until *al dente*. Drain, rinse under cold water and drain again.
2 Combine the pasta, beans, peppers and the spring onions in a large bowl, mixing well. Drain the tuna, reserving the oil, and flake with a fork.
3 Combine the reserved tuna oil, oil, vinegar, lemon juice, garlic and sugar in a small screw top jar. Shake vigorously for 2 minutes, or until well combined.
4 Spoon the pasta into the centre of a large serving platter. Arrange the cucumber, egg and tomato around the edge of the platter, and drizzle with half the dressing. Scatter the flaked tuna, olives and basil over the salad and drizzle with the remaining dressing just before serving.

NUTRITION PER SERVE: *Protein 35 g; Fat 25 g; Carbohydrate 65 g; Dietary Fibre 10 g; Cholesterol 235 mg; 2650 kJ (630 cal)*

ON THE SIDE

POLENTA BREAD Stir ½ cup (50 g/1¾ oz) finely grated Parmesan, some chopped fresh herbs (basil, parsley, oregano, sage), a crushed clove of garlic and a little cream into some cooked polenta. Mix well and season, to taste. Pour into a baking dish and bake at moderately hot 200°C (400°F/Gas 6) until the crust is golden and the polenta well set. Cut into slices and serve warm.

KUMERA AND PARSNIP CHIPS

Peel and cut kumera (orange sweet potato) and parsnip into very thin slices or ribbons, using a sharp vegetable peeler. Deep-fry in batches, in hot oil, until crisp. Drain and keep warm in a moderate 180°C (350°F/Gas 4) oven whilst cooking the remainder. Serve with a garlic mayonnaise.

ABOVE: Tuna and pasta salad

TUNA, GREEN BEAN AND ONION SALAD

Preparation time: 20 minutes
Total cooking time: 10–15 minutes
Serves 4

☆

200 g (6½ oz) green beans, trimmed
   and cut into short lengths
300 g (10 oz) penne rigate
½ cup (125 ml/4 fl oz) olive oil
250 g (8 oz) fresh tuna steak, cut into
   thick slices
1 red (Spanish) onion, thinly sliced
1 tablespoon balsamic vinegar

1 In a large pan of boiling water, cook the prepared beans for 1–2 minutes, until tender but still crisp. Remove with a slotted spoon and rinse under cold water. Drain and transfer to a serving bowl.
2 Cook the pasta in a large pan of rapidly boiling salted water until *al dente*. Drain, rinse under cold water and drain again before adding to the beans.
3 Heat half the oil in a frying pan. Add the tuna and onion and gently sauté until the tuna is just cooked through. Stir the tuna carefully to prevent it from breaking up. Add the vinegar, turn heat to high and quickly cook until the dressing has reduced and lightly coats the tuna. Transfer the tuna and onion to a bowl, leaving behind any bits on the bottom of the pan.
4 Toss the beans, pasta, tuna and onion together lightly and mix with the remaining oil, and salt and pepper, to taste. Cool to room temperature before serving.

NUTRITION PER SERVE: *Protein 25 g; Fat 30 g; Carbohydrate 55 g; Dietary Fibre 6 g; Cholesterol 45 mg; 2535 kJ (605 cal)*

PASTRAMI, MUSHROOM AND CUCUMBER SALAD

Preparation time: 20 minutes
Total cooking time: 5–10 minutes
Serves 4

☆

200 g (6½ oz) lasagnette, broken
   into quarters
250 g (8 oz) sliced pastrami,
   cut in strips
1 celery stick, sliced
2 small tomatoes, cut into wedges
1 Lebanese cucumber, thinly sliced
80 g (2¾ oz) button mushrooms,
   thinly sliced
1 tablespoon finely chopped fresh
   coriander, to garnish

Dressing

¼ cup (60 ml/2 fl oz) olive oil
2 tablespoons red wine vinegar
½ teaspoon Dijon mustard
1 clove garlic, crushed
¼ teaspoon hot chilli oil

1 Cook the lasagnette in a large pan of rapidly boiling salted water until *al dente*. Drain, rinse under cold water and drain again. Allow to cool and transfer to a large salad bowl.
2 Add the pastrami, celery, tomato wedges, cucumber and mushrooms to the pasta.
3 To prepare the dressing, combine all the ingredients in a screw top jar and shake until well blended.
4 Toss the dressing through the salad and refrigerate, covered, for several hours. Adjust the seasoning and sprinkle with the fresh coriander before serving.

NUTRITION PER SERVE: *Protein 15 g; Fat 55 g; Carbohydrate 35 g; Dietary Fibre 4 g; Cholesterol 280 mg; 3050 kJ (725 cal)*

PASTRAMI

Pastrami is a cured, highly seasoned cut of lean beef made popular in the United States. It is believed to have originated in the Balkans and is closely related to the pastirma of Turkey. Spiced with paprika, pepper, cumin and garlic, and sometimes smoked, pastrami is delicious sliced thinly and eaten cold.

OPPOSITE PAGE: Tuna, green bean and onion salad (top); Pastrami, mushroom and cucumber salad

ARTICHOKE HEARTS

Artichokes are a thistle and the edible part of a globe artichoke is the flower head. In the centre of this is the choke, a mass of hairs which is, in fact, the flower, and this sits on a tender cup-like base. It is surrounded by fleshy leaves of which the tough, outer ones are discarded to reveal the artichoke's heart, the lower section of delicate inner leaves surrounding the choke and bottom cup. Canned or bottled artichoke hearts retain a good flavour and are a time-saving substitute for fresh ones.

ABOVE: Italian-style chicken and pasta salad

ITALIAN-STYLE CHICKEN AND PASTA SALAD

Preparation time: 30 minutes
 + 3 hours marinating
Total cooking time: 10 minutes
Serves 8

☆

3 chicken breast fillets
1/4 cup (60 ml/2 fl oz) lemon juice
1 clove garlic, crushed
100 g (3 1/2 oz) thinly sliced prosciutto
1 Lebanese cucumber
2 tablespoons seasoned lemon pepper
2 tablespoons olive oil
1 1/2 cups (135 g/4 1/2 oz) penne, cooked
1/2 cup (80 g/2 3/4 oz) thinly sliced sun-dried
  tomatoes
1/2 cup (70 g/2 1/4 oz) pitted black olives, halved
1/2 cup (110 g/3 1/2 oz) halved bottled
  artichoke hearts
1/2 cup (50 g/1 3/4 oz) shaved fresh Parmesan

Creamy basil dressing
1/3 cup (80 ml/2 3/4 fl oz) olive oil
1 tablespoon white wine vinegar
1/4 teaspoon seasoned pepper
1 teaspoon Dijon mustard
3 teaspoons cornflour
2/3 cup (170 ml/5 1/2 fl oz) cream
1/3 cup (20 g/3/4 oz) shredded fresh basil

1 Remove the excess fat and sinew from the chicken. Flatten the chicken slightly with a mallet or rolling pin.
2 Combine the lemon juice and garlic in a bowl. Add the chicken and stir until it is coated. Cover with plastic wrap and refrigerate for at least 3 hours or overnight, turning occasionally.
3 Cut the prosciutto into thin strips. Cut the cucumber in half lengthways and cut each half into slices.
4 Drain the chicken and coat in seasoned pepper. Heat the oil in a large heavy-based frying pan. Cook the chicken for 4 minutes on

each side, or until lightly browned and cooked through. Remove from the heat, allow to cool and then cut into small pieces.

5 To make the creamy basil dressing, combine the oil, white wine vinegar, pepper and mustard in a medium pan. Blend the cornflour with ⅓ cup (80 ml/2¾ fl oz) of water in a small bowl or jug until smooth. Add to the pan. Whisk over medium heat for 2 minutes, or until the sauce boils and thickens. Add the cream, basil and salt, to taste. Stir until heated through.

6 Combine the pasta, chicken pieces, cucumber slices, prosciutto, sun-dried tomato, olives and artichoke hearts in a large serving bowl. Pour in the warm creamy basil dressing and toss gently to combine. Serve the salad warm or cold, topped with shaved Parmesan.

NUTRITION PER SERVE: *Protein 15 g; Fat 30 g; Carbohydrate 15 g; Dietary Fibre 2 g; Cholesterol 60 mg; 1555 kJ (370 cal)*

CREAMY SEAFOOD SALAD

Preparation time: 30 minutes
Total cooking time: 5–10 minutes
Serves 8 as a first course, 4 as a main meal

★

400 g (13 oz) medium-sized conchiglie (shells)
1 cup (250 g/8 oz) whole-egg mayonnaise
3 tablespoons fresh or 2 tablespoons
    dried tarragon
1 tablespoon finely chopped
    fresh parsley
cayenne pepper, to taste
1 teaspoon fresh lemon juice, or to taste
1 kg (2 lb) cooked shellfish flesh: prawns,
    lobster, crab (any one of these or a
    combination), cut into bite-sized pieces
2 mild red radishes, thinly sliced
1 small green pepper (capsicum), julienned

1 Cook the pasta in rapidly boiling salted water until *al dente*. Drain, rinse under cold water and drain again. Place in a large bowl and stir through 1–2 tablespoons of mayonnaise. Cool to room temperature, stirring occasionally to prevent sticking.

2 If using dried tarragon, simmer it in ¼ cup (60 ml/2 fl oz) of milk for 3–4 minutes and then drain. Combine the tarragon, parsley, cayenne pepper and lemon juice in a bowl, with the remaining mayonnaise, and mix well.

3 Add the shellfish to the pasta with the radishes and peppers, and salt and pepper, to taste. Mix with the tarragon mayonnaise, tossing gently to coat. Cover and chill before serving, adding more mayonnaise or extra lemon juice if the mixture is a little dry.

NOTE: To make your own mayonnaise, in a bowl, whisk together 2 egg yolks, 1 teaspoon of Dijon mustard and 2 teaspoons of lemon juice for 30 seconds, until light and creamy. Add 1 cup (250 ml (8 fl oz) of light olive oil, about a teaspoon at a time, whisking continuously. Increase the amount of oil as the mayonnaise thickens. When all the oil has been added, stir in an extra 2 teaspoons of lemon juice and season, to taste, with salt and white pepper. Alternatively, you can use a food processor. Use the same ingredients, but process the yolks, mustard and juice for 10 seconds. With the motor running, add the oil in a slow, thin stream until combined.

NUTRITION PER SERVE (8): *Protein 35 g; Fat 10 g; Carbohydrate 40 g; Dietary Fibre 3 g; Cholesterol 245 mg; 1755 kJ (415 cal)*

ABOVE: Creamy seafood salad

ROCKET, CHERRY TOMATO AND SPICY SALAMI PASTA SALAD

Preparation time: 20 minutes
Total cooking time: 18 minutes
Serves 6

☆

350 g (11 oz) orecchiette
6 slices (50 g/1³/₄ oz) spicy Italian salami, cut into strips
150 g (5 oz) rocket, shredded
200 g (6¹/₂ oz) cherry tomatoes, halved
4 tablespoons olive oil
3 tablespoons white wine vinegar
1 teaspoon sugar

1 Cook the pasta in a large pan of rapidly boiling salted water until *al dente*. Drain, rinse under cold water and drain again. Allow to cool.
2 Heat a frying pan over medium heat, add the prepared salami and cook until crisp. Drain well on paper towels.
3 Combine the salami, pasta, rocket and cherry tomatoes in a large bowl.
4 In a small food processor, combine the oil, vinegar, sugar and ¼ teaspoon each of salt and pepper, for 1 minute. Drizzle over the salad just before serving.

NUTRITION PER SERVE: *Protein 9 g; Fat 15 g; Carbohydrate 45 g; Dietary Fibre 4 g; Cholesterol 9 mg; 1505 kJ (360 cal)*

ON THE SIDE

DAMPER Sift 4 cups (500 g/1 lb) of self-raising flour with 1 teaspoon of salt and 1 teaspoon of caster sugar into a large bowl. Use a knife to mix in enough milk, about 1½ cups (375 ml/12 fl oz), to make a fairly stiff dough which leaves the side of the bowl. Knead the dough for about 1 minute, on a floured surface, and form into a ball. Place the ball on a greased baking tray and flatten slightly, cut 2 slits across the top, brush with milk and bake at hot 210°C (415°F/Gas 6–7) for 15 minutes, then turn the oven down to moderate 180°C (350°F/Gas 4) and bake for 20 minutes, or until the damper is golden and the base sounds hollow when tapped.

CHICKEN, PEAR AND PASTA SALAD

Preparation time: 35 minutes
Total cooking time: 30 minutes
Serves 6

☆

350 g (11 oz) gemelli or fusilli
200 g (6¹/₂ oz) chicken breast fillets
2 ripe pears
3 spring onions, finely sliced
2 tablespoons toasted slivered almonds
100 g (3¹/₂ oz) creamy blue cheese
3 tablespoons sour cream
3 tablespoons ice-cold water

1 Cook the pasta in a large pan of rapidly boiling salted water until *al dente*. Drain, rinse under cold water and drain again. Allow to cool.
2 Place the chicken breasts in a frying pan, cover with cold water and simmer gently for 8 minutes, or until tender, turning the chicken over occasionally. Remove from the pan, allow to cool, slice into fine pieces and place in a bowl with the cooled pasta.
3 Halve the pears and remove the cores. Cut the pears into thin slices, about the same size as the chicken pieces and add to the chicken with the spring onion and almonds.
4 Mix the creamy blue cheese and the sour cream with 3 tablespoons of ice-cold water and ¼ teaspoon each of salt and pepper, in a food processor until smooth. Pour the mixture over the salad and stir to combine. Transfer the salad to a serving bowl or arrange on a platter. Garnish with slivers of spring onion, if you like.

NUTRITION PER SERVE: *Protein 20 g; Fat 15 g; Carbohydrate 50 g; Dietary Fibre 5 g; Cholesterol 45 mg; 1655 kJ (395 cal)*

PEARS
The pear is a very versatile fruit. It can be eaten fresh, used in desserts and sweets, or cooked in savoury dishes. The crisp, firm texture reacts well to heat and the flavour is compatible with many other foods. Poultry, cheeses, salad greens and strangely enough, olive oil, make particularly good companions. There is a huge selection of local varieties grown They can be categorised into dessert pears, those with a clear, crisp sweet flesh intended for eating fresh, and cooking pears, which have a firm, often granular flesh and a more tart taste.

OPPOSITE PAGE: Rocket, cherry tomato and spicy salami pasta salad (top); Chicken, pear and pasta salad

BARBECUED CHICKEN AND PASTA SALAD

Preparation time: 15 minutes
Total cooking time: 15 minutes
Serves 6

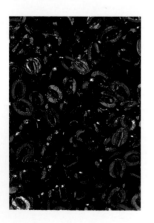

1 barbecued chicken
500 g (1 lb) penne
1/4 cup (60 ml/2 fl oz) olive oil
2 tablespoons white wine vinegar
200 g (6 1/2 oz) cherry tomatoes, halved
1/3 cup (20 g/3/4 oz) chopped fresh
   basil leaves
1/2 cup (75 g/2 1/2 oz) chopped pitted
   black olives
freshly ground black pepper, to taste

1 Pull the meat and skin from the barbecued chicken. Cut into fine shreds.
2 Cook the penne in a large pan of rapidly boiling salted water until *al dente*. Drain and transfer to a serving bowl. Combine the oil and vinegar and toss through while the pasta is still warm.
3 Add the chicken, cherry tomatoes, basil and olives to the pasta, and toss thoroughly to combine. Sprinkle with freshly ground black pepper. Serve warm, as a main meal, or at room temperature as part of a selection of salads.
NOTE: The salad can be prepared up to 2 hours in advance. Refrigerate the chicken until close to serving time and add it to the salad at the last minute. Chop and add the basil close to serving time as well, as it discolours when cut.

NUTRITION PER SERVE: *Protein 30 g; Fat 20 g; Carbohydrate 60 g; Dietary Fibre 5 g; Cholesterol 70 mg; 2500 kJ (595 cal)*

ABOVE: Barbecued chicken and pasta salad

LEMON AND VEGETABLE PASTA SALAD

Preparation time: 20 minutes
Total cooking time: 15 minutes
Serves 4

★

250 g (8 oz) farfalle

1/3 cup (80 ml/2¾ fl oz) olive oil

250 g (8 oz) broccoli, cut into small florets

125 g (4 oz) snow peas (mangetout), topped and tailed

150 g (5 oz) small yellow button squash, cut into quarters

2 tablespoons sour cream

1 tablespoon lemon juice

2 teaspoons finely grated lemon rind

1 celery stick, finely sliced

1 tablespoon chopped chervil

chervil sprigs, to garnish

1 Cook the farfalle in a large pan of rapidly boiling salted water until *al dente*. Drain well, toss with 1 tablespoon of the olive oil and set aside to cool.

2 Combine the broccoli, snow peas and squash in a large bowl, cover with boiling water and leave for 2 minutes. Drain, plunge into iced water, drain again and pat dry with paper towels.

3 Put the sour cream, lemon juice, rind and the remaining oil in a screw top jar and shake for 30 seconds, or until combined. Season with salt and pepper, to taste.

4 Combine the cooled pasta, sliced celery and drained vegetables in a large bowl; sprinkle with chervil. Drizzle the dressing over and toss to combine. Garnish with chervil sprigs. Serve at room temperature.

NUTRITION PER SERVE: *Protein 10 g; Fat 25 g; Carbohydrate 50 g; Dietary Fibre 5 g; Cholesterol 15 mg; 1910 kJ (455 cal)*

CHERVIL

An umbelliferous plant cultivated as a pot-herb, chervil has a delicate, slightly aniseed flavour. It has stiff stems and dainty, curly leaves, which can be chopped for use but are often left whole, like little petals. Its aroma evaporates quickly, so the leaves are best used fresh or added to hot dishes at the last minute. Chervil is folded through omelettes, sprinkled over soup and used as a garnish.

ABOVE: Lemon and vegetable pasta salad

BREAD
Crusty and fresh, in all its delightful varieties, bread is the perfect accompaniment to most meals. Serve plain, or dress it up with garlic, cheese, fresh basil, parsley and other herbs.

GARLIC GRISSINI STICKS
Preheat the oven to moderately hot 200°C (400°F/Gas 6). Combine 2 crushed cloves of garlic with 1 tablespoon of olive oil. Brush over 1 packet of grissini sticks and wrap each in paper-thin strips of prosciutto. Bake for 5 minutes, until the ends crisp. Cool on trays before serving. Makes about 25.

NUTRITION PER SERVE: *Protein 2 g; Fat 2 g; Carbohydrate 6 g; Dietary Fibre 0 g; Cholesterol 4 mg; 210 kJ (50 cal)*

CHEESY HERB ROLLS
Preheat the oven to 220°C (425°F/Gas 7). Combine 125 g (4 oz) of softened butter with 1 tablespoon each of chopped fresh basil, parsley and chives and 1/4 cup (30 g/1 oz) of grated Cheddar cheese.

Season with salt and pepper. Cut 4 crusty rosetta rolls into thin slices, but don't cut all the way through. Spread each side of each slice with flavoured butter. Bake for 15 minutes, or until the rolls are crisp and golden. Serves 4.

NUTRITION PER SERVE: *Protein 10 g; Fat 30 g; Carbohydrate 45 g; Dietary Fibre 3 g; Cholesterol 90 mg; 2055 kJ (490 cal)*

CRISPY FOCACCIA TOASTS WITH PESTO

Cut a square of focaccia, about 20 cm (8 inches) in diameter, in half horizontally. Combine 1 cup (50 g/ 1¾ oz) of basil leaves, 2 cloves of garlic, 3 tablespoons of toasted pine nuts and 4 tablespoons of freshly grated Parmesan in a food processor until roughly chopped. With the motor running, gradually add ¼ cup (60 ml/2 fl oz) of olive oil and process until the mixture forms a smooth paste. Brush the focaccia squares with olive oil and toast both sides until golden brown. Spread the pesto over the focaccia and cut into small rectangles. Makes 16–20.

NUTRITION PER SERVE: *Protein 2 g; Fat 6 g; Carbohydrate 4 g; Dietary Fibre 0 g; Cholesterol 3 mg; 340 kJ (80 cal)*

ROASTED PEPPER (CAPSICUM) BRUSCHETTA

Cut a red and a yellow pepper (capsicum) in half, removing the seeds and membrane. Place, skin-side-up, under a hot grill until the skin blackens and blisters. Cover with a damp tea towel and allow to cool. Peel away the skin and cut the flesh into thin strips. Cut 1 loaf of woodfired Italian bread into thin slices and toast lightly until golden. Rub each side of the slices with halved cloves of garlic and brush lightly with extra virgin olive oil. Top with a little of the pepper and sprinkle with fresh lemon thyme. Makes about 30 slices.

NUTRITION PER SERVE: *Protein 2 g; Fat 2 g; Carbohydrate 10 g; Dietary Fibre 1 g; Cholesterol 0 mg; 315 kJ (75 cal)*

ANCHOVY AND TOMATO CROSTINI

Cut 1 French baguette into thick diagonal slices. Brush lightly with olive oil and toast until golden. Spread with 250 g (8 oz) of sun-dried tomato pesto and sprinkle with 50 g (1¾ oz) of drained, thinly sliced anchovy fillets, 50 g (1¾ oz) of chopped black olives and some shredded fresh basil. Makes about 15 pieces.

NUTRITION PER SERVE: *Protein 4 g; Fat 5 g; Carbohydrate 15 g; Dietary Fibre 1 g; Cholesterol 4 mg; 535 kJ (125 cal)*

ABOVE, FROM LEFT: Garlic grissini sticks; Cheesy herb rolls; Crispy focaccia toasts with pesto; Roasted pepper bruschetta; Anchovy and tomato crostini

FRESH BABY CORN

Fresh baby corn is available from greengrocers and some supermarkets. It should be crisp and dry, have a soft yellow colour with no blemishes and be no longer than 8 cm (3 inches). It tastes of sweet, fresh corn and the cob is eaten whole. Although made popular in Asian dishes, it is now used in many cooking styles, for the sweet flavour and crunchy texture.

ABOVE: Pasta with Thai-style vegetables

PASTA WITH THAI-STYLE VEGETABLES

Preparation time: 20 minutes
Total cooking time: 15 minutes
Serves 6

★

350 g (11 oz) plain or tomato and herb fettucine

100 g (3½ oz) fresh baby corn, cut in half lengthways

1 carrot, cut into julienne strips

200 g (6½ oz) broccoli, cut into small florets

1 red pepper (capsicum), cut into thin strips

3 tablespoons sweet chilli sauce

2 tablespoons honey

2 teaspoons fish sauce

3 spring onions, julienned

2 teaspoons sesame seeds

1 Cook the pasta in a large pan of rapidly boiling salted water until *al dente*. Drain, rinse under cold water and drain again. Allow to cool.
2 In another pan of boiling water, blanch the corn for 1 minute. Use a slotted spoon to transfer the corn to a bowl of iced water. Blanch the carrot, broccoli and red pepper for 30 seconds, drain and add to the cold water. When the vegetables have cooled, drain and combine with the pasta in a bowl.
3 Whisk together the sweet chilli sauce, honey and fish sauce until well combined. Drizzle over the salad and mix well. Garnish with the spring onion and sesame seeds.

NUTRITION PER SERVE: *Protein 10 g; Fat 2 g; Carbohydrate 60 g; Dietary Fibre 6 g; Cholesterol 0 mg; 1210 kJ (290 cal)*

PASTA WITH MEDITERRANEAN-STYLE VEGETABLES

Preparation time: 30 minutes
Total cooking time: 15 minutes
Serves 6

☆

350 g (11 oz) macaroni
200 g (6½ oz) fried and marinated eggplant
(aubergine) slices (see note)
100 g (3½ oz) sun-dried or semi-dried
tomatoes
60 g (2 oz) Kalamata olives, pitted
200 g (6½ oz) double-smoked sliced or
shaved ham
2 tablespoons sweet chilli sauce
1 tablespoon white wine vinegar
1 tablespoon olive oil
2 tablespoons chopped fresh parsley

1 Cook the pasta in a large pan of rapidly
boiling salted water until *al dente*. Drain, rinse
under cold water and drain again. Allow to cool
and transfer to a bowl.
2 Slice the eggplant, tomato, olives and ham
into strips and add to the pasta. Shaved ham can
just be separated into smallish pieces.
3 Whisk together the sweet chilli sauce, vinegar,
oil, and salt and pepper, to taste, until well
combined. Drizzle the dressing over the pasta
and vegetables and toss well. Serve scattered
with the fresh parsley.
NOTE: Marinated vegetables are available from
delicatessens. If preferred, red or green peppers
(capsicums) or zucchini (courgettes) can be used.

NUTRITION PER SERVE: *Protein 15 g; Fat 8 g;
Carbohydrate 45 g; Dietary Fibre 4 g; Cholesterol 15 mg;
1280 kJ (305 cal)*

SHAVED HAM
Very finely sliced ham is
known as shaved ham. It
should be wafer-thin, but
still in discernible pieces
that fall into a loosely
bulky heap. This method
of preparation gives the
ham a delicate texture.
Shaved ham is available
from delicatessens and
should be eaten as soon as
possible, as it spoils more
quickly than unshaved.

*ABOVE: Pasta with
Mediterranean-style
vegetables*

BALSAMIC VINEGAR

Balsamic vinegar, *aceto balsamico*, is a speciality of the area around Modena in central northern Italy. It is made from the newly pressed juice of selected white grapes, which is slowly boiled down to one third of its volume. The resulting syrup is aged over a number of years, in a series of wooden casks, until it becomes concentrated, mellow and highly aromatic. It is a dense, almost black sauce which is used sparingly not as a regular vinegar, but as a condiment. A good balsamic vinegar should be sweet and syrupy but not cloying, with an intense fragrance and flavour. There are many imitations being manufactured and a cheap copy bears little resemblance to the real thing. Here is an instance where it is truly worth spending extra for the genuine article.

OPPOSITE PAGE:
Conchiglie salad with bocconcini, asparagus and oregano (top);
Warm garlic prawn and fettucine salad

CONCHIGLIE SALAD WITH BOCCONCINI, ASPARAGUS AND OREGANO

Preparation time: 25 minutes
Total cooking time: 10–15 minutes
Serves 4–6

⭐

350 g (11 oz) conchiglie (shell pasta)
155 g (5 oz) fresh asparagus
200 g (6½ oz) bocconcini cheese, thinly sliced
100 g (3½ oz) cherry tomatoes, quartered
2 tablespoons fresh oregano leaves
4 tablespoons walnut oil
1 tablespoon white wine vinegar
1 tablespoon balsamic vinegar
¼ teaspoon each salt and freshly ground
   black pepper

1 Cook the conchiglie in a large pan of rapidly boiling salted water until *al dente*. Drain, rinse under cold water and drain again. Allow to cool.
2 Cut the asparagus into short lengths. Bring a small pan of water to the boil, add the asparagus and blanch for 1 minute. Drain, transfer to a bowl of iced water to cool and then drain again.
3 In a large bowl, combine the conchiglie, asparagus, bocconcini, tomato and oregano. In a small bowl, whisk together the walnut oil, vinegars, salt and pepper until well combined.
4 Drizzle the dressing over the salad and toss thoroughly before serving.

NUTRITION PER SERVE (6): *Protein 15 g; Fat 25 g; Carbohydrate 40 g; Dietary Fibre 5 g; Cholesterol 35 mg; 1900 kJ (455 cal)*

WARM GARLIC PRAWN AND FETTUCINE SALAD

Preparation time: 30 minutes
Total cooking time: 25 minutes
Serves 4–6

⭐⭐

300 g (10 oz) fettucine
2 tablespoons olive oil
4 cloves garlic, crushed
300 g (10 oz) raw prawn meat
2 tablespoons whisky
½ cup (125 ml/4 fl oz) cream
3 spring onions, chopped

1 Cook the fettucine in a large pan of rapidly boiling salted water until *al dente*. Drain, rinse under cold water and drain again. Allow to cool and set aside.
2 Heat the olive oil in a heavy-based frying pan. Add the garlic and cook for 30 seconds. Add the prawns and stir-fry over high heat until they change colour. Add the whisky and cook until it evaporates. Add the cream and spring onion and simmer for 2 minutes.
3 Drizzle the sauce over the pasta. Season with plenty of salt and pepper.

NUTRITION PER SERVE (6): *Protein 15 g; Fat 15 g; Carbohydrate 35 g; Dietary Fibre 5 g; Cholesterol 125 mg; 1530 kJ (365 cal)*

ON THE SIDE

PARMESAN BISCUITS Sift 2 cups (250 g/8 oz) of plain flour with 1 teaspoon of baking powder, ¼ teaspoon of paprika and ½ teaspoon of salt into a bowl. Rub in 60 g (2 oz) of butter. Add ¼ cup (25 g/¾ oz) of finely grated Parmesan and ¾ cup (185 ml/6 fl oz) of milk and bring the mixture together. Roll out the mixture to about 2 cm (¾ inch) thick and cut out the biscuits. Sprinkle with some more Parmesan and bake in a hot 220°C (425°F/Gas 7) oven for 15 minutes.

RIGATONI

Rigatoni is a pasta with many uses: good for salads but also great for serving with chunky sauces, particularly tomato- or meat-based ones. When it is well tossed through, sauce catches inside the tubes and clings to the ribs on the outside surface. Tortiglioni is similar, with a slight bend in the middle.

ABOVE: Rigatoni with tomato, haloumi and spinach

RIGATONI WITH TOMATO, HALOUMI AND SPINACH

Preparation time: 30 minutes
Total cooking time: 1 hour
Serves 6

★

6 egg (Roma) tomatoes, halved
sugar, to sprinkle
4 cloves garlic, chopped
400 g (13 oz) rigatoni
1/4 cup (60 ml/2 fl oz) lemon juice
1/4 cup (60 ml/2 fl oz) olive oil
200 g (6 1/2 oz) haloumi cheese,
    thinly sliced
100 g (3 1/2 oz) baby English spinach

1 Preheat the oven to moderate 180°C (350°F/Gas 4). Put the tomatoes on a non-stick baking tray, lined with foil if you like, and sprinkle generously with salt, sugar, pepper and the garlic. Bake for 1 hour, or until quite dehydrated and shrunken. Allow to cool. Cut in half again.
2 While the tomatoes are cooking, cook the pasta in a large pan of rapidly boiling salted water until *al dente*. Drain, rinse under cold water and drain again. Allow to cool.
3 Combine the lemon juice and olive oil. Season, to taste, with salt and pepper.
4 Toss the lemon dressing through the cooked, cold pasta and lightly toss the tomato, haloumi cheese and spinach through. Serve sprinkled with freshly cracked black pepper, to taste.

NUTRITION PER SERVE: *Protein 20 g; Fat 35 g; Carbohydrate 50 g; Dietary Fibre 5 g; Cholesterol 25 mg; 2530 kJ (605 cal)*

DATES

Date palms grow in desert regions and have been cultivated for thousands of years. Fresh dates have a fruity, moist pulp and are an excellent source of iron, folic acid and vitamin B6, as well as having a high fibre content. There are hard and soft dates, the latter being preferred for table use. Both dry well, with soft dates maintaining succulent, soft flesh. Fresh and soft dried dates are interchangeable in recipes but dried are sweeter, with a slightly more concentrated flavour.

LEMON AND DATE ZITI

Preparation time: 15–20 minutes
Total cooking time: 25 minutes
Serves 4–6

☆

2 cups (360 g/12 oz) dried pitted
  dates, halved
1 1/2 cups (375 ml/12 fl oz) port
375 g (12 oz) ziti
1/4 cup (60 ml/2 fl oz) balsamic vinegar
1/2 cup (125 ml/4 fl oz) olive oil
150 g (5 oz) rocket, trimmed
rind from 3 preserved lemons (see note),
  finely chopped

1 Place the dates and port in a pan. Bring to the boil, reduce the heat and simmer for 10 minutes. Strain the dates, reserving the port. Set aside to cool.
2 Cook the ziti in a large pan of rapidly boiling salted water until *al dente*. Drain, rinse in cold water and drain again. Allow to cool.
3 Combine the balsamic vinegar, reserved port and olive oil in a bowl. Season with a little sugar if necessary.
4 Toss the dressing through the pasta with the dates, rocket and lemon rind.
NOTE: Preserved lemons can be purchased at any good delicatessen or speciality food shop. They are available either per lemon or bottled. This salad is also wonderful served warm.

NUTRITION PER SERVE (6): *Protein 10 g; Fat 20 g; Carbohydrate 95 g; Dietary Fibre 10 g; Cholesterol 0 mg; 2715 kJ (650 cal)*

ABOVE: Lemon and date ziti

191

and blistered. Remove from the heat and cover with a damp tea towel. When cool, peel away the skin and cut the flesh into thin strips.

3 In a large salad bowl, combine the pasta, pepper strips, onion, parsley, anchovies, oil, lemon juice, and salt and pepper, to taste. Toss until well combined and serve immediately.

NOTE: To prevent pasta sticking together, after rinsing under cold water add a little of the oil to pasta and toss well.

NUTRITION PER SERVE: *Protein 10 g; Fat 10 g; Carbohydrate 65 g; Dietary Fibre 5 g; Cholesterol 0 mg; 1675 kJ (400 cal)*

WARM PASTA AND CRAB SALAD

Preparation time: 20 minutes
Total cooking time: 10 minutes
Serves 6

✫

200 g (6¹/₂ oz) spaghetti
2 tablespoons olive oil
30 g (1 oz) butter
3 × 200 g (6¹/₂ oz) cans crab meat, drained
1 large red pepper (capsicum), cut into
   thin strips
2 teaspoons finely grated lemon rind
3 tablespoons grated fresh Parmesan
2 tablespoons chopped chives
3 tablespoons chopped fresh parsley

1 Break the spaghetti in half and cook it in a large pan of rapidly boiling salted water until *al dente*. Drain.
2 Place the spaghetti in a large serving bowl and toss with the oil and butter. Add all the remaining ingredients and toss to combine. Sprinkle with pepper and serve warm.
NOTE: Substitute 500 g (1 lb) of fresh crab meat for canned if you prefer.

NUTRITION PER SERVE: *Protein 20 g; Fat 15 g; Carbohydrate 25 g; Dietary Fibre 2 g; Cholesterol 100 mg; 1245 kJ (295 cal)*

GRILLED PEPPERS (CAPSICUMS) AND ANCHOVY SALAD

Preparation time: 15 minutes
Total cooking time: 25 minutes
Serves 6

✫

500 g (1 lb) penne or spiral pasta
2 large red peppers (capsicums)
1 small red onion, finely chopped
1 cup (20 g/³/₄ oz) fresh flat-leaf parsley leaves
2–3 anchovies, whole or chopped
¹/₄ cup (60 ml/2 fl oz) olive oil
2 tablespoons lemon juice

1 Cook the pasta in a large pan of rapidly boiling salted water until *al dente*. Drain, rinse under cold water and drain again.
2 Cut the peppers in half and remove seeds and membrane. Place skin-side-up under a hot grill and cook for 8 minutes, or until the skin is black

ABOVE: Grilled peppers and anchovy salad

TUSCAN WARM PASTA SALAD

Preparation time: 15 minutes
Total cooking time: 15 minutes
Serves 6

★

500 g (1 lb) rigatoni
1/3 cup (80 ml/2 3/4 fl oz) olive oil
1 clove garlic, crushed
1 tablespoon balsamic vinegar
425 g (14 oz) can artichoke hearts, drained and quartered
8 thin slices prosciutto, chopped
1/2 cup (80 g/2 3/4 oz) sun-dried tomatoes in oil, drained and thinly sliced
1/4 cup (15 g/1/2 oz) fresh basil leaves, shredded
2 cups (70 g/2 1/4 oz) rocket leaves, washed and drained well
1/4 cup (40 g/1 1/4 oz) pine nuts, lightly toasted
1/4 cup (45 g/1 1/2 oz) small black Italian olives

1 Add the rigatoni to a large pan of rapidly boiling water and cook until *al dente*. Drain the pasta thoroughly and transfer to a large serving bowl.
2 While the pasta is cooking, whisk together the oil, garlic and balsamic vinegar.
3 Toss the dressing through the hot pasta. Allow the pasta to cool slightly. Add the artichoke hearts, prosciutto, sun-dried tomato, basil, rocket, pine nuts and olives.
4 Toss all the ingredients together until well combined. Season, to taste, with salt and freshly ground black pepper.
NOTE: To toast the pine nuts, cook in a dry frying pan over medium heat for 1–2 minutes, until lightly golden. Allow to cool.

NUTRITION PER SERVE: *Protein 15 g; Fat 20 g; Carbohydrate 60 g; Dietary Fibre 10 g; Cholesterol 15 mg; 2145 kJ (510 cal)*

SALT

There are two sources of salt, or sodium chloride: rock salt, found in crystalline form in the ground, and sea salt, extracted from sea water. Refined sea salt is available in pure crystal form, which must be ground, in thin flakes ready to use, or already ground. This free running table salt has had products such as phosphate of lime added to prevent the pure salt reverting to crystal form when in humidity. Pure salt provides the best flavour.

ABOVE: Tuscan warm pasta salad

193

SMOKED SALMON, DILL AND EGG PASTA SALAD

Preparation time: 20 minutes
Total cooking time: 15 minutes
Serves 4–6

⭐

350 g (11 oz) farfalle or fusilli
2 eggs
200 g (6½ oz) smoked salmon, cut into
    thin strips
1 tablespoon finely chopped fresh dill
3 tablespoons sour cream
2 tablespoons lemon juice
¼ teaspoon each salt and freshly ground
    black pepper
1 tablespoon chopped fresh parsley, to garnish

1 Cook the pasta in a large pan of rapidly boiling salted water until *al dente*. Drain, rinse under cold water and drain again. Allow to cool.
2 While the pasta is cooking, cook the eggs for 12 minutes, or until hard-boiled. Allow to cool and then peel, finely grate or chop and set aside.
3 Place the pasta in serving bowls and scatter the strips of smoked salmon and the chopped fresh dill over the top.
4 In a small bowl, whisk together the sour cream, lemon juice, salt and pepper. Drizzle the dressing over the pasta. Sprinkle the egg and parsley over the top and serve immediately.

NUTRITION PER SERVE (6): *Protein 15 g; Fat 10 g; Carbohydrate 40 g; Dietary Fibre 3 g; Cholesterol 90 mg; 1280 kJ (305 cal)*

ON THE SIDE

GARLIC PIZZA BREAD Make up a pizza base using a pizza base mix and roll it out to a thin circle on a baking tray. Brush the surface of the dough with olive oil and sprinkle it with crushed garlic, chopped fresh parsley and coarse salt. Bake until golden brown. Cut into strips with a sharp knife or a pizza cutter.

ORANGE AND OLIVE SALAD Cut 8 peeled oranges into thick slices. Layer the oranges with thinly sliced red (Spanish) onion and chopped fresh mint on a plate. Top with olives and drizzle with a dressing made from orange juice, crushed garlic and a little sesame oil.

MIDDLE-EASTERN HUMMUS, TOMATO AND OLIVE PASTA SALAD

Preparation time: 25 minutes
Total cooking time: 15 minutes
Serves 6

⭐

350 g (11 oz) macaroni elbows or
    conchiglie (shell pasta)
200 g (6½ oz) cherry tomatoes, cut
    into quarters
1 large zucchini (courgette), grated
1 small onion, grated
50 g (1¾ oz) black olives, pitted and chopped

Hummus dressing

2 tablespoons hummus
2 tablespoons natural yoghurt
1 tablespoon olive oil
1 clove garlic, finely chopped
1 teaspoon finely grated lemon rind
1 tablespoon chopped fresh parsley

1 Cook the pasta in a large pan of rapidly boiling salted water until *al dente*. Drain, rinse under cold water and drain again. Allow to cool. Place the pasta in a large bowl with the tomato, zucchini, onion and olives.
2 To make the hummus dressing, in a blender or food processor, combine the hummus, yoghurt, olive oil, garlic and lemon rind. Add plenty of salt and pepper and process again briefly.
3 Pour the dressing over the salad, add the parsley and toss well to combine.

NUTRITION PER SERVE: *Protein 8 g; Fat 7 g; Carbohydrate 45 g; Dietary Fibre 5 g; Cholesterol 1 mg; 1145 kJ (270 cal)*

DILL
Dill is a native of the Mediterranean and has been used since ancient times for its medicinal properties and culinary flavours. All of the upper plant is aromatic, but the delicate leaves have the most subtle taste and aroma. Their bitter-sweet flavour nicely complements dairy produce such as cream, butter and cheese, and it enhances fish particularly well. Because its essential oil is extremely volatile, it will quickly evaporate in temperatures above 30°C (86°F), so this means dill should be added to a cooked dish just before serving.

OPPOSITE PAGE:
Smoked salmon, dill and egg pasta salad (top); Middle-eastern hummus, tomato and olive pasta salad

GNOCCHI

Simplicity and adaptability are the two characteristics to which gnocchi owes its popularity. While making your own spaghetti may be a daunting task, making gnocchi is a skill that anyone can master. And, once you've perfected the basic potato recipe, you can experiment with other vegetables, such as pumpkin, carrot, spinach or parsnip. Gnocchi also lends itself to buttery, creamy or tomato sauces. Whatever the combination, these little dumplings are simply divine.

GNOCCHI ROMANA
(SEMOLINA GNOCCHI WITH RICH CHEESE SAUCE)

Preparation time: 20 minutes
+ 1 hour refrigeration
Total cooking time: 40 minutes
Serves 4

★★

3 cups (750 ml/24 fl oz) milk
1/2 teaspoon ground nutmeg
2/3 cup (85 g/3 oz) semolina
1 egg, beaten
1 1/2 cups (150 g/5 oz) freshly
  grated Parmesan
60 g (2 oz) butter, melted
1/2 cup (125 m/4 fl oz) cream
1/2 cup (75 g/2 1/2 oz) freshly grated
  mozzarella cheese

1 Line a deep Swiss roll tin with baking paper. Combine the milk, half the nutmeg, and salt and freshly ground pepper, to taste, in a medium pan. Bring to the boil, reduce the heat and gradually stir in the semolina. Cook, stirring occasionally, for 5–10 minutes, or until the semolina is very stiff.
2 Remove the pan from the heat, add the egg and 1 cup of the Parmesan. Stir to combine and then spread the mixture in the tin. Refrigerate for 1 hour, or until the mixture is firm.
3 Preheat the oven to moderate 180°C (350°F/Gas 4). Cut the semolina into rounds using a floured 4 cm (1 1/2 inch) cutter and arrange in a greased shallow casserole dish.
4 Pour the melted butter over the top, followed by the cream. Combine the remaining grated Parmesan with the mozzarella cheese and sprinkle them on the rounds. Sprinkle with the remaining nutmeg. Bake for 20–25 minutes, or until the mixture is golden. You can serve garnished with a sprig of fresh herbs.
NOTE: Some claim that this traditional dish from Rome can be traced as far back as Imperial Roman times. A crisp garden salad is the ideal accompaniment for this lovely rich recipe.

NUTRITION PER SERVE: *Protein 30 g; Fat 50 g; Carbohydrate 25 g; Dietary Fibre 1 g; Cholesterol 200 mg; 2790 kJ (670 cal)*

SEMOLINA

Semolina is a term that describes a particular meal milled from grain. Usually applied to wheat, it has a coarse, discernible bead, unlike flour which is fine and powdery. It is higher in protein than flour and has a firmer texture that gives 'bite' to the pasta or dough it goes into. Different grades are milled, with fine semolina preferred for the making of gnocchi and a medium grain for baked desserts and puddings.

*ABOVE: Gnocchi
Romana*

ON THE SIDE

TURNIPS WITH TOMATO, WINE AND GARLIC Heat a little olive oil in a frying pan, add some chopped garlic, chilli and onion and cook over low heat until golden. Add a can of peeled, crushed Italian tomatoes in their juice and a little red wine, bring to the boil then reduce the heat to a simmer. Add some thickly sliced turnips and simmer until the sauce thickens and the turnips are tender. Do not overcook or the turnips will start to break up. Stir through some shredded fresh basil just before serving.

POTATO GNOCCHI WITH TOMATO AND BASIL SAUCE

Preparation time: 1 hour
Total cooking time: 45–50 minutes
Serves 4–6

★ ★

Tomato sauce

1 tablespoon oil
1 onion, chopped
1 celery stick, chopped
2 carrots, chopped
2 x 425 g (14 oz) cans crushed tomatoes
1 teaspoon sugar
1/2 cup (30 g/1 oz) fresh basil, chopped

Potato gnocchi

1 kg (2 lb) old potatoes
30 g (1 oz) butter
2 cups (250 g/8 oz) plain flour
2 eggs, beaten

freshly grated Parmesan, for serving

1 To make the tomato sauce, heat the oil in a large frying pan, add the onion, celery and carrot and cook for 5 minutes, stirring regularly. Add the tomato and sugar and season with salt and pepper, to taste. Bring to the boil, reduce the heat to very low and simmer for 20 minutes. Cool slightly and process, in batches, in a food processor until smooth. Add the basil; set aside.

2 To make the potato gnocchi, peel the potatoes, chop roughly and steam or boil until very tender. Drain thoroughly and mash until smooth. Using a wooden spoon, stir in the butter and flour, then beat in the eggs. Cool.

3 Turn onto a floured surface and divide into two. Roll each into a long sausage shape. Cut into short pieces and press each piece with the back of a fork.

4 Cook the gnocchi, in batches, in a large pan of boiling salted water for about 2 minutes, or until the gnocchi rise to the surface. Using a slotted spoon, drain the gnocchi, and transfer to serving bowls. Serve with the tomato sauce and freshly grated Parmesan. Garnish with fresh herbs if you like.

NUTRITION PER SERVE (6): *Protein 15 g; Fat 10 g; Carbohydrate 60 g; Dietary Fibre 5 g; Cholesterol 75 mg; 1680 kJ (400 cal)*

POTATO

The best potatoes for gnocchi are old, starchy ones that have a low water content. Their mealy flesh results in a gnocchi that is tender and light. If the potatoes hold a lot of moisture, more flour will be required for the dough, which in turn will cause the gnocchi to be rubbery. The potatoes are best baked, steamed or boiled, and they should not be puréed in a processor as this only results in a gluey texture that is unsuitable for gnocchi dough.

LEFT: Potato gnocchi with tomato and basil sauce

GNOCCHI WITH TOMATO AND FRESH BASIL

Preparation time: 10 minutes
Total cooking time: 15 minutes
Serves 4

★

1 tablespoon olive oil

1 onion, finely chopped

2 cloves garlic, crushed

410 g (13 oz) can tomatoes

2 tablespoons tomato paste (tomato purée, double concentrate)

1 cup (250 ml/8 fl oz) cream

1/4 cup (40 g/1 1/4 oz) chopped sun-dried tomatoes

375 g (12 oz) fresh potato gnocchi

1 tablespoon finely chopped fresh basil

60 g (2 oz) pepato cheese, grated

1 Heat the oil in a pan and cook the onion for 2 minutes, or until soft. Add the garlic and cook for another minute. Stir in the tomato and tomato paste, increase the heat and cook for about 5 minutes.
2 Reduce the heat, add the cream and sun-dried tomatoes and stir through. Simmer gently for another 3 minutes.
3 Meanwhile, lower batches of the fresh potato gnocchi into a large pan of boiling salted water. Cook for about 2 minutes, or until the gnocchi rise to the surface. Drain, using a slotted spoon, and add to the sauce with the fresh basil. Season with salt and freshly ground black pepper. Transfer to an ovenproof dish and sprinkle with the pepato cheese. Cook under a hot grill for 5 minutes, until bubbling. Garnish with fresh herbs, if you like.
NOTE: Pepato cheese is quite a pungent pepper cheese. Use a milder cheese if you prefer.

NUTRITION PER SERVE: *Protein 10 g; Fat 40 g; Carbohydrate 30 g; Dietary Fibre 5 g; Cholesterol 130 mg; 2160 kJ (515 cal)*

GNOCCHI

Gnocchi are little dumplings, sometimes as tiny as peas, but never bigger than a mouthful. Traditionally based on semolina flour, ricotta cheese or potato, they are now made with different grains such as buckwheat, and vegetables including pumpkin and artichokes. Although nearly always served with a sauce as a first course, they make a good accompaniment. Once made, they should be cooked and eaten as quickly as possible.

ABOVE: Gnocchi cheese bake

GNOCCHI CHEESE BAKE

Preparation time: 10 minutes
Total cooking time: 15 minutes
Serves 4

★

500 g (1 lb) fresh potato gnocchi

30 g (1 oz) butter, chopped

1 tablespoon chopped fresh parsley

100 g (3 1/2 oz) fontina cheese, sliced

100 g (3 1/2 oz) provolone cheese, sliced

1 Preheat the oven to moderately hot 200°C (400°F/Gas 6). Cook the fresh gnocchi, in batches, in a large pan of boiling water for about 2 minutes, or until the gnocchi rise to the surface. Carefully remove from the pan with a slotted spoon and drain well.
2 Put the gnocchi in a lightly greased ovenproof dish. Scatter with the butter and parsley. Lay the fontina and provolone cheeses over the top of the gnocchi. Season with sea salt and cracked black pepper. Bake for 10 minutes, or until the cheese has melted.

NUTRITION PER SERVE: *Protein 25 g; Fat 30 g; Carbohydrate 10 g; Dietary Fibre 1 g; Cholesterol 115 mg; 1755 kJ (420 cal)*

PUMPKIN GNOCCHI WITH SAGE BUTTER

Preparation time: 45 minutes
Total cooking time: 1 hour 30 minutes
Serves 4

★

500 g (1 lb) pumpkin
1 1/2 cups (185 g/6 oz) plain flour
1/2 cup (50 g/1 3/4 oz) freshly grated Parmesan
1 egg, beaten
100 g (3 1/2 oz) butter
2 tablespoons chopped fresh sage

1 Preheat the oven to warm 160°C (315°F/ Gas 2–3). Brush a baking tray with oil or melted butter. Cut the pumpkin into large pieces, leaving the skin on, and put on the tray. Bake for 1 1/4 hours, or until very tender. Cool slightly. Scrape the flesh from the skin, avoiding any tough or crispy parts. Transfer to a large bowl.

Sift the flour into the bowl, add half the Parmesan, the egg and a little black pepper. After mixing thoroughly, turn onto a lightly floured surface and knead for 2 minutes, or until smooth.
2 Divide the dough in half. Using floured hands, roll each half into a sausage about 40 cm (16 inches) long. Cut into 16 equal pieces. Form each piece into an oval shape and press firmly with the floured prongs of a fork, to make an indentation.
3 Lower batches of gnocchi into a large pan of boiling salted water. Cook for about 2 minutes, or until the gnocchi rise to the surface. Drain with a slotted spoon and keep them warm.
4 To make the sage butter, melt the butter in a small pan, remove from the heat and stir in the chopped sage.
5 To serve, divide the gnocchi among four bowls, drizzle with sage butter and sprinkle with the remaining Parmesan.

NUTRITION PER SERVE: *Protein 20 g; Fat 35 g; Carbohydrate 55 g; Dietary Fibre 5 g; Cholesterol 115 mg; 2465 kJ (590 cal)*

PUMPKIN FOR GNOCCHI

Hard, richly coloured pumpkin is best for making gnocchi. The moist flesh and sweetness of a butternut, for instance, is not suitable. The best pumpkin is dry and vibrant orange and will give a light gnocchi full of flavour and colour. Work the dough quickly and lightly, and use as little flour as possible, to avoid toughness. Wherever practical, bake or steam the pumpkin, don't boil it, and mash it with a fork or a ricer, not a processor.

ABOVE: Pumpkin gnocchi with sage butter

MAKING GNOCCHI

Today, our favourite gnocchi are potato-based but variations can be made using

other vegetables such as pumpkin or parsnip, or traditional semolina or cheese.

Gnocchi are little dumplings. No matter what they are based on, the consistency of the dough should be soft and light. When cooking vegetables to be used for gnocchi, ensure that the cooking process doesn't result in soggy vegetables, otherwise you will have to add more flour, thus making the dough too heavy. Work quickly so the dough doesn't become too sticky or soft.

Gnocchi are best eaten as soon after cooking as possible and you should have any accompanying sauce ready before you cook the dumplings.

TRADITIONAL POTATO GNOCCHI

When making potato gnocchi, it is important to use floury potatoes, preferably old boiling potatoes, because they have a low moisture content. Traditionally, the potatoes are prepared by baking in their skins, thus keeping the potato dry. However, as this is quite time-consuming, most people prefer to steam or boil them. If you do this, make sure you don't overcook the potatoes or they will break up and absorb too much moisture. Also, drain them thoroughly.

Many recipes for potato gnocchi include eggs, to make the gnocchi easier to handle. However, eggs also require the addition of more flour to absorb the extra moisture, thus making the gnocchi a little tougher. Experiment to find which way you prefer to work. The traditional method follows. To make enough for 4–6 people, you will need 1 kg (2 lb) of floury old potatoes, unpeeled, and about 200 g (6½ oz) of plain flour.

1 Prick the unpeeled potatoes all over with a fork and bake in a moderately hot 200°C (400°F/Gas 6) oven for 1 hour, or until tender. Don't wrap in foil. When cool enough to handle but still hot, peel and mash in a bowl with a masher, or put through a ricer or food mill into a bowl.

2 Add three-quarters of the flour and gradually work it in with your hands. When a loose dough forms, transfer it to a lightly floured surface and knead gently. Work in the remaining flour as you knead, but only enough to give a soft, light dough that does not stick to your hands or the work surface, but is still damp to touch. Stop kneading at this stage. Lightly flour the work surface and dust the inside tines of a fork with flour. Take a portion of the dough, about one-fifth, and roll it with your hands on the floured surface to form a long, even rope the thickness of your ring finger. Cut it into 2 cm (¾ inch) pieces.

3 Put a piece on the tines of a fork and press down with your finger, flipping the gnocchi as you do so. It will be rounded into a concave shell shape, ridged on the outer surface. Form a

good hollow in the centre, as this allows the gnocchi to cook evenly and hold the sauce more easily. Continue with the remaining dough.

4 Lower the gnocchi in batches, about 20 at a time, into a large pan of boiling salted water. The gnocchi are cooked when they all rise to the surface, after 2–3 minutes cooking. Remove each batch with a slotted spoon and keep them warm while cooking the remainder. Sauce, and serve.

Potato gnocchi can be frozen, shaped but uncooked, for up to two months. They will need to be first frozen in a single layer, not touching, before being stored in airtight containers. When you are ready to use them, lower them gently, in batches, into boiling water straight from the freezer.

FONTINA CHEESE

A semi-hard cheese from the Italian Alps, fontina has a creamy texture and a sweet, nutty flavour. It is eaten as a table cheese, but is also ideal for cooking because it melts completely to give a thick, rich cream. It is used in sauces for pasta and vegetables, and is the star ingredient of the famous *fonduta*, the Piedmontese version of fondue.

ABOVE: Gnocchi with fontina sauce

GNOCCHI WITH FONTINA SAUCE

Preparation time: 10 minutes
Total cooking time: 15 minutes
Serves 4

★

200 g (6 1/2 oz) fontina cheese, finely chopped
1/2 cup (125 ml/4 fl oz) cream
80 g (2 3/4 oz) butter
2 tablespoons freshly grated Parmesan
400 g (13 oz) fresh potato gnocchi

1 Combine the fontina cheese, cream, butter and Parmesan in a bowl over a pan of simmering water. Heat, stirring occasionally, for 6–8 minutes, or until the cheese has melted and the sauce is smooth and hot.

2 When the sauce is halfway through cooking, lower the gnocchi, in batches, into a large pan of boiling salted water and cook for about 2 minutes, or until the gnocchi rise to the surface.

3 Drain the gnocchi, using a slotted spoon, and serve with sauce over the top. Can be garnished with fresh oregano leaves or other fresh herbs.

NUTRITION PER SERVE: *Protein 25 g; Fat 60 g; Carbohydrate 10 g; Dietary Fibre 0 g; Cholesterol 185 mg; 2790 kJ (670 cal)*

HERBED POTATO GNOCCHI WITH CHUNKY TOMATO

Preparation time: 1 hour
Total cooking time: 30 minutes
Serves 4

★ ★

500 g (1 lb) floury potatoes, chopped
1 egg yolk
3 tablespoons grated Parmesan
3 tablespoons chopped fresh herbs
  (parsley, basil and chives)
up to 1 cup (125 g/4 oz) plain flour
2 cloves garlic, crushed
1 onion, chopped
4 bacon rashers, roughly chopped
150 g (5 oz) sun-dried tomatoes,
  roughly chopped
425 g (14 oz) can peeled tomatoes
1 teaspoon soft brown sugar
2 teaspoons balsamic vinegar
1 tablespoon shredded fresh basil
shaved Parmesan, for serving

1 To make the gnocchi, steam or boil the potatoes until just tender. Drain thoroughly, cool and mash. Transfer 2 cups of the potato to a large bowl. Add the egg yolk, grated Parmesan and herbs and mix until combined. Gradually add enough flour to form a slightly sticky dough. Knead gently for 5 minutes, adding more flour if necessary, until smooth.

2 Divide the dough into four. Roll each portion on a lightly floured surface to form a sausage 2 cm (¾ inch) thick and cut into 2.5 cm (1 inch) pieces. Roll each piece into an oval shape and roll carefully over lightly floured prongs on the back of a fork. Put on a lightly floured non-stick baking tray and cover until ready to use.

3 To make the sauce, heat a tablespoon of olive oil in a large frying pan, add the garlic and onion and cook over medium heat for 5 minutes, or until the onion is soft and golden.

4 Add the bacon and cook, stirring occasionally, for 5 minutes, or until the bacon has browned.

5 Stir in the sun-dried tomato, tomato, sugar and vinegar, bring to the boil, reduce the heat and simmer for 15 minutes, or until the sauce has thickened. Stir the shredded basil through just before serving.

6 Cook the gnocchi, in batches, in a large pan of boiling salted water for about 2 minutes, or until the gnocchi rise to the surface. Drain well and serve topped with the tomato sauce and Parmesan shavings.

NUTRITION PER SERVE: *Protein 20 g; Fat 6 g; Carbohydrate 45 g; Dietary Fibre 6 g; Cholesterol 70 mg; 1340 kJ (320 cal)*

BELOW: Herbed potato gnocchi with chunky tomato

SPICED CARROT AND FETA GNOCCHI

Preparation time: 45 minutes
Total cooking time: 40 minutes
Serves 6–8

★★

1 kg (2 lb) carrots, cut into large pieces
200 g (6½ oz) feta cheese, crumbled
2¼ cups (280 g/9 oz) plain flour
¼ teaspoon ground nutmeg
¼ teaspoon garam masala
1 egg, lightly beaten

Minted cream sauce

30 g (1 oz) butter
2 cloves garlic, crushed
2 spring onions, sliced
1 cup (250 ml/8 fl oz) cream
2 tablespoons shredded fresh mint

1 Steam, boil or microwave the carrot until tender. Drain and allow to cool slightly before transferring to a food processor.
2 Process the carrot and the feta cheese together until smooth. Transfer the mixture to a large bowl. Stir in the sifted flour, spices and egg, and mix to form a soft dough.
3 Lightly coat your fingertips with flour and shape teaspoons of the mixture into flat circles.
4 To make the minted cream sauce, melt the butter in a frying pan, add the garlic and spring onion and cook over medium heat for 3 minutes or until the garlic is soft and golden. Add the cream, bring to the boil, reduce the heat and simmer for 3 minutes, or until the cream has thickened slightly. Remove from the heat, stir the mint through and drizzle over the gnocchi.
5 Cook the gnocchi, in batches, in a large pan of boiling salted water for about 2 minutes, or until they float to the surface. Use a slotted spoon to transfer to warmed serving plates.
NOTE: This mixture is not as firm as some other gnocchi recipes. Make sure the dough is put on a lightly floured surface and keep your fingertips coated in flour when you are shaping the gnocchi.

NUTRITION PER SERVE (8): *Protein 10 g; Fat 25 g; Carbohydrate 35 g; Dietary Fibre 5 g; Cholesterol 90 mg; 1615 kJ (385 cal)*

SPINACH AND RICOTTA GNOCCHI

Preparation time: 45 minutes
+ 1 hour refrigeration
Total cooking time: 30 minutes
Serves 4–6

★★

4 slices white bread
½ cup (125 ml/4 fl oz) milk
500 g (1 lb) frozen spinach, thawed
250 g (8 oz) ricotta cheese
2 eggs
½ cup (50 g/1¾ oz) freshly grated Parmesan, plus some shaved Parmesan, for serving

1 Remove the crust from the bread and soak the bread in the milk, in a shallow dish, for 10 minutes. Squeeze out all the excess liquid. Then squeeze excess liquid from the spinach.
2 Combine the bread in a bowl with the spinach, ricotta cheese, eggs, Parmesan and salt and pepper. Use a fork to mix thoroughly. Cover and refrigerate for 1 hour.
3 Lightly coat your fingertips in flour and roll rounded teaspoonsful of the mixture into little flat dumplings. Lower batches of the gnocchi into a large pan of boiling salted water. Cook for about 2 minutes, or until the gnocchi rise to the surface. Transfer to serving plates. Drizzle with foaming butter, if you wish, and serve with shaved Parmesan.

NUTRITION PER SERVE (6): *Protein 15 g; Fat 10 g; Carbohydrate 10 g; Dietary Fibre 3 g; Cholesterol 95 mg; 905 kJ (215 cal)*

ON THE SIDE

POPOVERS Process 1 cup (250 g/8 oz) of plain flour with 4 eggs in a food processor until the mixture forms crumbs. While the machine is running, add ½ cup (125 ml/4 fl oz) of cream, 1 cup (250 ml/ 8 fl oz) of milk and 45 g (1½ oz) of melted butter. Butter a muffin tin and divide the mixture among the holes. Bake in a moderately hot 200°C (400°F/Gas 6) oven for 35 minutes, or until golden and puffy.

FETA CHEESE

Feta originated in Greece where it was made in the mountains from ewe's milk. It is a semi-hard, pure white cheese with a crumbly texture, not matured but preserved in a liquid made up of its whey and brine. Its flavour is fresh, mild and slightly salty and this intensifies as the cheese gets older. Feta is an essential ingredient of the Greek salad and is used in fillings for stuffed vegetables, and in pies and tarts.

OPPOSITE PAGE:
Spiced carrot and feta gnocchi (top); Spinach and ricotta gnocchi

PARSNIPS

Although parsnips are root vegetables, they belong to the *umbelliferae* or parsley family. They are cultivated for their large, tapering ivory taproots, which have a fruity taste and smell. The starchy flesh purées well and whole parsnips add flavour to stews and casseroles. If the parsnip has developed a tough core, remove it before use.

ABOVE: Parsnip gnocchi

PARSNIP GNOCCHI

Preparation time: 1 1/2 hours
Total cooking time: 45 minutes
Serves 4

★★

500 g (1 lb) parsnip
1 1/2 cups (185 g/6 oz) plain flour
1/2 cup (50 g/1 3/4 oz) freshly grated Parmesan

Garlic herb butter

100 g (3 1/2 oz) butter
2 cloves garlic, crushed
3 tablespoons chopped fresh lemon thyme
1 tablespoon finely grated lime rind

1 Peel the parsnip and cut into large pieces. Cook in a large pan of boiling water for 30 minutes, or until very tender. Drain thoroughly and allow to cool slightly.
2 Mash the parsnip in a bowl until smooth. Sift the flour into the bowl and add half the Parmesan. Season with salt and pepper and mix to form a soft dough.
3 Divide the dough in half. Using floured hands, roll each half of the dough out on a lightly floured surface into a sausage 2 cm (3/4 inch) wide. Cut each sausage into short pieces, shape each piece into an oval and press the top gently with floured fork prongs.
4 Lower batches of gnocchi into a large pan of boiling salted water. Cook for about 2 minutes, or until the gnocchi rise to the surface. Use a slotted spoon to transfer to serving plates.
5 To make the garlic herb butter, combine all the ingredients in a small pan and cook over medium heat for 3 minutes, or until the butter is nutty brown. Drizzle over the gnocchi and sprinkle with the remaining Parmesan.

NUTRITION PER SERVE: *Protein 10 g; Fat 20 g; Carbohydrate 30 g; Dietary Fibre 4 g; Cholesterol 60 mg; 1450 kJ (345 cal)*

RED PEPPER (CAPSICUM) GNOCCHI WITH GOATS CHEESE

Preparation time: 1 hour
Total cooking time: 40 minutes
Serves 6–8

★★

1 large red pepper (capsicum)
500 g (1 lb) kumera (orange sweet potato), chopped
500 g (1 lb) old potatoes, chopped
1 tablespoon sambal oelek
1 tablespoon grated orange rind
2¾ cups (340 g/11 oz) plain flour
2 eggs, lightly beaten
2 cups (500 ml/16 fl oz) bottled pasta sauce
100 g (3½ oz) goats cheese
2 tablespoons finely shredded fresh basil leaves

1 Cut the red pepper in half and discard the seeds and membrane. Put, skin-side-up, under a hot grill and cook for 8 minutes, or until the skin is black and blistered. Remove from the heat and cover with a damp tea towel. When cool, peel away the skin. Process the pepper in a food processor to form a smooth purée.
2 Steam or boil the kumera and potato in a large pan until very soft. Drain thoroughly, transfer to a large bowl and mash until smooth. Allow to cool slightly.
3 Add the pepper purée, sambal oelek, orange rind, flour and eggs, and mix to form a soft dough. Using floured hands, roll heaped teaspoonsful of the dough into oval shapes. Indent one side using lightly floured prongs on the back of a fork.
4 Lower batches of gnocchi into a large pan of boiling salted water. Cook for about 2 minutes, or until the gnocchi rise to the surface. Remove the gnocchi with a slotted spoon and divide among warmed serving plates. Top with the warmed pasta sauce. Crumble the goats cheese and sprinkle over the top with the shredded basil.

NUTRITION PER SERVE (8): *Protein 15 g; Fat 7 g; Carbohydrate 75 g; Dietary Fibre 7 g; Cholesterol 70 mg; 1830 kJ (435 cal)*

ON THE SIDE

NASTURTIUM AND WATERCRESS SALAD Combine 1 bunch of watercress with the petals from 10 nasturtium flowers, 20 small nasturtium leaves and the separated leaves of 1 Belgian endive. Drizzle with a light Caesar salad dressing. Serve with chopped pecans.

WARM KUMERA, ROCKET AND CRISPY BACON SALAD Roast or boil kumera (orange sweet potato) chunks until tender. Combine with rocket and crispy bacon and sprinkle with crumbled goats cheese. Make up a dressing using wholegrain mustard, red wine vinegar and olive oil. Drizzle over the salad.

GOATS CHEESE
Goats cheese or chevre ranges from fresh, soft and mild to mature and very strong. For cooking, somewhere between these extremes is best, a creamy texture accompanied by a mild but piquant taste. Goats cheese has a fragile texture that tends to crumble. It is made in small loaves or little shapes like logs or pyramids.

ABOVE: Red pepper gnocchi with goats cheese

FILLED PASTA

Make your own pasta dough, shape it into delicate pillows of ravioli, wrap it round your finger to make horseshoe tortellini, or roll it out into cannelloni tubes. You can fill tiny parcels of pasta with just about any of your favourite ingredients, from puréed vegetable, spinach and ricotta, to robust meat sauces. In some parts of Italy, just wrapping leftovers in pasta is part of the heritage, so there are no limitations. Of course, if time is short, you can buy the pasta and simply add your own sauce... but that's not half as much fun.

1 egg, beaten

1 tablespoon chopped fresh parsley

1 clove garlic, crushed

1/4 teaspoon mixed spice

Tomato sauce

2 tablespoons olive oil

1 onion, finely chopped

2 cloves garlic, crushed

2 x 425 g (14 oz) cans tomatoes, crushed

3 tablespoons chopped fresh basil

1/2 teaspoon mixed dried herbs

herb sprigs, optional

1 To make the pasta, sift the flour and a pinch of salt into a large bowl and make a well in the centre. Whisk together the eggs, oil and 1 tablespoon of water, add gradually to the flour and combine until the mixture forms a ball. Knead on a floured surface for 5 minutes, or until smooth and elastic. Transfer to an oiled bowl, cover with plastic wrap and set aside for 30 minutes.

2 To make the filling, mix all the filling ingredients with salt and pepper, to taste, in a food processor until finely chopped.

3 To make the tomato sauce, heat the oil in a pan, add the onion and garlic and stir over low heat until the onion is tender. Increase the heat, add the tomato, basil, herbs and salt and pepper, to taste. Bring to the boil, reduce the heat and simmer for 15 minutes. Remove from the heat.

4 Roll out half the pasta dough until 1 mm (1/25 inch) thick. Cut with a knife or fluted pastry wheel into 10 cm (4 inch) wide strips. Place teaspoons of filling at 5 cm (2 inch) intervals down one side of each strip. Whisk the extra egg yolk with 3 tablespoons of water and brush along one side of the dough and between the filling. Fold the dough over the filling to meet the other side. Repeat with remaining filling and dough. Press the edges of the dough together firmly to seal. Cut between the mounds with a knife or a fluted pastry wheel. Cook, in batches, in a large pan of rapidly boiling salted water for 10 minutes. Reheat the sauce in a large pan. Add the ravioli and stir until heated through. Garnish and serve.

NUTRITION PER SERVE: *Protein 35 g; Fat 35 g; Carbohydrate 60 g; Dietary Fibre 7 g; Cholesterol 315 mg; 2850 kJ (680 cal)*

RAVIOLI WITH CHICKEN FILLING

Preparation time: 1 hour
 + 30 minutes standing
Total cooking time: 35 minutes
Serves 4

★★

Pasta

2 cups (250 g/8 oz) plain flour

3 eggs

1 tablespoon olive oil

1 egg yolk, extra

Filling

125 g (4 oz) chicken mince

75 g (2 1/2 oz) ricotta or cottage cheese

60 g (2 oz) chicken livers, trimmed and chopped

30 g (1 oz) prosciutto, chopped

1 slice salami, chopped

2 tablespoons freshly grated Parmesan

ABOVE: Ravioli with chicken filling

CHICKEN MEZZELUNE WITH CREAM SAUCE

Preparation time: 45 minutes
Total cooking time: 15 minutes
Serves 4–6 as a first course

★★

250 g (8 oz) packet gow gee wrappers

Chicken and ham filling

250 g (8 oz) chicken breast fillet
1 egg, beaten
90 g (3 oz) cooked ham or prosciutto
2 teaspoons finely snipped chives
2 teaspoons chopped fresh marjoram

Cream sauce

30 g (1 oz) butter
2 spring onions, finely chopped
2 tablespoons white wine
1 1/2 cups (375 ml/12 fl oz) cream

1 To make the filling, remove any excess fat and sinew from the chicken breast. Cut the flesh into pieces and chop in a food processor. Add the egg, 1/2 teaspoon of salt and a pinch of white pepper and process until finely chopped. Transfer to a bowl. Chop the ham or prosciutto finely and stir into the chicken with the herbs.

2 Lay the gow gee wrappers on a work surface, six at a time, and put a teaspoonful of chicken filling in the centre of each. Brush the edges with cold water, fold in half to form a half moon shape (mezzelune), and press the edges together firmly to seal. Place on a tea towel and continue with the remaining circles.

3 If making your own pasta, roll the dough as thinly as possible on a lightly floured surface, or use a pasta machine and pass the dough through 5 or 6 settings. Cut into circles with an 8 cm (3 inch) cutter, fill and seal as above.

4 To make the cream sauce, heat the butter in a small pan, add the spring onion and cook for 2–3 minutes. Add the wine and cream and simmer until reduced. Season, to taste.

5 Cook the mezzelune in batches, in rapidly boiling salted water. Don't crowd the pan. Simmer for 2–3 minutes, until the chicken is cooked. Don't overcook or the chicken will be dry. Drain.

6 Serve the sauce immediately with the mezzelune. Garnish, if you like.

NUTRITION PER SERVE (6): *Protein 10 g; Fat 30 g; Carbohydrate 30 g; Dietary Fibre 2 g; Cholesterol 120 mg; 1810 kJ (430 cal)*

BELOW: Chicken mezzelune with cream sauce

RICOTTA CHEESE

Ricotta is an unsalted, unripened cheese made from the whey of ewe's or cow's milk. It has a limited shelf life and can only be used when fresh. When kept too long it sours and develops an acid flavour. It has a delicate, creamy flavour and a light, crumbly texture that blends well with other ingredients, especially other dairy produce. Ricotta, literally recooked, takes its name from the method by which it is made. In ordinary cheese-making there is left-over hot whey of milk. When this is heated again and the solid milk parts skimmed off and drained, ricotta results.

ABOVE: Spinach and ricotta shells

SPINACH AND RICOTTA SHELLS

Preparation time: 20 minutes
Total cooking time: 15 minutes
Serves 4

★

20 giant conchiglie (shell pasta)
1 tablespoon oil
2 bacon rashers, finely chopped
1 onion, finely chopped
500 g (1 lb) English spinach, chopped
750 g (1 1/2 lb) ricotta cheese
1/3 cup (35 g/1 1/4 oz) freshly grated Parmesan
1 cup (250 g/8 oz) bottled tomato
    pasta sauce

1 Cook the conchiglie in a large pan of rapidly boiling salted water until *al dente*; drain.
2 Heat the oil in a pan, add the bacon and onion and stir over medium heat for 3 minutes, or until lightly browned. Add the spinach and stir over low heat until wilted. Add the ricotta cheese and stir until combined.
3 Spoon the mixture into the pasta shells and sprinkle with Parmesan. Put the shells on a cold, lightly oiled grill tray. Cook under medium-high heat for 3 minutes, or until lightly browned and heated through.
4 Put the tomato pasta sauce in a small pan and stir over high heat for 1 minute, or until heated through. Spoon the sauce onto serving plates and top with the shells.

NUTRITION PER SERVE: *Protein 45 g; Fat 40 g; Carbohydrate 80 g; Dietary Fibre 10 g; Cholesterol 110 mg; 3470 kJ (830 cal)*

PRAWN TORTELLONI

Preparation time: 40 minutes
Total cooking time: 20–30 minutes
Serves 4

★★

300 g (10 oz) raw prawns
20 g (³/₄ oz) butter
1 clove garlic, crushed
2 spring onions, chopped
125 g (4 oz) ricotta cheese
1 tablespoon chopped fresh basil
200 g (6¹/₂ oz) packet gow gee wrappers

Sauce

5 tablespoons olive oil
shells and heads of prawns
1 clove garlic, crushed
2 spring onions, including green part, chopped
1 dried chilli, crumbled
1 firm tomato, finely diced, or
  1 tablespoon diced sun-dried tomato

1 Shell the prawns, reserving the heads and shells to flavour the sauce. With a sharp knife, slit down the back of each prawn and discard the vein. Chop the prawns roughly.
2 Heat the butter and gently cook the garlic and spring onion until soft and golden. Allow to cool, mix with the prawns, ricotta and basil and season, to taste. Put a teaspoonful of the mixture on each gow gee wrapper, moisten the edges with water, fold over to form a semi-circle and press firmly to seal. Press the corners together to make a tortelloni shape. For a large circular shape, use more filling and cover with another circle of pasta.
3 To make the sauce, heat 3 tablespoons of the olive oil in a large frying pan. When hot, add the shells and heads of the prawns and toss over high heat until they turn red. Lower the heat and cook for a few minutes, pressing the heads to extract as much flavour as possible. Add ¹/₂ cup (125 ml/4 fl oz) of water, cover and cook over low heat for 5 minutes. Remove the shells and heads from the pan using a slotted spoon, pressing out as much of the flavoured oil as possible before discarding them.
4 In another pan, heat the remaining 2 tablespoons of olive oil, add the garlic, spring onion and dried chilli and stir over low heat until the garlic is pale golden. Add the prawn stock and diced tomato and heat through.

5 Bring a large pan of salted water to the boil. Drop the tortelloni into the boiling water and cook for 3–4 minutes. Drain, then add to the sauce and toss so the pasta is well coated.
NOTE: Tortelloni are large tortellini.

NUTRITION PER SERVE: *Protein 25 g; Fat 35 g; Carbohydrate 35 g; Dietary Fibre 4 g; Cholesterol 140 mg; 2260 kJ (540 cal)*

ABOVE: Prawn tortelloni

Gently twist the ends of the roll to make a shape that resembles a bow. Repeat with the remaining sheets and filling.

3 Lightly brush a large rectangular ovenproof dish with melted butter or oil. Place the bows in the dish, dot with butter and pour the pasta sauce over the centre of the bows, leaving the ends exposed. Cover and bake for 5 minutes, or until the bows are heated through. Serve immediately, generously sprinkled with freshly grated Parmesan and shredded fresh basil leaves.

NUTRITION PER SERVE: *Protein 10 g; Fat 15 g; Carbohydrate 15 g; Dietary Fibre 2 g; Cholesterol 80 mg; 1015 kJ (250 cal)*

SPINACH RAVIOLI WITH SUN-DRIED TOMATO SAUCE

Preparation time: 20 minutes
Total cooking time: 15 minutes
Serves 4

★★

3/4 cup (155 g / 5 oz) firmly packed, chopped, cooked English spinach
250 g (8 oz) ricotta cheese, well drained
2 tablespoons freshly grated Parmesan
1 tablespoon chopped fresh chives
1 egg, lightly beaten
200 g (6 1/2 oz) packet gow gee wrappers

Sauce

1/3 cup (80 ml/2 3/4 fl oz) extra virgin olive oil
3 tablespoons pine nuts
100 g (3 1/2 oz) sun-dried tomatoes, sliced

LASAGNE BOWS

Preparation time: 20 minutes
Total cooking time: 20 minutes
Serves 6

★★

four 16 x 24 cm (6 1/2 x 9 1/2 inch) fresh lasagne sheets
400 g (13 oz) fresh ricotta cheese
1 egg, lightly beaten
1/4 teaspoon ground nutmeg
1 cup (50 g/1 3/4 oz) chopped fresh herbs
30 g (1 oz) butter, chopped
300 g (10 oz) bottled tomato pasta sauce
freshly grated Parmesan, for serving
shredded fresh basil leaves, to garnish

1 Preheat the oven to moderately hot 200°C (400°F/Gas 6). Cook the lasagne sheets in a large pan of rapidly boiling salted water until *al dente*, stirring frequently to ensure that they do not stick together.

2 While the pasta is cooking, combine the ricotta cheese, beaten egg, nutmeg and herbs in a bowl. Drain the pasta and carefully lay one sheet on a flat surface. Put 2–3 tablespoons of the ricotta mixture in the centre of the sheet. Fold the top third of the lasagne sheet over the filling, then the bottom third over the top.

ABOVE: Lasagne bows
RIGHT: Spinach ravioli with sun-dried tomato sauce

1 Combine the spinach, ricotta and Parmesan, chives and half the beaten egg in a medium bowl. Mix well and season with salt and pepper, to taste. Place 1½ teaspoons of the mixture into the centre of a gow gee wrapper. Brush the edge of the wrapper lightly with some of the remaining beaten egg, then cover with another wrapper, until they are all used. Press the edges firmly to seal. Using a 7 cm (2¾ inch) plain scone cutter, cut the ravioli into circles.

2 Cook the ravioli, in batches, in a large pan of rapidly boiling salted water for 4 minutes, or until *al dente*. Don't crowd the pan. Keep each batch warm while cooking the remainder. Carefully drain the ravioli, add to the sauce and toss very gently.

3 To make the sauce, combine the ingredients in a large pan and heat slowly until warm.

NUTRITION PER SERVE: *Protein 20 g; Fat 40 g; Carbohydrate 35 g, Dietary Fibre 5 g; Cholesterol 80 mg; 2440 kJ (580 cal)*

PUMPKIN AND HERB RAVIOLI

Preparation time: 40 minutes
  + 30 minutes resting
Total cooking time: 1 hour 15 minutes
Serves 6

★★

500 g (1 lb) pumpkin, cut into chunks
1¾ cups (215 g/7 oz) plain flour
3 eggs, lightly beaten
¼ teaspoon ground nutmeg
15 sage leaves
15 fresh flat-leaf parsley leaves
125 g (4 oz) butter, melted
60 g (2 oz) freshly grated Parmesan

1 Preheat the oven to moderate 180°C (350°F/Gas 4). Bake the pumpkin on a baking tray for 1 hour, or until tender. Allow to cool before removing the skin.

2 Process the flour and eggs in a food processor for 30 seconds, or until the mixture forms a dough. Transfer to a lightly floured surface and knead for 3 minutes, until the dough is very smooth and elastic. Cover with a clean cloth and set aside for 30 minutes.

3 Transfer the pumpkin to a bowl with the nutmeg and mash with a fork. Roll out half the dough to a rectangle about 1 mm (1/25 inch) thick. Roll out the remaining half to a rectangle slightly larger than the first.

4 On the first rectangle of dough, put heaped teaspoonsful of pumpkin filling at intervals, in straight rows, about 5 cm (2 inches) apart. Flatten each pumpkin mound slightly and place one whole sage or parsley leaf on top of each spoonful of filling.

5 Brush lightly between the mounds of filling with water. Place the second sheet of dough on top, press down gently between pumpkin mounds to seal. Cut into squares with a knife or fluted cutter. Cook the ravioli, in batches, in a large pan of rapidly boiling salted water for 4 minutes, or until *al dente*. Don't crowd the pan. Drain well and serve sprinkled with salt and pepper, to taste, and tossed with melted butter and Parmesan.

NUTRITION PER SERVE: *Protein 15 g; Fat 25 g; Carbohydrate 35 g; Dietary Fibre 5 g; Cholesterol 155 mg; 1645 kJ (390 cal)*

ABOVE: Pumpkin and herb ravioli

FILLING PASTA The benefits of

making your own filled or stuffed pasta are many. You can determine the pasta

flavour, size and shape as well as the ingredients and texture of the filling.

FILLINGS

Ingredients for filled pasta are fresh and interesting. Some, such as cheeses and mashed pumpkin, are smooth, while foods such as shellfish are better in small, discernible pieces. As a general rule, the finer the filling, the smaller the shape. A binding ingredient is usually needed. This is often a soft cheese such as ricotta, but can be cream, sauce or gravy. The moisture content can be controlled by the addition of a little grated Parmesan, breadcrumbs, or even mashed potato. Within a short time, the moisture in the filling will begin to seep through the pasta causing it to become soggy. Therefore, the filling should be quite dry, particularly if the pasta isn't going to be cooked immediately. Fresh filled pasta should be eaten soon after being made.

EQUIPMENT

You will need a long sharp knife, a pastry brush and, ideally, a zig-zag pastry wheel, to give a good seal. A cutter-crimper wheel gives an excellent seal, but can be less manoeuvrable on curved edges. Ravioli stamps or cutters are sometimes available. Moulded ravioli trays give a uniform shape and enable you to make a lot of ravioli quickly, once the technique is mastered.

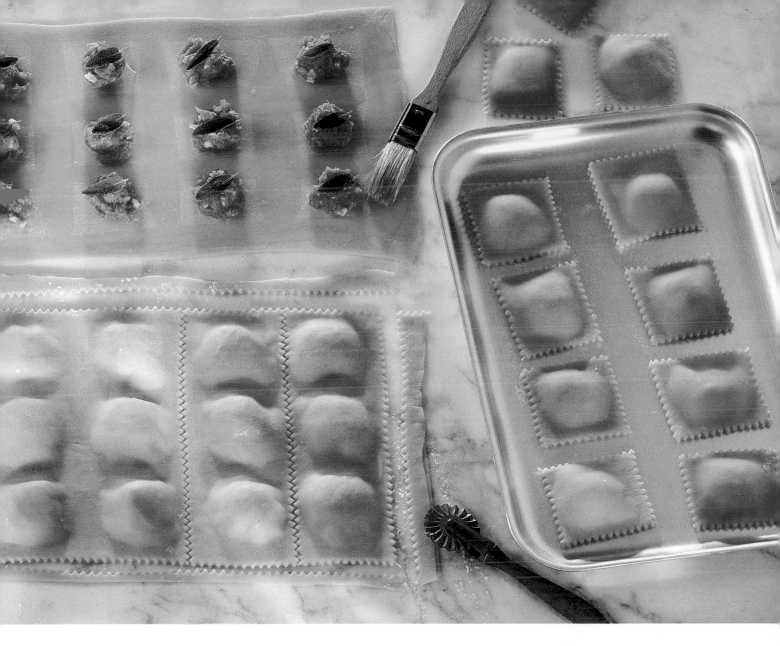

RAVIOLI

To serve 4–6, you will need one batch of basic pasta dough (page 17), about 1½ cups of filling and a beaten egg, for sealing the edges. There are two ways of hand-shaping ravioli: by cutting out the dough and individually folding each one over the filling, or by covering one sheet of dough and the filling with another sheet and cutting shapes from this. The folded method is very simple and has the advantage of a better seal, with only three cut edges which are firmly joined together by hand. The double-sheeted method is quicker, but results in a ravioli with all cut edges, increasing the likelihood of them opening up.

DOUBLE SHEETED METHOD

1 Lightly dust a large work surface with flour. Divide the dough into four. Roll two portions out into very thin (about 2.5 mm / ⅛ inch, or less) sheets, using a hand-cranked pasta machine, or with a rolling pin on the work surface. Roll one sheet slightly bigger than the other and cover this with a tea towel.

2 Spread the smaller sheet out on the work surface. In one corner, lightly mark out two or three ravioli squares for size. Spoon some filling into the centre of each and flatten slightly with the back of the spoon. This will help you determine the amount of filling per square and the spacing between each. The filling should cover about two-thirds of the area of each square. Now spoon equal amounts of filling, evenly spaced, over the sheet. Flatten lightly with the back of the spoon.

3 Brush beaten egg between the filling along the cutting lines. Take the larger sheet and, starting at one end, place it over the first, matching the sides and pressing it here and there so that it sticks to the bottom layer without slipping. Don't stretch it, but let it settle into position naturally.

4 Run your fingers along the cutting lines to press them together, or use the fine edge of a ruler which will also mark the lines as well as seal them. Now cut along these lines using a sharp knife or pastry wheel, or a zig-zag pastry wheel.

5 Transfer to a lightly floured baking tray or large platter and refrigerate while you work the remainder of the dough and filling. Don't put them on top of one another or they'll stick together. They can be refrigerated, covered, for up to 3 hours, depending on the moisture content of the filling. Cooking time varies according to the thickness of the pastry and type of filling.

FILLING PASTA

TORTELLINI

These small rounds of pasta dough are filled with anything from cooked meat, chicken and fish, to vegetables and soft cheeses, and then sealed and shaped into rings. To make tortellini for 4–6, you will need one batch of basic pasta dough (page 17), 1½ cups of smooth-textured filling and a beaten egg for sealing.

1 Lightly dust a large work surface with flour. Divide the dough into four, keeping all portions covered until needed. Using a hand-cranked pasta machine or with a rolling pin on the prepared surface, roll out one portion of dough very thinly, about 2.5 mm (¹/8 inch) or less.

2 Spread the pasta on a lightly floured work surface and avoid flouring it from now on. With a 6 cm (2½ inch) cutter or an upturned glass, cut out circles.

3 Lightly brush the edge of each circle with beaten egg or water, then spoon about ½ teaspoonful of filling onto the centre of each circle.

4 Working with one circle at a time, fold one side over the other to encase the filling. The cut sides should not match up exactly, but overlap slightly. Press the edges firmly together, slightly easing the filling along the length of the half-moon as you do so. Roll the rim of the cut edge back over itself, with the taller side uppermost. Now, with

the folded rim on the outside, wrap the shape around your index finger and press the two ends together. A dab of water might be needed to help seal them together.

5 Place the completed tortellini on a lightly floured baking tray or large plate and keep chilled while you work the remaining pasta and filling. Depending on the dryness of the filling used, they will keep in the refrigerator for up to 6 hours.

CANNELLONI

These filled tubes of pasta are not at all difficult to make. Suitable fillings include cooked meat with cheese, spinach with

ricotta or mashed pumpkin with pine nuts. As a rough guide, depending on the size of cannelloni you choose to make and the amount of filling you want to use, one batch of basic plain dough (page 17) will make about 20 tubes that are 10 cm (4 inches) long. Cut the pasta for cannelloni wide enough to wrap comfortably around the filling you want to use. Allow for a 2.5 cm (1 inch) overlap at the seam on larger tubes, down to half that on small, finger-sized tubes. Too little overlap, and the cannelloni may expand and open when baked, making serving difficult; too much, and the thickness of the pasta will be unpleasant. It is a good idea to cut one or two extra sheets in case some tear during cooking. To fill 20 tubes, you will need about 4 cups of filling.

1 Roll out fresh pasta sheets to about 2.5 mm (⅛ inch) thick, using a hand-cranked pasta machine or rolling pin.
2 Put a large pan of water on to boil and grease a shallow ovenproof dish.
3 Cut the pasta into sheets of the size you require, bearing in mind that they will increase slightly during cooking. The length of the tube runs with the grain of the pasta.
4 Keep uncooked sheets covered. Drop 3 or 4 at a time, depending on their size, into the water and keep boiling for 1½–2 minutes. Fish them out with a wide strainer or sieve and spread on dry tea towels while the rest of the sheets are being cooked. Turn the sheets over once when partially dry. Do not allow to dry too much as the edges crack when rolling. Trim if necessary. You might like to cut out a paper template to use

as a guide so they will be the same size.
5 Arrange some filling down the centre of each sheet, running it in the same direction as the grain. Roll the pasta tightly around the filling to form a tube. Place the tubes side by side, seam-side-down in the prepared dish, with the overlapping join on the bottom. Cannelloni are nearly always dressed with sauce and topped with cheese before being finished off in the oven, or under the grill.

FREEZING
Filled pastas freeze well and must be cooked straight from the freezer, not defrosted. To freeze filled or stuffed pasta, do so in a single layer or, if necessary, between sheets of baking paper. Cover with a tea towel. When frozen, transfer to an airtight container.

ABOVE: *Spinach and ricotta cannelloni*

1 Cut the lasagne sheets into 15 even-sized pieces and trim lengthways so that they will fit neatly into a deep-sided, rectangular ovenproof dish when filled. Bring a large pan of water to a rapid boil and cook 1–2 lasagne sheets at a time until just softened. The amount of time will differ, depending on the type and brand of lasagne, but is usually about 2 minutes. Remove the sheets carefully with a wide strainer or sieve and lay out flat on a clean damp tea towel. Return the water to the boil and repeat the process with the remaining pasta sheets.

2 Heat the oil in a heavy-based frying pan. Cook the onion and garlic until golden, stirring regularly. Add the washed spinach, cook for 2 minutes, cover with a tight-fitting lid and steam for 5 minutes. Drain, removing as much liquid as possible. The spinach must be quite dry or the pasta will be soggy. Combine the spinach with the ricotta, eggs, nutmeg and salt and pepper, to taste. Mix well and set aside.

3 To make the tomato sauce, heat the oil in a frying pan and cook the onion and garlic for 10 minutes over low heat, stirring occasionally. Add the chopped tomato including the juice, the tomato paste, sugar, ½ cup (125 ml/4 fl oz) of water and salt and pepper, to taste. Bring the sauce to the boil, reduce the heat and simmer for 10 minutes. If a smoother sauce is preferred, purée in a food processor until the desired consistency is reached.

4 Preheat the oven to moderate 180°C (350°F/Gas 4). Lightly brush the ovenproof dish with melted butter or oil. Spread about one-third of the tomato sauce over the base of the dish. Working with one piece of lasagne at a time, spoon 2½ tablespoons of the spinach mixture down the centre of the sheet, leaving a border at each end. Roll up and lay, seam-side-down, in the dish. Repeat with the remaining pasta and filling. Spoon the remaining tomato sauce over the cannelloni and scatter the mozzarella over the top.

5 Bake for 30–35 minutes, or until golden brown and bubbling. Set aside for 10 minutes before serving. Garnish with fresh herb sprigs if you like.

NOTE: Dried cannelloni tubes can be used instead of fresh lasagne sheets. The texture of the pasta will be firmer, but the dish will still be very successful.

NUTRITION PER SERVE: *Protein 35 g; Fat 30 g; Carbohydrate 50 g; Dietary Fibre 10 g; Cholesterol 130 mg; 2555 kJ (610 cal)*

SPINACH AND RICOTTA CANNELLONI

Preparation time: 1 hour
Total cooking time: 1 hour 15 minutes
Serves 6

★★★

375 g (12 oz) fresh lasagne sheets

2 tablespoons olive oil

1 large onion, finely chopped

1–2 cloves garlic, crushed

1 kg (2 lb) English spinach, finely chopped

650 g (1 lb 5 oz) fresh ricotta cheese, beaten

2 eggs, beaten

¼ teaspoon freshly ground nutmeg

Tomato sauce

1 tablespoon olive oil

1 medium onion, chopped

2 cloves garlic, finely chopped

500 g (1 lb) very ripe tomatoes, chopped

2 tablespoons tomato paste (tomato purée, double concentrate)

1 teaspoon soft brown sugar

150 g (5 oz) grated mozzarella cheese

CANNELLONI

Cannelloni are simply rectangles of pasta rolled around a filling. The pasta can be sheets of fresh egg dough, or dried lasagne sheets or tubes, which need to be blanched before filling. The dried product is also available in a form that requires no pre-cooking. Once the tubes are filled they may be sauced, then baked with cheese on top.

CONCHIGLIE WITH CHICKEN AND PESTO

Preparation time: 45 minutes
Total cooking time: 30 minutes
Serves 4

★★

20 giant conchiglie (shell pasta)
    (about 5 cm/2 inches long)
2 tablespoons oil
2 leeks, thinly sliced
500 g (1 lb) chicken mince
1 tablespoon plain flour
1 cup (250 ml/8 fl oz) chicken stock
4 tablespoons chopped pimiento
1/2 cup (50 g/1 3/4 oz) freshly grated Parmesan

Pesto

1 cup (50 g/1 3/4 oz) fresh basil
3 tablespoons pine nuts
2 cloves garlic, crushed
1/4 cup (60 ml/2 fl oz) olive oil

1 Preheat the oven to moderate 180°C (350°F/Gas 4). Brush a shallow baking dish with melted butter or oil. Cook the conchiglie in a large pan of rapidly boiling salted water until *al dente*. Drain well.

2 Heat the oil in a heavy-based pan, add the leek and stir-fry over medium heat for 2 minutes. Add the mince and stir until well browned and all the liquid has evaporated. Use a fork to break up any lumps as the mince cooks. Add the flour and stir over heat for 1 minute. Add the stock and pimiento and stir over medium heat until boiling. Reduce the heat and simmer for 1 minute, or until the mixture has reduced and thickened.

3 To make the pesto, blend the basil, pine nuts, garlic and oil in a food processor or blender for 30 seconds, or until smooth. Spoon into a small bowl or jug and press plastic wrap over the surface to exclude any air.

4 To assemble, spoon the chicken mixture into the cooled pasta shells, transfer to the prepared baking dish and cover with aluminium foil. Bake for 15 minutes, or until heated through. Serve topped with a spoonful of pesto and sprinkled with Parmesan.

NUTRITION PER SERVE: *Protein 45 g; Fat 55 g; Carbohydrate 75 g; Dietary Fibre 10 g; Cholesterol 110 mg; 4090 kJ (975 cal)*

ON THE SIDE

WILD RICE WITH ROASTED PEPPER Seed, quarter and grill 2 red peppers (capsicums) and cut them into thin slices. Cook some mixed wild and long-grain rice until it is tender and then drain. Put 2 tablespoons of olive oil, 2 tablespoons of balsamic vinegar, 1 crushed clove of garlic, 2 chopped spring onions and 2 finely chopped tomatoes in a large bowl. Add the rice mixture and the peppers, season with salt and pepper, to taste, and mix well. Scatter a handful of fresh coriander leaves over the top before serving.

CARAMELIZED LEEKS AND CRISPY BACON Cut leeks in half lengthways and then into long pieces, taking care to keep the leaves together. Cook the leeks over low heat in butter and a little soft brown sugar, turning occasionally, until the leeks are very tender and caramelized. Take care not to overcook them or they will fall apart. Top with pieces of crispy bacon and roughly chopped flat-leaf parsley.

Conchiglie with chicken and pesto

ABOVE: Chicken ravioli with buttered sage sauce

CHICKEN RAVIOLI WITH BUTTERED SAGE SAUCE

Preparation time: 15 minutes
Total cooking time: 10 minutes
Serves 4

★

500 g (1 lb) fresh or dried chicken-filled
   ravioli or agnolotti
60 g (2 oz) butter
4 spring onions, chopped
2 tablespoons fresh sage, chopped
1/2 cup (50 g/13/4 oz) freshly grated Parmesan,
   for serving
fresh sage leaves, extra, for garnish

1 Cook the ravioli in a large pan of rapidly boiling salted water until *al dente*. Drain and return to the pan.

2 While the ravioli is cooking, melt the butter in a heavy-based pan. Add the spring onion and sage and stir for 2 minutes. Add salt and pepper, to taste.

3 Add the sauce to the pasta and toss well. Pour into warmed serving bowls and sprinkle with Parmesan. Serve immediately, garnished with fresh sage leaves.

NUTRITION PER SERVE: *Protein 20 g; Fat 25 g; Carbohydrate 20 g; Dietary Fibre 2 g; Cholesterol 120 mg; 1590 kJ (380 cal)*

TORTELLINI WITH MUSHROOM CREAM SAUCE

Preparation time: 15 minutes
Total cooking time: 10 minutes
Serves 4

★

500 g (1 lb) tortellini
185 g (6 oz) button mushrooms
1 small lemon
60 g (2 oz) butter
1 clove garlic, crushed
1¼ cups (315 ml/10 fl oz) cream
pinch of nutmeg
3 tablespoons freshly grated Parmesan

1 Cook the tortellini in a large pan of rapidly boiling salted water until *al dente*. Drain, return to the pan and keep warm. Slice the mushrooms finely. Grate the lemon rind.

2 Melt the butter in a pan and cook the mushrooms over medium heat for 2 minutes. Add the garlic, cream, lemon rind, nutmeg and freshly ground black pepper, to taste. Stir over low heat for 1–2 minutes. Stir in the grated Parmesan and cook gently for 3 minutes.

3 Add the sauce to the tortellini and stir gently to combine well. Spoon into serving dishes and top with extra pepper.

NUTRITION PER SERVE: *Protein 10 g; Fat 50 g; Carbohydrate 35 g; Dietary Fibre 5 g; Cholesterol 155mg; 2570 kJ (610 cal)*

CREAM

Cream results from allowing milk to settle. Fats rise to the top and when skimmed off are a pourable single cream with a fat content of 10–20%, or in some countries 35%. Double cream, which contains at least 30% fat, has to be separated mechanically, to give a spoonable cream. Other natural creams, thick and stiff, will contain as much as 60% fat. Thickened cream has had a starch or gelatine added to it.

ABOVE: Tortellini with mushroom cream sauce

FRESH CHILLIES
There are many different
types of fresh chilli, ranging
from small and fiery to fat
and mildly hot. The seeds
and the membrane, which
are the hottest parts, are
generally removed from all
but the tiniest. Where a
recipe simply calls for
fresh chilli, use your
experience to select which
type. The most fiery are
usually small chillies such
as birds eye, available
in red or green. Serranos,
which are red, green
or yellow, are also small
and very hot. Jalapenos
are plump, green or red,
and as hot as the serranos
weight for weight.
Correctly identifying
chillies is quite difficult,
especially since even
growers disagree and the
names vary internationally.

*RIGHT: Basil tortellini
with bacon and
tomato sauce*

BASIL TORTELLINI WITH BACON AND TOMATO SAUCE

Preparation time: 15 minutes
Total cooking time: 25 minutes
Serves 4

⭐

500 g (1 lb) fresh or dried basil
  tortellini
1 tablespoon olive oil
4 bacon rashers, chopped
2 cloves garlic, crushed
1 medium onion, chopped
1 teaspoon chopped fresh chillies
425 g (14 oz) can tomatoes
1/2 cup (125 ml/4 fl oz) cream
2 tablespoons chopped fresh basil

1 Cook the pasta in a large pan of rapidly boiling salted water until *al dente*. Drain and return to the pan.

2 While the pasta is cooking, heat the oil in a medium heavy-based pan. Add the bacon, garlic and onion and cook for 5 minutes over medium heat, stirring regularly.
3 Add the chilli and undrained, chopped tomato. Reduce the heat and simmer for 10 minutes. Add the cream and basil and cook for 1 minute. Add the sauce to the pasta and toss well. Serve immediately.

NUTRITION PER SERVE: *Protein 25 g; Fat 25 g; Carbohydrate 95 g; Dietary Fibre 9 g; Cholesterol 60 mg; 2990 kJ (710 cal)*

ON THE SIDE

GREEN BEANS WITH GARLIC AND CUMIN Fry a sliced onion and a crushed clove of garlic in a little olive oil and add a 425 g (14 oz) can of chopped tomatoes and a pinch of ground cumin. Cook this mixture until it has reduced by half and add 300 g (10 oz) of sliced green beans. Cook the beans in the tomato mixture until tender but still vibrant green. Sprinkle with toasted cumin seeds.

MUSHROOM RAVIOLI

Preparation time: 30 minutes
Total cooking time: 15 minutes
Serves 4

★

½ cup (70 g/2¼ oz) hazelnut kernels,
  toasted and skinned
90 g (3 oz) unsalted butter
150 g (5 oz) mushrooms
1 tablespoon olive oil
200 g (6½ oz) packet won ton wrappers

1 Chop the hazelnuts in a food processor. Heat the butter in a pan over medium heat until it sizzles and turns nutty brown. Remove from the heat, stir in the chopped hazelnuts and season with salt and pepper, to taste.

2 Wipe the mushrooms with paper towel. Chop the stems and caps finely. Heat the oil in a pan, add the mushrooms and stir until soft. Add salt and pepper, to taste, and cook until the liquid has evaporated. Allow to cool.

3 Lay 12 won ton wrappers on a work surface and put a small teaspoonful of the mushroom filling on six of them. Brush the edges of the wrappers with water and place another wrapper on top. Press firmly to seal. If desired, trim the edges with a pasta cutter. Lay the ravioli on a tray lined with a clean tea towel and cover with another tea towel. Repeat with 12 more squares. Filling and sealing a few at a time prevents the ravioli from drying out.

4 When all the ravioli are made, cook in batches in a large pan of rapidly boiling salted water. Don't crowd the pan. Very thin pasta will be done in about 2 minutes after the water returns to the boil, so lift out with a slotted spoon and drain in a colander while the next batch is cooking. Serve with the hazelnut sauce.

NOTE: If you can't get toasted and skinned hazelnuts from your health food store, spread the nuts on a baking tray and roast in a moderate oven for 10–12 minutes. Cool, then rub in a tea towel to remove as many of the skins as possible. Won ton wrappers made with egg are best.

NUTRITION PER SERVE: *Protein 10 g; Fat 35 g; Carbohydrate 35 g; Dietary Fibre 5 g; Cholesterol 60 mg; 2070 kJ (490 cal)*

RAVIOLI

It is thought that ravioli originated in the seaport of Genoa, when thrifty housewives used pasta to wrap around little spoonfuls of leftovers in the hope of disguising it. The sailors happily took their *rabiole* to sea, unaware of the origins of the filling. Today, we are more discerning about the fillings we put in ravioli, and they are stuffed with well-considered combinations of meats, cheese or vegetables.

ABOVE: Mushroom ravioli

BAKED PASTA

Sheets of pasta layered with ragu or rich tomato sauce and a smooth, creamy béchamel, then finished with grated Parmesan and left in the oven to bubble and melt until the smell becomes irresistible... lasagne is undoubtedly the most famous (and perhaps the favourite) baked pasta dish of our times. But what about pasticcio, cannelloni and macaroni cheese? If you've perfected your lasagne, it could be time to try another little bit of pasta magic.

1 Lightly brush a deep 23 cm (9 inch) round springform tin with oil or butter and line it with baking paper. Cook the macaroni in a large pan of rapidly boiling salted water until *al dente*. Drain and set aside.

2 Arrange the eggplant on trays, sprinkle with salt and allow to stand for 20 minutes. Rinse well and pat dry with paper towels. Heat 2 tablespoons of oil in a frying pan, add the eggplant and cook, in batches, in a single layer, until golden on each side. Add more oil as required. Drain on paper towels.

3 Add the onion and garlic to the same pan and stir over low heat until the onion is tender. Add the mince and brown, breaking up any lumps with a spoon or fork as it cooks. Add the tomato, tomato paste and salt and pepper, to taste, and stir well. Bring to the boil. Reduce the heat and simmer for 15–20 minutes. Set aside.

4 In a bowl, mix together the peas, macaroni, mozzarella and Cheddar cheeses, egg and half the Parmesan. Set aside.

5 Preheat the oven to moderate 180°C (350°F/Gas 4). Place a slice of eggplant in the centre on the base of the prepared tin. Arrange three-quarters of remaining eggplant in an overlapping pattern to completely cover the base and sides of the tin. Sprinkle with half the remaining Parmesan.

6 Combine the mince mixture with the macaroni mixture. Carefully spoon the filling into the eggplant case, packing down well. Arrange the remaining eggplant slices, overlapping, over the filling. Sprinkle with the remaining Parmesan.

7 Bake, uncovered, for 25–30 minutes, or until golden. Allow to rest for 5 minutes before unmoulding onto a serving plate. Serve with salad, if desired.

NOTE: You can omit the mince and add chopped cooked Italian sausage and chopped cooked chicken to the tomato mixture.

Extra tomato sauce can be served with this dish. Make it by simmering canned, crushed tomato with a little garlic, pepper and chopped basil until thickened.

NUTRITION PER SERVE: *Protein 35 g; Fat 20 g; Carbohydrate 20 g; Dietary Fibre 5 g; Cholesterol 115 mg; 1780 kJ (425 cal)*

MACARONI EGGPLANT (AUBERGINE) CAKE

Preparation time: 1 hour
Total cooking time: 1 hour
Serves 6

★★

¾ cup (115 g/4 oz) macaroni

2–3 eggplant (aubergine), sliced thinly lengthways

1 onion, chopped

1 clove garlic, crushed

500 g (1 lb) pork, beef or chicken mince

425 g (14 oz) can crushed tomatoes

2 tablespoons tomato paste (tomato purée, double concentrate)

½ cup (80 g/2¾ oz) frozen peas

1 cup (150 g/5 oz) freshly grated mozzarella cheese

½ cup (60 g/2 oz) freshly grated Cheddar cheese

1 egg, beaten

½ cup (50 g/1¾ oz) freshly grated Parmesan

ABOVE: Macaroni eggplant cake

RICOTTA LASAGNE

Preparation time: 1 hour
Total cooking time: 1 hour 30 minutes
Serves 8

★ ★

500 g (1 lb) fresh spinach lasagne sheets
1/2 cup (30 g/1 oz) fresh basil leaves, chopped
2 tablespoons fresh breadcrumbs
3 tablespoons pine nuts
2 teaspoons paprika
1 tablespoon freshly grated Parmesan

Ricotta filling

750 g (1 1/2 lb) fresh ricotta
1/2 cup (50 g/1 3/4 oz) freshly grated Parmesan
pinch of nutmeg

Tomato sauce

1 tablespoon olive oil
2 onions, chopped
2 cloves garlic, crushed
800 g (1 lb 10 oz) can crushed tomatoes
1 tablespoon tomato paste (tomato purée,
    double concentrate)

Béchamel sauce

60 g (2 oz) butter
1/2 cup (60 g/2 oz) plain flour
2 cups (500 ml/16 fl oz) milk
2 eggs, lightly beaten
1/3 cup (35 g/1 1/4 oz) freshly grated Parmesan

1 Lightly brush a 25 x 32 cm (10 x 13 inch)
baking dish with melted butter or oil. Cut the
pasta sheets into large pieces and cook, 2–3 at
a time, in boiling water for 3 minutes. Drain
and spread on damp tea towels until needed.
2 To make the ricotta filling, mix the ricotta and
Parmesan, nutmeg and a little freshly ground
black pepper in a bowl. Set aside.
3 To make the tomato sauce, heat the oil in
a frying pan, add the onion and cook for
10 minutes, stirring occasionally, until very soft.
Add the garlic and cook for another minute.
Add the tomato and tomato paste and stir until
well combined. Stir until the mixture comes
to the boil. Reduce the heat and simmer,
uncovered, for 15 minutes, or until thickened,
stirring occasionally.

4 To make the béchamel sauce, heat the butter
in a small pan. Add the flour and stir for about
1 minute, until golden and smooth. Remove
from the heat and gradually stir in the milk.
Return to the heat and stir until the sauce boils
and begins to thicken. Remove from the heat
and stir in the eggs. Return to medium heat and
stir until almost boiling, but do not boil. Add
the cheese and season, to taste. Put plastic wrap
onto the surface to prevent a skin forming.
Preheat the oven to moderately hot 200°C
(400°F/Gas 6).
5 Put a layer of lasagne sheets in the dish. Spread
with a third of the ricotta filling, sprinkle with
basil, then top with a third of the tomato sauce.
Repeat the layers, finishing with pasta.
6 Pour the béchamel sauce over the top and
spread until smooth. Sprinkle with the
combined breadcrumbs, pine nuts, paprika
and Parmesan. Bake for 45 minutes, or until
browned. Set the lasagne aside for 10 minutes
before serving.
NOTE: Allowing the lasagne to stand before
serving makes it easier to cut.

NUTRITION PER SERVE: *Protein 30 g; Fat 30 g;
Carbohydrate 60 g; Dietary Fibre 5 g; Cholesterol 130 mg;
2670 kJ (635 cal)*

PAPRIKA
Ground paprika is the
dried and pounded form
of sweet red peppers,
capsicum annuum. It is
bright reddish-orange and
gives a rosy hue to dishes
when used in any quantity.
With a slightly pungent
taste, paprika is the
distinctive flavour in
Hungarian Goulash, and
benefits from slow cooking
to maximise its impact. It
is available in varying
strengths, from very sweet
and mild to fully flavoured
and highly fragrant.

ABOVE: Ricotta lasagne

SEAFOOD WITH PASTA

Preparation time: 30 minutes
Total cooking time: 45 minutes
Serves 6

✴ ✴

250 g (8 oz) packet instant lasagne sheets
500 g (1 lb) boneless fish fillets
125 g (4 oz) scallops, cleaned
500 g (1 lb) raw prawns, shelled
   and deveined
125 g (4 oz) butter
1 leek, chopped
2/3 cup (85 g/3 oz) plain flour
2 cups (500 ml/16 fl oz) milk
2 cups (500 ml/16 fl oz) dry white wine
1 cup (125 g/4 oz) freshly grated
   Cheddar cheese
1/2 cup (125 ml/4 fl oz) cream
1/2 cup (50 g/13/4 oz) freshly grated Parmesan
2 tablespoons chopped fresh parsley

1 Preheat the oven to moderate 180°C (350°F/Gas 4). Line a greased deep lasagne dish, approximately 30 x 30 cm (12 x 12 inch) with lasagne sheets, breaking them to fill any gaps. Set aside.
2 Chop the fish and scallops into even-sized pieces. Chop the prawns.
3 Melt the butter in a large pan. Add the leek and cook, stirring, for 1 minute. Add the flour and cook, stirring, for 1 minute. Gradually blend in the milk and wine, stirring until the mixture is smooth. Cook, stirring constantly, over medium heat until the sauce boils and thickens. Reduce the heat and simmer for 3 minutes. Remove from the heat and stir in the cheese and salt and pepper, to taste. Add the seafood and simmer for 1 minute. Remove from the heat.
4 Spoon half the seafood mixture over the lasagne sheets. Top with a layer of lasagne sheets. Continue layering, finishing with lasagne sheets.
5 Pour the cream over the top. Sprinkle with the combined Parmesan and parsley. Bake, uncovered, for 30 minutes, or until bubbling and golden.
NOTE: Lasagne sheets are available in straight or ridged sheets.

NUTRITION PER SERVE: *Protein 50 g; Fat 45 g; Carbohydrate 45 g; Dietary Fibre 5 g; Cholesterol 290 mg; 3460 kJ (825 cal)*

CHEDDAR
Cheddar, the most well loved of English cheeses, originated in the small Somerset village of Cheddar. It is a hard cow's milk cheese matured to give well balanced flavours with a mellow aftertaste.

ABOVE: Seafood with pasta

ON THE SIDE

SWEET CHILLI POTATO AND CORIANDER SALAD Cut 1 kg (2 lb) peeled Desiree potatoes into wedges, drizzle with olive oil and sprinkle with sea salt. Roast in a hot oven until crisp and golden. Transfer to a bowl and drizzle generously with sweet chilli sauce. Add about 3 tablespoons of chopped fresh coriander and toss until mixed through.

PASTA PIE

Preparation time: 20 minutes
Total cooking time: 1 hour
Serves 4

★★

250 g (8 oz) macaroni

1 tablespoon olive oil

1 onion, sliced

125 g (4 oz) pancetta, chopped

125 g (4 oz) ham, chopped

4 eggs

1 cup (250 ml/8 fl oz) milk

1 cup (250 ml/8 fl oz) cream

2 tablespoons snipped fresh chives

1 cup (125 g/4 oz) grated Cheddar cheese

125 g (4 oz) bocconcini (approximately 4),
chopped

1 Preheat the oven to moderate 180°C (350°F/Gas 4). Cook the macaroni in a large pan of rapidly boiling salted water until *al dente*. Drain. Spread evenly over the base of a 5 cm (2 inch) deep casserole dish.

2 Heat the oil in a large pan, add the onion and stir over low heat until just tender. Stir in the pancetta and cook for 2 minutes. Add the ham to the mixture and stir well. Remove from the heat and allow to cool.

3 In a bowl, whisk together the eggs, milk, cream, chives and salt and pepper, to taste. Mix in the Cheddar cheese, bocconcini and pancetta mixture, stirring thoroughly. Spread evenly over the top of the macaroni. Bake for 35–40 minutes, or until the mixture is set.

NUTRITION PER SERVE: *Protein 40 g; Fat 75 g; Carbohydrate 50 g; Dietary Fibre 5 g; Cholesterol 470 mg; 4335 kJ (1035 cal)*

ABOVE: Pasta pie

233

DURUM WHEAT

Durum wheat is a hard wheat with high levels of protein and therefore more gluten. It is considered the best wheat for pasta making and by law, all dried pasta made in Italy must be from 100% pure durum wheat semolina, *pasta di semola di grano duro*. As well as the nutritional benefits it provides, it gives pasta good colour, from pale lemon to golden, and more flavour. Durum wheat is necessary for the resilient texture of quality pasta and its presence helps to achieve the desired cooked state known as *al dente*.

BELOW: Pasta souffle

PASTA SOUFFLE

Preparation time: 35 minutes
Total cooking time: 55 minutes
Serves 4

★★

2 tablespoons freshly grated Parmesan
60 g (2 oz) butter
1 small onion, finely chopped
2 tablespoons plain flour
2 cups (500 ml/16 fl oz) milk
1/2 cup (125 ml/4 fl oz) chicken stock
3 eggs, separated
3/4 cup (115 g/4 oz) small macaroni, cooked
210 g (7 oz) can salmon, drained and flaked
1 tablespoon chopped fresh parsley
grated rind of 1 lemon

1 Preheat the oven to hot 210°C (415°F/Gas 6–7). Brush a round 6-cup capacity (18 cm/7 inch) soufflé dish with oil. Coat the base and sides with Parmesan. Shake off excess.
2 To collar a soufflé dish, cut a piece of aluminium foil or greaseproof paper 5 cm (2 inches) longer than the circumference of the soufflé dish. Fold the foil in half lengthways. Wrap the foil around the outside of the soufflé dish; it should extend 5 cm (2 inches) above the rim. Secure the foil with string.
3 Heat the butter in a large pan. Add the onion and cook over low heat until tender. Add the flour and stir for 2 minutes, or until the mixture is lightly golden. Remove from the heat. Gradually blend in the milk and stock, stirring until the mixture is smooth. Return to the heat. Stir constantly over medium heat until the mixture boils and thickens. Reduce the heat and simmer for 3 minutes. Add the egg yolks and whisk until smooth. Add the macaroni, salmon, parsley, lemon rind and salt and pepper, to taste. Stir until combined. Transfer the mixture to a large bowl.
4 Using electric beaters, beat the egg whites in a small dry mixing bowl until stiff peaks form. Using a metal spoon, fold gently into the salmon mixture. Spoon into the prepared dish. Bake for 40–45 minutes, or until well risen and browned. Serve immediately.
NOTE: Hot soufflés should be made just before you want to serve them as they will collapse very quickly after removal from the oven. The base mixture can be prepared, up to the end of Step 3, well in advance. Soften the mixture before folding in the beaten egg whites. Whites should be folded into the mixture just before cooking.

NUTRITION PER SERVE: *Protein 25 g; Fat 25 g; Carbohydrate 20 g; Dietary Fibre 1 g; Cholesterol 200 mg; 1690 kJ (405 cal)*

CLASSIC LASAGNE

Preparation time: 40 minutes
Total cooking time: 1 hour 40 minutes
Serves 8

★★★

2 tablespoons oil
30 g (1 oz) butter
1 large onion, finely chopped
1 carrot, finely chopped
1 celery stick, finely chopped
500 g (1 lb) beef mince
150 g (5 oz) chicken livers, finely chopped
1 cup (250 ml/8 fl oz) tomato purée
1 cup (250 ml/8 fl oz) red wine
2 tablespoons chopped fresh parsley
375 g (12 oz) fresh lasagne sheets

Béchamel sauce

60 g (2 oz) butter
1/3 cup (40 g/1 1/4 oz) plain flour
2 1/4 cups (560 ml/18 fl oz) milk
1/2 teaspoon nutmeg
1 cup (100 g/3 1/2 oz) freshly grated Parmesan

1 Heat the oil and butter in a heavy-based pan and cook the onion, carrot and celery over medium heat until softened, stirring constantly. Increase the heat, add the mince and brown well, breaking up any lumps with a fork. Add the chicken livers and cook until they change colour. Add the tomato purée, wine, parsley, and salt and pepper, to taste. Bring to the boil, reduce the heat and simmer for 45 minutes; set aside.

2 To make the béchamel sauce, melt the butter in a medium pan over low heat. Add the flour and stir for 1 minute. Remove from the heat and gradually stir in the milk. Return to the heat and stir constantly until the sauce boils and begins to thicken. Simmer for another minute. Add the nutmeg and salt, pepper, to taste. Place

a piece of plastic wrap on the surface of the sauce to prevent a skin forming; set aside.

3 Cut the lasagne sheets to fit snugly into a deep, rectangular ovenproof dish. Sometimes the sheets require precooking, so follow the instructions from the manufacturer and drain well before use.

4 To assemble, preheat the oven to moderate 180°C (350°F/Gas 4). Brush the ovenproof dish generously with melted butter or oil. Spread a thin layer of the meat sauce over the base and follow with a thin layer of béchamel. If béchamel has cooled and become too thick, warm it gently to make spreading easier. Lay lasagne sheets on top, gently pressing to push out any air. Continue the layers, finishing with the béchamel. Sprinkle with Parmesan and bake for 35–40 minutes, or until golden brown. Set aside 15 minutes before cutting.

NOTE: A packet of instant lasagne can be used instead of fresh. Follow the manufacturer's instructions. If you prefer, you can leave out the chicken livers and increase the amount of mince.

NUTRITION PER SERVE: *Protein 30 g; Fat 30 g; Carbohydrate 45 g; Dietary Fibre 5 g; Cholesterol 160 mg; 2415 kJ (575 cal)*

BÉCHAMEL SAUCE
Béchamel is known today as a white sauce made by adding milk to a roux, although originally it was produced by adding cream to a thick velouté. The sauce owes its name to a certain Marquis Louis de Béchameil, a rich handsome gourmet who acted as chief steward to Louis XIV. It is unlikely that he created the sauce, but more probable that one of the King's cooks, rather ingratiatingly, named it in his honour.

ABOVE: Classic lasagne

CINNAMON

The best quality cinnamon comes from the Sri Lankan cinnamon tree, *cinnamomum zeylanicum*, which has the most fragrant scent and a delicate and fresh flavour. It is made from the dried inner bark of young shoots where, once exposed, thin layers curl up into a cylinder as they dry. These are slipped together in rolls of ten, then cut into quills of equal length. It is more costly than Chinese cinnamon, *cassia*, where older, outer bark is collected for drying. Cinnamon is used whole, broken into pieces or ground to flavour sweet dishes and baked foods, and it is an ingredient of curry powder and garam masala.

ABOVE: Macaroni cheese

MACARONI CHEESE

Preparation time: 20 minutes
Total cooking time: 35 minutes
Serves 4

☆

2 cups (500 ml/16 fl oz) milk
1 cup (250 ml/8 fl oz) cream
1 bay leaf
1 whole clove
1/2 cinnamon stick
60 g (2 oz) butter
2 tablespoons plain flour
2 cups (250 g/8 oz) freshly grated
    Cheddar cheese
1/2 cup (50 g/1 3/4 oz) freshly grated Parmesan
375 g (12 oz) elbow macaroni
1 cup (80 g/2 3/4 oz) fresh breadcrumbs
2 rashers rindless bacon, chopped and fried
    until crisp

1 Preheat the oven to moderate 180°C (350°F/Gas 4). Pour the milk and cream into a medium pan with the bay leaf, clove and cinnamon stick. Bring to the boil, then remove from the heat and set aside for 10 minutes. Strain into a jug; remove and discard the flavourings.

2 Melt the butter in a medium pan over low heat. Add the flour and stir for 1 minute. Remove from the heat and gradually add the milk and cream mixture, stirring until smooth. Return to the heat and stir constantly until the sauce boils and thickens. Simmer for 2 minutes, then remove from the heat and add half the Cheddar cheese, half the Parmesan and salt and pepper, to taste. Set aside.

3 Cook the macaroni in a large pan of rapidly boiling salted water until *al dente*. Drain and return to the pan. Add the sauce and mix well. Spoon into a deep casserole dish. Sprinkle with combined breadcrumbs, bacon and remaining cheeses. Bake for 15–20 minutes, or until golden. Serve.

NOTE: You can add chopped cooked chicken to the white sauce before mixing with the pasta.

NUTRITION PER SERVE: *Protein 45 g; Fat 70 g; Carbohydrate 90 g; Dietary Fibre 5 g; Cholesterol 185 mg; 4960 kJ (1185 cal)*

CONCHIGLIE WITH CHICKEN AND RICOTTA

Preparation time: 15 minutes
Total cooking time: 1 hour 10 minutes
Serves 4

★★

500 g (1 lb) conchiglie (shell pasta)

2 tablespoons olive oil

1 onion, chopped

1 clove garlic, crushed

60 g (2 oz) prosciutto, sliced

125 g (4 oz) mushrooms, chopped

250 g (8 oz) chicken mince

2 tablespoons tomato paste (tomato purée, double concentrate)

425 g (14 oz) can crushed tomatoes

1/2 cup (125 ml/4 fl oz) dry white wine

1 teaspoon dried oregano

250 g (8 oz) ricotta cheese

1 cup (150 g/5 oz) grated mozzarella cheese

1 teaspoon snipped fresh chives

1 tablespoon chopped fresh parsley

3 tablespoons freshly grated Parmesan

1 Cook the conchiglie in a large pan of rapidly boiling salted water until *al dente*. Drain well.
2 Heat the oil in a large frying pan. Add the onion and garlic and stir over low heat until the onion is tender. Add the prosciutto and stir for 1 minute. Add the mushrooms and cook for 2 minutes. Add the chicken mince and brown well, breaking up with a fork as it cooks.
3 Stir in the tomato paste, tomato, wine, oregano and salt and pepper, to taste. Bring to the boil, reduce the heat and simmer for 20 minutes.
4 Preheat the oven to moderate 180°C (350°F/Gas 4). Combine the ricotta, mozzarella, chives, parsley and half the Parmesan. Spoon a little of the mixture into each shell. Spoon some of the chicken sauce into the base of a casserole dish. Arrange the conghiglie on top. Spoon the remaining sauce over the top. Sprinkle with the remaining Parmesan. Bake for 25–30 minutes, or until golden.
NOTE: Conchiglie (shell pasta) vary in size—medium or large shells are best for this dish.

NUTRITION PER SERVE: *Protein 50 g; Fat 40 g; Carbohydrate 95 g; Dietary Fibre 9 g; Cholesterol 115 mg; 3945 kJ (940 cal)*

ON THE SIDE

RASPBERRY BEETROOT SALAD
Cook 1 bunch beetroot in a pan of simmering water until tender, peel and cut into wedges. Make a dressing using raspberry vinegar, orange juice and honey. Toss the beetroot wedges in the dressing and sprinkle with a few caraway seeds.

BABY SPINACH, WALNUT AND CHEDDAR SALAD Combine baby spinach leaves, toasted walnut halves and shavings of vintage Cheddar cheese in a salad bowl. Drizzle with a good-quality French dressing.

CHICKEN MINCE
A good chicken mince will be made of meat from all parts of the chicken. It will have a good proportion of fat and include both white and dark meat. Use it soon after it is made as it will spoil more quickly than regular cuts of meat. Avoid buying pre-minced chicken that looks grey and patchy.

ABOVE: Conchiglie with chicken and ricotta

ABOVE: Baked spaghetti frittata

BAKED SPAGHETTI FRITTATA

Preparation time: 30 minutes
Total cooking time: 35 minutes
Serves 4

★★

30 g (1 oz) butter
125 g (4 oz) mushrooms, sliced
1 green pepper (capsicum), seeded
  and chopped
125 g (4 oz) ham, sliced
1/2 cup (80 g/2³/4 oz) frozen peas
6 eggs
1 cup (250 ml/8 fl oz) cream or milk
100 g (3¹/2 oz) spaghetti, cooked and chopped
2 tablespoons chopped fresh parsley
1/4 cup (25 g/³/4 oz) freshly grated Parmesan

1 Preheat the oven to moderate 180°C (350°F/Gas 4). Lightly brush a 23 cm (9 inch) flan dish with oil or melted butter.
2 Melt the butter in a frying pan, add the mushrooms and cook over low heat for 2–3 minutes. Add the pepper and cook for 1 minute. Stir in the ham and peas. Remove the pan from the heat and allow the mixture to cool slightly.
3 In a small bowl, whisk the eggs, cream and salt and pepper, to taste. Stir in the spaghetti, parsley and mushroom mixture and pour into the prepared dish. Sprinkle with Parmesan and bake for 25–30 minutes.
NOTE: Serve with chargrilled vegetables and leafy salad greens.

NUTRITION PER SERVE: *Protein 25 g; Fat 20 g; Carbohydrate 10 g; Dietary Fibre 5 g; Cholesterol 300 mg; 1320 kJ (315 cal)*

BAKED CANNELLONI MILANESE

Preparation time: 40 minutes
Total cooking time: 1 hour 50 minutes
Serves 4

☆

500 g (1 lb) pork and veal mince
½ cup (50 g/1¾ oz) dry breadcrumbs
1 cup (100 g/3½ oz) freshly grated Parmesan
2 eggs, beaten
1 teaspoon dried oregano
12–15 cannelloni tubes
375 g (12 oz) fresh ricotta cheese
½ cup (60 g/2 oz) freshly grated Cheddar
  cheese

Tomato sauce

425 ml (14 fl oz) can tomato purée (passata)
425 g (14 oz) can crushed tomatoes
2 cloves garlic, crushed
3 tablespoons chopped fresh basil

1 Preheat the oven to moderate 180°C
(350°F/Gas 4). Lightly brush a rectangular
casserole dish with melted butter or oil.
2 In a bowl, combine the pork and veal mince,
breadcrumbs, half the Parmesan, egg, oregano
and salt and pepper, to taste. Use a teaspoon to
stuff the cannelloni tubes with the mince
mixture. Set aside.
3 To make the tomato sauce, bring the tomato
purée, tomato and garlic to the boil in a
medium pan. Reduce the heat and simmer
for 15 minutes. Add the basil and pepper, to
taste, and stir well.
4 Spoon half the tomato sauce over the base of
the prepared dish. Arrange the stuffed cannelloni
tubes on top. Cover with the remaining sauce.
Spread with ricotta cheese. Sprinkle with the
combined remaining Parmesan and Cheddar
cheeses. Bake, covered with foil, for 1 hour.
Uncover and bake for another 15 minutes, or
until golden. Cut into squares for serving.

NUTRITION PER SERVE: *Protein 60 g; Fat 40 g;
Carbohydrate 40 g; Dietary Fibre 5 g; Cholesterol 255 mg;
3190 kJ (762 cal)*

ON THE SIDE
INDIVIDUAL CAULIFLOWER
CHEESE Boil, steam or microwave
baby cauliflower, allowing 1 per person,
until tender. Drain and transfer to an
ovenproof dish. Top with a béchamel sauce
made by melting 30 g (1 oz) of butter in a
small pan and stirring in 1 tablespoon of
plain flour. Add 1⅓ cups (350 ml/11 fl oz)
of milk and stir over medium heat for
1 minute, or until the sauce boils and
thickens. Add ½ cup (60 g/2 oz) of finely
grated Cheddar cheese and ¼ teaspoon of
Dijon mustard and mix to combine. Pour
the sauce over the cauliflower, top with
finely grated Cheddar cheese and bake in a
hot 210°C (415°F/Gas 6–7) oven for
10 minutes, or until the cheese is golden.

*ABOVE: Baked
cannelloni Milanese*

3 Add the tomato, oregano, cayenne pepper and olives and simmer gently for 5 minutes. Pour the vegetable sauce over the pasta and toss through with one-third of the mozzarella cheese. Season, to taste, with freshly ground black pepper. Sprinkle with Parmesan and distribute the remaining mozzarella evenly over the top.
4 Bake for 10 minutes, or until the cheese has melted and the top is lightly browned. Serve.

NUTRITION PER SERVE: *Protein 30 g; Fat 35 g; Carbohydrate 75 g; Dietary Fibre 10 g; Cholesterol 45 mg; 3030 kJ (720 cal)*

PASTA AND SPINACH TIMBALES

Preparation time: 25 minutes
Total cooking time: 45 minutes + resting
Serves 6

★ ★

30 g (1 oz) butter
1 tablespoon olive oil
1 onion, chopped
500 g (1 lb) English spinach, steamed
   and well-drained
8 eggs, beaten
1 cup (250 ml/8 fl oz) cream
100 g (3 1/2 oz) spaghetti or tagliolini, cooked
1/2 cup (60 g/2 oz) grated Cheddar cheese
1/2 cup (50 g/1 3/4 oz) freshly grated Parmesan

RIGATONI GRATIN

Preparation time: 20 minutes
Total cooking time: 30 minutes
Serves 4

★ ★

375 g (12 oz) rigatoni
1/4 cup (60 ml/2 fl oz) light olive oil
300 g (10 oz) slender eggplant
   (aubergine), chopped
4 small zucchini (courgettes), thickly sliced
1 onion, sliced
410 g (13 oz) can tomatoes
1 teaspoon chopped fresh oregano
pinch of cayenne pepper
8–10 black olives, pitted and sliced
250 g (8 oz) mozzarella cheese, cut into
   small cubes
2 tablespoons freshly grated Parmesan

1 Preheat the oven to moderate 180°C (350°F/Gas 4). Cook the rigatoni in a large pan of rapidly boiling salted water until *al dente*. Drain the pasta thoroughly and transfer to an oiled, shallow ovenproof dish.
2 While the pasta is cooking, heat the oil in a large pan and fry the eggplant, zucchini and onion for 5 minutes, or until lightly browned.

ABOVE: Rigatoni gratin
RIGHT: Pasta and spinach timbales

1 Preheat the oven to moderate 180°C (350°F/Gas 4). Brush six 1-cup capacity dariole moulds with melted butter or oil. Line the bases with baking paper. Heat the butter and oil together in a frying pan. Add the onion and stir over low heat until the onion is tender. Add the well-drained spinach and cook for 1 minute. Remove from the heat and allow to cool. Whisk in the eggs and cream. Stir in the spaghetti or tagliolini, grated cheeses, and salt and freshly ground pepper, to taste; stir well. Spoon into the prepared moulds.

2 Place the moulds in a baking dish. Pour boiling water into the baking dish to come halfway up the sides of the moulds. Bake for 30–35 minutes or until set. Halfway through cooking, you may need to cover the top with a sheet of foil to prevent excess browning. Near the end of cooking time, test the timbales with the point of a knife. When cooked, the knife should come out clean.

3 Allow the timbales to rest for 15 minutes before turning them out. Run the point of a knife around the edge of each mould. Invert onto serving plates.

NUTRITION PER SERVE: *Protein 20 g; Fat 16 g; Carbohydrate 7 g; Dietary Fibre 3 g; Cholesterol 330 mg; 1860 kJ (440 cal)*

BAKED CREAMY CHEESY PASTA

Preparation time: 10–15 minutes
Total cooking time: 35–40 minutes
Serves 4

☆

500 g (1 lb) fusilli

2½ cups (600 ml/20 fl oz) cream

3 eggs

250 g (8 oz) feta, crumbled

2 tablespoons plain flour

2 teaspoons ground nutmeg

1 cup (125 g/4 oz) grated Cheddar or
   mozzarella cheese

1 Cook the fusilli in a large pan of rapidly boiling salted water until *al dente*. Drain, reserving 1 cup (250 ml/8 fl oz) of the cooking water. Set the pasta aside to cool a little.

2 Preheat the oven to moderate 180°C (350°F/ Gas 4) and brush a 7-cup capacity ovenproof dish with olive oil.

3 Whisk the cream, eggs and reserved water in a large bowl until thoroughly combined. Stir in the crumbled feta, flour, ground nutmeg and salt and pepper, to taste.

4 Transfer the cooled pasta to the prepared dish. Pour the cream mixture over the top and sprinkle with the grated cheese. Bake for 30–35 minutes, or until the mixture is just set and the top is lightly golden.

NUTRITION PER SERVE: *Protein 40 g; Fat 85 g; Carbohydrate 95 g; Dietary Fibre 6 g; Cholesterol 380 g; 5520 kJ 1315 (cal)*

WHITE PEPPER

White peppercorns come from the same tropical vine as black peppercorns, but the berries are treated differently to give a more subdued flavour and a lighter colour. These features are desirable in some dishes, particularly with white sauces and those which are cream based, so the appearance is not spoilt. Surprisingly, white pepper is more aromatic than black.

ABOVE: Baked creamy cheesy pasta

MOZZARELLA CHEESE

Most mozzarella made outside Italy today is intended for cooking, to be sprinkled over pizzas and put into lasagnes and baked dishes. It is a matured, sometimes processed cheese with a rubbery texture, but with great melting qualities. When heated, it breaks down completely and becomes smooth and runny, and forms long strands when stretched, much to the delight of children. It is not eaten as a table cheese. Fresh mozzarella (bocconcini), on the other hand, is enjoyed fresh. It is pure white, has a creamy taste and a limited shelf-life. In Italy, it is sometimes still made from the milk of buffaloes, as it has been for centuries.

ABOVE: Meatballs and pasta

MEATBALLS AND PASTA

Preparation time: 40 minutes
Total cooking time: 55 minutes
Serves 4

★★

2/3 cup (100 g/3 1/2 oz) macaroni
500 g (1 lb) beef mince
1 onion, finely chopped
1 cup (80 g/2 3/4 oz) fresh breadcrumbs
2 tablespoons freshly grated Parmesan
1 tablespoon chopped fresh basil
1 egg, beaten
2 tablespoons olive oil
1 cup (150 g/5 oz) freshly grated
   mozzarella cheese

Sauce

1 onion, sliced
1 clove garlic, crushed
1 pepper (capsicum), seeded
   and sliced
125 g (4 oz) mushrooms, sliced
1/4 cup (60 ml/2 fl oz) tomato paste (tomato
   purée, double concentrate)
1/2 cup (125 ml/4 fl oz) red wine

1 Cook the macaroni in a large pan of rapidly boiling salted water until *al dente*. Drain thoroughly and set aside.
2 In a bowl, combine the mince, onion, half the breadcrumbs, Parmesan, basil and egg. Form heaped teaspoonsful into small balls.
3 Heat the oil in a frying pan. Add the meatballs and cook until well browned. Drain on paper towels. Transfer to an ovenproof dish. Preheat the oven to moderate 180°C (350°F/Gas 4).
4 To make the sauce, add the onion and garlic to the same pan and stir over low heat until the onion is tender. Add the pepper and mushrooms and cook for 2 minutes. Stir in the tomato paste and then the wine and 1 cup (250 ml/8 fl oz) of water. Bring to the boil, stirring continuously. Mix in the macaroni and salt and pepper, to taste. Pour over the top of the meatballs.
5 Bake, uncovered, for 30–35 minutes. Sprinkle with combined mozzarella cheese and remaining breadcrumbs. Bake for another 10 minutes, or until golden.

NUTRITION PER SERVE: *Protein 45 g; Fat 35 g; Carbohydrate 40 g; Dietary Fibre 5 g; Cholesterol 150 mg; 2840 kJ (680 cal)*

PASTA-FILLED VEGETABLES

Preparation time: 40 minutes
Total cooking time: 45 minutes
Serves 6

★★

150 g (5 oz) rissoni
1 tablespoon olive oil
1 onion, finely chopped
1 clove garlic, crushed
3 rindless bacon rashers, finely chopped
1 cup (150 g/5 oz) freshly grated
    mozzarella cheese
1/2 cup (50 g/1 3/4 oz) freshly grated Parmesan
2 tablespoons chopped fresh parsley
4 large red peppers (capsicums), halved
    lengthways, seeds removed
425 g (14 oz) can crushed tomatoes
1/2 cup (125 ml/4 fl oz) dry white wine
1 tablespoon tomato paste (tomato purée,
    double concentrate)
1/2 teaspoon ground oregano
2 tablespoons shredded fresh basil

1 Cook the rissoni in a large pan of boiling salted water until *al dente*. Drain.
2 Preheat the oven to moderate 180°C (350°F/Gas 4). Lightly oil a large shallow ovenproof dish.
3 Heat the oil in a pan. Add the onion and garlic and stir over low heat until the onion is tender. Add the bacon and stir until crisp. Transfer to a large bowl and combine with the rissoni, cheeses and parsley. Spoon the mixture into the pepper halves and arrange in the dish.
4 In a bowl, combine the tomato, wine, tomato paste, oregano and salt and pepper, to taste. Spoon over the rissoni mixture. Sprinkle with basil. Bake for 35–40 minutes.

NUTRITION PER SERVE: *Protein 20 g; Fat 15 g; Carbohydrate 25 g; Dietary Fibre 5 g; Cholesterol 35 mg; 1345 kJ (320 cal)*

ON THE SIDE

BUTTERY CARAWAY CABBAGE
Finely shred cabbage and boil, steam or microwave until tender. Lightly fry some sliced onion with some caraway seeds in lots of butter until the onion is very soft and the caraway seeds are fragrant. Add the cabbage to the pan and toss to combine. Drizzle with a little malt vinegar and season generously with salt and pepper.

RISSONI
Rissoni is dried pasta in the shape of rice. It is good in soups and is perfect for stuffing vegetables. Used in stews, it contributes body and substance without bulk and for this reason it is also ideal as an ingredient of stuffing for poultry.

ABOVE: Pasta-filled vegetables

GARLIC

How garlic is prepared depends on the degree of flavour required for the intended dish. If the cloves are finely chopped or mashed, they will be the most intense as more oils are released this way. For a mild taste without garlicky undertones, the cloves are used whole, often unpeeled, and discarded before the dish is eaten. A stronger flavour without pungency comes from cloves which are peeled and halved.

CANNELLONI

Preparation time: 45 minutes
Total cooking time: 1 hour 10 minutes
Serves 6

★★

Beef and spinach filling

1 tablespoon olive oil

1 onion, chopped

1 clove garlic, crushed

500 g (1 lb) beef mince

250 g (8 oz) packet frozen spinach, thawed

3 tablespoons tomato paste (tomato purée, double concentrate)

1/2 cup (125 g/4 oz) ricotta cheese

1 egg

1/2 teaspoon ground oregano

Béchamel sauce

1 cup (250 ml/8 fl oz) milk

1 sprig of fresh parsley

5 peppercorns

30 g (1 oz) butter

1 tablespoon plain flour

1/2 cup (125 ml/4 fl oz) cream

Tomato sauce

425 g (14 oz) can tomato purée

2 tablespoons chopped fresh basil

1 clove garlic, crushed

1/2 teaspoon sugar

12–15 instant cannelloni tubes

1 cup (150 g/5 oz) freshly grated mozzarella cheese

1/2 cup (50 g/1 3/4 oz) freshly grated Parmesan

1 Preheat the oven to moderate 180°C (350°F/Gas 4). Lightly oil a large shallow ovenproof dish. Set aside.
2 To make the beef and spinach filling, heat the oil in a frying pan, add the onion and garlic and stir over low heat until the onion is tender. Add the mince and brown well, breaking up with a fork as it cooks. Add the spinach and tomato paste. Stir for 1 minute and then remove from the heat. In a small bowl, mix the ricotta, egg, oregano and salt and pepper, to taste. Stir the mixture through the mince until combined. Set aside.
3 To make the béchamel sauce, combine the milk, parsley and peppercorns in a small pan. Bring to the boil. Remove from the heat and

RIGHT: Cannelloni

allow to stand for 10 minutes. Strain, discarding the flavourings. Melt the butter in a small pan over low heat, add the flour and stir for 1 minute, or until smooth. Remove from the heat and gradually stir in the strained milk. Return to the heat and stir constantly over medium heat until the sauce boils and begins to thicken. Reduce the heat, simmer for another minute, then stir in the cream and salt and pepper, to taste.

4 To make the tomato sauce, stir all the ingredients in a pan until combined. Bring to the boil, reduce the heat and simmer for 5 minutes. Season, to taste, with salt and pepper.

5 Spoon the beef and spinach filling into a piping bag and fill the cannelloni tubes or fill using a teaspoon.

6 Spoon a little of the tomato sauce in the base of the casserole dish. Arrange the cannelloni on top. Pour the béchamel sauce over the cannelloni, followed by the remaining tomato sauce. Sprinkle the combined cheeses over the top. Bake, uncovered, for 35–40 minutes, or until golden.
NOTE: Serve with a mixed green salad or steam some vegetables such as broccoli or beans, if desired.

NUTRITION PER SERVE: *Protein 35 g; Fat 40 g; Carbohydrate 25 g; Dietary Fibre 5 g; Cholesterol 150 mg; 2475 kJ (590 cal)*

ITALIAN OMELETTE

Preparation time: 20 minutes
Total cooking time: 15 minutes
Serves 4

☆

2 tablespoons olive oil
1 onion, finely chopped
125 g (4 oz) ham, sliced
6 eggs
1/4 cup (60 ml/2 fl oz) milk
2 cups cooked fusilli or spiral pasta
   (150 g/5 oz uncooked)
3 tablespoons grated Parmesan
2 tablespoons chopped fresh parsley
1 tablespoon chopped fresh basil
1/2 cup (60 g/2 oz) freshly grated
   Cheddar cheese

1 Heat half the oil in a frying pan. Add the onion and stir over low heat until softened. Add the sliced ham to the pan and stir for 1 minute. Transfer to a plate and set aside.

2 In a bowl, whisk the eggs, milk and salt and pepper, to taste. Stir in the pasta, Parmesan, herbs and onion mixture.

3 Heat the remaining oil in the same pan. Pour the egg mixture into the pan. Sprinkle with cheese. Cook over medium heat until the mixture begins to set around the edges. Place under a hot grill to complete the cooking. Cut into wedges for serving.
NOTE: This omelette goes well with a crisp green or mixed salad.

NUTRITION PER SERVE: *Protein 25 g; Fat 25 g; Carbohydrate 30 g; Dietary Fibre 2 g; Cholesterol 310 mg; 1925 kJ (460 cal)*

ABOVE: Italian omelette

1 tablespoon chopped fresh oregano

1/4 teaspoon nutmeg

1/2 cup (50 g/1 3/4 oz) freshly grated Parmesan

Béchamel sauce

60 g (2 oz) butter

2 tablespoons plain flour

1 1/2 cups (375 ml/12 fl oz) cold milk

150 g (5 oz) bucatini

1 Put the flour, butter, sugar and egg yolk in a food processor with 1 tablespoon of water. Process lightly until the mixture forms a ball, adding more water if necessary. Lightly knead the dough on a floured surface until smooth. Wrap in plastic wrap and refrigerate.

2 To make the filling, heat the oil in a heavy-based pan and cook the onion and garlic until softened and lightly golden. Increase the heat, add the mince and cook until browned, breaking up any lumps with a fork. Add the livers, tomato, red wine, stock, oregano and nutmeg, then season well with salt and pepper. Cook the sauce over high heat until it boils, then reduce to a simmer and cook, covered, for 40 minutes; cool. Stir in the Parmesan.

3 To make the béchamel sauce, heat the butter in a medium pan over low heat. Add the flour and stir for 1 minute, or until the mixture is golden and smooth. Remove from the heat and gradually stir in the milk. Return to the heat and stir constantly until the sauce boils and begins to thicken. Simmer for another minute. Add salt and pepper, to taste.

4 Cook the bucatini in a pan of rapidly boiling salted water until *al dente*. Drain and cool. Brush a 23 cm (9 inch) deep pie dish with melted butter or oil and preheat the oven to warm 160°C (315°F/Gas 2–3). Divide the pastry into two and roll out one piece to fit the base of the prepared dish, overlapping the sides. Spoon about half of the meat mixture into the dish, top with the bucatini and slowly spoon the béchamel sauce over the top, allowing it to seep down and coat the bucatini. Top with the remaining meat. Roll out the remaining pastry and cover the pie. Trim the edges and pinch lightly to seal. Bake for 50–55 minutes, or until dark golden brown and crisp. Set aside for 15 minutes before cutting.

NUTRITION PER SERVE: *Protein 35 g; Fat 50 g; Carbohydrate 65 g; Dietary Fibre 5 g; Cholesterol 270 mg; 3595 kJ (860 cal)*

PASTICCIO

Preparation time: 1 hour
Total cooking time: 1 hour 50 minutes
Serves 6

★★

2 cups (250 g/8 oz) plain flour

125 g (4 oz) cold butter, chopped

1/4 cup (60 g/2 oz) caster sugar

1 egg yolk

Filling

2 tablespoons olive oil

1 onion, chopped

2 cloves garlic, finely chopped

500 g (1 lb) beef mince

150 g (5 oz) chicken livers

2 tomatoes, chopped

1/2 cup (125 ml/4 fl oz) red wine

1/2 cup (125 ml/4 fl oz) rich
   beef stock

ABOVE: Pasticcio

PASTITSIO

Preparation time: 1 hour
Total cooking time: 1 hour 25 minutes
Serves 8

★★

2 tablespoons olive oil

4 cloves garlic, crushed

3 onions, chopped

1 kg (2 lb) lamb mince

800 g (1 lb 10 oz) can peeled tomatoes, chopped

1 cup (250 ml/8 fl oz) red wine

1 cup (250 ml/8 fl oz) chicken stock

3 tablespoons tomato paste (tomato purée,
    double concentrate)

2 tablespoons fresh oregano leaves

2 bay leaves

350 g (11 oz) ziti

2 eggs, lightly beaten

750 g (1 1/2 lb) Greek-style yoghurt

3 eggs, extra, lightly beaten

200 g (6 1/2 oz) kefalotyri or manchego cheese,
    grated

1/2 teaspoon ground nutmeg

1/2 cup (50 g/1 3/4 oz) freshly grated Parmesan

1 cup (80 g/2 3/4 oz) fresh breadcrumbs

1 Preheat the oven to moderately hot 200°C (400°F/Gas 6). To make the meat sauce, heat the oil in a large heavy-based pan and cook the garlic and onion over low heat for 10 minutes, or until the onion is soft and golden.

2 Add the mince and cook over high heat until browned, stirring constantly and breaking up any lumps. Add the tomato, wine, stock, tomato paste, oregano and bay leaves. Bring to the boil, reduce the heat and simmer, covered, for 15 minutes. Remove the lid and cook for 30 minutes. Season with salt and pepper.

3 While the meat is cooking, cook the ziti in a large pan of rapidly boiling salted water until *al dente*. Drain well. Transfer to a bowl and stir the eggs through. Spoon into a lightly greased 4-litre capacity ovenproof dish. Top with the meat sauce.

4 Whisk the yoghurt, extra eggs, cheese and nutmeg in a jug to combine and pour the mixture over the meat sauce. Sprinkle with the combined Parmesan and breadcrumbs. Bake for 30–35 minutes, or until the top is crisp and golden brown. Allow to stand for 20 minutes before slicing. Serve with a green salad.

NOTE: Kefalotyri and manchego are firm, grating cheeses. Use Parmesan if they are unavailable.

NUTRITION PER SERVE: *Protein 50 g; Fat 40 g; Carbohydrate 45 g; Dietary Fibre 5 g; Cholesterol 250 mg; 3275 kJ (780 cal)*

PASTICCIO AND PASTITSIO

It is easy to be confused by the terms pasticcio and pastitsio (*pastizio*, or *pastetseo*). In Italian cooking, pasticcio is a generic term used to describe a pie in which the composite parts such as meat, pasta and vegetables are baked in layers. Lasagne is, in fact, one type of pasticcio, and some have a pastry crust. Pasticcio is made for special occasions and can be plain and simple, or quite elaborate in its composition and the ingredients used. It is eaten as a main course and is traditionally served unaccompanied, with a salad or vegetable course following. Pastitsio is the Greek version, and the two are often so similar that it's hard to tell from the recipe which country the cook hails from. Pastitsio is likely to be made with lamb instead of beef, and often Greek favourites such as olives and yoghurt will feature.

LEFT: Pastitsio

BUTTERNUT PUMPKIN FILLED WITH PASTA AND LEEKS

Preparation time: 30 minutes
Total cooking time: 1 hour
Serves 2 as a light meal, or 4 as
an accompaniment

★ ★

1 medium butternut pumpkin
20 g (³/₄ oz) butter
1 leek, thinly sliced
¹/₂ cup (125 ml/4 fl oz) cream
pinch of nutmeg
60 g (2 oz) cooked linguine or stellini
¹/₄ cup (60 ml/2 fl oz) olive oil

1 Preheat the oven to moderate 180°C (350°F/Gas 4). Cleanly cut a quarter off the top end of the butternut pumpkin (where the stalk attaches), to make a lid. Level off the other end so that it stands evenly. Scrape out the seeds and sinew from the pumpkin and discard. Hollow out the centre to make room for filling. Sprinkle salt and pepper over the cut surfaces and then transfer the pumpkin to a small baking dish.
2 Melt the butter in a small frying pan and gently cook the leek until softened. Add the cream and nutmeg and cook over low heat for 4–5 minutes, or until thickened. Season with salt and white pepper, to taste, and stir in the pasta.
3 Fill the butternut pumpkin with the pasta mixture, place the lid on top and drizzle with the olive oil. Bake for 1 hour, or until tender. Test by inserting a skewer through the thickest part of the vegetable.
NOTE: Choose a butternut which is round and fat, not one with a long stem of flesh.

NUTRITION PER SERVE (4): *Protein 10 g; Fat 30 g; Carbohydrate 30 g; Dietary Fibre 6 g; Cholesterol 50 mg; 1885 kJ (450 cal)*

CHICKEN AND VEAL LOAF WITH MUSHROOMS AND SOUR CREAM

Preparation time: 20 minutes
Total cooking time: 1 hour
Serves 6

★ ★

100 g (3¹/₂ oz) pappardelle
¹/₄ cup (20 g/³/₄ oz) fresh breadcrumbs
1 tablespoon white wine
375 g (12 oz) chicken mince
375 g (12 oz) veal mince
2 cloves garlic, crushed
100 g (3¹/₂ oz) button mushrooms,
finely chopped
2 eggs, beaten
pinch of nutmeg
pinch of cayenne pepper
¹/₄ cup (60 ml/2 fl oz) sour cream
4 spring onions, finely chopped
2 tablespoons chopped fresh parsley

1 Grease a 6-cup capacity loaf tin. Cook the pappardelle in a large pan of rapidly boiling salted water until *al dente*. Drain.
2 Preheat the oven to moderately hot 200°C (400°F/Gas 6).
3 Soak the breadcrumbs in the wine. Mix the crumbs in a bowl with the chicken and veal minces, garlic, mushrooms, eggs, nutmeg, cayenne pepper, and salt and freshly ground black pepper, to taste. Mix in the sour cream, spring onion and parsley.
4 Place half the mince mixture into the prepared tin with your hands. Form a deep trough along the entire length. Fill the trough with the pappardelle. Press the remaining mince mixture over the top. Bake for 50–60 minutes, draining the excess fat and juice from the tin twice during cooking. Cool slightly before slicing.
NOTE: Mushrooms can be chopped in a food processor. Don't prepare too far in advance or they will discolour and darken the loaf.

NUTRITION PER SERVE: *Protein 35 g; Fat 20 g; Carbohydrate 15 g; Dietary Fibre 2 g; Cholesterol 205 mg; 1545 kJ (365 cal)*

BUTTERNUT PUMPKIN
Butternut pumpkins or squash are well named, for they have sweet, buttery and slightly nutty taste. When young, they should be evenly firm, with no cracks or blemishes on the skin. The flesh inside will be crisp, with a good bright colour and a low water content.

OPPOSITE PAGE:
Butternut pumpkin filled with pasta and leeks (top); Chicken and veal loaf with mushrooms and sour cream

GREEN OLIVE PASTE

When the pulp of green olives is mixed with olive oil, salt and herbs, the resulting purée is known as green olive paste or pâté. As is, it makes an excellent dip or spread for bread and it can be used to dress pasta and vegetables. Stirred through soups and sauces, it adds flavour and colour, and is delicious rubbed into the skin of poultry.

ABOVE: Pasta with green olive paste and three cheeses

PASTA WITH GREEN OLIVE PASTE AND THREE CHEESES

Preparation time: 10 minutes
Total cooking time: 20 minutes
Serves 4

☆

400 g (13 oz) mafalda or pappardelle

2 tablespoons olive oil

2 cloves garlic, crushed

1/2 cup (125 g/4 oz) green olive paste

4 tablespoons cream

1/2 cup (50 g/1 3/4 oz) freshly grated Parmesan

1/2 cup (60 g/2 oz) grated Cheddar cheese

1/2 cup (50 g/1 3/4 oz) grated Jarlsberg cheese

1 Preheat the oven to moderately hot 200°C (400°F/Gas 6). Lightly brush a deep ovenproof dish with oil.

2 Cook the pasta in a large pan of rapidly boiling salted water until *al dente*. Drain and return to the pan.

3 Toss the olive oil, garlic and green olive paste through the pasta and then mix in the cream. Season with black pepper. Transfer to the prepared dish.

4 Sprinkle the top with the cheeses. Bake, uncovered, for 20 minutes, or until the top is crisp and cheeses have melted.

NUTRITION PER SERVE: *Protein 25 g; Fat 40 g; Carbohydrate 70 g; Dietary Fibre 6 g; Cholesterol 65 mg; 3055 kJ (725 cal)*

GIANT CONCHIGLIE WITH RICOTTA AND ROCKET

Preparation time: 50 minutes
Total cooking time: 1 hour
Serves 6

★★

40 giant conchiglie (shell pasta)

Filling

500 g (1 lb) ricotta cheese
1 cup (100 g/3½ oz) grated Parmesan
150 g (5 oz) rocket, finely shredded
1 egg, lightly beaten
180 g (6 oz) marinated artichokes,
  finely chopped
½ cup (80 g/2¾ oz) sun-dried tomatoes,
  finely chopped
½ cup (95 g/3 oz) sun-dried pepper
  (capsicum), finely chopped

Cheese sauce

60 g (2 oz) butter
30 g (1 oz) plain flour
3 cups (750 ml/24 fl oz) milk
100 g (3½ oz) Gruyère cheese, grated
2 tablespoons chopped fresh basil

600 ml (20 fl oz) bottled pasta sauce
2 tablespoons fresh oregano leaves,
  chopped
2 tablespoons fresh basil leaves,
  finely shredded

1 Cook the giant conchiglie in a large pan of rapidly boiling salted water until *al dente*. Drain and arrange the shells on 2 non-stick baking trays to prevent them sticking together. Cover lightly with plastic wrap.
2 To make the filling, mix all the ingredients in a large bowl. Spoon the filling into the shells, taking care not to overfill them or they will split.
3 To make the cheese sauce, melt the butter in a small pan over low heat. Add the flour and stir for 1 minute, or until golden and smooth. Remove from the heat and gradually stir in the milk. Return to the heat and stir constantly until the sauce boils and begins to thicken. Simmer for another minute. Remove from the heat and stir in the Gruyère cheese with the basil and salt and pepper, to taste.

4 Preheat the oven to moderate 180°C (350°F/Gas 4). Spread 1 cup of the cheese sauce over the base of a 3-litre capacity ovenproof dish. Arrange the filled conchiglie over the sauce, top with the remaining sauce and bake for 30 minutes, or until the sauce is golden.
5 Place the bottled pasta sauce and oregano in a pan and cook over medium heat for 5 minutes, or until heated through. To serve, divide the sauce among the warmed serving plates, top with the conchiglie and sprinkle with the shredded fresh basil leaves.

NUTRITION PER SERVE: *Protein 35 g; Fat 35 g; Carbohydrate 70 g; Dietary Fibre 8 g; Cholesterol 145 mg; 3165 kJ (755 cal)*

ABOVE: Giant conchiglie with ricotta and rocket

PASTA PRONTO

Forget packet meals and takeaways: pasta is the ultimate convenience food. All of these dishes can be ready in around 30 minutes, some of them so fast they are on the table before the family's had time to sit down. Who knows when friends might call in unexpectedly? A good hoard of dried pasta is the key to quick, fuss-free meals and should be part of every well-stocked store-cupboard. Was that the doorbell? Start grating the Parmesan.

GREEN OLIVES

As the name suggests, green olives are the unripe fruit of the olive tree. When olives begin forming they contain no oil, just sugars and organic acids and it is these which give green olives their tangy flavour. As olives mature, they change from pale green through bright green, rose, deep purple to black, and the oil content increases. The flesh goes from being hard and crisp, to soft and slightly spongy. For these reasons, green olives need to be treated differently to black olives to become edible, and it also helps explain why there is such a contrast in flavour and texture between them.

ABOVE: Linguine with anchovies, olives and capers

LINGUINE WITH ANCHOVIES, OLIVES AND CAPERS

Ready to eat in 30 minutes
Serves 4

★

500 g (1 lb) linguine

2 tablespoons olive oil

2 cloves garlic, crushed

2 very ripe tomatoes, peeled and chopped

3 tablespoons capers

1/2 cup (75 g/2 1/2 oz) pitted black olives, finely chopped

1/4 cup (55 g/2 oz) pitted green olives, finely chopped

1/4 cup (60 ml/2 fl oz) dry white wine

3 tablespoons chopped fresh parsley or basil

90 g (3 oz) can anchovies, drained and chopped

1 Cook the linguine in a large pan of rapidly boiling salted water until *al dente*. Drain and return to the pan.

2 While the pasta is cooking, heat the oil in a large frying pan. Add the garlic and stir over low heat for 1 minute. Add the tomato, capers and olives and cook for 2 minutes.

3 Stir in the wine, parsley or basil, and freshly ground black pepper, to taste. Bring to the boil, reduce the heat and simmer for about 5 minutes. Remove from the heat. Add the anchovies and stir gently to combine.

4 Add to the warm pasta in the pan and toss well to distribute the sauce evenly.

NOTE: For variation or on special occasions, you may like to serve this dish with the following topping. Heat a little olive oil in a small pan and add some fresh breadcrumbs and a crushed clove of garlic. Toss over the heat until crisp and golden and sprinkle over the top with freshly grated Parmesan.

NUTRITION PER SERVE: *Protein 20 g; Fat 15 g; Carbohydrate 90 g; Dietary Fibre 8 g; Cholesterol 15 mg; 2525 kJ (600 cal)*

FETTUCINE WITH SPINACH AND PROSCIUTTO

Ready to eat in 20 minutes
Serves 4–6

☆

500 g (1 lb) spinach or plain fettucine
2 tablespoons olive oil
8 thin slices prosciutto, chopped
3 spring onions, chopped
500 g (1 lb) English spinach
1 tablespoon balsamic vinegar
1/2 teaspoon caster sugar
1/2 cup (50 g/1 3/4 oz) freshly grated Parmesan

1 Cook the pasta in a large pan of rapidly boiling salted water until just *al dente*. Drain and return to the pan.
2 While the pasta is cooking, heat the oil in a large heavy-based deep pan. Add the prosciutto and the spring onion and cook, stirring occasionally, over medium heat for 5 minutes or until crisp.
3 Trim the stalks from the spinach, roughly chop the leaves and add them to the pan. Stir in the vinegar and the sugar, cover and cook for 1 minute or until the spinach has softened. Add salt and pepper, to taste.
4 Add the sauce to the pasta and toss well to distribute sauce evenly. Sprinkle with Parmesan and serve immediately.

NUTRITION PER SERVE (6): *Protein 20 g; Fat 10 g; Carbohydrate 60 g; Dietary Fibre 7 g; Cholesterol 25 mg; 1825 kJ (435 cal)*

PASTA WITH FRAGRANT LIME AND SMOKED TROUT

Ready to eat in 30 minutes
Serves 4

☆

500 g (1 lb) spinach and white linguine
1 tablespoon extra virgin olive oil
3 cloves garlic, crushed
1 tablespoon grated lime rind
2 tablespoons poppy seeds
250 g (8 oz) smoked trout, skin and
   bones removed
400 g (13 oz) camembert cheese, chopped
2 tablespoons chopped fresh dill
lime wedges, for serving

1 Cook the linguine in rapidly boiling salted water until *al dente*. Drain.
2 Heat the olive oil in a large heavy-based frying pan. Add the garlic, cook over low heat for 3 minutes or until fragrant. Add the rind, poppy seeds and pasta to the pan and toss to coat.
3 Fold the trout, camembert and dill through the mixture and cook over low heat until the camembert begins to melt. Toss gently through the pasta and serve immediately with a squeeze of lime.

NUTRITION PER SERVE: *Protein 50 g; Fat 40 g; Carbohydrate 90 g; Dietary Fibre 6 g; Cholesterol 140 mg; 3870 kJ (920 cal)*

ENGLISH SPINACH
English spinach has medium to dark green leaves, smaller than those of swiss chard or silverbeet. The stalks are thin and only the tough lower end needs to be removed. It can be steamed, fried, lightly boiled or baked in a gratin or pie.

ABOVE: Fettucine with spinach and prosciutto

CHICKEN RAVIOLI WITH LIME BALSAMIC DRESSING

Ready to eat in 30 minutes
Serves 4

☆

250 g (8 oz) chicken mince
1 egg, lightly beaten
1 teaspoon finely grated orange rind
1/2 cup (50 g/1 3/4 oz) freshly grated Parmesan
1 tablespoon finely shredded fresh basil
275 g (9 oz) won ton wrappers
2 tablespoons lime juice
2 tablespoons balsamic vinegar
1/2 teaspoon honey
1 tablespoon oil

1 Combine the chicken mince, egg, orange rind, Parmesan and basil in a bowl. Place a heaped tablespoon of chicken mixture in the centre of a won ton wrapper, lightly brush the edges with water and top with another wrapper. Press the edges together to seal. Repeat with remaining filling and wrappers. (This is a quick way to make ravioli.)
2 Cook the chicken ravioli in a large pan of rapidly boiling salted water for 5 minutes.
3 Meanwhile, combine the lime juice, balsamic vinegar, honey and oil in a small jug and whisk to combine. Drain the ravioli. Serve drizzled with the dressing and sprinkled with finely chopped fresh chives. Garnish with lime slices, if you like.

NUTRITION PER SERVE: *Protein 30 g; Fat 20 g; Carbohydrate 50 g; Dietary Fibre 2 g; Cholesterol 120 mg; 2020 kJ (480 cal)*

ZITI WITH ROASTED TOMATOES AND OVOLINI

Ready to eat in 30 minutes
Serves 4

☆

200 g (6 1/2 oz) yellow teardrop tomatoes
200 g (6 1/2 oz) red cherry tomatoes
500 g (1 lb) ziti
200 g (6 1/2 oz) ovolini cheese
100 g (3 1/2 oz) capers
3 tablespoons fresh marjoram leaves
3 tablespoons fresh lemon thyme leaves
2 tablespoons extra virgin olive oil
3 tablespoons balsamic vinegar

1 Preheat the oven to moderately hot 200°C (400°F/Gas 6). Cut all the tomatoes in half and bake, cut-side-up, on an oven tray for 15 minutes.
2 While the tomatoes are baking, cook the ziti in a large pan of rapidly boiling salted water until *al dente*. Drain and return to the pan.
3 Add the tomatoes and remaining ingredients to the drained pasta and toss thoroughly. Serve immediately.
NOTE: Use smaller quantities of fresh herbs if you prefer. Ovolini is a type of small fresh cheese available from speciality shops and some supermarkets. Use bocconcini cut into small pieces, if ovolini is unavailable.

NUTRITION PER SERVE: *Protein 30 g; Fat 30 g; Carbohydrate 90 g; Dietary Fibre 10 g; Cholesterol 50 mg; 3110 kJ (740 cal)*

LIMES

The lime is a tropical citrus tree. The fruit are small, distinctive yellowish-green and almost perfectly rounded, with a thin skin. The taste is pleasantly sharp, with tropical overtones. Slices of the unpeeled fruit make an attractive garnish, while the juice and rind are used to enhance both sweet and savoury dishes. Lime juice works well as a curing agent and is particularly effective on fresh seafood.

OPPOSITE PAGE: Chicken ravioli with lime balsamic dressing (top); Ziti with roasted tomatoes and bocconcini

---

ON THE SIDE

HERB SALAD Combine fresh basil leaves, rocket, flat-leaf parsley, coriander and baby English spinach leaves in a bowl. Drizzle with a dressing made of crushed garlic, lemon juice, honey and olive oil. Toss well and serve immediately with loads of freshly cracked black pepper.

MIXED TOMATO SALAD Combine cherry, teardrop and sliced egg (Roma) tomatoes in a bowl with chopped red (Spanish) onion and loads of finely shredded basil leaves. Toss in a little red wine vinegar and olive oil.

FARFALLE WITH PEAS

Ready to eat in 20 minutes
Serves 4

✦

500 g (1 lb) farfalle
1 1/2 cups (235 g/7 1/2 oz) frozen baby peas
8 thin slices pancetta
60 g (2 oz) butter
2 tablespoons each shredded fresh
    basil and mint

1 Cook the farfalle in a large pan of rapidly boiling salted water until *al dente*. Drain and return to the pan.
2 While the pasta is cooking, steam, microwave or lightly boil the baby peas until just tender and drain. Chop the pancetta and cook in the butter over medium heat for 2 minutes. Toss the butter and pancetta mixture through the pasta with the peas, basil and mint. Season with cracked black pepper and serve.

NUTRITION PER SERVE: *Protein 20 g; Fat 40 g; Carbohydrate 90 g; Dietary Fibre 10 g; Cholesterol 220 mg; 3470 kJ (830 cal)*

PENNE WITH ROCKET

Ready to eat in 20 minutes
Serves 4

✦

500 g (1 lb) penne
100 g (3 1/2 oz) butter
200 g (6 1/2 oz) rocket, roughly chopped
3 tomatoes, finely chopped
1/2 cup (45 g/1 1/2 oz) grated pecorino cheese
freshly grated Parmesan, for serving

1 Cook the penne in a large pan of rapidly boiling salted water until *al dente*. Drain and return to the pan. Place the pan over low heat. Add the butter, tossing it through until it melts and coats the pasta.
2 Add the rocket leaves to the pasta along with the tomato. Toss through to wilt the rocket. Stir in the pecorino cheese and season with salt and pepper, to taste. Serve sprinkled with freshly grated Parmesan.

NUTRITION PER SERVE: *Protein 20 g; Fat 25 g; Carbohydrate 90 g; Dietary Fibre 10 g; Cholesterol 80 mg; 2885 kJ (690 cal)*

ABOVE, FROM LEFT:
Farfalle with peas; Penne with rocket; Penne with olive and pistachio pesto

258

PENNE WITH OLIVE AND PISTACHIO PESTO

Ready to eat in 20 minutes
Serves 4

☆

500 g (1 lb) penne
125 g (4 oz) unsalted, shelled
  pistachio nuts
4 cloves garlic
1 tablespoon green peppercorns
2 tablespoons lemon juice
150 g (5 oz) pitted black olives
1 1/2 cups (150 g/5 oz) freshly grated Parmesan
  plus extra, shaved, for serving
1/2 cup (125 ml/4 fl oz) light olive oil

1 Cook the penne in a large pan of rapidly boiling salted water until *al dente*. Drain and return to the pan.
2 While the penne is cooking, combine the pistachio nuts, garlic, peppercorns, lemon juice, black olives and Parmesan in a food processor for 30 seconds, or until roughly chopped.

3 While the motor is running, gradually pour in the olive oil in a thin stream. Blend until the mixture is smooth. Toss the pesto through the hot pasta and serve topped with extra Parmesan.

NUTRITION PER SERVE: *Protein 40 g; Fat 60 g; Carbohydrate 90 g; Dietary Fibre 10 g; Cholesterol 35 mg; 4420 kJ (1055 cal)*

ON THE SIDE

TOMATO, EGG AND OLIVE SALAD Cut 6 ripe tomatoes into thick slices and arrange on a large plate, top with 1 thinly sliced red (Spanish) onion, 6 peeled and sliced hard-boiled eggs, 1/2 cup (90 g/ 3 oz) of marinated black olives and scatter a few torn fresh basil leaves over the top. Drizzle with some extra virgin olive oil and sprinkle generously with sea salt and freshly cracked black pepper.

SPAGHETTI WITH RICH BEEF AND MUSHROOM SAUCE

Ready to eat in 30 minutes
Serves 6

✭

1 tablespoon light olive oil

1 large onion, finely chopped

2 cloves garlic, crushed

500 g (1 lb) lean beef mince

350 g (11 oz) button mushrooms, halved

1 tablespoon dried mixed herbs

1/2 teaspoon paprika

1/2 teaspoon cracked black pepper

825 g (1 lb 11 oz) can crushed tomatoes

1/2 cup (125 g/4 oz) tomato paste (tomato purée, double concentrate)

1/2 cup (125 ml/4 fl oz) dry red wine

1/2 cup (125 ml/4 fl oz) beef stock

500 g (1 lb) spaghetti

freshly grated Parmesan, for serving

1 Heat the oil in a large, deep pan. Add the onion, garlic and beef and cook for 5 minutes, using a fork to break up any lumps of mince. Add the mushrooms, herbs, paprika and cracked pepper. Reduce the heat to low and stir in the crushed tomato, tomato paste, red wine and stock. Cover and simmer for 15 minutes.
2 While the sauce is cooking, cook the spaghetti in a large pan of rapidly boiling salted water until *al dente*. Drain. Serve the sauce spooned over the spaghetti and top with freshly grated Parmesan.

NUTRITION PER SERVE: *Protein 30 g; Fat 15 g; Carbohydrate 70 g; Dietary Fibre 10 g; Cholesterol 55 mg; 2300 kJ (550 cal)*

ON THE SIDE

PROSCIUTTO, CAMEMBERT AND FIG SALAD Arrange curly oak leaf lettuce leaves on a large plate and top with 4 quartered fresh figs, 100 g (3 1/4 oz) of thinly sliced camembert cheese and 60 g (2 oz) of thinly sliced prosciutto that has been grilled until crisp. Make up a vinaigrette by whisking together 1 crushed clove of garlic, 1 tablespoon of mustard, 2 tablespoons of white wine vinegar and 1/3 cup (80 ml/2 3/4 fl oz) of olive oil. Drizzle over the salad.

PENNE WITH ROASTED PEPPERS (CAPSICUMS)

Ready to eat in 30 minutes
Serves 4

✭

1 red pepper (capsicum)

1 green pepper (capsicum)

1 yellow or orange pepper (capsicum)

1 tablespoon olive oil

2 cloves garlic, crushed

6 anchovy fillets, finely chopped

1 teaspoon seasoned cracked pepper

1/3 cup (80 ml/2 3/4 fl oz) dry white wine

1 cup (250 ml/8 fl oz) vegetable stock

2 tablespoons tomato paste (tomato purée, double concentrate)

500 g (1 lb) penne

1 tablespoon chopped fresh parsley

1 Cut the peppers into large flat pieces and discard the seeds and membrane. Grill, skin-side up, for 8 minutes, or until the skin is black and blistered. Remove from the heat and cover with a damp tea towel. When cool, peel the skin away and cut the flesh into thin strips.
2 Heat the oil in a large pan, add the garlic and anchovy fillets and cook over low heat for 2–3 minutes. Add the strips of pepper, seasoned pepper and wine. Bring to the boil, reduce the heat and simmer for 5 minutes. Stir in the stock and tomato paste and simmer for 10 minutes.
3 While the sauce is cooking, cook the penne in a large pan of rapidly boiling water until *al dente*. Drain, add to the pepper sauce and toss until well combined. Stir in the fresh parsley and serve immediately with crusty Italian bread.
NOTE: If you can't find yellow peppers, use an extra red one, as they are sweeter than green.

NUTRITION PER SERVE: *Protein 20 g; Fat 10 g; Carbohydrate 95 g; Dietary Fibre 10 g; Cholesterol 5 mg; 2245 kJ (535 cal)*

THE DIFFERENCE BETWEEN PEPPERS
Red, yellow, green and purple peppers belong to the same pepper (capsicum) family but have different characteristics. Colour is the most obvious, but texture, flavour and digestive properties also vary. Red peppers have a sweeter flavour and softer flesh, properties which change when subjected to heat. This makes them the best for roasting or grilling. Gold and yellow come next, with green and purple peppers chosen where a crisp flesh and clean taste are required, such as for use in salads and stir-fries.

OPPOSITE PAGE:
Spaghetti with rich beef and mushroom sauce (top); Penne with roasted peppers

SPAGHETTI WITH GARLIC AND CHILLI

Ready to eat in 20 minutes
Serves 4

⭐

500 g (1 lb) spaghetti
1/2 cup (125 ml/4 fl oz) extra virgin olive oil
3 cloves garlic, crushed
1 red chilli, finely chopped

1 Cook the spaghetti in a large pan of rapidly boiling salted water until *al dente*. Drain and return to the pan.
2 Just before the spaghetti is cooked, heat the olive oil in a small pan until warm. Add the garlic and red chilli and stir over low heat for 2 minutes. Add the flavoured oil to the pasta and toss to combine.

NUTRITION PER SERVE: *Protein 15 g; Fat 30 g; Carbohydrate 90 g; Dietary Fibre 10 g; Cholesterol 0 mg; 2900 kJ (690 cal)*

FUSILLI WITH SAGE AND GARLIC

Ready to eat in 20 minutes
Serves 4

⭐

500 g (1 lb) fusilli
60 g (2 oz) butter
2 cloves garlic, crushed
1/2 cup (10 g/1/4 oz) fresh sage leaves
2 tablespoons cream
freshly grated Parmesan, for serving

1 Cook the fusilli in a large pan of rapidly boiling salted water until *al dente*. Drain and return to the pan.
2 While the pasta is cooking, melt the butter in a frying pan. Add the garlic and fresh sage leaves. Cook over low heat for 4 minutes, stirring frequently.
3 Stir in the cream and season with some salt and freshly ground black pepper, to taste. Stir

the sauce through the drained pasta until thoroughly coated. Top each serving with freshly grated Parmesan.

NUTRITION PER SERVE: *Protein 15 g; Fat 20 g; Carbohydrate 90 g; Dietary Fibre 5 g; Cholesterol 55 mg; 2510 kJ (600 cal)*

RUOTE WITH LEMON, OLIVES AND BACON

Ready to eat in 25 minutes
Serves 4

☆

500 g (1 lb) ruote
6 bacon rashers
1 cup (125 g/4 oz) black olives, sliced
1/3 cup (80 ml/2³/4 fl oz) lemon juice
2 teaspoons finely grated lemon rind
1/3 cup (80 ml/2³/4 fl oz) olive oil
1/3 cup (20 g/³/4 oz) chopped fresh parsley

1 Cook the ruote in a large pan of rapidly boiling salted water until *al dente*. Drain and return to the pan.
2 While the pasta is cooking, discard the bacon rind and cut the bacon into thin strips. Cook in a frying pan until lightly browned.
3 In a bowl, combine the black olives, lemon juice, lemon rind, olive oil, chopped parsley and the bacon. Gently toss the olive and bacon mixture through the pasta until it is evenly distributed. Serve with freshly ground black pepper, to taste.
NOTE: Ruote is a very attractive pasta resembling wagon wheels. Small chunks of sauce are trapped between the spokes.

NUTRITION PER SERVE: *Protein 25 g; Fat 25 g; Carbohydrate 90 g; Dietary Fibre 10 g; Cholesterol 30 mg; 2900 kJ (690 cal)*

BELOW, FROM LEFT: Spaghetti with garlic and chilli; Fusilli with sage and garlic; Ruote with lemon, olives and bacon

PARSLEY

Curly-leafed and flat-leafed parsley are commonly used in everyday cooking. Parsley adds flavour as well as colour to a dish, is equally at home fresh or cooked, and is ideal as a garnish for savoury foods. If you don't grow your own, buy parsley with unwilted leaves and firm stems. For storage, immerse the stalks in cold water for up to a week, or put the parsley in the vegetable section of the refrigerator, wrapped in paper towels. Parsley is a rich source of iron as well as vitamins A, B and C.

ABOVE: Spaghetti puttanesca

SPAGHETTI PUTTANESCA

Ready to eat in 25 minutes
Serves 4–6

★★

500 g (1 lb) spaghetti
2 tablespoons olive oil
3 cloves garlic, crushed
2 tablespoons chopped fresh parsley
1/4–1/2 teaspoon chilli flakes or powder
2 x 425 g (14 oz) cans crushed tomatoes
1 tablespoon capers
3 anchovy fillets, chopped
3 tablespoons black olives
freshly grated Parmesan, for serving

1 Cook the spaghetti in a large pan of rapidly boiling salted water until *al dente*. Drain and return to the pan.
2 While the spaghetti is cooking, heat the oil in a large heavy-based frying pan. Add the garlic, parsley and chilli flakes and cook, stirring constantly, for 1 minute, over medium heat.
3 Add the crushed tomato to the pan, bring to the boil, reduce the heat and simmer for 5 minutes.
4 Add the capers, anchovies and olives and cook, stirring, for 5 minutes. Season with black pepper. Toss gently with the pasta until the sauce is evenly distributed. Serve with Parmesan.

NUTRITION PER SERVE (6): *Protein 15 g; Fat 10 g; Carbohydrate 65 g; Dietary Fibre 5 g; Cholesterol 5 mg; 1650 kJ (395 cal)*

SPAGHETTI WITH PEAS AND ONIONS

Ready to eat in 25 minutes
Serves 4–6

☆

500 g (1 lb) spaghetti or vermicelli

1 kg (2 lb) large bulb spring onions

1 tablespoon olive oil

4 bacon rashers, chopped

2 teaspoons plain flour

1 cup (250 ml/8 fl oz) chicken stock

1/2 cup (125 ml/4 fl oz) white wine

1 cup (155 g/5 oz) shelled fresh peas

1 Cook the pasta in a large pan of rapidly boiling salted water until *al dente*. Drain and return to the pan.

2 While the pasta is cooking, trim the outer skins and ends from the onions, leaving only a small section of the green stem attached.

3 Heat the oil in a large heavy-based pan. Add the bacon and onions and stir over low heat for 4 minutes or until golden. Sprinkle the flour lightly over the top and stir for 1 minute.

4 Add the combined stock and wine and stir until the mixture boils and thickens slightly. Add the peas and cook for 5 minutes or until the onions are tender. Add black pepper, to taste. Add the mixture to the pasta and toss gently. Garnish with sprigs of fresh herbs if you like.

NUTRITION PER SERVE (6): *Protein 20 g; Fat 5 g; Carbohydrate 70 g; Dietary Fibre 10 g; Cholesterol 15 mg; 1770 kJ (420 cal)*

ABOVE: Spaghetti with peas and onions

SPICY SAUSAGE AND FENNEL RIGATONI

Ready to eat in 25 minutes
Serves 4–6

★

500 g (1 lb) rigatoni
30 g (1 oz) butter
1 tablespoon oil
500 g (1 lb) chorizo sausage, thickly
   sliced diagonally
1 bulb fennel, thinly sliced
2 cloves garlic, crushed
1/3 cup (80 ml/2³/4 fl oz) lime juice
400 g (13 oz) can red pimientos, sliced
100 g (3¹/2 oz) small rocket leaves, chopped
shavings of fresh Parmesan, for serving

1 Cook the rigatoni in a large pan of rapidly boiling salted water until *al dente*. Drain and return to the pan.
2 While the rigatoni is cooking, heat the butter and oil in a large frying pan. Add the chorizo sausage slices and cook over medium heat until well browned. Add the fennel to the pan and cook, stirring occasionally, for 5 minutes.
3 Add the garlic to the pan and stir for 1 minute. Stir in the lime juice and pimientos, bring to the boil, reduce the heat and simmer for another 5 minutes.
4 Add the sausage mixture and rocket to the pasta and toss to combine. Serve topped with shavings of fresh Parmesan.
NOTE: Chorizo is a spicy dried sausage, heavily flavoured with garlic and chilli. It is similar to salami, which can be substituted if chorizo sausage is not available.

NUTRITION PER SERVE (6): *Protein 25 g; Fat 35 g; Carbohydrate 60 g; Dietary Fibre 5 g; Cholesterol 80 mg; 2945 kJ (705 cal)*

FUSILLI WITH VEGETABLES

Ready to eat in 30 minutes
Serves 4–6

★

500 g (1 lb) fusilli
3 tablespoons olive oil
6 yellow squash, sliced
3 zucchini (courgettes), sliced
2 cloves garlic, crushed
3 spring onions, chopped
1 red pepper (capsicum), cut into strips
1/3 cup (65 g/2¹/4 oz) corn kernels
4 tomatoes, chopped
2 tablespoons chopped fresh parsley

1 Cook the fusilli in a large pan of rapidly boiling salted water until *al dente*. Drain and return to the pan.
2 While the fusilli is cooking, heat 2 tablespoons of the oil in a wok or frying pan, add the squash and zucchini and stir-fry for 3 minutes, or until the vegetables are just tender. Add the garlic, spring onion, red pepper and corn kernels to the wok and stir-fry for another 2–3 minutes. Add the tomato and stir until combined.
3 Add the remaining olive oil and fresh parsley to the pasta and toss well. Serve the pasta topped with the vegetable mixture.
NOTE: This is a good recipe to use up any vegetables you have on hand. Mushrooms, broccoli, snow peas (mangetout) and asparagus are all suitable, and other fresh herbs such as chives or coriander can be added.

NUTRITION PER SERVE (6): *Protein 20 g; Fat 20 g; Carbohydrate 100 g; Dietary Fibre 15 g; Cholesterol 5 mg; 2740 kJ (654 cal)*

ON THE SIDE

ASPARAGUS AND PARMESAN SALAD Cook 300 g (10 oz) of asparagus in a pan of boiling water until bright green and tender. Refresh in iced water and drain well. Arrange the asparagus on a plate and top with shavings of Parmesan cheese. Drizzle with a little balsamic vinegar and extra virgin olive oil and sprinkle generously with cracked black pepper.

BABY YELLOW SQUASH
Baby yellow squash belong to the vegetable marrow family. They are chosen for their colour, size and texture and are easy to prepare, with no wastage. They lend themselves equally well to baking, steaming, boiling and stir-frying and this versatility has made them popular in many cuisines.

OPPOSITE PAGE: Spicy sausage and fennel rigatoni (top); Fusilli with vegetables

CREAM OF ONION PASTA

Ready to eat in 30 minutes
Serves 4

★

500 g (1 lb) fettucine or linguine
50 g (1 3/4 oz) butter
6 onions, thinly sliced
1/2 cup (125 ml/4 fl oz) beef stock
1/2 cup (125 ml/4 fl oz) cream
shavings of Parmesan cheese, for serving
spring onion, to garnish, optional

1 Cook the fettucine in a large pan of rapidly boiling salted water until *al dente*. Drain and return to the pan.
2 While the pasta is cooking, melt the butter, add the onion and cook over medium heat for 10 minutes, until soft. Stir in the stock and cream and simmer for 10 minutes. Season with salt and pepper, to taste.
3 Stir the sauce through the fettucine and serve with shavings of Parmesan. Garnish with chopped spring onion if you wish.

NUTRITION PER SERVE: *Protein 20 g; Fat 25 g; Carbohydrate 95 g; Dietary Fibre 10 g; Cholesterol 80 mg; 2935 kJ (700 cal)*

ORIENTAL FRICELLI

Ready to eat in 30 minutes
Serves 4–6

★

500 g (1 lb) multicoloured fricelli
2 tablespoons peanut oil
1 teaspoon sesame oil
2 garlic cloves, crushed
1 tablespoon grated fresh ginger
1/2 Chinese cabbage, finely shredded
1 red pepper (capsicum), thinly sliced
200 g (6 1/2 oz) sugar snap peas
3 tablespoons soy sauce
3 tablespoons sweet chilli sauce
2 tablespoons chopped fresh coriander
chopped peanuts or cashews,
  to garnish

1 Cook the fricelli in a large pan of rapidly boiling salted water until *al dente*. Drain and keep warm.

2 While the fricelli is cooking, heat the oils in a pan, add the garlic and ginger and cook over medium heat for 1 minute.
3 Add the cabbage, red pepper and peas to the wok and stir-fry for 3 minutes over high heat. Stir in the sauces and coriander and cook for 3 minutes, or until heated through. Add the fricelli to the wok and toss to combine. Serve sprinkled with chopped peanuts or cashews.

NUTRITION PER SERVE (6): *Protein 15 g; Fat 10 g; Carbohydrate 65 g; Dietary Fibre 10 g; Cholesterol 0 mg; 1780 kJ (425 cal)*

SPAGHETTI WITH CREAMY LEMON SAUCE

Ready to eat in 20 minutes
Serves 4

★

500 g (1 lb) spaghetti
1 cup (250 ml/8 fl oz) cream
3/4 cup (185 ml/6 fl oz) chicken stock
1 tablespoon finely grated lemon rind plus
  some shredded, to garnish
2 tablespoons finely chopped fresh parsley
2 tablespoons chopped fresh chives

1 Cook the spaghetti in a large pan of rapidly boiling salted water until *al dente*. Drain and return to the pan.
2 While the spaghetti is cooking, combine the cream, chicken stock and lemon rind in a pan over medium heat. Bring to the boil, stirring occasionally. Reduce the heat and simmer gently for 10 minutes, or until the sauce is reduced and thickened slightly.
3 Add the sauce and herbs to the spaghetti and toss to combine. Serve immediately, garnished with finely shredded lemon rind.

NUTRITION PER SERVE: *Protein 15 g; Fat 30 g; Carbohydrate 90 g; Dietary Fibre 5 g; Cholesterol 85 mg; 2850 kJ (680 cal)*

CHIVES
Chives are related to the onion, but used as a herb, either for seasoning or for garnishing. Only the green stalks, with their mild flavour, are eaten and they should be freshly cut as you need them. If they are intended as a garnish for hot food, sprinkle them on just before serving. Dried chives bear little resemblance in taste or texture to fresh.

OPPOSITE PAGE, FROM TOP: Cream of onion pasta; Oriental fricelli; Spaghetti with creamy lemon sauce

269

SORREL

Sorrel is a bitter leaf vegetable rich in vitamins A and C, as well as in essential minerals. Young, glossy leaves are simply rinsed and trimmed of their tough stems before being tossed in a green salad. Sorrel's clean, sharp flavour makes it a good companion to fish and rich poultry such as goose and duck, and it is used to flavour stews and sauces. When subjected to prolonged heat, it breaks down to a pulp, so it is good for puréeing. Avoid iron or aluminium pans when cooking with sorrel, as the chemical reaction that results leaves the sorrel acrid.

TORTELLINI BROTH

Ready to eat in 20 minutes
Serves 4

★

250 g (8 oz) tortellini
4 cups (1 litre) good-quality beef stock
1/2 cup (30 g/2 oz) sliced spring onions, plus
    extra, for garnish

1 Cook the tortellini in a large pan of rapidly boiling salted water until *al dente*. Drain and divide among 4 deep soup bowls.
2 While the tortellini is cooking, bring the beef stock to the boil in a pan. Add the spring onion and simmer for 3 minutes. Ladle the stock over the tortellini and garnish with the extra spring onion, finely sliced.

NUTRITION PER SERVE: *Protein 10 g; Fat 1 g; Carbohydrate 45 g; Dietary Fibre 3 g; Cholesterol 0 mg; 945 kJ (225 cal)*

ARTICHOKE, EGG AND SORREL PASTA

Ready to eat in 25 minutes
Serves 4

★

500 g (1 lb) conchiglie (shell pasta)
2 tablespoons oil
3 cloves garlic, crushed
315 g (10 oz) marinated artichoke hearts, halved
3 tablespoons chopped fresh parsley
160 g (5 1/2 oz) sorrel leaves, roughly chopped
4 hard-boiled eggs, chopped
fresh Parmesan shavings, for serving

1 Cook the conchiglie in a large pan of rapidly boiling salted water until *al dente*. Drain and keep warm.
2 While the pasta is cooking, heat the oil in a frying pan, add the garlic and cook over medium heat until golden. Add the artichoke hearts and chopped parsley and cook over low

heat for 5 minutes, or until the artichoke hearts are heated through.

3 Transfer the pasta to a large bowl. Add the sorrel leaves, eggs and artichoke hearts and toss to combine. Serve immediately, topped with shavings of fresh Parmesan and cracked black pepper, to taste.

NUTRITION PER SERVE: *Protein 25 g; Fat 20 g; Carbohydrate 90 g; Dietary Fibre 10 g; Cholesterol 210 mg; 2620 kJ (625 cal)*

CHEESY BUCKWHEAT AND BEAN PASTA

Ready to eat in 30 minutes
Serves 4

☆

500 g (1 lb) buckwheat fusilli
1 tablespoon oil
2 cloves garlic, crushed
1 onion, chopped
300 g (10 oz) bottled pasta sauce
1/3 cup (80 ml/2¾ fl oz) orange juice
400 g (13 oz) can kidney beans, drained
1 cup (125 g/4 oz) grated Cheddar cheese plus extra, for serving
3 tablespoons chopped fresh herbs

1 Cook the fusilli in a large pan of rapidly boiling salted water until *al dente*. Drain and return to the pan.
2 While the pasta is cooking, heat the oil in a frying pan. Add the garlic and onion and cook over medium heat for 3 minutes, or until the onion is golden but not brown.
3 Add the pasta sauce, orange juice and kidney beans. Bring to the boil, reduce the heat and simmer for 5 minutes, or until the sauce is heated through.
4 Add the sauce to the pasta with the Cheddar cheese and fresh herbs. Stir until the cheese melts and serve immediately. Top with extra grated Cheddar cheese.

NUTRITION PER SERVE: *Protein 20 g; Fat 15 g; Carbohydrate 65 g; Dietary Fibre 15 g; Cholesterol 25 mg; 2015 kJ (480 cal)*

ABOVE, FROM LEFT: Tortellini broth; Artichoke, egg and sorrel pasta; Cheesy buckwheat and bean pasta

271

PREPARING AND COOKING BLACK MUSSELS

Black mussels are a variety of bivalve mollusc with a rounded black shell and plump, succulent flesh. Like all shellfish, they must be bought and eaten fresh and cleaned before cooking. First, discard those which have already opened. Scrub the unopened mussels with a stiff brush and remove the beard. If the mussels are gritty, they can be soaked in clean, salted water for 1–2 hours to make them expel grit and sand. After a final rinse, put them in a pan to steam open. By the time they have all opened, they will be cooked. Before using, discard any unopened mussels and those with flat and dried out flesh.

OPPOSITE PAGE: Tomato mussels on spaghetti (top); Gorgonzola and toasted walnuts on linguine

TOMATO MUSSELS ON SPAGHETTI

Ready to eat in 30 minutes
Serves 4

★★

16 fresh black mussels
500 g (1 lb) spaghetti
4 tablespoons olive oil
1 large onion, finely chopped
2 cloves garlic, crushed
850 g (1 lb 12 oz) can crushed tomatoes
1/2 cup (125 ml/4 fl oz) white wine

1 Scrub the mussels thoroughly and remove the beards. Discard any open mussels.
2 Cook the spaghetti in a large pan of rapidly boiling salted water until *al dente*. Drain, return to the pan and toss with half the olive oil.
3 While the pasta is cooking, heat the remaining olive oil in a pan, add the onion and cook until soft, but not brown. Add the garlic and cook for another minute. Stir in the tomato and wine and bring to the boil. Reduce the heat and simmer gently.
4 Meanwhile, put the mussels in a large pan and just cover with water. Cook over high heat for a few minutes, until the mussels have opened. Shake the pan often and discard any mussels that have not opened after 5 minutes.
5 Add the mussels to the tomato sauce and stir to combine. Serve the pasta with mussels and sauce over the top. Garnish with sprigs of thyme, if desired.

NUTRITION PER SERVE: *Protein 20 g; Fat 20 g; Carbohydrate 95 g; Dietary Fibre 10 g; Cholesterol 8 mg; 2825 kJ (670 cal)*

ON THE SIDE

SPINACH, PANCETTA AND PECAN NUT SALAD Mix together 250 g (8 oz) of baby spinach leaves, 50 g (1 3/4 oz) of toasted pecan nuts and 3 peeled and chopped hard-boiled eggs. Fry or grill 6 paper-thin slices of pancetta until crispy. Break the pancetta into bite-size pieces and toss through the salad. To make the dressing, thoroughly combine 100 g (3 1/2 oz) of blue cheese with 1/4 cup (60 ml/2 fl oz) of cream, 2 tablespoons of milk and 2 tablespoons of oil. When mixed, drizzle over the salad and serve immediately.

GORGONZOLA AND TOASTED WALNUTS ON LINGUINE

Ready to eat in 25 minutes
Serves 4

★

3/4 cup (75 g/2 1/2 oz) walnut halves
500 g (1 lb) linguine
75 g (2 1/2 oz) butter
150 g (5 oz) gorgonzola cheese, chopped
  or crumbled
2 tablespoons cream
1 cup (155 g/5 oz) shelled fresh peas

1 Preheat the oven to moderate 180°C (350°F/Gas 4). Lay the walnuts on an oven tray in a single layer and bake for about 5 minutes, until lightly toasted. Set the walnuts aside to cool.
2 Cook the linguine in a large pan of rapidly boiling water until *al dente*. Drain and return to the pan.
3 While the pasta is cooking, melt the butter in a small pan over low heat and add the gorgonzola, cream and peas. Stir gently for 5 minutes, or until the sauce has thickened. Season, to taste, with salt and pepper. Add the sauce and the walnuts to the pasta and toss until well combined. Serve immediately, sprinkled with freshly ground black pepper.
NOTE: You can use frozen peas if you prefer. Don't bother to thaw them, just add them as directed in the recipe. Use a milder blue cheese such as Castello in place of the gorgonzola, if you don't like really strong blue cheese.

NUTRITION PER SERVE: *Protein 30 g; Fat 50 g; Carbohydrate 90 g; Dietary Fibre 10 g; Cholesterol 95 mg; 3870 kJ (920 cal)*

SPAGHETTI WITH HERBS

Ready to eat in 20 minutes
Serves 4

☆

500 g (1 lb) spaghetti
50 g (1³/₄ oz) butter
¹/₂ cup (30 g/1 oz) shredded fresh basil
¹/₃ cup (10 g/¹/₄ oz) chopped fresh oregano
¹/₃ cup (20 g/³/₄ oz) chopped fresh chives

1 Cook the spaghetti in a large pan of rapidly boiling salted water until *al dente*. Drain and return to the pan.
2 Add the butter to the pan, tossing it through until it melts and coats the strands of spaghetti. Add the basil, oregano and chives to the pan and toss the herbs through the buttery pasta until well distributed. Season, to taste, and serve immediately.

NUTRITION PER SERVE: *Protein 15 g; Fat 10 g; Carbohydrate 90 g; Dietary Fibre 5 g; Cholesterol 30 mg; 2175 kJ (520 cal)*

BELOW, FROM LEFT:
Spaghetti with herbs;
Pasta with pesto
and Parmesan;
Calabrian spaghetti

PASTA WITH PESTO AND PARMESAN

Ready to eat in 15 minutes
Serves 4

☆

500 g (1 lb) linguine or taglierini
¹/₄ cup (40 g/1¹/₄ oz) pine nuts
2 firmly packed cups (100 g/3¹/₂ oz) fresh basil leaves
2 cloves garlic, chopped
¹/₄ cup (25 g/³/₄ oz) freshly grated Parmesan plus shavings, to garnish
¹/₂ cup (125 ml/4 fl oz) extra virgin olive oil

1 Cook the pasta in a large pan of rapidly boiling salted water until *al dente*. Drain and return to the pan.
2 While the pasta is cooking, mix the pine nuts, fresh basil leaves, garlic and Parmesan in a food processor until finely chopped. With the motor running, add the extra virgin olive

oil in a slow stream until a smooth paste is formed. Season with salt and freshly ground black pepper, to taste. Toss the pesto through the hot pasta until it is thoroughly distributed. Garnish with shavings of fresh Parmesan.

NUTRITION PER SERVE. *Protein 20 g; Fat 45 g; Carbohydrate 90 g; Dietary Fibre 5 g; Cholesterol 15 mg; 3390 kJ (810 cal)*

CALABRIAN SPAGHETTI

Ready to eat in 20 minutes
Serves 4

★

500 g (1 lb) spaghetti
1/3 cup (80 ml/2 3/4 fl oz) olive oil
3 cloves garlic, crushed
50 g (1 3/4 oz) anchovy fillets, finely chopped
1 teaspoon finely chopped fresh
    red chillies
3 tablespoons chopped fresh parsley

1 Cook the spaghetti in a large pan of rapidly boiling salted water until *al dente*. Drain and return to the pan.
2 While the spaghetti is cooking, heat the olive oil in a small pan. Add the garlic, anchovy fillets and red chillies and cook over low heat for 5 minutes. Be careful not to burn the garlic or brown it too much as it will become bitter. Add the parsley to the garlic mixture and cook for a few more minutes. Season with salt and freshly ground black pepper, to taste.
3 Add the sauce to the pasta and toss through until well combined. Serve garnished with extra anchovies and sliced red chillies as well as a sprig of fresh herbs, if desired.

NUTRITION PER SERVE: *Protein 15 g; Fat 20 g; Carbohydrate 90 g; Dietary Fibre 5 g; Cholesterol 10 mg; 2600 kJ (620 cal)*

PESTO
When a fully made pesto is stored for any length of time, the composition of the ingredients alters. The cheese component reacts with other ingredients, in particular the basil, and starts to turn rancid. It will keep, at best, for 5–7 days, if refrigerated in an airtight jar with a layer of olive oil or plastic wrap covering the exposed surface. A more successful option when making pesto to put away is to leave out the cheeses and stir them through when the sauce is to be used. In this way, your pesto will keep for 2–3 months refrigerated, or 5–6 months frozen.

RAVIOLI WITH PEAS AND ARTICHOKES

Ready to eat in 30 minutes
Serves 4

✩

650 g (1 lb 5 oz) fresh cheese and
    spinach ravioli
1 tablespoon olive oil
8 marinated artichoke hearts, quartered
2 large cloves garlic, finely chopped
1/2 cup (125 ml/4 fl oz) dry white wine
1/2 cup (125 ml/4 fl oz) chicken stock
2 cups (310 g/10 oz) frozen peas
125 g (4 oz) thinly sliced prosciutto, chopped
1/4 cup (7 g/1/4 oz) chopped fresh flat-leaf parsley
1/2 teaspoon seasoned cracked pepper

1 Cook the ravioli in a large pan of rapidly boiling salted water until *al dente*. Drain.
2 While the ravioli is cooking, heat the olive oil in a pan and cook the artichoke hearts and garlic over medium heat for 2 minutes, stirring frequently. Add the wine and stock and stir until well mixed. Bring to the boil, reduce the heat slightly and simmer for 5 minutes. Add the peas (they don't need to be thawed first) and simmer for another 2 minutes.
3 Stir the prosciutto, parsley and pepper into the artichoke mixture. Serve the ravioli topped with the artichoke mixture.
NOTE: You can buy marinated artichoke hearts in jars from supermarkets and delicatessens.

NUTRITION PER SERVE: *Protein 25 g; Fat 15 g; Carbohydrate 30 g; Dietary Fibre 10 g; Cholesterol 45 mg; 1540 kJ (370 cal)*

BRANDIED CREAM AND SALMON FUSILLI

Ready to eat in 30 minutes
Serves 2

✩

375 g (12 oz) fusilli
45 g (1 1/2 oz) butter
1 leek, finely sliced
1 large clove garlic, crushed
1/4 cup (60 ml/2 fl oz) brandy
1/2 teaspoon sambal oelek
2 tablespoons finely chopped fresh dill
1 tablespoon tomato paste (tomato purée, double concentrate)
1 cup (250 ml/8 fl oz) cream
250 g (8 oz) smoked salmon, thinly sliced
red caviar or lumpfish roe, to garnish, optional

1 Cook the fusilli in a large pan of rapidly boiling salted water until *al dente*. Drain.
2 Heat the butter in a large pan and cook the leek over medium heat for a few minutes, until soft. Add the garlic and cook for another minute. Add the brandy and cook for another minute. Stir in the sambal oelek, dill, tomato paste and cream. Simmer gently for 5 minutes, until the sauce reduces and thickens slightly.
3 Add the pasta and smoked salmon to the sauce. Toss to combine and season with freshly ground black pepper, to taste. Divide the mixture between two serving bowls. Garnish with a spoonful of caviar, if you like, and a sprig of dill. Serve immediately.
NOTE: Wash the leek thoroughly, as dirt and grit can sometimes be difficult to remove from the inner leaves.

NUTRITION PER SERVE: *Protein 55 g; Fat 80 g; Carbohydrate 140 g; Dietary Fibre 10 g; Cholesterol 290 mg; 6500 kJ (1550 cal)*

SAMBAL OELEK

Sambal oelek is an indispensable paste used in Indonesian cooking. Traditionally, it is made from red chillies and salt. The commercially available product is often mixed with vinegar. As well as being used to flavour dishes, sambal oelek can be served as a dipping sauce or an accompaniment. Sometimes labelled sambal ulek, it can be found in supermarkets and Asian food stores. It is handy to have to use whenever chilli is called for. Store in the refrigerator.

ON THE SIDE

PEACH SALSA SALAD Cut 6 large fresh peaches into wedges and put them in a bowl. Add 1 thinly sliced red (Spanish) onion, 6 quartered egg (Roma) tomatoes, 1 cup (200 g/6½ oz) of corn kernels and 1 sliced green pepper (capsicum). Make a dressing by thoroughly mixing 1 crushed clove of garlic, 1 teaspoon of ground cumin, 1 finely chopped red chilli, 2 tablespoons of freshly squeezed lime juice and 1/4 cup (60 ml/2 fl oz) of oil. Pour over the salad and toss to combine. Fold through 1/2 cup (15 g/1/2 oz) of fresh coriander leaves just before serving.

OPPOSITE PAGE: Ravioli with peas and artichokes (top); Brandied cream and salmon fusilli

ABOVE, FROM LEFT:
Pasta Niçoise; Garlic
bucatini; Spaghetti
Mediterranean

PASTA NIÇOISE

Ready to eat in 25 minutes
Serves 4

☆

500 g (1 lb) farfalle
350 g (11 oz) green beans
1/3 cup (80 ml/2¾ fl oz) olive oil
60 g (2 oz) sliced anchovy fillets
2 garlic cloves, finely sliced
250 g (8 oz) cherry tomatoes, halved
freshly grated Parmesan, for serving

1 Cook the farfalle in a large pan of rapidly
boiling salted water until *al dente*. Drain and
return to the pan.
2 While the pasta is cooking, place the beans in
a heatproof bowl and cover with boiling water.
Set aside for 5 minutes, drain and rinse under
cold water.
3 Heat the olive oil in a frying pan and stir-fry
the beans and anchovy fillets for 2–3 minutes.
Add the garlic and cook for 1 minute. Add the
cherry tomatoes and stir through.

4 Add the sauce to the pasta, toss well and warm
through. Serve with freshly grated Parmesan.

NUTRITION PER SERVE: *Protein 20 g; Fat 25 g;*
Carbohydrate 90 g; Dietary Fibre 10 g; Cholesterol 15 mg;
2810 kJ (670 cal)

GARLIC BUCATINI

Ready to eat in 15 minutes
Serves 4

☆

500 g (1 lb) bucatini
1/3 cup (80 ml/2¾ fl oz) olive oil
8 garlic cloves, crushed
2 tablespoons chopped fresh parsley
freshly grated Parmesan, for serving

1 Cook the bucatini in a large pan of rapidly
boiling water until *al dente*. Drain and return
to the pan.
2 When the pasta is almost finished cooking,
heat the olive oil over low heat in a frying pan
and add the garlic. Cook for 1 minute before

removing from the heat. Add the garlic oil and the parsley to the pasta and toss to distribute thoroughly. Serve with Parmesan.

NOTE: Olives or diced tomato can be added. Do not overcook the garlic or it will be bitter.

NUTRITION PER SERVE: *Protein 15 g; Fat 20 g; Carbohydrate 90 g; Dietary Fibre 5 g; Cholesterol 5 mg; 2605 kJ (620 cal)*

SPAGHETTI MEDITERRANEAN

Ready to eat in 30 minutes
Serves 4–6

☆

500 g (1 lb) spaghetti

750 g (1 1/2 lb) tomatoes

1/2 cup (125 ml/4 fl oz) extra virgin olive oil

2 garlic cloves, crushed

4 spring onions, finely sliced

6 anchovy fillets, chopped

1/2 teaspoon grated lemon rind

1 tablespoon fresh thyme leaves

12 stuffed green olives, thinly sliced

shredded fresh basil, for serving

1 Cook the spaghetti in a large pan of rapidly boiling salted water until *al dente*. Drain and return to the pan.

2 While the pasta is cooking, score small crosses in the bases of the tomatoes. Add to a pan of boiling water for 1–2 minutes, drain and plunge into cold water. Peel down from the cross and discard the skin. Cut the tomatoes in half horizontally. Place a sieve over a small bowl and squeeze the tomato seeds and juice into it; discard the seeds. Chop the tomatoes roughly and set aside.

3 In a bowl, combine the olive oil, garlic, spring onion, anchovies, lemon rind, thyme leaves and stuffed green olives. Add the chopped tomato and tomato juice, mix well and season with salt and freshly ground black pepper, to taste. Add the sauce to the pasta, toss to combine and sprinkle with shredded fresh basil.

NUTRITION PER SERVE (6): *Protein 10 g; Fat 20 g; Carbohydrate 60 g; Dietary Fibre 5 g; Cholesterol 3 mg; 2060 kJ (490 cal)*

THYME

There are many different types of thyme used in cooking and they range from having grey-green leaves and a pungent scent, to tiny bright green leaves with a more evasive perfume. In fact, the fragrance that thyme imparts to a dish is just as important as the flavour. Wild thyme is refined and aromatic while lemon thyme gives off a subtle lemony fragrance when heated. With small leaves of low moisture content, thyme is one herb which is easy to dry.

SPAGHETTI WITH TOMATO SAUCE

Ready to eat in 30 minutes
Serves 4

☆

500 g (1 lb) spaghetti
1 tablespoon olive oil
1 onion, finely chopped
2 cloves garlic, crushed
825 g (1 lb 11 oz) can crushed tomatoes
1 teaspoon dried oregano
2 tablespoons tomato paste (tomato purée, double concentrate)
2 teaspoons sugar
shavings fresh Parmesan, for serving

1 Cook the spaghetti in a large pan of rapidly boiling salted water until *al dente*. Drain.
2 Heat the oil in a pan, add the onion and cook for 3 minutes, until soft. Add the garlic and cook for another minute.
3 Add the tomato and bring to the boil. Add the oregano, tomato paste and sugar; reduce the heat and simmer for 15 minutes. Season with salt and pepper, to taste. Serve the pasta topped with the tomato sauce and shavings of fresh Parmesan.

NUTRITION PER SERVE: *Protein 20 g; Fat 10 g; Carbohydrate 100 g; Dietary Fibre 10 g; Cholesterol 5 mg; 2300 kJ (550 cal)*

RICOTTA AND BASIL WITH TAGLIATELLE

Ready to eat in 25 minutes
Serves 4

☆

500 g (1 lb) tagliatelle
1 cup (20 g/³⁄₄ oz) fresh flat-leaf parsley
1 cup (50 g/1³⁄₄ oz) fresh basil leaves
1 teaspoon olive oil
¹⁄₃ cup (50 g/1³⁄₄ oz) chopped sun-dried pepper (capsicum)
1 cup (250 g/8 oz) sour cream
250 g (8 oz) fresh ricotta cheese
¹⁄₄ cup (25 g/³⁄₄ oz) freshly grated Parmesan

1 Cook the tagliatelle in a large pan of rapidly boiling salted water until *al dente*. Drain and return to the pan.

2 While the pasta is cooking, process the parsley and basil in a food processor or blender until just chopped.
3 Heat the oil in a pan. Add the sun-dried pepper and fry for 2–3 minutes. Stir in the sour cream, ricotta and Parmesan and stir over low heat for 4 minutes, or until heated through. Do not allow to boil.
4 Add the herbs and sauce to the pasta, toss to combine and serve.

NUTRITION PER SERVE: *Protein 25 g; Fat 35 g; Carbohydrate 90 g; Dietary Fibre 5 g; Cholesterol 120 mg; 3330 kJ (800 cal)*

SPAGHETTI CARBONARA WITH MUSHROOMS

Ready to eat in 25 minutes
Serves 4

☆

500 g (1 lb) spaghetti
8 bacon rashers
2 cups (180 g/6 oz) sliced button mushrooms
2 teaspoons chopped fresh oregano
4 eggs, lightly beaten
1 cup (250 ml/8 fl oz) cream
²⁄₃ cup (65 g/2¹⁄₄ oz) freshly grated Parmesan

1 Cook the spaghetti in a large pan of rapidly boiling salted water until *al dente*. Drain and return to the pan.
2 While the spaghetti is cooking, trim the bacon and cut into small pieces. Fry until lightly browned and then set aside on paper towels. Add the mushrooms to the pan and fry for 2–3 minutes, until soft.
3 Add the mushrooms, bacon, oregano and the combined eggs and cream to the drained spaghetti. Cook over low heat, stirring, until the mixture starts to thicken slightly. Remove from the heat and stir in the cheese. Season with salt and cracked black pepper, to taste.

NUTRITION PER SERVE: *Protein 45 g; Fat 40 g; Carbohydrate 90 g; Dietary Fibre 5 g; Cholesterol 320 mg; 3844 kJ (920 cal)*

TOMATO PASTE
Tomato paste, also known in the U.K. as tomato purée, is made by simmering whole tomatoes until very thick, dark and no longer liquid. Only salt is added, and sometimes a little sugar. The resulting paste has an intense flavour that is used sparingly to flavour sauces, stocks, stews and soups. The many commercial brands have varying degrees of concentration, so it is a matter of trying different ones until you find one that best suits your needs. Italian tomato paste is graded, so look for *doppio concentrato* (double concentrate), or *triplo concentrato* (triple concentrate) on the label.

OPPOSITE PAGE, FROM TOP: Spaghetti with tomato sauce; Ricotta and basil with tagliatelle; Spaghetti carbonara with mushrooms

FARFALLE WITH PEAS, PROSCIUTTO AND MUSHROOMS

Ready to eat in 20 minutes
Serves 4

☆

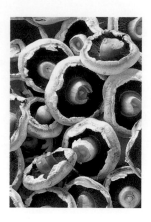

375 g (12 oz) farfalle
60 g (2 oz) butter
I onion, chopped
200 g (6½ oz) mushrooms,
  thinly sliced
250 g (8 oz) frozen peas
3 slices of prosciutto, sliced
I cup (250 ml/8 fl oz) cream
I egg yolk
fresh Parmesan, optional, for serving

I Cook the farfalle in a large pan of rapidly boiling salted water until *al dente*. Drain and return to the pan.
2 While the pasta is cooking, heat the butter in a pan, add the onion and mushrooms and stir over medium heat for 5 minutes or until tender.

3 Add the peas and prosciutto to the pan. Combine the cream and the yolk in a small jug and pour into the pan. Cover and simmer for 5 minutes or until heated through.
4 Mix the sauce through the pasta or serve the sauce over the top of the pasta. Can be topped with shaved or grated fresh Parmesan.

NUTRITION PER SERVE: *Protein 25 g; Fat 45 g; Carbohydrate 75 g; Dietary Fibre 10 g; Cholesterol 180 mg; 3280 kJ (785 cal)*

ON THE SIDE

FENNEL, ORANGE AND ALMOND SALAD Finely slice 1 or 2 fennel bulbs. Peel 3 oranges, removing all the white pith, and cut into segments. Toast 100 g (3½ oz) of flaked almonds in a frying pan until golden. Combine the fennel, oranges and almonds in a bowl. Add 150 g (5 oz) of crumbled creamy blue cheese and 50 g (1¾ oz) of thinly sliced sun-dried pepper (capsicum). Make a dressing by combining 3 tablespoons of orange juice, 1 teaspoon of sesame oil and 1 tablespoon of red wine vinegar. Drizzle over the salad and serve.

BELOW: Farfalle with peas, prosciutto and mushrooms

PENNE WITH SUN-DRIED TOMATOES AND LEMON

Ready to eat in 25 minutes
Serves 4

☆

250 g (8 oz) penne
¹/₄ cup (60 ml/2 fl oz) olive oil
3 bacon rashers, chopped
1 onion, chopped
¹/₃ cup (80 ml/2³/₄ fl oz) lemon juice
1 tablespoon fresh thyme leaves
¹/₃ cup (50 g/1³/₄ oz) chopped
   sun-dried tomatoes
¹/₂ cup (80 g/2³/₄ oz) pine nuts, toasted

1 Cook the pasta in a large pan of rapidly boiling salted water until *al dente*. Drain.
2 While the pasta is cooking, heat the olive oil in a large pan, add the chopped bacon and onion and stir over medium heat for 4 minutes or until the bacon is brown and the onion has softened.
3 Add the pasta to the pan with the lemon juice, thyme leaves, sun-dried tomato and pine nuts. Stir over low heat for 2 minutes, or until heated through.
NOTE: You can use pancetta instead of bacon, if preferred.

NUTRITION PER SERVE: *Protein 15 g; Fat 30 g; Carbohydrate 50 g; Dietary Fibre 5 g; Cholesterol 15 mg; 2200 kJ (530 cal)*

FARFALLE WITH PINK PEPPERCORNS AND SUGAR SNAP PEAS

Ready to eat in 30 minutes
Serves 4

☆

400 g (13 oz) farfalle
1 cup (250 ml/8 fl oz) white wine
1 cup (250 ml/8 fl oz) cream
100 g (3¹/₂ oz) pink peppercorns in
   vinegar, drained
300 ml (9¹/₂ fl oz) crème fraîche
200 g (6¹/₂ oz) sugar snap peas,
   topped and tailed

1 Cook the pasta in a large pan of rapidly boiling salted water until *al dente*. Drain and return to the pan.
2 While the pasta is cooking, pour the wine into a large saucepan, bring to the boil, reduce the heat and simmer until reduced by half.
3 Add the cream, bring to the boil, reduce the heat and simmer until reduced by half.
4 Remove from the heat and stir in the pink peppercorns and crème fraîche. Return to the heat and add the sugar snap peas, simmering until the peas turn bright green. Season with salt, if necessary. Stir through the pasta and serve immediately.

NUTRITION PER SERVE: *Protein 15 g; Fat 55 g; Carbohydrate 80 g; Dietary Fibre 8 g; Cholesterol 175 mg; 3855 kJ (915 cal)*

ABOVE: Penne with sun-dried tomatoes and lemon

PASTA DESSERTS

Never had pasta as a dessert? You're probably not alone. But once you've tasted these luscious desserts, you'll begin to wonder why. Combined with fresh fruit, cream or chocolate, pasta becomes the finale rather than the beginning. If you're a die-hard pasta fan you can even start and end your meal with pasta. While the concept is not strictly conventional, the possibilities are endless. As they say, the proof of the pudding's in the eating... so what are you waiting for?

CANDIED LEMON PEEL

Candied or crystallized lemon peel is fresh peel that has been preserved in sugar. A sugar syrup is introduced to replace the moisture content and this process is done gradually to allow the lemon rind to keep its shape and tenderness. When enough sugar has been absorbed, the peel is allowed to dry out so that it will be easy to store. Candied lemon peel is used in puddings and desserts, and as a decoration for cakes and sweets.

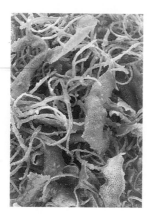

ABOVE: Sweet cheese in lemon pasta

SWEET CHEESE IN LEMON PASTA

Preparation time: 1 hour + standing
Total cooking time: 25 minutes
Serves 4–6

★★

2 cups (250 g/8 oz) plain flour

1/2 teaspoon salt

1 teaspoon caster sugar

grated rind of 2 lemons

2 tablespoons fresh lemon juice

2 eggs, lightly beaten

1 tablespoon currants

1 tablespoon brandy

600 g (1 1/4 lb) ricotta cheese

5 tablespoons icing sugar

3/4 teaspoon grated lemon rind

3/4 teaspoon vanilla essence

beaten egg, for glazing

4 tablespoons flaked almonds, toasted

vegetable oil, for frying

1 cup (250 ml/8 fl oz) cream, flavoured with brandy, to taste

mint leaves and thin strips of lemon rind or candied lemon peel, to garnish, optional

1 Pile the combined flour, salt, sugar and lemon rind on a work surface and make a well in the centre. Add 1–2 tablespoons of water, the lemon juice and egg and gradually blend them into the flour, using a fork. The dough can be made in a processor up to this point. When a loosely combined dough forms, use your hands and begin kneading. Incorporate a little extra flour if the dough feels moist. Knead for 5–8 minutes, or until smooth and elastic. Cover with plastic and set aside for 15 minutes.

2 Soak the currants in the brandy in a bowl. In a larger bowl, combine the ricotta cheese, icing sugar, lemon rind and vanilla. Set aside.

3 Divide the dough into eight equal portions. Roll each out to a thin sheet about 18 cm (7 inches) square. Cover each as it is completed.

4 Trim the pasta into neat squares. Working with a few at a time, brush around the edges with beaten egg. Add the currants and toasted almonds to the ricotta filling, then put one-eighth of the filling in the middle of each square of dough. Fold the edges over to completely enclose the filling. Press the edges down to seal.

5 Heat oil in a pan to 1–2 cm (about 1/2 inch) depth. Drop a piece of scrap pasta in to check that it turns golden without burning. Fry the parcels, two or three at a time, until golden. Remove with a slotted spoon, drain on paper towels and keep warm. Serve with brandy cream, sprinkled with icing sugar and garnished with mint leaves and lemon rind.

NUTRITION PER SERVE (6): *Protein 20 g; Fat 45 g; Carbohydrate 50 g; Dietary Fibre 3 g; Cholesterol 185 mg; 2965 kJ (705 cal)*

CREAMY FRESH STRAWBERRY ROLLS

Preparation time: 40 minutes
Total cooking time: 50 minutes
Serves 6

✷ ✷

250 g (8 oz) strawberries, hulled
60 g (2 oz) butter
2 egg yolks
1/3 cup (80 ml/2¾ fl oz) cream
1/3 cup (90 g/3 oz) sugar
1 teaspoon lemon juice
6 sheets fresh lasagne, 16 cm x 21 cm
   (6½ x 8½ inches)
1/3 cup (40 g/1¼ oz) toasted slivered almonds,
   plus 1 tablespoon for decoration
icing sugar, for dusting

1 Preheat the oven to moderate 180°C (350°F/Gas 4) and grease a gratin dish. Halve the strawberries, slicing from top to bottom. Melt 20 g (¾ oz) of butter in a pan and lightly toss the strawberries for 20 seconds. Remove from the pan. Melt another 20 g (¾ oz) of butter in the pan. Mix the egg yolks with the cream, then add to the pan with the sugar and lemon juice. Cook, stirring often, until very thick. Remove from the heat and stir in the strawberries. Cool.
2 Cook the fresh lasagne sheets, two at a time, in plenty of boiling water for 3 minutes, or until *al dente*. Transfer to a bowl of cold water and leave for 1 minute before placing on tea towels to dry.
3 Divide the strawberry mixture and the almonds among the pasta sheets, leaving a 3 cm (1¼ inch) border all around. Fold in the long edges first, then carefully fold up the end closest to you and roll. As the mixture begins to ooze, bring the top end over and towards you. Carefully place, seam-side-down, in the prepared dish. Position the rolls closely side-by-side.
4 Dot the top with pieces of the remaining butter. Sprinkle with extra almonds and 2 teaspoons of sifted icing sugar. Bake for 15 minutes, then place under a preheated grill for 5 minutes or until lightly browned.
NOTE: This dessert is delicious accompanied by vanilla ice cream and a strawberry coulis. For a change, you can use fresh raspberries when they are in season. They will not need to be cooked, so just add them to the prepared cream mixture. Blueberries can also be used and should be prepared the same way as the strawberries, but not sliced. You can use dry lasagne sheets instead of fresh, but they are often thicker, less pliable and slippery to handle. If you use them, cook them as they come from the packet, then trim to the dimensions above.

NUTRITION PER SERVE: *Protein 9 g; Fat 20 g; Carbohydrate 50 g; Dietary Fibre 4 g; Cholesterol 100 mg; 1775 kJ (420 cal)*

STRAWBERRIES
All the strawberry varieties grown today for the mass market are hybrids, descendants of an original cross between a large fruited North American berry and one with intense flavour from Chile.

ABOVE: Creamy fresh strawberry rolls

BLANCHED ALMONDS

Almonds which have had their skins removed are known as blanched almonds. They are readily available, sold in bulk or pre-packaged, but the skins can be easily removed at home. Drop the shelled almonds into boiling water and simmer for 1 minute. Drain, and as soon as they are cool enough to handle, squeeze each almond between your thumb and forefinger. The nut will pop out. Where ground almonds are called for in a recipe it might be worth buying them ready ground, as it is difficult to achieve a uniform and fine grind with most home equipment, and oil can be extracted which makes the almonds moist and clump into little balls. This problem can be partly avoided by adding about 2 tablespoons of the recipe's sugar to the almonds when grinding.

*ABOVE: Coconut
and lemon rissoni cake*

COCONUT AND LEMON RISSONI CAKE

Preparation time: 20 minutes
Total cooking time: 1 hour
Serves 6–8

⭐

1/3 cup (70 g/2 1/4 oz) rissoni
1/4 cup (30 g/1 oz) plain flour
3/4 cup (90 g/3 oz) self-raising flour
1/2 cup (95 g/3 1/4 oz) ground almonds
1/2 cup (45 g/1 1/2 oz) desiccated coconut
1 tablespoon firmly packed grated lemon rind
185 g (6 oz) butter
1/2 cup (160 g/5 1/2 oz) apricot jam
1 cup (250 g/8 oz) caster sugar
3 eggs, lightly beaten

1 Preheat the oven to warm 160°C (315°F/ Gas 2–3). Brush a deep 20 cm (8 inch) round cake tin with melted butter or oil. Line the base and sides with baking paper.
2 Cook the rissoni in a large pan of rapidly boiling water for 3–4 minutes, or until *al dente*. Drain well.
3 While the rissoni is cooking, combine the flours, almonds, coconut and lemon rind in a large bowl. Make a well in the centre.
4 Melt the butter, jam and sugar in a medium pan over low heat, or in a heatproof bowl in the microwave oven, until smooth. Stir in the rissoni, then using a large metal spoon, stir into the dry ingredients. Stir in the eggs until smooth. Pour into the tin and bake for 50–55 minutes or until firm and a skewer comes out clean when inserted in the centre. Leave in the tin for 10–15 minutes before turning out. Serve warm or cold, topped with candied lemon slices.

NUTRITION PER SERVE (8): *Protein 8 g; Fat 30 g; Carbohydrate 60 g; Dietary Fibre 3 g; Cholesterol 125 mg; 2280 kJ (540 cal)*

BAKED RISSONI PUDDING

Preparation time: 15 minutes
Total cooking time: 1 hour
Serves 4–6

★

1/4 cup (50 g/13/4 oz) rissoni
2 eggs, lightly beaten
1/3 cup (80 ml/23/4 fl oz) maple syrup
2 cups (500 ml/16 fl oz) cream
1/4 cup (30 g/1 oz) sultanas
1 teaspoon vanilla essence
pinch of nutmeg
1/4 teaspoon ground cinnamon

1 Preheat the oven to slow 150°C (300°F/ Gas 2). Cook the rissoni in a large pan of rapidly boiling water for 3–4 minutes, or until *al dente*. Drain well.
2 Whisk together the eggs, maple syrup and cream in a bowl.

3 Stir in the rissoni, sultanas, vanilla essence, nutmeg and cinnamon. Pour the mixture into a deep round or oval ovenproof dish. Sit the dish in a large baking dish and pour enough water into the baking dish to come halfway up the sides of the ovenproof dish. Bake for 50–55 minutes, or until a knife comes out clean when inserted into the centre.
NOTE: As a variation, replace the sultanas with chopped dried apricots or raisins. Or, use fresh pitted and chopped dates or whole raspberries and blueberries. The cooking time may need to be a little longer with the fresh fruit, because some of the juice will ooze out.

NUTRITION PER SERVE (6): *Protein 5 g; Fat 30 g; Carbohydrate 25 g; Dietary Fibre 1 g; Cholesterol 155 mg; 1700 kJ (405 cal)*

ABOVE: Baked rissoni pudding

ABOVE: Berries and cream pasta stack

BERRIES AND CREAM PASTA STACK

Preparation time: 15 minutes
Total cooking time: 15 minutes
Serves 4

☆

4 fresh or dried lasagne sheets
oil, for deep-frying
2 cups (500 ml/16 fl oz) cream
250 g (8 oz) punnet strawberries
250 g (8 oz) punnet blueberries
250 g (8 oz) punnet raspberries
4 passionfruit
icing sugar, for dusting

1 Cook the lasagne sheets two at a time in a large pan of rapidly boiling water until *al dente*. Add a little oil to the water to prevent the pasta from sticking together. Drain, then carefully rinse the pasta sheets under cold running water. Carefully cut each sheet into three, crossways. Pat dry with a tea towel.
2 Half fill a medium pan with oil. Heat the oil until moderately hot. Cook the pasta pieces one at a time until crisp and golden. Drain on paper towels.
3 Whip the cream until soft peaks form. Place one piece of fried lasagne sheet on each serving plate. Top with some cream, berries and passionfruit pulp. Dust with a little icing sugar. Continue layering once more for each, finishing with a lasagne sheet. Dust again with icing sugar and serve immediately.
NOTE: Any fruits in season are suitable to use for this dessert. Chop or slice the way you like. If you prefer, you can add a little sugar and vanilla to the whipped cream to sweeten.

NUTRITION PER SERVE: *Protein 7 g; Fat 50 g; Carbohydrate 35 g; Dietary Fibre 10 g; Cholesterol 145 mg; 2520 kJ (600 cal)*

PASTA CASES WITH FRUITY RICOTTA FILLING

Preparation time: 35 minutes
Total cooking time: 30 minutes
Serves 4

★ ★ ★

oil, for deep-frying
6 dried lasagne sheets

Ricotta fruit filling

350 g (11 oz) fresh ricotta cheese
1 tablespoon caster sugar
60 g (2 oz) mixed candied fruit (cherries,
    orange and lemon peel), chopped
30 g (1 oz) dark chocolate shavings

1 Heat the oil. It will need to be at least 10 cm (4 inches) deep. Cook the lasagne sheets one at a time in plenty of boiling salted water until *al dente*. Remove with a sieve and place in a bowl of cold water for a minute or two, then transfer to a tea towel and dry both sides. Trim the end of each sheet to make a square.
2 For the next step you will need 3 implements able to withstand boiling oil: a soup ladle of approximately 9 cm (3½ inch) diameter or a wire scoop of the same dimensions; a utensil such as an egg whisk or a mixmaster beater which fits into the scoop to hold the pasta in shape; a pair of tongs. Take one pasta square and gently push it into the ladle by hand. Form a cup shape, with the corners sticking out and with flutes between them.
3 Test the oil for frying by dropping in a piece of scrap pasta. It should bubble immediately and rise to the top. Lower the ladle into the oil. Use tongs to lift the pasta away from the ladle to prevent it sticking initially, then use the egg whisk to maintain the shape. The cases are quite sturdy so don't be afraid to manhandle them. They are ready when crisp and golden with bubbles forming on the surface. Practise with the first two, as these are spares.
4 As each case is ready, remove from the oil and drain upside-down on paper towels. Allow to cool before serving.
5 To make the sweet ricotta filling, mix the ricotta with the sugar until combined. Don't use a food processor as it will make the texture too smooth. Fold in the fruit and chocolate. Spoon into the pasta shells just before serving. Top with shaved curls of chocolate.

NOTE: If the cases become limp or have spots of surface oil, put them in a hot oven to crisp up again. These cases are perfect for turning a humble dessert such as ice cream or fruit salad into an elegant course. Dress the dish up further with a simple sauce and finish off with a dusting of icing sugar. Wire gaufrette baskets, suitable for making the pastry cases, are available from speciality kitchenware shops.

NUTRITION PER SERVE: *Protein 15 g; Fat 15 g; Carbohydrate 45 g; Dietary Fibre 2 g; Cholesterol 40 mg; 1585 kJ (375 cal)*

CASTER SUGAR
When granulated sugar is crushed to a very fine grain it is called caster sugar. Also known as superfine sugar, it is preferred in cooking because the grains melt quickly and dissolve completely. Caster sugar has good visual appeal and so is sprinkled on the top of cakes, puddings and sweet breads. It is also used to coat sweets and candies.

ABOVE: Pasta cases with fruity ricotta filling

HAZELNUTS

Hazelnuts are the edible nut of the hazel tree, *Corylus*, a member of the birch family. They are rich in oil and pleasant tasting, and are used in baking and confectionery. In recipes, skinned and roasted hazelnuts are often called for, and it is possible to do this at home. Spread them on a baking tray and bake at moderate 180°C (350°F/Gas 4) until the skins shrivel and flake, about 10 minutes. Wrap the hazelnuts in a tea towel for 5 minutes and then rub them vigorously with the tea towel to start dislodging the skins. Then each one has to be skinned separately, rubbing between your fingers.

ABOVE: Chocolate nut cake

CHOCOLATE NUT CAKE

Preparation time: 30 minutes
  + overnight refrigeration
Total cooking time: 5–10 minutes
Serves 6–8

★

250 g (8 oz) stellini
1 cup (140 g/5 1/2 oz) roasted hazelnuts, skinned
1 1/2 cups (150 g/4 1/2 oz) walnuts
3/4 cup (100 g/3 1/2 oz) blanched almonds
3 tablespoons cocoa powder
1 teaspoon ground cinnamon
2/3 cup (155 g/5 oz) sugar
1 tablespoon mixed peel
grated rind of 1 lemon
1 teaspoon vanilla essence
2 tablespoons Cognac
60 g (2 oz) butter
100 g (3 1/2 oz) dark chocolate, chopped

1 Grease and line the base of a deep 20 cm (8 inch) round springform tin. Cook the pasta in boiling water until *al dente*. Rinse under cold water to cool. Drain thoroughly.
2 Place the nuts, cocoa powder, cinnamon, sugar, mixed peel, rind, vanilla essence and Cognac in a food processor. Process in short bursts until finely ground.
3 Melt the butter and chocolate in a small pan over low heat or in the microwave, until smooth.
4 Combine the pasta, nut mixture and melted chocolate and butter. Mix well. Spoon the mixture into the prepared tin. Press down firmly with a wet hand. Smooth the surface with the back of a wet spoon. Refrigerate overnight to firm. Remove from the tin and cut into wedges. Dust with a little cocoa powder and icing sugar for serving. Delicious with whipped cream.

NUTRITION PER SERVE (8): *Protein 15 g; Fat 45 g; Carbohydrate 55 g; Dietary Fibre 7 g; Cholesterol 20 mg; 2795 kJ (665 cal)*

INDEX

Page numbers in *italics* refer to photographs. Page numbers in **bold** type refer to margin notes.

On the Side
Accompaniments

Antipasto Salad, 157

Asparagus and Parmesan Salad, 266

Asparagus with Lemon Hazelnut Butter, 63

Baby Spinach, Walnut and Cheddar Salad, 237

Bacon, Lettuce and Tomato Salad, 83

Bean Salad with Vinaigrette, 61

Beans with Parsley Butter, 91

Beetroot and Nectarine Salad, 131

Beetroot, Goats Cheese and Pistachio Nut Salad, 73

Black Beans with Tomato, Lime and Coriander, 97

Braised Leeks with Pine Nuts, 164

Buttery Caraway Cabbage, 243

Caramelized Leeks and Crispy Bacon, 223

Cauliflower Cheese, Individual, 239

Cherry Tomatoes with Butter and Dill, 89

Chive and Garlic Corn Cobs, 63

Crispy Zucchini Ribbons, 139

Cucumber with Toasted Sesame Seeds, 57

Damper, 181

Dilled Orange Carrots, 164

Fennel, Orange and Almond Salad, 282

Garlic Dill Mushrooms, 64

Garlic Pizza Bread, 195

Greek Salad, 146

Green Beans with Garlic and Cumin, 226

Green Herb Pilaf, 162

Herb Bread, 43

Herb Salad, 256

Kumera and Parsnip Chips, 175

Kumera, Yoghurt and Dill Salad, 150

Marinated Mushroom Salad, 96

Mixed Tomato Salad, 256

Nasturtium and Watercress Salad, 209

Orange and Olive Salad, 195

Panzanella, 91

Parmesan Biscuits, 188

Peach Salsa Salad, 276

Polenta Bread, 175

Popovers, 206

Potato Salad, 59

Potato, Egg and Bacon Salad, 113

Prosciutto, Camembert and Fig Salad, 261

Pumpkin and Sage Scones, 173

Raspberry Beetroot Salad, 237

Roast Broccoli with Cumin Seeds, 89

Roast Pumpkin with Sage, 57

Roasted Tomatoes Topped with Herbed Goats Cheese, 87

Roasted Vegetable and Brie Salad, 110

Sesame Coleslaw, 160

Spicy Cucumber Salad, 64

Spinach, Pancetta and Pecan Nut Salad, 272

Sweet Chilli Potato and Coriander Salad, 232

Tabouli, 107

Tomato and Bocconcini Salad, 157

Tomato and Feta Salad, 150

Tomato, Egg and Olive Salad, 259

Turnips with Tomato, Wine and Garlic, 198

Waldorf Salad, 130

Warm Broccoli Florets with Almonds, 131

Warm Ginger and Sesame Carrot Salad, 136

Warm Kumera, Rocket and Crispy Bacon Salad, 209

Warm Spring Vegetable Salad, 146

Warm Vegetable Salad, 120

Watercress, Salmon and Camembert Salad, 96

Wild Rice with Roasted Pepper, 223

Zucchini with Tomato and Garlic, 97

Pasta dishes

A

Alfredo, 25, *25*
Alfredo sauce, **162**
almonds, blanched, **288**
Amatriciana, 29, *29*
Anchovy and Tomato Crostini, 185, *185*
anchovy fillets, **152**
antipasto
  Balsamic Tomatoes, Slow-Roasted, 53, *53*
  Barbecued Sardines, 51, *51*
  Bruschetta, 53, *53*
  Cauliflower Fritters, 53, *53*
  Grilled Eggplant and Peppers, 52, *52*
  Mussels, Stuffed, 50, *50*
  Pesto Bocconcini Balls, 52, *52*
  Polenta Shapes with Chorizo and Salsa, 51, *51*
  Salami and Potato Frittata Wedges, 50, *50*
Arrabbiata, 32, *32*
Artichoke, Egg and Sorrel Pasta, 270, *270*
artichokes, **178**
  Farfalle and Olives, with, 117, *117*
  Ravioli with Peas and, 276, *277*
asiago, 169, *169*
asparagus, **154**
  Conchiglie Salad with Bocconcini, Asparagus and Oregano, 188, *189*
  Creamy Asparagus Linguine, 118, *119*
  Tagliatelle with Asparagus and Fresh Herbs, 154, *154*
aubergine *see* eggplants

B

bacon
  Basil Tortellini with Bacon and Tomato Sauce, 226, *226*
  Carbonara, 27, *27*
  Ruote with Lemon, Olives and, 263, *263*
  Spaghetti Carbonara, 155, *155*, **155**
  Spaghetti Carbonara with Mushrooms, *280,* 281
Bacon and Pea Soup, 43, *43*
Baked Cannelloni Milanese, 239, *239*
Baked Creamy Cheesy Pasta, 241, *241*
baked pasta
  Butternut Pumpkin Filled with Pasta and Leeks, *248,* 249
  Cannelloni, 244, *244*
  Cannelloni Milanese, 239, *239*
  Chicken and Veal Loaf with Mushrooms and Sour Cream, *248,* 249
  Classic Lasagne, 234, *235*
  Conchiglie with Chicken and Ricotta, 237, *237*
  Creamy Cheesy Pasta, 241, *241*
  Giant Conchiglie with Ricotta and Rocket, 251, *251*
  Italian Omelette, 245, *245*
  Macaroni Cheese, 236, *236*
  Macaroni Eggplant Cake, 230, *230*
  Meatballs and Pasta, 242, *242*
  Pasta and Spinach Timbales, 240, *240*
  Pasta Pie, 233, *233*
  Pasta Souffle, 234, *234*
  Pasta with Green Olive Paste and Three Cheeses, 250, *250*
  Pasta-filled Vegetables, 243, *243*
  Pasticcio, 246, *246,* **247**
  Pastitsio, 247, *247,* **247**
  Ricotta Lasagne, 231, *231*
  Rigatoni Gratin, 240, *240*
  Seafood with Pasta, 232, *232*
  Spaghetti Frittata, 238, *238*
Baked Pasta and Mince, 61, *61*
Baked Rissoni Pudding, 289, *289*
Baked Spaghetti Frittata, 238, *238*

balsamic vinegar, **188**
  Chicken Ravioli with Lime Balsamic Dressing, 256, *257*
  Slow-roasted Balsamic Tomatoes, 53, *53*
Barbecued Chicken and Pasta Salad, 182, *182*
Barbecued Sardines, 51, *51*
basil, **41**
  Fettucine with Zucchini and Crisp-fried, 116, *116*
  Gnocchi with Tomato and Fresh, 200
  Linguine in Honey Basil Cream, 158, *158*
  Potato Gnocchi with Tomato and Basil Sauce, 199, *199*
  Prawn and Basil Soup, 42, *42*
  Ricotta and Basil with Tagliatelle, *280,* 281
  Tomato and Basil Pasta Salad, 174, *174*
  Tomato Soup with Pasta and Basil, 41, *41*
  Vegetable Soup with Basil Sauce, 45, *45*
Basil Tortellini with Bacon and Tomato Sauce, 226, *226*
bay leaves, **80**
Bean Soup with Sausage, 39, *39*
beans
  and pasta, **46**
  borlotti, **37**
  broad, **45**
  Cheesy Buckwheat and Bean Pasta, 271, *271*
  Fettucine with Creamy Mushroom and Bean Sauce, 151, *151*
  Fusilli with Broad Bean Sauce, 146, *146*
  pasta and beans, **46**
  Pasta and Bean Soup, 46, *46*
  Rigatoni with Kidney Beans and Italian Sausage, 65, *65*
  Tuna, Green Bean and Onion Salad, 176, *177*
Béchamel sauce, 231, 235, **235,** 244, 246

beef
Meatballs Stroganoff, 76, *76*
Spaghetti with Rich Beef and
Mushroom Sauce, *260*, 261
Stir-fried Chilli Beef with
Spaghettini, 70, *71*
beef stock, **49**
bel paese, 168, *168*
Berries and Cream Pasta Stack,
290, *290*
black mussels, 272, *272*
black olives, **118**, *118*
sautéed, 135, *135*
black pepper, **148**
blue cheese
Caramelized Onion and Blue
Cheese Rissoni, 159, *159*
Blue Cheese and Broccoli with
Rigatoni, *138*, 139
bocconcini, 166, *167*
Conchiglie Salad with
Bocconcini, Asparagus and
Oregano, 188, *189*
Pesto Bocconcini Balls, 52, *52*
bolognese
Classic, 24, *24*
Quick Spaghetti, 60, *60*
Spaghetti, 56, *56*
Spaghetti with Chicken,
85, *85*
borlotti beans, **37**
Boscaiola, Creamy, 30, *30*
Brandied Cream and Salmon
Fusilli, 276, *277*
Brandy Chicken Fettucine,
91, *91*
breadcrumbs, **130**
broad beans, **45**
broccoli, **42**
Blue Cheese and Broccoli
with Rigatoni, *138*, 139
Conchiglie with Broccoli and
Anchovy, 152, *153*
Broccoli Soup, 42, *42*
Bruschetta, 53, *53*
Bucatini with Gorgonzola
Sauce, 150, *150*
butternut pumpkin, **249**
Butternut Pumpkin Filled with
Pasta and Leeks, *248*, 249
button mushrooms, **137**

C

Cacciatore, 67, *67*
Calabrian Spaghetti, 275, *275*
calamari, **94**

candied lemon peel, **286**
cannelloni, 220, *221*, **222**
Cannelloni, 244, *244*
cannelloni
Spinach and Ricotta,
222, *222*
capers, **125**
Linguine with Anchovies,
Olives and Capers,
254, *254*
Orecchiette with Tuna,
Lemon and Caper Sauce,
160, *161*
Spaghetti with Olives and
Capers, 125, *125*
cappelletti, **81**
capsicums *see* peppers
Caramelized Onion and
Blue Cheese Rissoni,
159, *159*
carbonara, 27, *27*, **155**
Carbonara
Grilled, 160, *161*
carbonara
Spaghetti, 155, *155*
Spaghetti Carbonara with
Mushrooms, *280*, 281
carrots
Spiced Carrot and Feta
Gnocchi, 206, *207*
caster sugar, **291**
Cauliflower Fritters, 53, *53*
caviar, red, **102**
cayenne pepper, **157**
celery, **43**
Pasta with Braised Oxtail and,
58, *58*
Cheddar, **232**
cheese dishes
Blue Cheese and Broccoli
with Rigatoni, *138*, 139
Caramelized Onion and Blue
Cheese Rissoni, 159, *159*
Fettucine with Smoked
Cheese and Salami,
156, 157
Gnocchi Cheese Bake,
200, *200*
Macaroni Cheese, 236, *236*
Pasta with Green Olive Paste
and Three Cheeses,
250, *250*
Red Pepper Gnocchi with
Goats Cheese, 209, *209*
Sweet Cheese in Lemon
Pasta, 286, *286*
Cheese sauce, 82, 123

cheeses
asiago, 169, *169*
bel paese, 168, *168*
bocconcini, 166, *167*
Cheddar, **232**
feta, **206**
fontina, 168, *168*, **204**
goats cheese, 169, *169*,
209
gorgonzola, **150**, *166*,
167
grana, 168, *169*
mascarpone, 167, *167*
mozzarella, 166, *166*, **242**
ovolini, 166, *167*
parmigiano reggiano, 168,
168
pecorino, 167, *167*
provolone, 167, *167*
ricotta, 166, *166*, **214**
taleggio, 169
Cheesy Buckwheat and Bean
Pasta, 271, *271*
Cheesy Herb Rolls, 184,
184
cherry tomatoes, **140**
chervil, **183**
chicken
Barbecued Chicken and Pasta
Salad, 182, *182*
Brandy Chicken Fettucine,
91, *91*
Conchiglie with Chicken and
Pesto, 223, *223*
Conchiglie with Chicken and
Ricotta, 237, *237*
Fettucine, and Mushroom
Sauce with, 86, *86*
Italian-style Chicken and
Pasta Salad, 178, *178*
Lasagnette with Mushrooms
and Chicken, 88, *88*
Lemon, Parsley and
Orecchiette, 83, *83*
mince, **237**
Oriental Chicken Pasta, 84,
84
Pear and Pasta Salad,
180, 181
Penne with Chicken and
Mushrooms, 148, *149*
Pesto Chicken Pasta, 87,
87
Ravioli with Chicken Filling,
212, *212*
Ravioli with Fresh Tomato
Sauce, 90, *90*

chicken *continued*
Spaghetti with Chicken
Meatballs, 80, *80*
Spaghetti with Chicken
Bolognese, 85, *85*
Spicy Chicken Broth with
Coriander Pasta, 40, *40*
Tagliatelle with Chicken
Livers and Cream, 147, *147*
Tortellini with Tomato Sauce,
81, *81*
Chicken and Macaroni Bake,
88, *88*
Chicken and Pasta Soup, 47, *47*
Chicken and Spinach Lasagne,
82, *82*
Chicken and Veal Loaf with
Mushrooms and Sour Cream,
248, 249
Chicken Livers with Penne,
89, *89*
Chicken Mezzelune with Cream
Sauce, 213, *213*
Chicken Ravioli with Buttered
Sage Sauce, 224, *224*
Chicken Ravioli with Fresh
Tomato Sauce, 90, *90*
Chicken Ravioli with Lime
Balsamic Dressing, 256, *257*
Chicken Tortellini with Tomato
Sauce, 81, *81*
Chicken with Lemon, Parsley
and Orecchiette, 83, *83*
Chicken, Barbecued, and Pasta
Salad, 182, *182*
Chicken, Leek and Chickpea
Soup, 36
Chicken, Pear and Pasta Salad,
180, 181
Chicken, Warm, and Pasta
Salad, 174, *174*
chickpeas, **132**
Conchiglie with, 132, *133*
chilli dishes
Spaghetti with Chilli
Calamari, 99, *99*
Spaghetti with Garlic and
Chilli, 262, *262*
Stir-fried Chilli Beef with
Spaghettini, 70, *71*
chilli garlic olives, 135, *135*
Chilli Seafood in Tomato Sauce,
103, *103*
chillies, **226**
chives, **269,** *269*
Chocolate Nut Cake,
292, *292*

chorizo, **62,** 67, *67*
Chunky Spaghetti Napolitana,
124, *124*
cinnamon, **236**
clams, **112**
Classic Bolognese, 24, *24*
Classic Lasagne, 234, *235*
Coconut and Lemon Rissoni
Cake, 288, *288*
cod
Tomato Pasta with Smoked
Cod and Sesame, *106,* 107
cold meats
cacciatore, 67, *67*
chorizo, 67, *67*
coppa, 67, *67*
finocchiona Toscana, 67, *67*
ham, shaved, **187**
Milano salami, 67, *67*
mortadella, 67, *67*
pancetta, 66, *66*
pastrami, **176,** *176*
pepperoni, 67, *67*
prosciutto, 66, *66*
salami, 67, *67*
speck, 67, *67*
conchiglie
Giant Conchiglie with
Ricotta and Rocket,
251, *251*
Conchiglie Salad with
Bocconcini, Asparagus and
Oregano, 188, *189*
Conchiglie with Broccoli and
Anchovy, 152, *153*
Conchiglie with Chicken and
Pesto, 223, *223*
Conchiglie with Chicken and
Ricotta, 237, *237*
Conchiglie with Chickpeas,
132, *133*
coppa, 67, *67*
coriander, **40**
Spicy Chicken Broth with
Coriander Pasta, 40, *40*
corn, **186**
Country Pumpkin and Pasta
Soup, 48, *48*
courgettes *see* zucchini
crab, **97**
Crab Cakes with Hot Salsa,
97, *97*
cream, **225**
Cream of Onion Pasta, *268,*
269
Creamy Asparagus Linguine,
118, *119*

Creamy Boscaiola, 30, *30*
creamy pasta
Alfredo, 25, *25*
Baked Creamy Cheesy Pasta,
241, *241*
Brandied Cream and Salmon
Fusilli, 276, *277*
Bucatini with Gorgonzola
Sauce, 150, *150*
Caramelized Onion and Blue
Cheese Rissoni, 159, *159*
Chicken and Veal Loaf with
Mushrooms and Sour
Cream, *248,* 249
Chicken Mezzelune with
Cream Sauce, 213, *213*
Conchiglie with Broccoli and
Anchovy, 152, *153*
Farfalle with Tuna,
Mushrooms and Cream,
95, *95*
Fettucine Alfredo, 162, *162*
Fettucine with Creamy
Mushroom and Bean Sauce,
151, *151*
Fusilli with Broad Bean
Sauce, 146, *146*
Grilled Carbonara, 160, *161*
Lemon Grass and Lime
Scallop Pasta, 165, *165*
Linguine in Honey Basil
Cream, 158, *158*
Linguine with Creamy
Lemon Sauce, 163, *163*
Orecchiette with Tuna,
Lemon and Caper Sauce,
160, *161*
Penne with Chicken and
Mushrooms, 148, *149*
Penne with Creamy Tomato
Sauce, 126, *126*
Pork and Veal Ravioli with
Cheesy Sauce, 164, *164*
Rigatoni with Sausage and
Parmesan, 148, *149*
Spaghetti with Creamy Garlic
Mussels, 110, *110*
Spaghetti with Creamy
Lemon Sauce, *268,* 269
Tagliatelle with Chicken
Livers and Cream, 147, *147*
Tagliatelle with Veal, Wine
and Cream, 57, *57*
Tortellini with Mushroom
Cream Sauce, 225, *225*
Creamy Prawns with Fettucine,
96, *96*

Creamy Seafood Ravioli,
108, *108*
Creamy Seafood Salad, 179, *179*
Crispy Focaccia Toasts with
Pesto, 185, *185*
cumin
Parsee Lamb with Cumin,
Eggs and Tagliatelle, 75, *75*

D

dates, **191**
desserts
Baked Rissoni Pudding,
289, *289*
Berries and Cream Pasta
Stack, 290, *290*
Chocolate Nut Cake,
292, *292*
Coconut and Lemon Rissoni
Cake, 288, *288*
Pasta Cases with Fruity
Ricotta Filling, 291, *291*
Strawberry Rolls, Creamy
Fresh, 287, *287*
Sweet Cheese in Lemon
Pasta, 286, *286*
dill, **195**
Smoked Salmon, Dill and Egg
Pasta Salad, *194*, 195
durum wheat, **234**

E

egg tomatoes, **122**
eggplants, **44**
Green Olive and Eggplant
Toss, 120, *120*
Grilled Eggplant and Peppers,
52, *52*
Macaroni Eggplant Cake,
230, *230*
Tortellini with Eggplant,
143, *143*
English spinach, **255**

F

Farfalle Salad with Sun-Dried
Tomatoes and Spinach,
172, *172*
Farfalle with Artichoke Hearts
and Olives, 117, *117*
Farfalle with Mushrooms, 126
Farfalle with Peas, 258, *258*
Farfalle with Peas, Prosciutto
and Mushrooms, 282, *282*

Farfalle with Pink Peppercorns
and Sugar Snap Peas, 283
Farfalle with Tuna, Mushrooms
and Cream, 95, *95*
fennel, **107**
Spicy Sausage and Fennel
Rigatoni, 266, *267*
Trout, Fettucine and Fennel
Frittata, *106*, 107
feta cheese, **206**
fettucine
Brandy Chicken, 91, *91*
with Chicken and Mushroom
Sauce, 86, *86*
Creamy Prawns with, 96, *96*
Spinach Fettucine with
Mushroom Sauce, 152, *153*
Trout, Fettucine and Fennel
Frittata, *106*, 107
Warm Garlic Prawn and
Fettucine Salad, 188, *189*
Fettucine Alfredo, 162, *162*
Fettucine Boscaiola, 137, *137*
Fettucine Primavera, 131, *131*
Fettucine with Caviar, 102,
102
Fettucine with Chicken and
Mushroom Sauce, 86, *86*
Fettucine with Creamy
Mushroom and Bean Sauce,
151, *151*
Fettucine with Smoked Cheese
and Salami, *156*, 157
Fettucine with Smoked Salmon,
111, *111*
Fettucine with Snow Peas and
Walnuts, 140, *141*
Fettucine with Spinach and
Prosciutto, 255, *255*
Fettucine with Zucchini and
Crisp-fried Basil, 116, *116*
filling pasta, 218-21, *218-21*
Basil Tortellini with Bacon
and Tomato Sauce,
226, *226*
Chicken Mezzelune with
Cream Sauce, 213, *213*
Chicken Ravioli with
Buttered Sage Sauce,
224, *224*
Conchiglie with Chicken and
Pesto, 223, *223*
Lasagne Bows, 216, *216*
Mushroom Ravioli, 227, *227*
Prawn Tortelloni, 215, *215*
Pumpkin and Herb Ravioli,
217, *217*

Ravioli with Chicken Filling,
212, *212*
Spinach and Ricotta
Cannelloni, 222, *222*
Spinach and Ricotta Shells,
214, *214*
Spinach Ravioli with Sun-
dried Tomato Sauce,
216, *216*
Tortellini with Mushroom
Cream Sauce, 225, *225*
Finocchiona Toscana, 67, *67*
fish stock, **99**
flour, seasoned, **73**
focaccia, crispy, toasts with
pesto, 185, *185*
fontina, 168, *168*, **204**
Fragrant Herb Tagliatelle with
Kaffir Lime and Prawns,
100, *101*
Fragrant Seafood Pasta,
102, *103*
Fricelli, Oriental, *268*, 269
frittata
Baked Spaghetti, 238, *238*
Salami and Potato Frittata
Wedges, 50, *50*
Trout, Fettucine and Fennel,
106, 107
fusilli
Brandied Cream and Salmon,
276, *277*
Lamb and Fusilli Soup, 49, *49*
Meatballs with, 73, *73*
Moroccan Lamb and Roasted
Pepper with, 70, *71*
Fusilli with Broad Bean Sauce,
146, *146*
Fusilli with Green Sauce,
128, 129
Fusilli with Sage and Garlic,
262, *262*
Fusilli with Vegetables, 266, *267*

G

garam masala, **75**
garlic, **77, 244**
chilli garlic olives, 135, *135*
Fusilli with Sage and,
262, *262*
Spaghetti with Creamy Garlic
Mussels, 110, *110*
Spaghetti with Garlic and
Chilli, 262, *262*
Spaghettini with Roasted
Salmon and, 104

garlic *continued*
    Warm Garlic Prawn and
      Fettucine Salad, 188, *189*
Garlic Bucatini, 278, *278*
Garlic Grissini Sticks, 184, *184*
Garlic, Pasta and Fish Soup, 47
Giant Conchiglie with Ricotta
    and Rocket, 251, *251*
ginger, **70**
gnocchi, **200**
    Herbed Potato Gnocchi with
      Chunky Tomato, 205, *205*
    Parsnip, 208, *208*
    potato, 202, *202*
    Potato Gnocchi with Tomato
      and Basil Sauce, 199, *199*
    Pumpkin Gnocchi with Sage
      Butter, 201, *201*
    Red Pepper Gnocchi with
      Goats Cheese, 209, *209*
    Spiced Carrot and Feta,
      206, *207*
    Spinach and Ricotta,
      206, *207*
Gnocchi Cheese Bake, 200, *200*
Gnocchi Romana, 198, *198*
Gnocchi with Fontina Sauce,
    204, *204*
Gnocchi with Tomato and
    Fresh Basil, 200
goats cheese, 169, *169*, **209**
    Red Pepper Gnocchi with,
      209, *209*
gorgonzola, **150**, *166*, 167
    Bucatini with Gorgonzola
      Sauce, 150, *150*
Gorgonzola and Toasted
    Walnuts on Linguine,
    272, *273*
grana, 168, *169*
Green Olive and Eggplant Toss,
    120, *120*
green olives, **254**
    paste, **250**
gremolata, **113**
Grilled Carbonara, 160, *161*
Grilled Eggplant and Peppers,
    52, *52*
Grilled Peppers and Anchovy
    Salad, 192, *192*
Grilled Vegetables on Pasta,
    122, *122*

H

ham, shaved, **187**
hazelnuts, **292**

Herb Tagliatelle with Kaffir
    Lime and Prawns, 100, *101*
Herbed Potato Gnocchi with
    Chunky Tomato, 205, *205*
honey, **158**
    Linguine in Honey Basil
      Cream, 158, *158*

I–J

Italian Omelette, 245, *245*
Italian sausages, **65**
Italian-style Chicken and Pasta
    Salad, 178, *178*

K

Kaffir lime leaves, **101**

L

lamb
    Moroccan Lamb and Roasted
      Pepper with Fusilli, 70, *71*
    Parsee Lamb with Cumin,
      Eggs and Tagliatelle, 75, *75*
    Pasta with Lamb and
      Vegetables, 77, *77*
    Turkish Ravioli, 69, *69*
Lamb and Fusilli Soup, 49, *49*
lasagne, **82**
    Chicken and Spinach, 82, *82*
    Classic, 234, *235*
    Ricotta, 231, *231*
    Vegetable, 123, *123*
Lasagne Bows, 216, *216*
Lasagnette with Mushrooms and
    Chicken, 88, *88*
leeks, **39**
    Butternut Pumpkin Filled
      with Pasta and, *248*, 249
    Chicken, Leek and Chickpea
      Soup, 36
Lemon and Date Ziti, 191, *191*
Lemon and Vegetable Pasta
    Salad, 183, *183*
lemon grass, **165**
Lemon Grass and Lime Scallop
    Pasta, 165, *165*
Lemon-Scented Broth with
    Tortellini, 36, *36*
lemons, **83**
    candied peel, **286**
    Coconut and Lemon Rissoni
      Cake, 288, *288*
    Linguine with Creamy
      Lemon Sauce, 163, *163*

Orecchiette with Tuna,
    Lemon and Caper Sauce,
    160, *161*
    Penne with Sun-dried
      Tomatoes and, 283, *283*
    Ruote with Lemon, Olives
      and Bacon, 263, *263*
    Spaghetti with Creamy
      Lemon Sauce, *268*, 269
    Sweet Cheese in Lemon
      Pasta, 286, *286*
limes, **256**
    Chicken Ravioli with Lime
      Balsamic Dressing, 256, *257*
    Herb Tagliatelle with Kaffir
      Lime and Prawns, 100, *101*
    Lemon Grass and Lime
      Scallop Pasta, 165, *165*
    Pasta with Fragrant Lime and
      Smoked Trout, 255
linguine
    Creamy Asparagus, 118, *119*
    Gorgonzola and Toasted
      Walnuts on, 272, *273*
Linguine in Honey Basil Cream,
    158, *158*
Linguine with Anchovies,
    Olives and Capers, 254, *254*
Linguine with Creamy Lemon
    Sauce, 163, *163*
Linguine with Red Pepper
    Sauce, *128*, 129
Linguine with Roasted
    Vegetable Sauce, 121

M

macaroni, **74**
    Chicken and Macaroni Bake,
      88, *88*
Macaroni Cheese, 236, *236*
Macaroni Eggplant Cake,
    230, *230*
Marinara, 33, *33*
    Spaghetti, 94, *94*
marjoram, **72**
mascarpone, 167, *167*
meat
    Baked Pasta and Mince, 61, *61*
    Basil Tortellini with Bacon and
      Tomato Sauce, 226, 226
    Bean Soup with Sausage, 39,
      39
    Carbonara, 27, *27*
    Chicken and Veal Loaf with
      Mushrooms and Sour
      Cream, *248*, 249

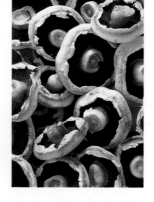

Classic Bolognese, 24, *24*
Classic Lasagne, 234, *235*
Farfalle with Peas, Prosciutto
  and Mushrooms, 282, *282*
Fettucine with Smoked
  Cheese and Salami,
  156, 157
Fettucine with Spinach and
  Prosciutto, 255, *255*
Italian sausages, **65**
Lamb and Fusilli Soup, 49, *49*
Moroccan Lamb and Roasted
  Pepper with Fusilli, 70, *71*
Parsee Lamb with Cumin,
  Eggs and Tagliatelle, 75, *75*
Pasta with Braised Oxtail and
  Celery, 58, *58*
Pasta with Lamb and
  Vegetables, 77, *77*
Penne with Prosciutto, 74, *74*
Pork and Veal Ravioli with
  Cheesy Sauce, 164, *164*
Pork, Paprika and Poppy
  Seeds with Pasta, 68, *68*
Quick Spaghetti Bolognese,
  60, *60*
Rigatoni with Chorizo and
  Tomato, 62, *62*
Rigatoni with Italian-style
  Oxtail Sauce, 64, *64*
Rigatoni with Kidney Beans
  and Italian Sausage, 65, *65*
Rigatoni with Salami and
  Fresh Herbs, 72, *72*
Rigatoni with Sausage and
  Parmesan, 148, *149*
Rocket, Cherry Tomato and
  Spicy Salami Pasta Salad,
  180, 181
Salami and Potato Frittata
  Wedges, 50, *50*
Spaghetti Bolognese, 56, *56*
Spaghetti with Rich Beef and
  Mushroom Sauce, *260*, 261
Spaghetti with Salami and
  Peppers, 59, *59*
Spicy Sausage and Fennel
  Rigatoni, 266, *267*
Stir-fried Chilli Beef with
  Spaghettini, 70, *71*
Tagliatelle with Veal Wine
  and Cream, 57, *57*
Ziti with Vegetables and
  Sausage, 63, *63*
Meatball and Pasta, 242, *242*
Meatballs Stroganoff, 76, *76*
Meatballs with Fusilli, 73, *73*

meats *see also* cold meats
Middle-Eastern Hummus,
  Tomato and Olive Pasta
  Salad, *194*, 195
Milano Salami, 67, *67*
Minestrone, 37, *37*
Moroccan Lamb and Roasted
  Pepper with Fusilli, 70, *71*
mortadella, 67, *67*
mozzarella cheese, 166, *166*,
  242 *see also* bocconcini
  Olive and Mozzarella
  Spaghetti, 116, *117*
Mushroom Ravioli, 227, *227*
mushrooms
  button, **137**, *137*
  Chicken and Veal Loaf with
    Mushrooms and Sour
    Cream, 248, 249
  Chicken Fettucine and
    Mushroom Sauce, 86, *86*
  Farfalle with, 126
  Farfalle with Peas, Prosciutto
    and, 282, *282*
  Farfalle with Tuna,
    Mushrooms and Cream,
    95, *95*
  Fettucine with Creamy
    Mushroom and Bean Sauce,
    151, *151*
  Lasagnette with Mushrooms
    and Chicken, 88, *88*
  Pastrami, Mushroom and
    Cucumber Salad, 176, *177*
  Rissoni and Mushroom
    Broth, 38, *38*
  Spaghetti Carbonara with,
    280, 281
  Spaghetti with Rich Beef and
    Mushroom Sauce, *260*, 261
  Spinach Fettucine with
    Mushroom Sauce, 152, *153*
  Tortellini with Mushroom
    Cream Sauce, 225, *225*
mussels
  black, **272**
  Spaghetti and Mussels in
    Tomato and Herb Sauce,
    113, *113*
  Spaghetti with Creamy Garlic,
    110, *110*
  Stuffed, 50, *50*
  Tomato Mussels on Spaghetti,
    272, *273*
  Mussels with Tomato Sauce,
    109, *109*
mustard, **147**

N
Napolitana, 26, *26*

O
octopus
  Tagliatelle with, 105, *105*
Olive and Mozzarella Spaghetti,
  116, *117*
Olive and Tomato Tapenade,
  135, *135*
olive oil, **60**
olives, **118**, 134, *134*, *135*, **254**
  and Mozzarella Spaghetti,
    116, *117*
  Farfalle with Artichoke Hearts
    and, 117, *117*
  Green Olive and Eggplant
    Toss, 120, *120*
  green olive paste, **250**
  Linguine with Anchovies,
    Olives and Capers,
    254, *254*
  Middle-Eastern Hummus,
    Tomato and Olive Pasta
    Salad, *194*, 195
  Pasta with Green Olive Paste
    and Three Cheeses,
    250, *250*
  Penne with Olive and
    Pistachio Pesto, 259, *259*
  Ruote with Lemon, Olives
    and Bacon, 263, *263*
  Spaghetti with Olives and
    Capers, 125, *125*
Omelette, Italian, 245, *245*
onions
  Caramelized Onion and Blue
    Cheese Rissoni, 159, *159*
  Spaghetti with Peas and
    Onions, 265, *265*
orecchiette
  Chicken with Lemon, Parsley
    and, 83, *83*
  Orecchiette with Tuna,
    Lemon and Caper Sauce,
    160, *161*
oregano, **172**
Oriental Chicken Pasta,
  84, *84*
Oriental Fricelli, 268, *269*
ovolini, 166, *166*
oxtail
  Pasta with Braised Oxtail and
    Celery, 58, *58*
  Rigatoni with Italian-style
    Oxtail Sauce, 64, *64*

P

Pancetta, 66, *66*
pappardelle, **104**
Pappardelle with Salmon, 104, *104*
paprika, **231**
Parmesan, **164**
   Pasta with Pesto and, 274, *274*
   Rigatoni with Sausage and, 148, *149*
parmigiano reggiano, 168, *168*
Parsee Lamb with Cumin, Eggs and Tagliatelle, 75, *75*
parsley, **264**
   Chicken with Lemon, Parsley and Orecchiette, 83, *83*
   flat-leaf, **124**
Parsnip Gnocchi, 208, *208*
parsnips, **208**
pasta
   cooking, 9
   dried, 10–13
   fresh, 14
   making, 16
   re-heating, **86**
Pasta and Bean Soup, 46, *46*
Pasta and Mince, Baked, 61, *61*
Pasta and Spinach Timbales, 240, *240*
Pasta Cases with Fruity Ricotta Filling, 291, *291*
Pasta Niçoise, 278, *278*
Pasta Pie, 233, *233*
Pasta Souffle, 234, *234*
Pasta with Braised Oxtail and Celery, 58, *58*
Pasta with Fragrant Lime and Smoked Trout, 255
Pasta with Green Olive Paste and Three Cheeses, 250, *250*
Pasta with Lamb and Vegetables, 77, *77*
Pasta with Mediterranean-style Vegetables, 187, *187*
Pasta with Pesto and Parmesan, 274, *274*
Pasta with Thai-style Vegetables, 186, *186*
Pasta-filled Vegetables, 243, *243*
Pasticcio, 246, *246*, **247**
Pastitsio, 247, *247*, **247**
pastrami, **176**, *176*
Pastrami, Mushroom and Cucumber Salad, 176, *177*
pears, **181**
pecorino, 167, *167*

penne
   Livers with, 89, *89*
   Spicy Penne with Peppers, 140, *141*
Penne with Chicken and Mushrooms, 148, *149*
Penne with Creamy Tomato Sauce, 126, *126*
Penne with Olive and Pistachio Pesto, 259, *259*
Penne with Prosciutto, 74, *74*
Penne with Pumpkin and Cinnamon Sauce, 132, *133*
Penne with Roasted Peppers, *260*, 261
Penne with Rocket, 258, *258*
Penne with Sun-dried Tomatoes and Lemon, 283, *283*
pepper
   black, **148**
   cayenne, **157**
   white, **241**
Pepperoni, 67, *67*
peppers, **261**
   Grilled Peppers and Anchovy Salad, 192, *192*
   Linguine with Red Pepper Sauce, *128*, 129
   Spicy Penne with, 140, *141*
pesto, 28, *28*, **275**
   Conchiglie with Chicken and, 223, *223*
   Pasta with Pesto and Parmesan, 274, *274*
   Penne with Olive and Pistachio, 259, *259*
   Pesto Bocconcini Balls, 52, *52*
   Pesto Chicken Pasta, 87, *87*
pine nuts, **139**
   Pumpkin and Pine Nut Tagliatelle, *138*, 139
Pistou Soupe au, 45
Polenta Shapes with Chorizo and Salsa, 51, *51*
Pomodoro, 23, *23*
pork
   Paprika and Poppy Seeds with Pasta, 68, *68*
   Pork and Veal Ravioli with Cheesy Sauce, 164, *164*
   Pork, Paprika and Poppy Seeds with Pasta, 68, *68*

potato gnocchi, 202, *202*
Potato Gnocchi with Tomato and Basil Sauce, 199, *199*
potatoes, **199**
   Herbed Potato Gnocchi with Chunky Tomato, 205, *205*
   Salami and Potato Frittata Wedges, 50, *50*
Prawn and Basil Soup, 42, *42*
Prawn Tortelloni, 215, *215*
prawns
   Creamy Prawns with Fettucine, 96, *96*
   Fragrant Herb Tagliatelle with Kaffir Lime and, 100, *101*
   Snow Pea, Prawn and Pasta Soup, 38, *38*
   Spicy Prawn Mexicana, 100, *100*
   Warm Garlic Prawn and Fettucine Salad, 188, *189*
Primavera, 22, *22*
   Fettucine, 131, *131*
prosciutto, 66, *66*, **160**
   Farfalle with Peas, Prosciutto and Mushrooms, 282, *282*
   Fettucine with Spinach and, 255, *255*
   Penne with, 74, *74*
provolone, 166, *167*
Pumpkin and Herb Ravioli, 217, *217*
Pumpkin and Pine Nut Tagliatelle, *138*, 139
Pumpkin Gnocchi with Sage Butter, 201, *201*
pumpkins, **48, 201**
   butternut, **249**
   Butternut Pumpkin Filled with Pasta and Leeks, *248*, 249
   Country Pumpkin and Pasta Soup, 48, *48*
   Penne with Pumpkin and Cinnamon Sauce, 132, *133*
   Rigatoni with Pumpkin Sauce, 127, *127*
Puttanesca, 31, *31*

Q

Quick Spaghetti Bolognese, 60, *60*

R

Ratatouille and Pasta Soup, 44, *44*
ravioli, 219, *219*, **227**
  Chicken Ravioli with Buttered Sage Sauce, 224, *224*
  Chicken Ravioli with Fresh Tomato Sauce, 90, *90*
  Chicken Ravioli with Lime Balsamic Dressing, 256, *257*
  Mushroom, 227, *227*
  Pork and Veal Ravioli with Cheesy Sauce, 164, *164*
  Pumpkin and Herb, 217, *217*
  Spinach Ravioli with Sun-dried Tomato Sauce, 216, *216*
  Turkish, 69, *69*
  Ravioli with Chicken Filling, 212, *212*
Ravioli with Mascarpone and Pancetta, *156*, 157
Ravioli with Peas and Artichokes, 276, *277*
red caviar, **102**
Red Pepper Gnocchi with Goats Cheese, 209, *209*
red wine, **64**
ricotta, 166, *167*
  Conchiglie with Chicken and, 237, *237*
  Giant Conchiglie with Ricotta and Rocket, 251, *251*
  Pasta Cases with Fruity Ricotta Filling, 291, *291*
  Spinach and Ricotta Cannelloni, 222, *222*
  Spinach and Ricotta Gnocchi, 206, *207*
  Spinach and Ricotta Shells, 214, *214*
Ricotta and Basil with Tagliatelle, *280*, 281
ricotta cheese, **214**
Ricotta Lasagne, 231, *231*
rigatoni, **190**
  Blue Cheese and Broccoli with, *138*, 139
  Spicy Sausage and Fennel, 266, *267*
Rigatoni Gratin, 240, *240*
Rigatoni with Chorizo and Tomato, 62, *62*
Rigatoni with Italian-style Oxtail Sauce, 64, *64*

Rigatoni with Kidney Beans and Italian Sausage, 65, *65*
Rigatoni with Pumpkin Sauce, 127, *127*
Rigatoni with Salami and Fresh Herbs, 72, *72*
Rigatoni with Sausage and Parmesan, 148, *149*
Rigatoni with Tomato, Haloumi and Spinach, 190, *190*
rissoni, **243**
  Baked Rissoni Pudding, 289, *289*
  Caramelized Onion and Blue Cheese, 159, *159*
  Coconut and Lemon Rissoni Cake, 288, *288*
  Rissoni and Mushroom Broth, 38
Roasted Pepper Bruschetta, 185, *185*
Rocket, Cherry Tomato and Spicy Salami Pasta Salad, *180*, 181
rosemary, **85**
Ruote with Lemon, Olives and Bacon, 263, *263*

S

saffron, **163**
salads
  Barbecued Chicken and Pasta Salad, 182, *182*
  Chicken, Pear and Pasta Salad, *180*, 181
  Conchiglie Salad with Bocconcini, Asparagus and Oregano, 188, *189*
  Grilled Peppers and Anchovy Salad, 192, *192*
  Italian-style Chicken and Pasta Salad, 178, *178*
  Lemon and Date Ziti, 191, *191*
  Lemon and Vegetable Pasta Salad, 183, *183*
  Middle-Eastern Hummus, Tomato and Olive Pasta Salad, *194*, 195
  Pasta with Mediterranean-style Vegetables, 187, *187*
  Pasta with Thai-style vegetables, 186, *186*

Pastrami, Mushroom and Cucumber Salad, 176, *177*
Rigatoni with Tomato, Haloumi and Spinach, 190, *190*
Rocket, Cherry Tomato and Spicy Salami Pasta Salad, *180*, 181
Seafood Salad, Creamy, 179, *179*
Smoked Salmon, Dill and Egg Pasta Salad, *194*, 195
Tuna, Green Bean and Onion Salad, 176, *177*
Tuscan Warm Pasta Salad, 193, *193*
warm, **174**
Warm Garlic Prawn and Fettucine Salad, 188, *189*
Warm Pasta and Crab Salad, 192
salami, **59**, 67, *67*
  Fettucine with Smoked Cheese and, *156*, 157
  Rigatoni with Salami and Fresh Herbs, 72, *72*
  Rocket, Cherry Tomato and Spicy Salami Pasta Salad, *180*, 181
  Spaghetti with Salami and Peppers, 59, *59*
Salami and Potato Frittata Wedges, 50, *50*
salmon, **98**
  Brandied Cream and Salmon Fusilli, 276, *277*
  Fettucine with Smoked Salmon, 111, *111*
  Pappardelle with Salmon, 104, *104*
  Smoked Salmon, Dill and Egg Pasta Salad, *194*, 195
  Spaghettini with Roasted Salmon and Garlic, 104
Salmon and Pasta Mornay, 98, *98*
salt, **193**
sambal oelek, **276**
Sardines, Barbecued, 51, *51*
sauces
  Alfredo, **162**
  Béchamel, 231, 235, **235**, 244, 246
  Cheese, 82, 123
  Tomato, 81, 94, 212, 231, 244

sausages
  Bean Soup with, 39, *39*
  fresh Italian, **65**
  Rigatoni with Sausage and
    Parmesan, 148, *149*
  Spicy Sausage and Fennel
    Rigatoni, 266, *267*
  Ziti with Vegetables and,
    63, *63*
scallops, **108**
seafood
  Anchovy and Tomato
    Crostini, 185, *185*
  anchovy fillets, **152**
  Barbecued Sardines, 51, *51*
  black mussels, **272**
  Brandied Cream and Salmon
    Fusilli, 276, *277*
  Chilli Seafood in Tomato
    Sauce, 103, *103*
  clams, **112**
  Creamy Prawns with
    Fettucine, 96, *96*
  Creamy Seafood Ravioli,
    108, *108*
  Creamy Seafood Salad,
    179, *179*
  Farfalle with Tuna,
    Mushrooms and Cream,
    95, *95*

  Fettucine with Smoked
    Salmon, 111, *111*
  Fragrant Herb Tagliatelle with
    Kaffir Lime and Prawns,
    100, *101*
  Fragrant Seafood Pasta,
    102, *103*
  Garlic, Pasta and Fish Soup,
    47
  Linguine with Anchovies,
    Olives and Capers, 254,
    254
  Orecchiette with Tuna,
    Lemon and Caper Sauce,
    160, *161*
  Pappardelle with Salmon, 104,
    104
  Pasta with Fragrant Lime and
    Smoked Trout, 255
  scallops, **108**, *108*
  Smoked Salmon, Dill and Egg
    Pasta Salad, *194,* 195
  Snow Pea, Prawn and Pasta
    Soup, 38, *38*
  Spaghetti and Mussels in
    Tomato and Herb Sauce,
    113, *113*

Spaghetti with Creamy Garlic
  Mussels, 110, *110*
Spaghetti with Olives and
  Capers, 125, *125*
Spaghettini with Roasted
  Salmon and Garlic, 104
Spicy Prawn Mexicana,
  100, *100*
Stuffed Mussels, 50, *50*
Tagliatelle with Octopus,
  105, *105*
Tomato Mussels on Spaghetti,
  272, *273*
Tomato Pasta with Smoked
  Cod and Sesame, *106,* 107
Trout, Fettucine and Fennel
  Frittata, *106,* 107
Tuna and Pasta Salad,
  175, *175*
Tuna, Green Bean and Onion
  Salad, 176, *177*
Warm Garlic Prawn and
  Fettucine Salad, 188, *189*
Seafood with Pasta, 232, *232*
semolina, **198**
silverbeet, **129**
Slow-roasted Balsamic
  Tomatoes, 53, *53*
Smoked Salmon, Dill and Egg
  Pasta Salad, *194,* 195
Snow Pea, Prawn and Pasta
  Soup, 38, *38*
snow peas, **84**
  Fettucine with Snow Peas and
    Walnuts, 140, *141*
sorrel, **270**
Souffle, Pasta, 234, *234*
Soupe au Pistou, 45, *45*
soups
  Bacon and Pea, 43, *43*
  Bean Soup with Sausage,
    39, *39*
  Beef Stock, **49**
  Broccoli, 42, *42*
  Chicken and Pasta,
    47, *47*
  Chicken, Leek and Chickpea,
    36
  Garlic, Pasta and Fish, 47
  Lamb and Fusilli, 49, *49*
  Lemon-Scented Broth with
    Tortellini, 36, *36*
  Minestrone, 37, *37*
  Pasta and Bean, 46, *46*
  Prawn and Basil, 42, *42*
  Rissoni and Mushroom
    Broth, 38

Snow Pea, Prawn and Pasta,
  38, *38*
Soupe au Pistou, 45, *45*
Spicy Chicken Broth with
  Coriander Pasta, 40, *40*
Tomato Soup with Pasta and
  Basil, 41, *41*
Vegetable Soup with Basil
  Sauce, 45, *45*
spaghetti, **110**
  Baked Spaghetti Frittata,
    238, *238*
  Calabrian, 275, *275*
  Chunky Spaghetti Napolitana,
    124, *124*
  Olive and Mozzarella,
    116, *117*
  Quick Spaghetti Bolognese,
    60, *60*
  Tomato Mussels on, 272, *273*
Spaghetti and Mussels in
  Tomato and Herb Sauce,
  113, *113*
Spaghetti Bolognese, 56, *56*
Spaghetti Carbonara, 155,
  155, **155**
Spaghetti Carbonara with
  Mushrooms, *280,* 281
Spaghetti Marinara, 94, *94*
Spaghetti Mediterranean,
  279, *279*
Spaghetti Puttanesca, 264, *264*
Spaghetti Siracusani, 136, *136*
Spaghetti Tomato Salad,
  173, *173*
Spaghetti Vongole, 112, *112*
Spaghetti with Chicken
  Bolognese, 85, *85*
Spaghetti with Chicken
  Meatballs, 80, *80*
Spaghetti with Chilli Calamari,
  99, *99*
Spaghetti with Creamy Garlic
  Mussels, 110, *110*
Spaghetti with Creamy Lemon
  Sauce, *268,* 269
Spaghetti with Fresh Tomato
  Sauce, 121, *121*
Spaghetti with Garlic and Chilli,
  262, *262*
Spaghetti with Herbs, 274, *274*
Spaghetti with Herbs and
  Tomato, 130, *130*
Spaghetti with Olives and
  Capers, 125, *125*
Spaghetti with Peas and Onions,
  265, *265*

Spaghetti with Rich Beef and
Mushroom Sauce, 260, 261
Spaghetti with Salami and
Peppers, 59, 59
Spaghetti with Tomato Sauce,
280, 281
spaghettini
Stir-fried Chilli Beef with
Spaghettini, 70, 71
Spaghettini with Roasted
Salmon and Garlic, 104
Speck, 67, 67
Spiced Carrot and Feta
Gnocchi, 206, 207
Spicy Chicken Broth with
Coriander Pasta, 40, 40
Spicy Penne with Peppers,
140, 141
Spicy Prawn Mexicana,
100, 100
Spicy Sausage and Fennel
Rigatoni, 266, 267
spinach
Chicken and Spinach Lasagne,
82, 82
English, 255
Farfalle Salad with Sun-Dried
Tomatoes and, 172, 172
Fettucine with Spinach and
Prosciutto, 255, 255
Pasta and Spinach Timbales,
240, 240
Rigatoni with Tomato,
Haloumi and, 190, 190
Spinach and Ricotta Cannelloni,
222, 222
Spinach and Ricotta Gnocchi,
206, 207
Spinach and Ricotta Shells,
214, 214
Spinach Fettucine with
Mushroom Sauce, 152, 153
Spinach Ravioli with Sun-dried
Tomato Sauce,
216, 216
squash, baby yellow, 266
Stir-Fried Chilli Beef with
Spaghettini, 70, 71
stocks
beef, 49
fish, 99
vegetable, 151
strawberries, 287
Strawberry Rolls, Creamy
Fresh, 287, 287
Stuffed Mussels, 50, 50
sugar, caster, 291

Sun-dried Tomato Sauce on
Tagliatelle, 118, 119
sun-dried tomatoes, 111
Sweet Cheese in Lemon Pasta,
286, 286

T

Tagliatelle with Asparagus and
Fresh Herbs, 154, 154
Tagliatelle with Chicken Livers
and Cream, 147, 147
Tagliatelle with Octopus,
105, 105
Tagliatelle with Tomato and
Walnuts, 142, 142
Tagliatelle with Veal
Wine and Cream,
57, 57
taleggio, 169, 169
thyme, 279
Tomato and Basil Pasta Salad,
174, 174
Tomato Mussels on Spaghetti,
272, 273
Tomato Pasta with Smoked
Cod and Sesame,
106, 107
Tomato Sauce, 81, 94, 212,
231, 244
Tomato Soup with Pasta and
Basil, 41, 41
tomatoes
Anchovy and Tomato
Crostini, 185, 185
Basil Tortellini with Bacon
and Tomato Sauce,
226, 226
cherry, 140
Chicken Ravioli with Fresh
Tomato Sauce, 90, 90
Chicken Tortellini with
Tomato Sauce, 81, 81
Chilli Seafood in Tomato
Sauce, 103, 103
egg, 122
Farfalle Salad with Sun-dried
Tomatoes and Spinach,
172, 172
Gnocchi with Tomato and
Fresh Basil, 200
Herbed Potato Gnocchi
with Chunky Tomato,
205, 205
Middle-Eastern Hummus,
Tomato and Olive Pasta
Salad, 194, 195

Olive and Tomato Tapenade,
135, 135
paste, 281
Penne with Creamy Tomato
Sauce, 126, 126
Penne with Sun-dried
Tomatoes and Lemon,
283, 283
Rigatoni with Chorizo and,
62, 62
Rigatoni with Tomato,
Haloumi and Spinach,
190, 190
Rocket, Cherry Tomato and
Spicy Salami Pasta Salad,
180, 181
Slow-roasted Balsamic,
53, 53
Spaghetti Tomato Salad,
173, 173
Spaghetti with Fresh Tomato
Sauce, 121, 121
Spaghetti with Herbs and,
130, 130
Spinach Ravioli with
Sun-dried Tomato Sauce,
216, 216
sun-dried, 111
Sun-dried Tomato Sauce on
Tagliatelle, 118, 119
Tagliatelle with Tomato and
Walnuts, 142, 142
Ziti with Roasted Tomatoes
and Ovolini, 256, 257
tortellini, 81, 143, 220, 220
Basil Tortellini with Bacon
and Tomato Sauce,
226, 226
Chicken Tortellini with
Tomato Sauce, 81, 81
Lemon-Scented Broth with,
36, 36
Prawn, 215, 215
Tortellini Broth, 270, 270
Tortellini with Eggplant,
143, 143
Tortellini with Mushroom
Cream Sauce, 225, 225
trout
Pasta with Fragrant Lime and
Smoked, 255
Trout, Fettucine and Fennel
Frittata, 106, 107
tuna, 95
Farfalle with Tuna,
Mushrooms and Cream,
95, 95

tuna *continued*
Orecchiette with Tuna,
Lemon and Caper Sauce,
160, *161*
Tuna and Pasta Salad, 175, *175*
Tuna, Green Bean and Onion
Salad, 176, *177*
Turkish Ravioli, 69, *69*
Tuscan Warm Pasta Salad,
193, *193*

U–V

veal
Chicken and Veal Loaf with
Mushrooms and Sour
Cream, *248,* 249
Pork and Veal Ravioli with
Cheesy Sauce, 164, *164*
Tagliatelle with Veal Wine
and Cream, 57, *57*
Vegetable Lasagne, 123, *123*
Vegetable Soup with Basil
Sauce, 45, *45*
vegetable stock, **151**
vegetables with pasta
Chunky Spaghetti Napolitana,
124, *124*
Conchiglie with Chickpeas,
132, *133*
Creamy Asparagus Linguine,
118, *119*
Farfalle with Artichoke Hearts
and Olives, 117, *117*
Farfalle with Mushrooms,
126

Fettucine with Zucchini and
Crisp-fried Basil, 116, *116*
Fusilli with Green Sauce,
128, 129
Fusilli with Vegetables,
266, *267*
Green Olive and Eggplant
Toss, 120, *120*
Grilled Vegetables on Pasta,
122, *122*
Lemon and Vegetable Pasta
Salad, 183, *183*
Linguine with Red Pepper
Sauce, 128, 129
Linguine with Roasted
Vegetable Sauce, 121
Olive and Mozzarella
Spaghetti, 116, *117*
Pasta with Mediterranean-
style Vegetables, 187, *187*
Pasta with Thai-style
Vegetables, 186, *186*
Pasta-filled Vegetables,
243, *243*
Penne with Creamy Tomato
Sauce, 126, *126*
Penne with Pumpkin and
Cinnamon Sauce, 132, *133*
Rigatoni with Pumpkin
Sauce, 127, *127*
Spaghetti with Herbs and
Tomato, 130, *130*
Spaghetti with Olives and
Capers, 125, *125*
Spicy Penne with Peppers,
140, *141*

Sun-dried Tomato Sauce on
Tagliatelle, 118, *119*

W

walnuts, **142**
Fettucine with Snow Peas
and Walnuts, 140, *141*
Tagliatelle with Tomato
and Walnuts, 142, *142*
Warm Chicken and Pasta
Salad, 174, *174*
Warm Garlic Prawn and
Fettucine Salad, 188, *189*
Warm Pasta and Crab Salad,
192, *192*
white pepper, **241**
white wine, **57**
wine, **57, 64**

Y

yoghurt, **69**

Z

Ziti with Roasted Tomatoes
and Ovolini, 256, *257*
Ziti with Vegetables and
Sausage, 63, *63*
zucchini, **116**
Fettucine with Zucchini
and Crisp-fried Basil,
116, *116*
Fettucine, and Crisp-fried
Basil with, 116, *116*

ACKNOWLEDGEMENTS

HOME ECONOMISTS: Jo Forrest, Michelle
Lawton, Kerrie Mullins, Justine Poole, Kerrie Ray,
Chris Sheppard, Dimitra Stais, Alison Turner,
Jody Vassallo

RECIPE DEVELOPMENT: Wendy Berecry,
Rebecca Clancy, Amanda Cooper, Alex Diblasi,
Michelle Earl, Joanne Glynn, Lulu Grimes,
Michelle Lawton, Barbara Lowery, Angela Nahas,
Sally Parker, Jennene Plumber, Tracey Port,
Jo Richardson, Tracy Rutherford, Dimitra Stais,
Jody Vassallo

PHOTOGRAPHY: Jon Bader, Ashley Barber, Joe
Filshie, Chris Jones, Luis Martin, Reg Morrison

STYLISTS: Amanda Cooper, Carolyn Fienberg,
Michelle Gorry, Mary Harris, Donna Hay,
Rosemary Mellish

The publisher wishes to thank the following for
their assistance in the photography for this book:
Antico's Northbridge Fruitworld, NSW;
Bush Wa Zee Pty Ltd Ceramics, NSW;
Dee Why Fruitworld, NSW;
Nick Greco Family Delicatessen, NSW;
Ma Maison en Provence, NSW; Pasta Vera, NSW.